Habsburg-Lorraine

(abdicated 1848)

Charles Louis d.1896
Margaret of Saxony
Maria Annunciata
of Bourbon-Naples
Maria Theresa of Portugal

Louis Victor d.1919

Otto d.1906
Maria Josefa of Saxony

Ferdinand
(renounced title 1911)

CHARLES I d.1922
Zita of Bourbon-Parma

Charles Louis
b.1918
Iolande de Ligne

Rudolph
b.1919
Xenia, Countess
Tschernitschew

Charlotte
b.1921
George, Duke of
Mecklenburg-
Strelitz

Elizabeth
b.1922
Henry of
Lichtenstein

The Coronation portrait of the Emperor Charles I and the Empress Zita
of Austro-Hungary.

The Last Habsburg

The
Last Habsburg

Gordon Brook-Shepherd

WEYBRIGHT AND TALLEY
NEW YORK

To the memory of a dear friend,
Count Ferdinand von Arco auf Valley,
whose world this was.

CONTENTS

ILLUSTRATIONS

MAPS

ACKNOWLEDGMENTS

Illustrations: frontispiece, 3, 4, 5, 6, 17, 18, 19, 20, 21, 24, 27, taken by kind permission from the family albums of the former Empress Zita of Austro-Hungary.

Illustrations: 1, 2, 7, 8, 9, 10, 11, 12, 13, 14, 15, 16, 22, 23, 26, reproduced by kind permission of the Austrian National Library.

FOREWORD

The venerable Franz Josef was not the last of the Habsburg Emperors. Nor, despite that chain of family suicides and assassinations stretching from Mayerling to Sarajevo – which prompted the heart-felt sigh 'I am spared nothing' – was he the most sorely tried.

It was his young great-nephew Charles, succeeding the eighty-six-year-old monarch in November 1916, who was to be afflicted, during a bare hundred weeks of power, with all the things that Franz Josef had, in fact, been spared in those phenomenal seven decades of rule. Charles had to endure the annihilation of his Empire at war and its dissolution at home; the loss of a crown which his ancestors had worn for six and a half centuries and which he himself cherished as a gift from God as well as a legacy from them; and finally, after the failure of two restoration attempts in Hungary, the second outbidding the first in drama and danger, a premature and poverty-stricken death in exile at the age of only thirty-five.

His is a tale of almost unparalleled royal tragedy, and tragedy of classical dimensions. No sovereign of modern times ascended the throne with nobler intentions than this young Habsburg Archduke. Certainly none was confronted with greater problems or contradictions. Charles loathed the war he was committed to finish; he distrusted and feared his German allies; he admired and secretly courted his Western enemies. At home, he sought to achieve what so many of the Empire's leaders had talked about and all had recoiled from – a truly federal programme of reform to drag Austro-Hungary by the scruff of its braided collar into the twentieth century.

Everything failed because everything was interlocked. He was defeated both as the 'Emperor of Peace' and as the 'Emperor of the people', to name the two popular titles that even his critics could never deny him. Yet, could he have fulfilled either title (which in practice would have meant fulfilling both) the Europe we live in today would be a very different continent, whatever might have happened in the end to his own eleven-nation Empire.

It was in a discussion with his eldest son, Archduke Otto, whose friendship I have enjoyed for many years, that the idea of writing a definitive biography of the Emperor Charles first arose. I said I would be happy to take it on, provided that I could get some special facilities, however modest, to help with original research.

A few months later, I learned that the help I would be offered was far from modest. The Habsburg family papers, which had never before been seen by an historian, or indeed by any 'outside eye', were to be made available to me as concerned all surviving political and biographical material about the Emperor Charles. Furthermore, unexpectedly and unasked on my part, his widow, the former Empress Zita of Austro-Hungary, had agreed to give her personal assistance in the re-telling of the story of her husband's life and struggles. This was precious testimony indeed. The ex-Empress, now seventy-six, had always declined, ever since going into exile fifty years ago, to speak of these events to anyone outside the family circle.

During the past two years, we have spent a total of some twenty-five full working days together, and a very detailed questionnaire has been sent ahead on each of my visits. In some cases, the Empress has kindly made available diaries written at the time, either in the form of brief jottings or, to cover one particular episode, an extensive narrative. For the rest she has relied on her memory. This is excellent, detailed and, so far as I can judge and check from a wealth of other sources, completely undistorted by either bitterness or bias. As a result, it has been possible to reconstruct the collapse of the old European order, as well as the Habsburg Empire itself, with the help of the only central eye-witness of those events who is still alive anywhere in the world today. My thanks for this privileged experience are due to a gracious lady who, like her husband, has been much maligned by her own people and widely misrepresented in the history of our times.

I am now tempted to agree with a remarkable compatriot of mine, Lieutenant-Colonel Edward Strutt, who figures prominently in this story, that she was 'one of the three great royal women' of the First World War.

Unique though all this help has been, it has formed only part of the research, which has been supplemented by a wide range of other unpublished documentary material. In Britain, by gracious permission of Her Majesty the Queen, I have been given access to all papers concerning the Emperor Charles in the Royal Archives at Windsor. These have included letters written by the Austrian Emperor to Her Majesty's grandfather, King George v (who once acted, in a remarkable way, as Charles's rescuer in an hour of peril); and some references to those secret wartime contacts between the two sides which have gone down in history as 'The Sixtus Affair'. I am grateful to Sir Michael Adeane, the Queen's Secretary, for putting this matter in train and subsequently to the Queen's Librarian, Mr Mackworth-Young, and Miss Jane Langton of his staff, for the patience and efficiency with which they met and often anticipated my requests.

In London I must also express thanks to the Trustees of the Beaverbrook Library for help in finding documents bearing on the Emperor Charles and his peace efforts among the papers of David Lloyd-George, the wartime Prime Minister. Everything that could be traced concerning the Emperor Charles (as sovereign and as exile) in the recently expanded archives of the Public Record Office has also been consulted, and, thanks to some devoted research help there, considerable use has been made of secret Cabinet minutes, Foreign Office telegrams, and other hitherto unpublished Whitehall material of the day.

In Austria my thanks are due to the Federal Chancellor himself, Dr Klaus, who, in his capacity as Head of the State Archives, issued me with a personal letter of authority to see all surviving material in Vienna concerning the last Emperor; also the Archives' Director Dr Blaas and his staff for their courtesy, speed and thoroughness in helping my research there. Extensive use has also been made of these archives, especially bearing on Charles's wartime secret diplomacy, his relations with his German ally, and the collapse of his Empire in the autumn of 1918.

From the other side of the Iron Curtain, in the Communist Budapest that was once the twin capital of Charles's Dual Monarchy, I am grateful to helpers, who had better remain anonymous, for tracing and making available much useful material on the late Emperor's two abortive restoration attempts of 1921.

I would also like to thank the executors of the late Lieutenant-Colonel Strutt for permission to see and quote extensively from the full text of the diary of his dramatic 'rescue mission' to the Emperor Charles in 1919; and Commander Charles Drage R.N. (retd.) for the use of his diary and pictures of the Imperial couple's final journey into exile aboard H.M.S. *Cardiff* in 1921.

There have been a great number of other minor eye-witness accounts, mostly in diary or letter form, from sources scattered over the former Austro-Hungarian Empire, as well as in Britain and France. This has all been pure grist to a willing mill. For imperfections in the end product, with whatever mistakes and misjudgements it may contain despite this array of special source material, I alone am responsible.

London, May 1968   GORDON BROOK-SHEPHERD

Chapter 1

A SKEIN OF CHANCE

᠅

The tragedy of Charles, last of the Habsburg Emperors, begins where the tragedy of the old Europe erupted: Sarajevo.

No one, on that 28 June 1914, sensed what the assassination by a Bosnian student of the Austrian heir-apparent, Archduke Franz Ferdinand, would bring in its train. Certainly no one dreamed that young Gavrilo Princip's bullets would go on to kill ten million more men in the World War they were to trigger off; would bring down four European dynasties and empires – the Romanov, Hohenzollern, Ottoman and the ancient Habsburg itself; would destroy a way of life as well as an order of life; and, by impoverishing the entire continent, would begin that slow shift of power from Europe to America which the Second World War was to finish. On the day, and for nearly a month afterwards, Sarajevo was seen as basically just another Austrian domestic crisis – something that would eventually be absorbed, as so much else had been absorbed during the six centuries of its existence, by the Empire's own vast porous mass.

Indeed, apart from the wretched assassin himself – who had in fact just killed the best Habsburg friend the South Slavs ever had – only two people in that old Europe had their lives instantly and unalterably transformed by the event. They were the dead man's twenty-six-year-old nephew, the Archduke Charles, and his twenty-two-year-old bride Zita. Little known even inside the Austro-Hungarian Empire, and almost totally unknown to the world outside, they became that morning the new heirs to the throne; and, as the ruling Emperor Franz Josef was then in his eighty-fourth year (and his sixty-sixth as sovereign), the forbidding heritage could at any moment fall on their young shoulders.

On 28 June they were with their family at Reichenau, their quiet country home some thirty miles south-west of Vienna. The then Archduchess and later Empress Zita of Austria has described what happened:

'It was midday, and beautiful summer weather, and we were having lunch outside in a little garden house which the Archduke had himself enjoyed helping to build.

'Suddenly there was a pause in the serving of the meal from the kitchens in the main house. It turned out to be a long one. For minutes on end, no more food appeared. Then a servant came out carrying, instead of the next course, a telegram in his hand which he handed to the Archduke.

'I remember asking: "What's the signature?" – but only out of idle curiosity. We often received and sent telegrams, as all members of the Imperial House could use the telegraph services all over the Monarchy free of charge.

'My husband opened it and, to answer my question, looked at the end first.

'"Rumerskirch," he replied, and added: "That's odd. He's with Uncle Franz. Why him?"

'Then he began to read out the brief message. The exact words I forget. But it was something like: "Deeply regret to report that His Imperial Highness and the Duchess were both assassinated here today."

'For a moment the Archduke hardly seemed to realize what he was reading. Then he went as white as a sheet in the sun and stood up without a word.

'We forgot all about food of course and went back into the house. The first thing was to get confirmation of the terrible news. In those days there was no wireless or television to switch on. The Emperor was the only one who would know for sure. So the Archduke got through on the telephone to Bad Ischl where he was staying.

'I heard him as the aide de camp simply, "Is it true?" and, when told that it was, he said "Shall I come to Ischl?"

'The Emperor passed back the message: "No, I'm leaving immediately for Vienna. You had better join me straight away there."

'The Archduke awaited the Emperor at Hietzing Station and drove with him in an open carriage the short distance to Schönbrunn Palace, where I was already waiting. It was the first time my husband had appeared in public as heir to the throne.

'He never forgot the stunned silence of the crowd lining the pavements and the tears in the eyes of almost everyone as the carriage slowly passed by on the brief journey. It was as though everyone shared the shock and grief with us.

'When they reached Schönbrunn and were alone at last the old Emperor's composure suddenly broke down and he burst into tears. It was then – and not on first hearing the news of the assassination, as is so often said – that he made the remark that was to become so well known:

"*Mir bleibt nichts erspart*" ("I am spared nothing"). But he also added, turning to my husband, some words that are never quoted: "*Auf jedenfall kann ich mich auf dich verlassen*" ("At least I can rely on you").

'As to our own feelings on that day, we were quite simply overwhelmed. We had always thought that, for us, the throne and its responsibilities were so far away. The Archduke Franz Ferdinand, after all, had only recently turned fifty. He was in good health and in the prime of life. Despite his own strange premonitions of violent death, we thought it would be twenty or thirty years before we would be called on. We felt so safe, so secure.

'Now, suddenly, the security was gone and it was upon us. We felt numbed by it all. We stood on the threshold of this frightful responsibility, and at a time when the whole Empire was shaking.'

The Sarajevo murder was not the only unexpected stroke of fate which brought the young Archduke Charles to the steps of the Habsburg throne. It was in fact the last of a long-drawn-out series of such strokes by which, one by one, all the other and higher limbs of the family tree had been lopped away from that seemingly indestructible stem which was the Emperor Franz Josef.

The Emperor's only son, the Crown Prince Rudolf, had taken his own life and that of his pretty and infinitely pathetic mistress Marie Vetsera at his shooting lodge at Mayerling on the night of 30 January 1889; and he had died without male issue. The man to whom the succession would then have reverted was the Emperor's next younger brother, the Archduke Maximilian. But, twenty-six years before, he had been tempted to become an Emperor of sorts on his own by accepting the crown of Mexico as an act of Catholic and dynastic faith. It proved a disastrous adventure. On 19 June 1867, he had ended up before a firing squad of his rebellious adopted subjects. The luckless Maximilian had also died without heirs.

On Rudolf's suicide, therefore, Franz Josef's second youngest brother, the Archduke Karl Ludwig, became the new heir-apparent. He also was killed far from home, also a victim of his deep religious convictions. He drank from the sacred but insanitary waters of the River Jordan while on a pilgrimage to the Holy Land in the spring of 1896, and died of typhoid on 17 May of that year.

The pilgrim Archduke, however, had left three sons behind him and the eldest of these, Franz Ferdinand of the Sarajevo tragedy, now became the fourth successive heir to the throne. The thought that his nephew Charles – then a boy nearly nine years old – would become Emperor of Austria only twenty years later would have seemed at the time too utterly remote even to entertain. For one thing, Franz Ferdinand himself was steadily recovering from the attack of tuberculosis which had made him like a doomed man the year before; he would now presumably marry and have children of his own. And even if he should die without issue, there was still his brother, Archduke Otto, father of the little Charles – an apparently healthy young man whose zest for high living was already a Vienna legend.

But at the turn of the century, after the most extraordinary family drama of even Franz Josef's long reign, another line of heirs presumptive was unexpectedly extinguished. This episode, which was to end in high tragedy, began like a novelette. In the summer of 1898, a servant in a castle at Pressburg brought to his mistress a gold pocket watch that Franz Ferdinand had left behind him on the tennis court. The *châtelaine* concerned, the Archduchess Isabella, had daughters of her own and had fondly assumed that her illustrious guest was courting one of these. But her curiosity was far from rewarded when she hopefully prised open the locket at the back of the watch. Instead of a daughter's picture, she found the face of her own lady-in-waiting, Countess Chotek, looking out. A romance that the heir to the throne had kept secret ever since he had first met his Bohemian Countess at a ball in Prague three years before was now exposed. The scandal was commensurate with the surprise, for by no stretch of the Habsburg family laws or standards could the Choteks be accepted as eligible for marriage into the Imperial house.

But Franz Ferdinand, a lonely and difficult man, had found the one woman with whom he wanted to share his life. Like a salmon leaping doggedly home against the torrent, he went after his heart's choice. The whole weight of court pressure, headed by the Emperor's personal opposition, could not prevail – even when bearing down on the Archduke's own passionate devotion to his dynasty. The result of one of the strangest protocol tussles of history was a ceremony in the Vienna Hofburg Palace on 28 June 1900. In return for permission to marry his Countess, Franz Ferdinand swore before the Emperor and all the Archdukes and principal dignitaries of the Empire that his marriage would be morganatic and that, among other renunciations, all children from it would be ineligible to succeed to the throne. Three days later the marriage took place. Though it had produced two sons by the time man and wife were killed side by side in the streets of Sarajevo fourteen years later, both had been eliminated before their birth from the succession.

It was his uncle's obstinate romance and the acceptance of the 1900 compromise which first brought the crown within the young Archduke Charles's range. Assuming the uncle did not marry again – and more suitably – the Hofburg ceremony now made the twelve-year-old Charles third in line of succession: after Franz Ferdinand himself and after Charles's own father, Otto. The throne was now in sight, though still a long way off.

Then came the penultimate stroke – the death of Archduke Otto on 1 November 1906 at the age of barely forty. The man who had asked too much of life came to a lingering and painful end, fighting for every breath with a tube in his larynx, in a Vienna villa specially adapted for him as a hospital. His son, then nineteen years old, received the news at eleven o'clock at night in Milan railway station, on the journey home with his mother from Cannes where they had been attending a family wedding.

From that day on, it became for Charles as good as certain that only his uncle Franz Ferdinand would wear the crown before him. The question now was not whether he would succeed, but when. Despite the already advanced age of the Emperor, the heir-apparent himself was still only in his mid-forties, and undergoing a new lease of happy morganatic married life divided between the Belvedere Palace in Vienna and his favourite estate at Konopischt in Bohemia. For the next eight years, young Charles could imagine himself succeeding his uncle probably as far ahead as 1935 or 1940, when he himself would be around fifty and in the prime of his own life.

Then finally, in 1914, came Sarajevo – a dark thunderbolt out of the blue, and one which was itself compounded of so much unpredictable coincidence. (Had the Archduke's chauffeur continued, as instructed, straight down the town's Appel Quay that June morning and not blundered by turning right into Franz Josef street he would not, for example, have stopped within point-blank range of Princip and his revolver.) But the wrong turn was made and the student determined to put Bosnia and the world at rights found his illustrious targets virtually looking at him down the short barrel of his pistol. The grievously wounded victims were driven at top speed (another blunder) to the Konak, the official residence of the Bosnian Imperial Governor, General Potiorek. Priests and doctors were summoned but by 11.30 A.M. both the Austrian heir-apparent and the woman he had sacrificed so much to marry were dead. From there the story passes to that lunch-time scene in the villa at the foot of the Rax mountains in Lower Austria.

Execution by a firing squad in Mexico; a suicide in a hunting lodge at Mayerling; poison from the waters of the River Jordan; a father's premature death in a Vienna villa; an uncle's unfitting romance in Bohemia and his assassination on the banks of the Milajca. Such was the long and tangled skein of chance that had drawn Franz Josef's fifth heir into the succession. One need not be a determinist to believe that fate had reserved something very special for a ruler selected in this remorseless way. Special it was: the story of Charles of Austria is one of personal and political tragedy almost unparalleled among the sovereigns of our time.

Chapter 2

BRIGHT MORNING

The beginning, at least, was sunny. Despite all that was to come down on his head later, with the Habsburg crown, Charles seemed to keep about him throughout his life that mark of serenity which comes from inward personal blessings. In his case, four were paramount: a strong faith, a clear conscience, a serene marriage and a happy childhood.

He was born on 17 August 1887 at the Danube castle of Persenbeug, some fifty miles upstream from Vienna. This lovely stretch of Lower Austria, where the great river twists its way through terraced vineyards with a ruined fortress perched on almost every crag above, was the very cradle of the Empire. It was the source, not only of much ancient Nibelungen saga, but of the Habsburgs' own temporal power. These lands north and south of the Central Danube were their first feudal domains as Archdukes of Austria. On this solid centre was based their gradual growth, from the thirteenth century onwards, into Emperors who ruled over nearly all the peoples that the river linked. There was no more fitting place for the infant who was to become the last of them to open his eyes.

There was also no more deceptively tranquil time to be born in. 1887 lay in the middle of the Empire's Indian summer. The dynasty's defeat by the Prussians in battle of 1866 and the ensuing defeat by the Hungarians in domestic politics of 1867 lay twenty years behind. The ultimate catastrophe of the World War lay twenty years ahead. The Emperor Franz Josef was still in his fifties. His son, Crown Prince Rudolf, had not yet committed suicide. His wife, the troubled Bavarian beauty Elizabeth, had not yet been murdered by an irrelevant fanatic on the shores of a Swiss lake. The Habsburg crown, and the old European universe around it, both seemed as stable as the Danube rocks on which Persenbeug was built.

Charles's father who, as we have seen, was the Emperor's nephew, was aptly nicknamed 'Handsome Otto' – a man who combined seemingly inexhaustible vitality with a seemingly insatiable appetite for life. He was a gay extrovert who could charm the legs off a donkey, let alone a beautiful

7

woman. Though he followed the formal career of a Habsburg Archduke in the army and fulfilled all the representational duties that came his way, he never seems to have worried his head unduly about the succession or even about politics as such. Living meant more to him than ruling; pleasure attracted more than power.

Unhappily, his wife formed that sort of contrast to her husband which does not blend in a marriage, as so many contrasts do. Like his father, the pious Karl Ludwig before him, Otto had gone to the court of Dresden for his bride; at twenty-one he married the nineteen-year-old Maria Josepha of Saxony, a niece of the ruling King. This blonde Saxon princess was pretty enough, well-born and well-educated. Yet once the first flush of passion had gone, she was simply not the woman who, by temperament or by guile, could have held her most restless of Habsburgs. She seems, indeed, to have been a sublimated archducal version of the ideal nineteenth-century German *Hausfrau* – deeply religious, placid, charitable, unassuming and determined to centre her whole life around her home and family. Though always respecting her, and perhaps in his fashion always loving her, 'Handsome Otto' was clearly stifled by such implacable domesticity. Their marriage never went right on the rocks. It just drifted with the years gently and sadly off course.

This estrangement still lay ahead when the young couple had their first child. The birth itself was of course noted in the Court circulars; but the event was quite swamped in the public mind by the fifty-seventh birthday anniversary of the Emperor Franz Josef, which fell on the following day, 18 August, and was duly celebrated by speeches, toasts and artillery salvoes all over the sprawling Empire from Innsbruck across to Lemberg and from Prague down to Mostar. The baptism was, indeed, postponed until the 19th in order to allow the various guests who had been engaged in the Imperial birthday celebrations time to assemble at Persenbeug. There, in the great hall of the castle which had been converted into a chapel for the occasion, the dynasty's newest Archduke was christened with his seven names. To give them as they were given to him: Karl, Franz, Josef, Ludwig, Hubert, Georg, Maria.

They must have been wonderful childhood years. There were the twin anchors of home always to come back to: the yellow castle at Persenbeug on the Danube and later the Villa Wartholz at Reichenau at the foot of the Rax mountains as well – each a contrast in everything but tranquillity. But in between there were constant exciting moves with his parents, wherever the garrison duty of his soldier-father took them. Thus, even as he learned to walk and talk, the child saw much of the Empire he was later to rule and to lose.

The first such move was to Brunn in Moravia, where his father was posted as Captain (*Rittmeister*) in the 6th Dragoons. Then in 1890 came a longer spell at home when Archduke Otto was transferred back to the 4th Dragoons at Enns in Upper Austria. In 1891 there began a memorable stay in the Hradcin palace of Prague where Otto, now a Lieutenant-Colonel, had been sent to command an Infantry Regiment. The old Bohemian castle high over the city, where Charles was himself to return as a young man, made an instant and indelible appeal of romantic grandeur to the boy.

The last of these early childhood moves was to Ödenburg in Western Hungary where Archduke Otto, now returned to the cavalry, was posted with the 9th Hussars. For this tour of provincial garrison duty, the family rented the small but comfortable palace of Count Pejacsvics which, if less imposing than the Hradcin they had just left, was also more homely. Charles, now five years old, thus had a tranquil first glimpse of that Hungary, and of that very town in Hungary, which was to bring him such high drama as its King.

From his earliest years, the child showed an exceptional sweetness of character and a spontaneous concern for his fellow-creatures, especially the unluckier ones, that even the example of his mother – renowned for her charitable works – could not wholly explain. At the tender age of four, for example, he asked his father's estate steward to give him some sort of work to do so that he could earn a little money to give to the old and the poor of Persenbeug. There, and later at Reichenau, he was always selling fruit and flowers from his own little garden for this purpose; taking round money-boxes; organizing lotteries; and even, when all else failed, giving away clothes which he had furtively removed from his own none too elaborate wardrobe.

It might be as well at the very beginning to put into its longer per-spective this matter of the goodness of Charles – whether as Archduke, Emperor, or exile. The promise of the child was to be fulfilled in the man. He grew up without a moral blemish worthy of the name in his character. This is not just a portrait drawn by doting parents or adulating courtiers. It is one on which relatives, close or distant, and both his political sup-porters and critics at home and abroad were all agreed. Yet, even when convinced of its authenticity, it is a difficult picture for the biographer to present. It could also be an easy one for the reader to tire of. Goodness in human beings is only in rare circumstances absorbing.

Such rare circumstances are, however, present in this case. In 1949, twenty-seven years after his death, and two world wars away from the universe of Persenbeug and Reichenau we are describing, a 'Process for the Beatification of the Servant of God, Charles of the House of Habsburg' was introduced at the Vatican. The young Archduke was, in fact, to be blessed with something close to saintliness as a man. As an Emperor caught up in a murderous war he was perhaps to be burdened with it. This is what gives a poignancy and an irony even to those first radiant gestures of the child.

Until the age of seven, he was mainly in the hands of the ladies – above all his mother and her lady-in-waiting, Countess Pallavicini; his young aunt, the Archduchess Annunciata; and his Irish governess, Miss Casey, from whom he first learned to read and write – in English, not in German.

But in 1894, when he had reached that end-of-nursery age, the ladies retired to the background and, overnight, his toys were withdrawn – even the stuffed monkeys of which he was particularly fond. The business of educating a Habsburg Archduke who was by now fourth in line for the throne had begun. It was an exhausting as well as an exhaustive process.

He was put in the overall charge of Count George Wallis Carighmain, who had already served as tutor to the child's father and before that to his uncle Franz Ferdinand. A spartan regime was now introduced: out of bed at six o'clock, summer and winter, and each day, after a cold bath which also took no account of the seasons, packed full of tuition in that wide variety of subjects a young Habsburg was expected to master. Modern languages alone included, apart from his native German, the English of Miss Casey, the French of M. Mathieu and the principal tongues of the Empire, above all the Hungarian of Herr Tormassy.

Constitutional law and political science were the most important subjects of all for a possible future ruler to master; and the enormously detailed care with which Charles's long-term studies were prepared can be seen from the draft programme drawn up as early as 20 March 1906 for these two themes alone. Not only was the exact balance between canon law and church law, civil law and criminal law, economics and finance, weighed out in the syllabus with the care of a chemist's prescription; detailed arguments were advanced for and against each individual professor suggested for the specialized instruction, and the very sensible directive was issued that the young Archduke should be given an overall insight into every important aspect of the material but without ever being submerged in legalistic detail. 'He will never, after all, be called upon actually to sit in judgement in a court of law,' wrote Arthur von Polzer, who was later to play a key role in the first stages of Charles's reign.

This was, of course, still a programme for the future in 1906. For the next few years, apart from intensive modern language instruction, a grounding in the classics, and general reading, the boy was lucky enough to be able to learn, in both work and sport, from the countryside around his two lovely homes and the various garrison posts of his father. Zoology was learned with shooting; botany came with riding. His friend and mentor in all this outdoor instruction was his immediate house-tutor, Dr Holzlechner (soon known to all in the family, for some inscrutable reason, as 'Nisi'). He was an orphan of fairly modest origins who had got the job, without any wire-pulling, by the simple process of applying for it.

Charles's early education was rounded off in what was then an unusual way for a young Archduke in eventual line of succession. In 1899 he was sent for two years as an ordinary pupil to the Vienna Schottengymnasium, where he appears to have won the hearts of his fellow pupils by his total lack of 'side' or arrogance, and those of his professors by his quick perception and retentive memory. On 27 June 1901, 'Arch-Charles' ('*Erzkarl*') as he was nicknamed by his class-mates, put the seal on his days as a schoolboy by passing the intermediate examinations of the Schotten with flying colours. But any question of him going on to take the state Matriculation (*Matura*) was ruled out by no less a person than the Emperor himself. Franz Josef forbade it on the fair-minded grounds that young Charles had enjoyed special advantages of private tuition over the other boys. He also opposed it on the (to modern eyes) old-fashioned grounds that the young Archduke would be entering into public competition with those who were likely to become his future subjects. The twentieth century had only just dawned; the seventy-year-old Emperor was emphatically a man of the nineteenth, if not earlier.

The next few years must have been mainly memorable for the journeys – not any longer as an infant in the train of his soldier-father, but as a teenage boy travelling to see for himself the wide Habsburg Empire and something of the wider continent around it. The raw but cosy little world of 'Nisi's' tuition was now left behind, as the stuffed monkeys in the nursery had been laid aside before that. Count Wallis came on most of these journeys himself, so that the boy should see life through the tutor's wise eyes, as well as through his own.

In 1901 they travelled eastwards to Galicia and then through most of the 'Hungarian half' of the Dual Monarchy, including the provinces of Bukovina and Transylvania on the Rumanian border. 1902 saw a long journey through France – Paris, Brittany, Trouville, Lyon, Chamonix – with calls at the courts of Stuttgart (his uncle Duke Albrecht) and Dresden (his mother's birth-place) on the way. In 1903, France was visited again and, on this occasion, a brief excursion was made across the Channel to England.

On these westward trips, the disputed border territories of Alsace-Lorraine – at that time, of course, in German hands – were studied with particular care. Whichever country claimed these provinces or ruled them in 1903, the Habsburgs had been the dynastic heads of the house of that name ever since the future Empress Maria Theresa had married her Duke Francis of Lorraine in 1736. The young Archduke Charles was now shown every cultural and economic facet of these distant lands whose name he still bore, and talked to many of their inhabitants. Whether it was partly the influence of Count Wallis, his guide, and of Professor Mathieu, his French teacher, or whether it was wholly the judgement of his own fresh mind, Charles came away convinced that the people of Alsace-Lorraine were French, rather than German, in their roots and their proper destiny.

This almost unknown episode of his youth has its importance for his years of power later on. From the first weeks of his brief wartime reign, he strove to return these provinces from the hands of his ally, Germany, to those of his enemy, France. The attempt ran right across the thread of the alliances and ruffled them in the process; but it ran parallel to his own early beliefs and experiences.

The year 1905 marked another clear and predestined rung upwards in the dynastic ladder. Though he had formally been appointed Lieutenant two years before at the age of sixteen, he now began his active service with the 7th Dragoons (called, incidentally, the Duke of Lorraine's) at a small garrison near Bilin in Bohemia. He settled down quickly and happily in his two-room quarters in the old barracks of Kostelitz, and took part as an illustrious though still humble subaltern in the ordinary life of his regiment. Little did he guess that, just eleven years later, he would as Emperor assume the supreme command over all the forces of the Dual Monarchy, in the middle of the disastrous war that was to destroy it.

It was in 1905 also that Charles received the highest accolade of the dynasty, the Order of the Golden Fleece, bestowed, of course, by his great-uncle Franz Josef. The Archduke was staying at Brixen at the time and so, by a coincidence, was the same Polzer who was soon to draw up that blueprint for his education. Despite the difference of nearly twenty years in their ages, the two had already become close companions, and Charles sent for his friend when the despatch arrived from Vienna with the Imperial autograph letter and the rules of the Order. Polzer describes the scene:

Together we undid the seals of the enormous envelope and plunged into the reading of the rules which were by no means easy to read as they were drawn up in old French. The young Archduke, however, was very thorough and took it as a matter of course that he must not sign the oath to observe the rules until he was perfectly clear about the obligations he would thereby undertake. Our study of them therefore lasted several days. The Archduke remarked that certain of these provisions were completely out-of-date and impossible, with the best will in the world, to carry out.*

The episode, slight in itself, has a double significance: first, that this youngest recipient of the Golden Fleece should devote days to studying his obligations under the Order; and second, that, with due respect to his venerable great-uncle, he had decided that this most coveted of all Habsburg distinctions belonged to a vanished age. Both characteristics – the conscientiousness and the urge to modernize – stayed with Charles when the Golden Fleece became his to bestow.

All so far had gone to plan – the nursery stage of the family and Miss Casey; the post-nursery stage of 'Nisi'; the spell as an ordinary schoolboy; the first travels abroad; the beginning of military training – each step on time and as arranged. But on 1 November 1906 the time-table was upset. The early death of his father (for whom he had retained a close affection despite the family estrangement) brought the nineteen-year-old Charles within two lives of the throne, and the rhythm of his own life had to be quickened accordingly. Shortly after the funeral, the Archduke, instead of returning to his regiment, was installed with Count Wallis and a bevy of professors in the Hradcin Castle at Prague. There, for the next two years, he worked his way throughout the elaborate syllabus which had been devised by Polzer six months before.

Charles was barely installed in the Hradcin when, on 13 November 1906, he invited his adviser to pay him a visit. It was the first of several such visits Polzer made and, after one particularly lively encounter, he has left us this further glimpse of the way the young Archduke's mind was forming:

In his studies he was not merely receptive; he often gave vent to sharp and bold criticism of political conditions and many state institutions. On one occasion discussion was so heated that it ended in our both losing our temper. I had been stubbornly defending a conservative point of view. The arguments on both sides became more and more violent and our attitudes more and more irreconcilable until, finally, the Archduke broke off the discussion with the words: 'It's impossible to argue with you. You are an incorrigible bureaucrat.' That got me on the raw, for I had always hated bureaucratism.

Next day at lunch, tempers were still strained to start with. But suddenly a smile stole over the face of the Archduke. He raised his glass and said laughingly: 'May the wretched bureaucrat live and learn!'

* Polzer-Hoditz, *The Emperor Charles*, p. 38.

That broke the ice. I joined in the laugh and replied: 'I confess I made a very poor showing in yesterday's debate. My point of view was a thankless one to defend . . . but I could not leave such ultra-modern ideas unopposed in one so near to the throne.'*

Charles was clearly growing up with a mind of his own. And, despite all the stiff brocade of tradition that had enfolded him since infancy, it was a mind not of the nineteenth century in which he had been born, but of the twentieth century which he and the old Empire were now facing.

* From Polzer, *op. cit.*, pp. 43–4.

Chapter 3

WHITE LILIES AND BLACK EAGLE

Apart from following with interest one fascinating and unexpected piece of news about his personal life, Charles's future subjects were made little aware of him in these last years of his young manhood before Sarajevo. His majority had been declared on his twentieth birthday in 1907 and, as another predestined rung up the ladder, he had duly acquired on that day a Head of Household (Prince Lobkowitz) and a gentleman-in-waiting (Count Ledebuhr) in the place of his tutors. In theory, he was now ready to take his place close to the centre of the Vienna stage. Yet after the completion of his Prague studies, he went back full-time into the army and, for the next six years, the pleasant anonymity of a regimental life spent mostly in provincial garrisons kept him well out of the public eye. This was perhaps just as well. The Empire had its immediate heir-apparent in the person of Franz Ferdinand and he always kept himself, if anything, too much in the public eye.

The event which temporarily thrust his young nephew into the limelight was the surprise announcement on 13 June 1911 that Archduke Charles was engaged to be married to Princess Zita, daughter of Duke Robert of Bourbon-Parma – one of the many separate Italian states liquidated in the great *Risorgimento* which had been completed forty years before. The news came from Pianore, a property which the Duke had still kept in Tuscany and where Zita herself had been born on 9 May 1892.

The stir of interest was caused partly by the intrinsic importance of the event: Charles was, after all, second in line to the throne, and his engagement was a reminder that it would be his children, not those of Franz Ferdinand, to whom the crown would presumably pass. The most unusual name and the semi-Italian background of the bride-to-be also aroused popular curiosity.

But apart from all this, by now any new Habsburg wedding was in itself likely to cause another bout of somewhat morbid speculation. The Imperial House, from the old Emperor downwards, had been plagued by such appalling bad luck or bad judgement with its marriages. So often, the brides they had chosen were either dynastically suitable but personally incompatible; or personally suitable but dynastically incompatible. Rarely, if ever, had the Archdukes squared the circle of bliss and duty by combining both.

Indeed, had he ever thought about it – and one must presume he did – Charles's own immediate ancestors had, between the three of them, run the entire gamut of the dynasty's marital misfortunes. His own father Otto, as we have seen, had married a Saxon princess whose religion, politics and lineage were all above reproach but whose life and tastes he simply could not share. Uncle Franz Ferdinand in his romance had struggled to a very painful compromise. The woman of his heart was noble, but insufficiently so, and he had been forced to pay for a happy married life with all renunciations of the 1900 settlement – after which both of them sat on a perpetual pin-cushion of tiny protocol pricks.

Less momentous but even more alarming had been the fate of his other uncle, Otto's younger brother Ferdinand. This unfortunate soul had fallen desperately in love with one Berta Czuber, the daughter of a Vienna university professor and – like his eldest brother Franz – was determined to marry his sweetheart of redder blood. This time, however, the Emperor proved immovable in his shocked opposition. A Countess Chotek perhaps, though with weighty reservations and only to put an end to a ruinous public conflict with his own immediate heir. But a plain Miss Czuber never, and especially as the infatuated prince concerned was the youngest of the Emperor's three nephews with no position of his own to bargain from. Poor Ferdinand went on regardless and married his 'Milly', and all the wrath of dynastic excommunication fell upon his head accordingly. The final stage was to come in 1912 when (having already been deprived of his title, his military rank and his income) his name was deleted from the official genealogy of the Imperial house and he became a Habsburg 'nonperson'. The second half of that name he clung to. After a pathetic odyssey he died in 1915 and was buried in Munich as 'Mr Burg'.

The examples of father and both uncles – one more shattering than the other – could not have been absent from the young Charles's mind when he first turned to thoughts of marriage. But as it turned out, no calculation entered into his choice, and no sacrifices had to follow it. He combined the blessings and avoided the woes of all three ancestors by falling genuinely and lastingly in love with a princess of equal blood. How the old Emperor must have sighed with relief when he heard that his favourite greatnephew, so exemplary already as child, student and soldier, had now done the exemplary thing in marriage!

Charles had first met his future bride when she was still in the nursery and he barely out of it, on visits with his parents to and from Persenbeug or Wartholz and the Bourbon-Parmas' Austrian home at Schwarzau. Her father, Duke Robert, had been blessed with no fewer than twenty-four children, of whom some died, but there were twenty alive at any one time (nine by his first wife, Maria Pia of Sicily, and eleven by his second, Maria Antonia of Braganza). In this household – large even by the copious standards of the day – it really does seem to have been a case of 'the more the merrier'.

The Duke was himself a good-natured and liberal-minded man, much given to literature and the arts. So far from pining after the past, he was happily resigned to the fact that he would never again wear the crown of the tiny Italian kingdom where his father had been murdered on the streets in 1854 and whence he had fled, an eleven-year-old boy, with his mother five years later. He still had property in Italy, France and Switzerland and the links with Austria were so close that it was a second home rather than a place of exile. Schwarzau itself was a solid but unpretentious castle set in a pleasant park on the edge of the great Neunkirchen forest. It was ideally situated for his purpose. Vienna was less than twenty miles away to the north, while the main road and rail routes to Italy and the south ran almost past the park gates. To the east are the soft round hills of the *Bucklige Welt* or 'Humped-back world' – which are the last thrust of the great Alpine massif before it flounders for good in the Central European plain. Enough space and enough horizon even for twenty children.

The little princess who was to become the last Empress of Austria has given these memories of those childhood days and of her first impressions of the Habsburg boy who was to become her husband:

'It was a peaceful, happy time. We spent about six months of the year at Schwarzau – usually beginning in July, when the heat got intense in Italy, and staying over Christmas and New Year until early January, when the real winter cold set in in Austria. Then we would go down to Pianore and stay there through the spring and early summer until moving back north again.

'And what moves they were! Every year and for each journey back and forth we had our special train. When fully assembled for the trip it must have had fifteen or sixteen coaches, and two engines were needed to pull it over the Semmering Pass just south of Schwarzau. Today, of course, anything like that sounds enormous, yet it was always full, for virtually the entire household was moved – my father with many of his books and personal belongings, us twenty children, all the servants and administrative staff, and even our riding horses in special box-cars. These journeys were for us the most exciting events of the year.

'We were a lively and also a united family: the fact that the children came from different mothers made not the slightest difference. There were always plenty of interesting guests at Schwarzau because our father had such a variety of interests – especially anything to do with history and geography. So, apart from the usual visitors, there were also professors and writers of several nationalities frequently at the castle.

'Indeed, we grew up internationally. My father thought of himself first and foremost as a Frenchman, and spent a few weeks every year with the elder children at Chambord, his main property on the Loire. I once asked him how we should describe ourselves. He replied: "We are French princes who reigned in Italy." In fact, of the twenty-four children only three were actually born in Italy. The three included me, though both my sister before me and my brother after me were born in Austria.

'I distinctly remember meeting the young Archduke Charles at Schwarzau – but just as one of the many cousins and friends who came. He was, of course, four years older than I, and at that age those four years make a big difference. He usually played with his own age group and I with mine. But I do recall how carefully he always looked after his own tiny brother Max when he came on these visits – making sure the right food was given and so on – and I thought to myself "How conscientious he is!"'

For more than ten years, Charles and Zita were separated by their education in different countries. Then, in 1909, Charles was with his Dragoon regiment at Brandeis on the Elbe from where he could easily visit his favourite aunt, the Archduchess Annunciata at Franzensbad. It was on one of these trips that he met again his childhood playmate – now an attractive dark-haired and vivacious seventeen-year-old, fresh from her convent schooling at Zangberg in Bavaria and Ryde in the Isle of Wight.

The Empress takes up the story of this reunion and what followed:

'We were of course glad to meet again and became close friends. On my side feelings developed gradually over the next two years. He seemed to have made up his mind much more quickly, however, and became even more keen when, in the autumn of 1910, a rumour spread about that I had got engaged to a distant Spanish relative, Don Jaime, the Duke of Madrid.

'On hearing this, the Archduke came down post-haste from his regiment at Brandeis and sought out his grandmother, the Archduchess Maria Theresa (who was also my great-aunt) and the natural "confidante" in such matters. He asked her whether the rumour was true and when told it was not replied: "Well, I had better hurry in any case or else she really will get engaged to someone else."'

Another event during this same period which spurred the young Archduke on was an unexpected summons from his Emperor about affairs of
the heart. For some years, Franz Josef had been taking the closest interest
in his great-nephew's marriage plans. One of his first thoughts had been to
link young Charles with his own grand-daughter Ella (the later Countess
Waldburg). This plan fell through, largely because of the objections of
Charles's mother, who went to the Emperor and pleaded that, as the two
were related twice over, a marriage would be unsuitable for them and
could well prove unfortunate for their children. It was an argument that
carried great weight, for it seemed then that those children might well be
carrying the Habsburg crown in the second half of the twentieth century.

Soon after this, Charles's name had become linked in Vienna with
Princess 'Belli' Hohenlohe. The rumoured romance appears to have been
the product of the mother's and the daughter's joint ambitions and not of
any wooing on the Archduke's part. But the Emperor was determined to
make sure. He summoned his great-nephew and asked point-blank what
was behind the gossip. Charles answered with absolute truth for himself –
and perhaps with a gallant little white lie on the young lady's behalf – that
neither he nor Princess Hohenlohe had ever dreamt of marrying.

As Charles later told his real fiancée, Franz Josef replied that this was
just as well, for he would never have sanctioned the match. For good
measure, he then went on to warn Charles that he would not be allowed to
marry into any noble family, however ancient and illustrious (as indeed the
Hohenlohes were). The Archduke was told he would have to choose his
bride from among the Imperial or Royal houses of Europe; and he was
further warned that he had better lose no time about it and must inform
his Emperor immediately of his proposed choice.

Fortunately Charles had already spared himself any prolonged and
calculating search around the courts of Europe. Though he does not
appear even to have hinted at it at this audience, he had already made a
private choice that would solve both his problems and the Emperor's. The
problem was to make the private choice speedily a public one.

Again Charles went to his grandmother and explained that, as the
Emperor had just virtually ordered him to marry both suitably and swiftly,
the engagement with Princess Zita should surely now be hurried along.
The good Maria Theresa needed no persuading of the case and it was only
the hesitations of Charles's own mother which delayed the formal betrothal a little longer.

This pious lady, since 1906 a widow, had yet again expressed anxiety at
a family relationship between the couple concerned though in fact the
link, which went back to a step-grandmother of Charles's, was by marriage

only. Finally, however, Maria Josepha's last misgivings were overcome – not, it seems, without some quiet work behind the scenes by the old Emperor – and the Pianore announcement could be made.

Once again, the white lilies of Bourbon and the black double-headed eagle of Habsburg had crossed threads in the heraldic tapestry of the old Europe. The unions between these two ancient dynasties had not always been happy ones: one need only think of the Austrian Archduchess Maria Antonia who, as Marie Antoinette, perished at the scaffold of the French Revolution together with her husband, Louis xvi. But, politics apart, it seemed that nothing would trouble this match. Both shared the same deep faith, the same simple tastes, the same love of home and – not so far behind these three in enduring value for a marriage – the same sense of humour. The strains of the throne never weakened these personal bonds; those of exile only strengthened them.

The couple were not allowed long together in Pianore to celebrate their engagement. On 17 June, only four days after the announcement, Charles had to set out on his first important mission abroad, to represent the Emperor at the Coronation of King George v in London. The heir-apparent, his uncle Franz Ferdinand, should by rights have gone, as indeed he had attended the Coronation of Edward vii ten years before. But there had already been difficulties on that occasion because of his morganatic marriage; and where his beloved Sophie was concerned, Franz Ferdinand was never disposed to turn the other cheek – let alone offer the same cheek for another slap. So the freshly engaged young nephew was despatched instead. It was to be his last visit to England,* and it had a significance that neither he nor anyone else could have guessed at the time. London was displaying its official panoply of Empire for the last time in the old world, like a peacock opening out its feathers against the setting sun.

Delegations from fifty-eight countries – all the adult and 'accepted' nations of the world – converged on London for the occasion with the representatives of the Austrian Emperor and his suite. On 19 June, the day Charles arrived at Victoria Station, no fewer than twenty-eight princes and other foreign notabilities with their retinues travelled up with him from Dover in two special trains. The grimy terminus was carpeted and draped in crimson for the occasion; and a blaze of hydrangeas and carnations replaced the usual paraphernalia of mail bags. As one eye-witness account proudly put it: 'Never in the history of railways has such an assemblage been seen upon one platform. . . . Every known language of two hemispheres was

---

* Three years later, in the summer of 1914, he fell in gladly with his wife's plan to make a second and purely private trip to see the convent on the Isle of Wight where she had finished her education. The war put a stop to the idea.

being spoken at one and the same time.' Justified or not, the boast was understandable. Every state from the Argentine to Zanzibar had sent its emissaries and under the glass dome of Victoria were brought together such present-day incompatibles as the United States and China, Russia and Spain, Greece and Bulgaria, and Persia and Egypt.

For the next few days, Charles was plunged into festivities. The house at 41 Belgrave Square was put at his disposal for the stay and from here, on his first night in London, he left for a banquet at Buckingham Palace followed by a ball given by the Duchess of Sutherland at Stafford House which lasted until the small hours. On 22 June, Coronation Day, he drove to the Abbey in a carriage placed immediately in front of the British Royal Family's procession, a distinction he shared with the German Crown Prince and Princess and the Crown Prince of Egypt. The ceremony itself – a litany of England's history with its blend of medieval rites and the Christian symbolism of kingship – made a deep impression on the young man for whose head the crown of another Empire was destined. He little imagined it was to be placed there only five years later in the middle of a war in which his present gracious hosts were to be his enemies.

Charles later told his fiancée that, apart from the actual Coronation service, it was the great naval review at Spithead on 24 June he found most impressive. He always remembered those scores of men-of-war of all nations lined up in parade off-shore: columns of grey steel by day; turrets of light by night when each lay illuminated overall on the dark water. Like the Coronation, it was a symbol of Britain's might; the experts of the day reckoned, in that calm and confident summer of 1911, that there were sixty-three British battleships built or building, compared with the forty-one of her nearest rival, Germany.

More official receptions followed at which Charles met the leading British statesmen of the time – Asquith, Haldane and the same Edward Grey who was to take Britain into war against him. There was little call or occasion for political discussion, and this suited Charles well. He had no mandate from the Emperor for such talks, and even less desire to poach on the preserves of his very sensitive uncle Franz Ferdinand, who would be reading every detail of his movements back in Vienna.

It was also noticed that, while obviously enjoying the round of pleasures, the young Austrian Archduke held himself back a little at the social festivities. He stayed late at all the balls, for example, but was never seen to dance with anyone. This was interpreted as a gallant homage to Princess Zita, whose portrait he showed with pride to the newly-crowned Queen Mary. Such gestures, and his own unaffected gaiety, seem to have won him all hearts.

On 28 June, after a final ball for the Coronation guests given by Lord Derby, Charles left England for home via Paris. Another solemn festivity, that of his own marriage, now lay ahead. Like the one he had just attended in London, this too was to be almost the last happy parade of a dynasty in its old setting.

The wedding took place on 21 October 1911, at the same Schwarzau where the couple had first met and played as children. The quiet baroque castle on the Steinfeld, which had been preparing for the great event for weeks, was transformed for the occasion from the retreat of a literary *grand seigneur* into an Imperial Aladdin's cave. The wedding gifts alone took up two large rooms to display. At the centre of the main table stood the diadem in diamonds given by the Emperor; next to it the twenty-two-row pearl necklace which was Charles's present to his bride; and grouped around those a brooch from Charles's mother, a ring from Franz Ferdinand, and the silver statue of a Spanish fountain from Don Alfonso of Bourbon.

The gifts on the other tables, though not matching these in conventional splendour were able to surpass them in ingenuity. There was, for example, the bronze statue of a youth on an eagle, the present of the near-by military airfield at Wiener Neustadt. It had been personally delivered two days before by one of the pilots who had circled the castle grounds dropping flowers and then landed in its near-by meadows – no ordinary happening in 1911. But the most remarkable of all these varied 'gifts of homage' came from much farther out in space, so far indeed as to be quite invisible. It was a small new planet just discovered by the Viennese astronomer Dr Palisa, which he had named 'Zita' and 'presented' to the bride for the occasion.

The day before – a Friday – had seen the celebration of the villagers of Schwarzau itself, whose low-roofed yellow houses now seemed happily drowned under a deluge of blue-red and black-yellow streamers (the house colours of Parma and Habsburg respectively), chains of coloured paper and autumn flowers, flags, cardboard coats of arms and pictures of Franz Josef and the bridal couple. After the early October darkness fell, a long procession carrying torches and *lampions* blazed and twinkled its way around the park – the ranks of the villagers now swollen a hundred-fold by groups of war veterans and fire-brigade units from all over the district. It was perhaps as well that all those firemen – who had come with their local mayors as 'official' representatives of their communities – were on the scene. For while all the village bands joined forces for a deafening mass offering described as 'a patriotic sound picture', firework displays crackled into life to outshine the torches and then the *Böller*, or festive mortars, opened up to swamp everything with their thunder of blank charge. Inside the castle, the bride and the groom-to-be each held, separate from each other, the customary last supper parties of their single lives. They were eaten off silver plate. Duke Robert's gold plate was waiting in reserve, ready polished for tomorrow's wedding banquet, laid out on five tables in the great dining-hall on the first floor.

Apart, of course, from the wedding ceremony itself in the gold and white castle chapel, the great event of the great day was the arrival of the eighty-one-year-old Emperor. He had travelled from Vienna by train to the little branch-line station of St Egyden near-by and from there by car to Schwarzau. Punctual to the minute as always, he drove at 11 A.M. through the main gate of the park, which had been shut ever since his last visit and only opened again for him now.

The old monarch was in exceptionally high spirits. Next to the bridal couple, it was indeed his day, for this wedding seemed to him to give his Empire and his dynasty a worthy and stable line of succession stretching into the second half of the century. After the service (which was conducted by Monsignore Bisletti as the personal representative of Pope Pius x), it was the Emperor who proposed the bridal toast to this newest member of his house; later, it was he again who grouped the principal wedding guests together in their proper order before the lens of the court photographer. The bride of that happy day even noticed one occasion on which the Emperor laughed out heartily and loud in front of everyone – a most unusual indulgence for him. The cause was one of the many august telegrams of congratulations brought to him to read. This particular one had come from Victor Emmanuel, King of that *Italia Unita* which had cost Duke Robert his Parma throne. 'That,' declared Franz Josef, 'was certainly not despatched with a willing heart.'

But there was one spectre at this historic feast. He was a spectre unbeknown to everyone, even to himself, for he was the shadow of a then unimaginable future. Seated respectfully upright next to the Emperor as the imperial automobile had entered the castle park that morning was a young Hungarian naval officer called Nicholas von Horthy. He was one of the monarch's many aides-de-camp and it just happened that he had been selected for duty on that day. Horthy was later heard boasting in Vienna that he was the only wedding guest at Schwarzau of non-princely blood. It was a lie, or a self-deception – as so much else was to be in his long and turbulent life.

The real significance of his presence there on that day was quite different. He was destined to become the political executioner of the bridegroom, after this ill-fated Archduke had first worn and then lost the Emperor's crown. For it was Nicholas von Horthy, promoted Vice-Admiral by Charles after a brilliant war career, who, as Regent of post-war Hungary, drove that same Charles and Zita from the outskirts of Budapest when the royal couple came back from their Swiss exile in the second of two desperate bids to recapture at least their Hungarian throne. And the date of this second and final betrayal was October 1921 – ten years almost to the day after the ambitious aide-de-camp had danced obsequious attendance in that other universe of the Schwarzau wedding.

From their marriage to the outbreak of war there were less than three years to go. These were in fact the only peaceful, untroubled years the young couple were ever to know. At least they were able to enjoy them without any premonition of that chain of disasters which was to begin for both Charles and the House of Habsburg in 1914.

After a honeymoon which began at Reichenau and then continued via the South Tyrol to Grado on the Adriatic and then down the Dalmatian coast to Bosnia, they returned to the tranquil routine of provincial garrison life. Tranquil but not uneventful. After barely four months' duty back at Brandeis on the Elbe, which was one of the more attractive of the Empire's military stations, Charles was abruptly transferred to one of the least attractive – Kolomea in remote eastern Galicia, where the Habsburg and Romanov empires touched shoulders. Though the distance was over 500 miles by the zig-zag route followed, Charles rode with his squadron of the Dragoons every yard of the way, his wife going ahead by rail to welcome him at the town or village appointed for the end of each day's journey. In this way, throughout March and early April of 1912, they travelled from west to east across virtually the whole of the Empire's northern border, including those Carpathian foothills where Charles was to serve again in bitter times in the war ahead.

They had an unpleasant surprise in store for him even now. In August 1912 the Austro-Hungarian Army held large-scale cavalry manoeuvres in Galicia in which Charles and his regiment took part. His horse slipped on wet ground, threw him, and he was severely concussed. Back he went to Vienna and then on to the mountain woods of his beloved Reichenau to convalesce.

A change of regiment was anyway due for him and the Emperor took this opportunity to carry it out. On 1 November 1912 the Archduke was posted as Major to the 39th Infantry Regiment in Vienna. This was not merely a transfer to a new branch of the army, which Charles, as a future Emperor, was expected to know more thoroughly than any ordinary Archduke. It was also, for him and his wife, the end of the relative obscurity of provincial garrison duty. The pleasant palace of Hetzendorff –

close to Schönbrunn itself – had been placed at their disposal by the Emperor. From now on they would live in the political glare of the capital.

There was doubtless another reason why the Emperor chose this particular moment to make this change for the young married couple. On 20 November, three weeks after the new posting was announced, Zita gave birth to a son – the first of eight children to be born in wildly fluctuating fortunes in the decade ahead. The baby prince was christened five days later with a formidable series of names which sounded like a seventeen-gun salute to the dynasties of Habsburg, Bourbon-Parma and Saxony combined: Francis Josef, Otto, Robert, Maria Antonia, Charles Maximilian, Henry, Sixtus, Xavier, Felix, René, Ludwig, Gaetus, Pius and Ignatius.

For the eighty-two-year-old Emperor, the birth of this healthy boy must really have seemed like a grappling-iron which the dynasty could throw far ahead of it into a slippery future. As one contemporary commentator put it, 'he could now see no fewer than three future Emperors of Austria around him' – his nephew Franz Ferdinand, his great-nephew Charles, and his great-great-nephew, the infant prince. It was a happy vision compared with the harsh truth that after him only one of those three would wear the crown – and that for barely two years.

The birth of a male heir to Charles and Zita heightened the significance of their installation at Hetzendorff. They had now begun to be presented – discreetly but unmistakably – as the rulers of the future. Discreetly it had to be, for the heir-apparent, Franz Ferdinand, was a touchy man by any standards and had become almost pathologically sensitive about his rights and dignity since that famous morganatic marriage. His own Vienna palace, the great two-tiered Belvedere, originally built by the seventeenth-century warrior Prince Eugene, had been for years a rival power centre to the Emperor's own court at Schönbrunn. Franz Ferdinand had his own ideas – which we shall come to later – about solving the conundrums of the multi-racial Empire. Nor was he content to wait patiently for his own accession to propound them. Aided by a brilliant and devoted personal staff, he was tirelessly at work to prepare for that event by placing his own nominees wherever and whenever possible in the key military and civilian posts of the Empire. Small wonder that his relations with Franz Josef, which had never been particularly cordial, grew more strained as the last years of peace went by. To the old ruler, his successor must have appeared at times like his undertaker.

Both Charles and Zita were determined on one thing: that Hetzendorff should never become a third centre of power in Vienna nor a second centre of intrigue against the Emperor. While personally liking his uncle, and admiring much in that stubborn, complex nature of his, young Charles was convinced that the heir-apparent was making a grave error in trespassing on sovereign preserves that were not yet his to tread. He knew that as and when Franz Ferdinand became Emperor, he would never stand for such behaviour from his own heir, who would be Charles himself. The rather daunting prospect of spending twenty years or more under the imperial shadow of his uncle was certainly one reason why Charles was so resolved not to 'blot his copybook' in advance. But another and perhaps more powerful argument was ethical – the conviction that the undivided authority of the crown was the best guarantee of the Empire's well-being. As he once commented during this time: 'Better a ruling hand that does not always steer the right course than government that seeks the good of the people along different paths. These can only lead in opposite directions or else cross one another.'

But for all these firm resolves, the eighteen months that now followed to the outbreak of war were exceptionally delicate ones for the young couple. All the obligations that the Emperor passed to them had to be discharged to the hilt, yet without ever if possible offending the sensibilities of the immediate heir. It was, in the Austrians' own phrase, 'a dance on eggs'.

That they succeeded without breaking many, if any, shells was due firstly to the tactful way in which Charles was launched by the Emperor on the Vienna stage. Thus, in the military sphere, he was given, from January 1913 onwards, intensive General Staff studies which filled part of every working day of his life. This, however, was training, not power. There was no excessively premature promotion and no special assignments which might have aroused the suspicions of his uncle. But Charles came through this difficult pre-war Vienna début unscathed mainly because his own straightforwardness and loyalty were soon seen to be beyond question. Even Franz Ferdinand's apprehensions were dispelled and he came to confide things to his young nephew that he would never have breathed to his Emperor. One of these confidences was disturbing and bizarre, as the following recollection of the then Archduchess Zita shows:

'At the beginning of May 1914, we were in Vienna and uncle Franz Ferdinand rang up one evening asking us to come over to the Belvedere for supper. It was just a small family meal with the heir-apparent, his wife and children, and ourselves as the only guests.

'Everything passed off normally – indeed quite gaily – until after supper, when the Duchess of Hohenberg [a title bestowed on the Countess

Chotek by the Emperor] went to take the children up to bed. After his wife left the room, the Archduke Franz Ferdinand suddenly turned to my husband and said:

' "I have something to say but I must say it quickly as I don't want your aunt to hear anything of this when she comes down. *I know that I shall soon be murdered.* In this desk are papers which concern you. When it happens, take them. They are for you."

'My husband protested: "Surely, you must be joking." But his uncle replied: "No, I am serious. After all, everything is ready. The crypt in Arstetten* is now finished."

'Before anything more could be said, the Duchess reappeared and we all did our best to pass the rest of the evening as though nothing out of the ordinary had happened.'

It was a staggering premonition. The following month, Franz Ferdinand and his wife left that same Belvedere for the last time, on the journey that was to take them down to Sarajevo and their deaths, and make the incredulous and horrified young nephew of that May supper party the new heir to the throne.

---

* The Lower Austrian castle of Franz Ferdinand's, on the Danube very close to Charles's own birthplace at Persenbeug.

Chapter 4

THE CRIPPLING LEGACY

For centuries, the Habsburg Empire had been treated, even by its rivals, as a historical necessity – a contrivance that Europe 'would have to have invented had it not existed' to keep this most turbulent and tangled part of Christendom in some sort of order. By the time Charles was born, however, the rise of nationalism among the eleven basic racial groups of the Empire was already turning the necessity into something of an improbability. This was not because those groups ever thought of themselves before 1914 as a substitute for the crown. They were, however, becoming a divisive challenge to an organism that had to be either united or dead.

From a necessity to an improbability then, even as the twentieth century dawned. But it was war – or rather, defeat in war – that first made the Empire a political impossibility. Sweeping domestic reforms that might have stood a chance of success in peacetime had to be postponed by a dynasty fighting for survival on the battlefield. At the other end of the scale, the separate nations now, for the first time, looked seriously to an existence outside the shell of the sinking Empire, which they were finally to bring down under the waves for ever in their own struggles to swim alone. In modern parlance, the First World War destroyed the 'image' of the Habsburg crown just as the Second World War destroyed that of the British Raj.

By 1914, Franz Josef had lived through eighty-four years of this rising nationalist tide and had ruled over it for an incredible sixty-six years. Throughout that time, though he must often have despaired of finding a lasting solution to the Empire's problems, he had never been known to utter one word which suggested that, at heart, he also despaired of its existence. There is now first-hand evidence that, after Sarajevo, even the old Emperor saw the writing on the wall. The then Archduchess Zita, wife of the man who had become the Emperor's immediate heir, recalls this remarkable conversation with Franz Josef in Vienna on 17 August 1914, a bare fortnight after the fighting had begun:

28

'It was the Archduke Charles's birthday and he was already away serving on the Russian front. I was by then living in Schönbrunn, for the Emperor had asked us to move in with him there from Hetzendorff for greater safety.

'Suddenly the Emperor appeared in my room in the east wing and said how much, on this of all days, he was thinking of the Archduke Charles and of me.

'It so happened that, on that same day, a big Austro-Hungarian victory had been reported against the Russians – the first one of the war. I congratulated the Emperor on it.

'He replied, in a resigned tone of voice: "Yes, it is a victory, but that is the way my wars have always begun, only to finish in defeat. *And this time it will be even worse. They will say I am old and cannot cope any more, and after that revolutions will break out and then it will be the end.*"

'I was absolutely shattered by his words and replied: "But that's surely not possible – the war we are fighting is such a just one!"

'At that, the Emperor smiled and, putting his head on one side, answered quietly:

'"Yes, one can see you are very young that you still believe in the victory of the just!"'

Like his murdered nephew Franz Ferdinand, the Emperor too had felt the future in his bones.

What were the problems of which even Franz Josef, the very incarnation of the dynasty, had secretly begun to despair? They spring to life again today to any reader who takes a look at the racial map of the Empire on pp. 32–3. Indeed, whenever in later chapters this book deals with Charles's own efforts, as Emperor, towards domestic reform and with his famous bid, launched one minute before midnight in 1918, to legitimize and therefore control the disintegration that had already begun, a glance back at that map may help to explain his actions and check gratuitous criticism of them. Not that, in the fifty years that have passed since his reign, his successors in Central and South-Eastern Europe have fared any better. Quite the contrary. After the Empire tore itself apart, the difficulty of matching the resulting fragments harmoniously together again was experienced first by the new nation-states themselves, then by Hitler, and finally, down to our own day, by the Kremlin. The failure of the Habsburgs is perhaps best explained by the fiasco of their successors.

There are two things to note about that incredible patchwork of the Empire's eleven peoples – all of whom, by 1918, were demanding greater independence from their neighbours or from the crown. The first, which is obvious, is the complexity of the pattern: look, for example, at those clumps of Germans isolated in southern Hungary and again in the extreme south-east corner of the Empire in Transylvania, where they lived cheek by jowl with other uprooted communities. Any attempt to superimpose the dotted lines of nation-states over this jumble would tend only to make confusion worse confounded – as the treaty-makers of Versailles discovered to their cost in 1919–20, when they created across the Habsburg lands more racial 'minorities' than the old Empire had ever known. (Significantly, it also never used that word; a people, however small, scattered and underprivileged, was still always a 'nation'.)

But the second problem which bedevilled all reform plans does not emerge from the map. It is the antiquity of all those component parts and the great pull of tradition that this created. If I may quote something I wrote on this theme ten years ago:

The confused racial tangle of the Danube Basin . . . had roots too deep to be pulled apart by force. It was the result of the exposed position of the area itself, the crossroads of primitive Europe towards which the horses' hoofs automatically picked their way. The minorities of the nineteenth century were the nomad tribes of the fifth century who reined their mounts at the entrance to an inviting valley. They were the horde of a Teuton chieftain made leaderless in battle; the artisan and merchant colonies of the Middle Ages; or the mercenaries of a feudal prince stranded too far away from home to return.

There are few regions on earth where traditions are so alive, so compressed, and so irreconcilable. It was the complete failure of President Wilson to understand this which produced most of the errors committed in 1918 under the name of 'self-determination'; and a similar naïveté of President Roosevelt's during the Second World War helped on the Danubian tragedy of 1945. In both cases, there was a certain bewildered impatience that Europe could not arrange her internal frontiers with the same ease with which America had arranged hers. But the United States had no history and too much space with which to redraw her boundaries, while the lands of the Austrian Empire had too much history and too little space.*

It was this conflict between the old historic demands of his various peoples (which they were very clear about) and their new democratic demands (which they were mostly very vague about) which had frustrated Franz Josef as it was to frustrate Charles after him. Both sovereigns' advisers were never short of theoretical solutions to solve the problems of the present. But not one of them could show his ruler a way round Austria's past.

* *The Austrian Odyssey*, pp. 56–7.

Admittedly, it was a formidable past to surmount. Thus the Hungarians, the most lethal adversaries both Emperors had to tackle, entered history 'Well-nigh full panoplied, by a single act' (as their British chronicler puts it)* in the last years of the ninth century when Arpad brought the seven Magyar tribes in from the east to the mid-Danube basin. Precisely in the year A.D. 1000, Arpad's great-great-grandson Stephen, pressed by family rivals for the Magyar leadership, applied in desperation to Rome for recognition as a Christian king. The Pope, Sylvester II, agreed to be his patron, and, according to legend, sent back an apostolic cross and a crown for Stephen's coronation on Christmas Day of that same Millenium year. At one stroke, the Magyars thus ceased to be tribal outlaws and became a princely people, whose throne and whose lands were henceforth held inviolable because they had been granted as a papal fief.

All the stubborn emotional mysticism of the Hungarians and their political resistance, in the modern age of nationalism, to redrawing boundaries held by them on a sacred trust, goes back to that far-distant coronation. And the papal regalia which had first given them freedom as a people was ever afterwards preserved as the symbol of their statehood. In December 1916, as we shall see, Charles was to be crowned in Budapest (as Charles IV of Hungary) with parts of that very same crown placed 916 Christmases before on the head of Stephen.† It brought with it unique obligations from which he could never free himself while in power, as well as unique opportunities which he could never quite exploit while in exile.

The Magyars were by far the biggest of the non-German nations under the Habsburg crown (over ten million out of the Empire's total population of fifty-one million). They were also always the most articulate, the most insistent, and the most persistent in their demand for a separate identity. But they were by no means alone in the depth and pull of their historic roots. The Croats, for example, who were eventually placed under their control as a 'secondary' race of the Empire, had been an independent multi-national kingdom before the Austrians themselves. As far back as 924, the Croat King Tomislav had held part of the Dalmatian coast, only to lose it eventually to Venice (a foretaste of the Italian–Yugoslav rivalry of the 1950s over Trieste). One reason why, despite this pedigree, the Hungarians 'claimed' these lands was again historical: in 1097 the Croat kingdom itself had been absorbed by the Magyars under King Kalman.

* *Hungary, A Short History*, by C. A. Macartney, p. 1.

† The crown was taken to the West at the end of the Second World War and is now in American safe-keeping. One of the most impressive tributes to its power as a non-political symbol of Magyar nationhood is the tireless campaign of the Communist regime of Hungary to get it returned.

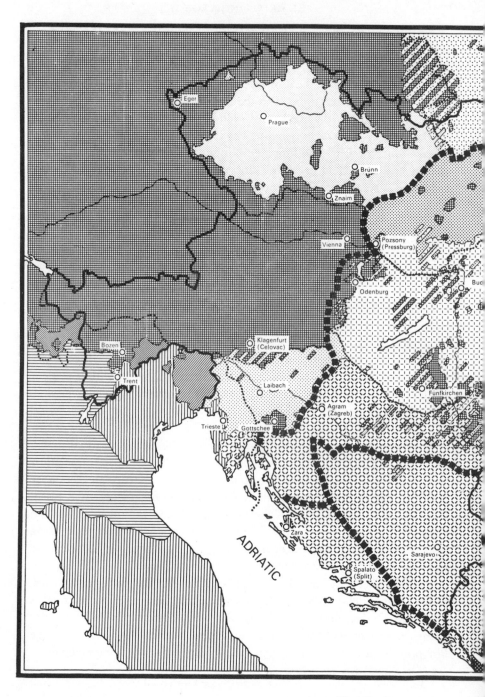

The distribution of races wit[h

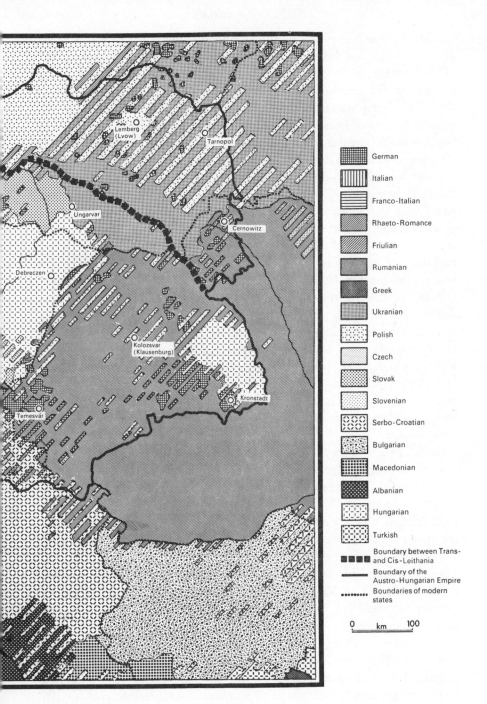

German	
Italian	
Franco-Italian	
Rhaeto-Romance	
Friulian	
Rumanian	
Greek	
Ukranian	
Polish	
Czech	
Slovak	
Slovenian	
Serbo-Croatian	
Bulgarian	
Macedonian	
Albanian	
Hungarian	
Turkish	

Boundary between Trans- and Cis-Leithania
Boundary of the Austro-Hungarian Empire
Boundaries of modern states

0   km   100

Lemberg (Lvow)
Tarnopol
Ungarvar
Cernowitz
Debreczen
Kolozsvar (Klausenburg)
Temesvár
Kronstadt

Austro-Hungarian Empire

It was the same story among the Slav peoples in the northern half of the Empire. There had been a 'Greater Moravian' kingdom as early as the ninth century under the Moravian chieftain Svatopluk. The other element in the traditional racial strife of this area, the Germans, was almost as deeply rooted. The first German craftsmen had settled in the wooded fringes of Bohemia by the tenth century – anticipating Hitler and his Sudeten problem by a thousand years. The tension between these two seemingly unmixable races often had to be fought out on the battlefield: it was the victory of Rudolf I, the founder of the Habsburg dynasty, over the Bohemian King Ottokar II in 1278 which first established the pre-dominance of Vienna over Prague, though the battle had to be fought again four centuries later.

And to the north of this Czech–Moravian belt, the Poles had, of course, had *their* age of glory in the fifteenth century, when the Jagellon dynasty had challenged the Habsburgs for the mastery of all Central Europe. Indeed, after the Austro-Germans and the Magyars, and together with the Bohemians, the Poles were the 'historic' nation of the Empire *par excellence*. The other racial groups counted for much less. The monarchy's Italian subjects living south of the Brenner, for example, were coveted by an Italy which, though united, had less than two generations of statehood behind it, even by 1914. The Serbo-Croats, Ruthenes, Slovaks and the like were all races without continuous pedigree, the so-called 'non-historic' peoples which were constitutionally weaker because their political roots were shorter.

Some of these lands the Habsburgs had won in battle. Others they had first gained by marriage, like the crowns of Bohemia and Hungary, which fell to them in the sixteenth century through the most spectacular double-wedding of all time. But even these great prizes, though easily won, were hard defended. The personal union of the two neighbour kingdoms with the Habsburg crown only became fully effective in the case of Prague after 1620 (the Battle of the White Mountain), and in the case of Budapest after 1687, when the Emperor's armies, having crushed the Turkish invaders before the gates of Vienna, counter-attacked and drove them out of Hungary as well. The Habsburg Empire entered the modern age united by the sword as well as by the wedding ring.

One final point about this tangle of races – more knots than string – that Charles was to inherit. It concerns the danger of reading twentieth-century slogans like 'parliamentary democracy' and 'self-determination' into a setting where they had no place. Throughout the nineteenth century, the nationalist agitation with which Vienna had to contend was basically a demand, not for autonomy outside the Empire, but for greater power and privilege inside it. It was a struggle for personal and racial *status* rather than for political freedom. At the administrative level, the burning issues were likely to be which tongues should be taught in which primary schools. At the local level, the nationality of the new post-master usually meant more than the right to vote. Apart from a few bands of political demons, freedom to the masses before 1914 meant hearing the sound of your own language and getting a fair share of the Emperor's uniforms.

It was only the war which transformed this, as it transformed so much else. After the Russian revolution of March 1917 social and ideological pressures were added, *for the first time*, to the Empire's chronic racial tensions. This mixture was to prove as explosive as it was unfamiliar. It was Charles's misfortune to be sitting on the throne when it developed; but it did not exist, as so many historians have blandly assumed, before his time. Right down to his accession, history and race remained the realities of the Empire, with the crown as their only common symbol. No one *felt* himself a 'South Slav' (let alone a Yugoslav!). As for the Czechoslovakia (without the hyphen in between) that was soon to emerge in the north, this contradicted history as well as race. It started life not as a nation at all but as a confidence trick played by the Czech exiles on President Wilson.

Such were the formidable domestic problems Charles was to inherit. What were the solutions that had been tried out before his time, in an attempt, not to remove all discontent, but to make as many of the eleven nations as contented as possible?

In the first half of his long reign, Franz Josef had tried to shuffle and cut the racial pack in any number of ways – providing always the court cards did not drop out. The first proposal in the year of his accession (1848) was the so-called Kremsier Constitution which would have divided the existing provinces of the Empire into administrative sub-districts of separate nationalities where each people would enjoy the use of its own tongue in schools and law-courts. (Another glance at that racial map of the Empire shows the practical difficulties confronting this admirable aim.) Twelve years later, in the so-called 'October Diploma' of 1860, the Emperor and his advisers sought stability by sharing out more power among aristocratic Diets of the 'historic' nations – which, of course, would have left the rest unsatisfied.

A year after this, in the so-called 'February Patent', new-fangled democratic devices were imported in an attempt to reconcile the rival races with what was essentially borrowed political magic. A two-chambered Parliament was set up in Vienna to which, in theory, all the peoples of the

Empire would send their delegates – elected on a complicated curial system which in fact favoured the Austro-Germans. This was a return to centralism, with a genuine legislative body now installed to help the crown in the unifying role it had hitherto played alone. The trouble was that the new Parliament was the crown's creation, not the people's. It was a rootless plant set in a deep-rooted world, and it languished accordingly. Some nations, like the Hungarians, simply ignored it. Others, like the Czechs, turned up to walk out. Those who both came and stayed remained only to squabble. It was an unhappy, inorganic start to modern political life, and its consequences were far-reaching. The Austrian Republic of today is still labouring to make proper use of the Parliament which a harassed Emperor hopefully presented to Vienna a century ago.

Then, in 1867, Franz Josef finally took his historic plunge with a reform that was to end all other reforms. It did this, not by making them unnecessary, but by making them impossible. In the so-called *Ausgleich* or Compromise with Hungary, he split the orb of his Empire into two: an Austrian 'half' which was in fact a vast outer crescent sweeping from Galicia west to Bohemia, then curving down through Vienna to Bosnia in the far south; and a Hungarian 'half', the compact central mass enclosed by this crescent which was, in essence, the old lands of St Stephen's crown.* In internal affairs, the Magyars henceforth enjoyed what amounted to domestic autonomy and direct rule over all the peoples of their portion – Croats and Transylvanians included.

Though still under Franz Josef's sceptre, they were now given their own Prime Minister, their own government, their own law. Only in the three 'imperial' fields of foreign policy, defence and finance did they share power with Vienna, through three special joint ministries created for the purpose and made technically responsible to 'Delegations' of sixty members drawn from the Parliaments of the two partner states. A ludicrous little river called the Leitha, which trickles down through the Burgenland just east of Vienna, entered history at this point to define the cumbrous transformation. Everything on the Hungarian side was henceforth known as 'Transleithania' and everything on the Austrian side as 'Cisleithania'. On 8 June 1867, after the Hungarian Parliament had voted this 'Dual Settlement' with Austria, Franz Josef was crowned King of Hungary in Budapest.

For the Magyars, all this spelt the triumph of national over imperial thinking. For the Austrians it spelt the long-term ruin of the Imperial idea itself. An organism that could only survive in unity had voluntarily cut itself in half in the search for stability. Almost as fateful as this internal

* See map on pp. 32–3 for this Dualist division.

cleavage was the damage to be done as the years passed to the Empire's reputation abroad. The Magyars, now masters in their own multi-racial house, chose to go on running it along feudal and chauvinist lines. In doing so, they drove the two segments of the Dualist Empire further apart. By 1914, the 'Austrian half' had become politically and socially capable of adjustment to modern conditions; it had established both universal suffrage and a balance of wealth and influence between town and country, industry and the plough. The Hungarian half had neither and was thus doomed to go under. Of the 413 seats in the Budapest 'Parliament', no fewer than 407 were held by Magyars, though these represented little more than fifty per cent of the population. And in a basically agricultural economy, no less than one-third of the land was owned (and under-cultivated) by some 4,000 of its nineteen million inhabitants.*

This was the sixteenth century trying to struggle on defiantly into the twentieth. Having renounced their right of direct control in the 1867 Compromise, the Austrians were powerless to drag the Hungarians forward with them. Franz Josef's Dualist experiment began by destroying the internal unity of the Habsburg Empire. It ended by destroying its standing in the world outside.

The old Emperor, as though exhausted by the one bold stroke of his cautious life, clung to his Dualist solution despite all the long-term hazards it revealed, and all the pressures for reform from Austrian conservatives and Magyar liberals alike. But his nephew, Franz Ferdinand, had other ideas about the Empire's future and, as he was heir-apparent for eighteen years before his assassination, he had plenty of time to develop them. In essence, his plan was to break up the Dualist state of his uncle, restore centralized power to the hands of the Emperor in Vienna, and reduce the Magyars from their position as haughty equals to a status of privileged servants in a unified Empire run again by the Austro-Germans. And the main method chosen for demoting the Magyars was to promote to greater independence their Slav fellow-citizens in the 'Hungarian half' – above all the Croats.

All this was revealed in those papers which Franz Ferdinand had hurriedly mentioned to the young Archduke Charles in that after-supper conversation in the Belvedere in May 1914.† Franz Ferdinand has gone down in history as the great champion of 'Trialism' – that is, the creation

---

* An even more striking statistic was that the 324 largest private estates – which averaged some 41,000 acres each – accounted alone for over nineteen per cent of the country's total agricultural land.

† The papers, which Charles did not manage to see until his own accession in 1916, were deposited as the *Nachlass Erzherzog Franz Ferdinand* in the Haus-Hof-und Staatsarchiv in Vienna, where they still are.

of a separate South Slav state as a third basic unit of the Monarchy to exist together with an enhanced Austria and a chastened Hungary. He certainly favoured this idea at the turn of the century and neither he nor his principal advisers ever abandoned it publicly, if only because it was the corner-stone of his anti-Hungarian policy.

But those 'secret papers'* left behind for his nephew reveal that the Belvedere planners, long before the murder of their chief, had developed serious doubts about the South Slav 'solution', as it was optimistically called. This was partly due to misgivings about the supposedly undying loyalty of the Serbo-Croats to Vienna; partly to the sheer cumbrousness of the projected Trialist state (*three* joint ministries; *three* Parliaments; *three* joint delegations); and partly to the familiar fears that 'promotion' for any new nation of the Empire would only increase the clamour from the others – in this case, of course, above all from the ancient Slav kingdom of Bohemia in the north.

It is thus doubtful whether fully-fledged Trialism would have worked. It is even doubtful whether Franz Ferdinand as Emperor would ever have tried to make it work. We can never know. Princip's bullets came between the Archduke and such hazy dreams of power as he had cherished.

Like anyone close to the throne – and indeed anyone in power in the old Empire – Charles grew up with all these theories and counter-theories dinning in his ears. Centralization or decentralization; racial units versus historical ones; Dualism versus Trialism. For the politicians and pundits these were the ceaseless debates of the time. But for Charles, as for Franz Ferdinand, there was an inheritance as well as an argument at stake. The young Archduke had wasted no time developing ideas of his own on the subject, nor in discussing them with the woman who was to become his wife and later his Empress. The then Princess Zita has recalled these political views of Charles, uttered when he was twenty-three years old and still her fiancé:

'I first heard his ideas about the Empire from his lips in April 1911, when we were just getting engaged and the throne seemed very, very remote. We were staying at the time at St Jakob in Styria with the Archduchess Maria Theresa and went out together shooting capercailzie.

'On one such outing the talk turned to politics and he said to me: "Dualism cannot be saved. Trialism is not just and anyway doesn't go far enough. The only solution is a truly federal one to give all the peoples a chance."

* Especially the set of political instructions worked out for the *Thronwechsel* – the detailed programme for the accession that never came.

'That summed up his whole approach and he never wavered in it. He wanted to come back again to the old Habsburg tradition – before the centralization measures of the Empress Maria Theresa – and ensure that every nation should have its freedom within the state as a whole. On another occasion I heard him say, speaking of an Emperor's duties: "A father makes no distinction between his children."

'This meant that he had no personal prejudices. He was certainly not anti-Hungarian as has been alleged. For him all nations were the same. But he was convinced that one group could not be favoured above the rest – as the Magyars and Germans were favoured under Dualism.

'We had up to seventeen nationalities, if one counted the tiny ones as well as the eleven main groups. He was prepared to give *all seventeen* their individual freedom if they wanted it – for example, Bosnia-Herzegovina separated from Croatia as well as, of course, from Hungary.

'And he went even further. He always stressed to me that it wouldn't even matter if one or the other nation wanted to declare itself a Republic in this process. He used to point out to me that the three Hansa towns were, after all, Republics within the German Reich. The essential thing for him was that, whatever constitutional form they chose, the nations should maintain their link with the monarchy and their identity within the state as a whole.'

Three points of interest arise out of this account of the future Emperor's views. The first is the precocity of his thinking. His mind was clearly made up when still an unmarried man in his early twenties, with the crown apparently a generation or more ahead. The second is its consistency: when he came to wear that crown, he never wavered one inch from the ideals he had nurtured as a relatively unknown aspirant to the throne. The third and most important is its 'progressiveness' – measured by the cautious conservative standards of his own dynasty and day. The Indian leader, Mr Nehru, speaking nearly fifty years later of another dynasty and day, claimed he had been the first to 'invent' the modern concept of Empire after India had become the first Republic under the British crown. A young Austrian Archduke had beaten him by half a century – though, unlike the Kashmiri Hindu, it was not to be his happy fate to put his ideas into practice.

This basic philosophy of Charles's explains his attitude to the steadily rising growth of nationalism. He did not oppose it, as did at heart Franz Josef, who would echo the famous question 'Is he a patriot for *me*?' He did not treat it as an instrument of imperial policy, anti-Hungarian or otherwise, as did Franz Ferdinand. He wanted to do with it something quite different and perhaps quite impossible: to absorb it into the existing Empire.

This was why the shrill chauvinistic undertones of the new mood always jarred on his ears. The Austrian 'credo' was conciliation. That of the nationalist era was hate. The dynasty could only live, could only survive, on the first. Yet both inside and outside the Empire – in Hungary to the east, Italy to the south and Wilhelmian Germany to the north – it was surrounded by nations who fed on the second. This was the terrible and unique dilemma Charles faced in war. His allies, as well as his enemies, were fighting for aims that could only destroy his own.

He did not live to see this national egotism which he feared so much become mistrusted by the world at large – a world indeed which was to seek protection from it in a United Nations or a united Europe. His tragedy was that of his own Imperial House. He was international too early in history; national too late.

Chapter 5

THE THRONE

Whatever visions the young Archduke may have had about the future of Austro-Hungary, June 1914 was not the time to float them. All eyes and minds were turned to the crisis that faced the Empire as a result of his uncle's murder, the crisis that slid during the following six weeks inexorably over the abyss into war. Charles, though now heir-apparent, played no role in shaping the uncompromising policy Vienna now adopted, culminating in the fateful ultimatum to Serbia of 23 July. Indeed, he does not even appear to have been consulted about the tone or terms of this *démarche* which proved the diplomatic genesis of the great conflict.

This was perhaps just as well. To have been called upon by the Emperor to take a stand would have caught him in a conflict of emotions. On the one hand, it was an Archduke of his own house, and his uncle at that, who had just been struck down by assassins certainly encouraged and probably controlled by the Belgrade government. Charles would have been less than human had he not also been touched by the white-hot anger that was sweeping Vienna. On the other hand, with his whole being he already loathed war, and already dreaded its consequences for his Empire. One imagines therefore that, had he been able to shape Austrian policy at this cataclysmic point, he would have restrained some of those hot-heads who were busy turning the demand for justice into a cry for vengeance. But he was not yet steering what Bismarck had once called 'the worm-eaten galleon of the Austrian Empire'. This enabled him, two years later, to take over the helm without any taint of personal responsibility for the disaster course on which it had been set, and without any reproach of inconsistency when he immediately tried to steer a new course.

He was, however, quickly to realize his new and delicate responsibilities in a number of ways, some of them seemingly trivial. The then Archduchess Zita recalls the following episode which took place within a few days of his becoming heir:

'When the bodies of the Archduke Franz Ferdinand and his wife were brought back to Vienna to be buried, protests got around that the Duchess Sophie was being deprived of her proper share of pomp at the funeral. The Archduke Charles finally agreed to be the spokesman for this group. So he went to the Emperor Franz Josef and asked for "a bit more ceremony" on the dead woman's behalf.

'He told me afterwards that the old Emperor, after listening to his plea, had looked at him in silent astonishment for a while, and had then replied sadly:

'"What more do they want? I have ordered for her exactly the same ceremony as I did for my own Empress – and she was also murdered!"' *

'And when this reply was taken back and the protocol experts were told to look it all up, they found that the Emperor was right.'

Charles soon found himself the centre of far weightier court intrigue. It spun around the exact part he should play as heir-apparent of an Empire now at war. Should his duties be basically political, at his Emperor's side in Vienna; or was his proper place as a soldier at the front, where he would learn more about fighting but not about ruling? And if he was to be sent to the battlefield, what position was he to hold and what safeguards could be laid down to ensure that he would never be taken prisoner by the enemy?

The same tug-of-war over his great-nephew's role was going on in the Emperor's mind too, and, fortunately for Charles, the result was a compromise. He saw enough of active service and high command in both of the Empire's main fronts (Russia; then, after Italy's declaration of war, the south Tyrol, and finally Russia again) to earn the respect of the army and to fill out, from personal experience, his own inner loathing of war. But between these spells in the field came long intervals back in the capital where he could be personally introduced by the aged sovereign to the mechanism of power.

His first period on the north-east Galician front lasted only a few weeks. He had been attached to the Austro-Hungarian headquarters established in what was fondly believed to be the impregnable fortress town of Przemysl. Though the nominal Commander-in-Chief there was Charles's uncle, the Archduke Frederick, it was the Emperor's able but overbearing Chief of Staff, Conrad von Hötzendorff, who ruled the roost. Young Charles soon realized that, under the formidable Conrad, he too could only become a static figurehead. When in September the headquarters was moved back to Teschen, he therefore asked the Emperor

* Elizabeth of Bavaria, stabbed to death as the motiveless deed of an Italian anarchist on 10 September 1898, as she was about to board a lake steamer at Geneva, on the quay-side opposite the Hôtel Beau Rivage.

whether he might be given a new and more mobile role as the link between Franz Josef and all his armies. The request was granted and it began the most fruitful period of Charles's training.

For the next year and a half, his special missions brought him to nearly all the battlefronts, and taught him at first hand the problems of co-operating with Austria's allies, as well as those of fighting the common enemy. The weeks and even months when he was based on Vienna for these trips were used to gain equally first-hand knowledge of the political aspects of the war. Every day, on Franz Josef's orders, the same ministers or officials who made their regular reports to the Emperor repeated them separately to the young Archduke, who went daily to the Hofburg palace in the centre of Vienna for the purpose.

More than this. The then Archduchess Zita recalls that, despite the enormous demands on his time, Franz Josef devoted part of each day to a personal 'tutorial' in which he would teach his great-nephew the arts of government as he had learned them over the past sixty-five years.

'Every night or morning, the Emperor would give the Archduke Charles some of the files for him to deal with. And the next day, when he reported on the decisions he had taken or recommended, the Emperor would question him on his reasons and comment on his conclusions.

'So close and regular did this contact become indeed that quite a large clique of people at court began to protest that the Archduke was spending too much time in Vienna when he should have been at the front. Those involved were largely the former advisers of his late uncle Franz Ferdinand, though Conrad also wanted Archduke Charles back "under observation" at Army Headquarters and not out of his reach in the capital.

'All this put the Emperor in a dilemma. He was a soldier himself and so was his great-nephew. Yet now he wanted his successor near at hand.'

It was the Italian front which finally solved the Emperor's dilemma. Italy, of course, had been allied with Austria and Germany by the Triple Alliance system of 1879–82. But she had ominously opted for neutrality when war broke out. It was the beginning of a treachery which reached its climax on 23 May 1915, when Rome, bribed by secret promises from France and Britain of vast territorial awards at Austria's expense,* put greed before loyalty and joined the fighting on the Western powers' side. There had always existed a very taut relationship – racial, political and dynastic – between the Austrians and the Italians. The temper and patience of Vienna now broke for good. The Italian war now became the only really 'popular' one; the Italian front the only battle-line where the Emperor's troops fought with their hearts as well as their heads. It was

* The so-called Secret Treaties of London.

here that in March 1916 he finally sent Charles, as Commander of the XXth Army Corps * which had been newly formed, to take part in the planned spring offensive.

To take over an *élite* Corps for a major attack in war was a big step for a man who had hitherto only held command of a battalion in peacetime. But the military histories of both Austria and Italy show that the young Archduke, for all his hatred of bloodshed, acquitted himself well. Within a week of the start of the great Austrian offensive on 15 May 1916, his Corps had captured its first objective (the fortified area of Arsiero) and by the end of May his troops had fought their way against bitter resistance to within five miles of their second target (Schio).

Then, just as fresh Italian reserves had begun to slow the pace of this southern advance, a savage blow struck the Emperor's forces far away to the north-east. On 4 June the Russians under General Brusilov overwhelmed two entire Austro-Hungarian armies and tore a great rent across the whole Galicia–Bukovina front. It was the worst military crisis the war had brought so far to Vienna. The offensive in Italy – which was anyway slowing – was now called off and a retreat to shorter lines ordered. Early in July, Charles was himself transferred to the threatened northeast front, where he was further promoted and given command of an army.

Here he served out the last few months that lay ahead of him as heir-apparent, mixing military operations with an ever-increasing degree of political activity. This latter was not confined to the regular pouches of state documents which – up here as down in Italy – the Emperor sent him for study and comment from Vienna. Charles was now being consulted more and more by Franz Josef on decisions vital for the whole conduct of the war. Thus in September 1916 the Archduke was asked for his opinion as to whether Conrad, with whom the Emperor was becoming increasingly disillusioned, should remain on as Chief of Staff or not. Though sharing many of these misgivings, Charles recommended that Conrad 'should for the time being be left at his post, in view of his great military reputation which was acknowledged also by the Germans'. His advice was accepted, though the other reforms he mentioned in that same memorandum of 29 September had to wait for his own accession to be carried out.

Finally, on his periodic trips back to the capital for consultation, Charles found himself being launched increasingly on an independent political

---

* Its four regiments were a typical cross-section of the Empire: the *Kaiserjäger* of Tyrol; the Upper Austrian No. 14 from Linz; the Czech No. 21 from Caslau; and the 50th Hungarian–Rumanian.

programme as heir-apparent. On 8 October, for example, after his own audience with the Emperor, the Archduke is recorded as having received the three leading members of the Government (the Prime Minister Stürgkh, the Foreign Minister Burian and the War Minister Krobatin) for separate discussions. And the day after that, he left for the German head-quarters at Pless where he held top-level discussions on Franz Josef's behalf with his ally, the German Emperor William, and with the real rulers of wartime Germany, the Generals Hindenburg and Ludendorff. It was not the first time Charles had met the German Emperor (they had talked very frankly to one another in January 1915, when the German headquarters was at Charleville); but this was the most wide-ranging dis-cussion that the young Archduke had so far conducted with William or any other foreign leader.

It can have brought him no encouragement over an alliance about which already, after two years of war, he had few illusions. One topic of discus-sion was a joint peace move to the Western powers. For weeks, Vienna had been urging Berlin to agree to including some concrete statement of Austro-German war aims – as precise and as moderately worded as possible – in the formal approach it was agreed to make to the enemy side. Charles failed now with the Emperor as the Austrian ministers had failed at their level. As a result, when the joint peace appeal was issued, it was couched in terms which were both tough and vague, and it forfeited any prospect of success accordingly.

This was one sobering omen for the future to come out of the Pless talks. There were others: a clear clash of views as to whether a reconsti-tuted Poland should come under Berlin's influence or Vienna's; and a suggestion of the Emperor William's that Germany and Austria-Hungary should, in peacetime, bind themselves more closely together even than in war – plans which Charles resisted now as he was to resist them from the throne. All in all, this visit to Pless and the spectacle of the vain and emotionally unstable German sovereign strutting around on the iron lead of his generals, must have been a disturbing one. There were to be many more such experiences later on, some of them bitter as well.

After Pless, Charles returned to the Eastern front, where, on 13 October, he took a new and still higher command over an Austro-Hungarian Army Group. This was a key post on the vital front and seemed as if it would absorb most of his energies. But in fact he had less than four weeks left both as an Archduke and as a field commander.

Late in the afternoon of 11 November, a telegram from Vienna arrived for Charles at his headquarters in the little Saxon town of Schässburg. It was from the Court Chamberlain, Prince Montenuovo, and urged the immediate return of the heir-apparent to the capital 'in view of the condition of the Emperor'.

Franz Josef lived on for ten more days after Charles's arrival in Vienna. It was not only his iron constitution, but also the iron bands of routine and hard work – forged by nearly seven decades of rule – which still held him up. Until the last hours of his life he laboured away, an imperial Sisyphus, pushing at the ever-recurring mound of state documents which piled up on his desk. But, unlike that unfortunate of the classical legend, his hopeless task was not to be for all eternity. The end came at five minutes past nine on the evening of 21 November 1916, in his plainly-furnished bedroom in Schönbrunn. The old heart that, ever since 1848, had also been the heart-beat of an Empire, stopped at last.

This is how the young woman who became Empress of Austro-Hungary at that same moment remembers the final day:

'My husband and I saw the Emperor for the last time shortly before noon on the day of his death. By then he had been fighting off bronchitis and afterwards pneumonia for more than a fortnight, but he insisted on carrying on as usual. That morning, for example, he had a temperature of 102°, but was working on some documents about recruitment when we called.

'When he heard that I as well as my husband was coming into his room, he asked us to wait until he had changed into his formal military jacket to receive us. But I sent word back insisting that he did not, and he reluctantly agreed.

'When we went in, the Emperor still made a normal impression and talked quite normally, despite his fever and his weakness. He told us how happy he was to have received the blessing of the Pope,* and also what joy the victories that our armies had just won in Rumania had brought him. We left after a general conversation of this sort, not thinking a crisis was imminent.

'Later that day, when he was obviously expecting the end, we were told he had said this: "I took over the throne under the most difficult conditions and I am leaving it under even worse ones. I would like to have spared Charles this. But he is made of the right stuff, and will know how to cope."

'Then, that night, came the sudden collapse and the end. The Archduke and I had been summoned, of course, to his bedside, but when we arrived he was already in the last deep sleep from which he never woke.

'When it was all over and we all filed out of the death chamber into the crowded ante-room no one knew what to say or what to do. No one

* Pope Benedict xv.

wanted to speak first and so for a few moments there was utter silence. Then I remember the dear plump figure of Prince Lobkowitz going up to my husband and, with tears in his eyes, making the sign of the cross on Charles's forehead. As he did so he said: "May God bless your Majesty!"

'It was the first time we had heard the Imperial title used to us.'

That 'frightful responsibility' whose shadow Charles and Zita had first felt in their peaceful garden at Reichenau two and a half years before had now enveloped them. She was twenty-four years old. Her husband, the new Emperor, was barely five years older.

Chapter 6

YOUNG EMPEROR, ANCIENT CROWN

Charles had stepped into the shoes of a living legend. There was much to be said for and against this. The disadvantage, of course, was that he could never hope, in the two years ahead that were to be his slim portion of power, to exert anything like the personal dominance of his great-uncle. Franz Josef, for all his courtliness and charm, had anyway been a man of far more authoritarian stamp; and this sterner nature of his had been stiffened seven-fold by those seven decades of rule. He had sat on the throne, after all, for longer than the bulk of his fifty million subjects had lived. As for his ministers, there was not one of them with a shred of his experience. Whatever course of action at home or abroad any one of them proposed, the old sovereign could draw a parallel and point a moral – usually a disillusioned one – from something he had lived through since 1848, and they had not.

Charles had little of this practical knowledge and none of this mystique. He had been prepared for office as well as any heir could have been in the midst of a war that gave military considerations priority over political ones. But there had been less than two and a half years even of this difficult apprenticeship; and, by adamantly refusing to follow Franz Ferdinand's example and set up a 'rival court' of his own, Charles had never snatched at one single ounce of extra responsibility that the Emperor did not freely give him. It is quite wrong to say that in 1916 he was unprepared for power, or that his training had been neglected. But it is undeniable that this training had been limited in time and constricted by the straitjacket of war.

There was also, however, a brighter side to the accession picture. Franz Josef may have been the bedrock of the Empire, but there were many who complained that, in the end, the rock had become so fossilized that nothing green and living could grow out of it. Now the throne was occupied by a handsome and sincere young couple with a four-year-old son who looked the picture-book image of a Crown Prince. As the trio walked through the streets of Vienna behind the Emperor's coffin, not a heart could fail to be stirred with hope for new beginnings, as well as touched with nostalgia for the past that they were all following to its grave.

The proclamation which Charles issued the day after his accession succeeded only partially in capturing this hopeful mood. There was not a hint, let alone an outright mention, of internal political reform. The key sentence on domestic affairs ran:

I desire to be a just and benign ruler to my peoples. I will hold high their constitutional freedoms and other dues and carefully preserve the equality of everyone before the law. It will be my ceaseless endeavour to promote the moral and spiritual welfare of my peoples, to protect freedom and order in my lands and to ensure for all productive branches of society the fruits of honest work....

The one unconventional thing about these hallowed platitudes was something no ordinary citizen could have known. The new sovereign really meant them with all his young heart.

It was only in the passage on war and peace that something of Charles's own personality came through and a new note was struck accordingly. After some ritual references to his 'unbreakable resolve to fight the battle through' comes the following significant sentence:

I will do everything to banish in the shortest possible time the horrors and sacrifices of war, to win back for my peoples the sorely-missed blessings of peace, insofar as this can be reconciled with the honour of our arms, the essential living requirements of my lands and their loyal allies and the defiance of our enemies.

This sentence, we know on the Empress's authority, was inserted at Charles's own command. It was the first round, on his first day of power, in the long losing struggle for peace. The lack of anything novel or arresting in the remainder of the proclamation is explained by the Empress as being due above all to the fact that, throughout Charles's time as heir-apparent and now at the moment of his accession, his advisers and friends were either scattered along the battlefronts or – like Polzer – had not yet emerged as 'confidants'. Unlike Franz Ferdinand, Charles did not have eighteen years of peace in which to prepare his proclamation down to the last comma; nor did he have an established secretariat of brilliant men like the 'Belvedere clique' to do his preliminary labours for him. The explanation is convincing. Yet it remains a pity that, in the vital field of the Empire's internal reform, no new trumpet call could have been sounded in November 1916. The enemy powers abroad, as well as the still loyal peoples at home, would have pricked up their ears at it. And, as we shall see, there was a vital – and ultimately fatal – link between the two.

Barely twelve hours after becoming Emperor, Charles first came face to face with the central domestic problem which overshadowed that accession proclamation, and indeed his whole reign: Hungary. At 11 A.M. on the morning of 22 November, Count Stefan Tisza, the Hungarian Prime Minister, came to be received in audience at Schönbrunn Palace, at his own urgent request, by his new sovereign. Tisza was a Calvinist whose nine-teenth-century title of nobility was, by Hungary's mellow standards, as raw as an unboiled egg. But he did not yield to the oldest and proudest names in his country in the fierceness of his Magyar patriotism and in his Messianic determination to preserve intact the ancient heritage of King Stephen – whose name, indeed, he bore. It was concern for this heritage that had brought him post-haste from Budapest and into the imperial audience-chambers of Vienna.

How much of the murdered uncle's anti-Hungarian and pro-Slav philosophy had his new master absorbed? Did the young monarch and his advisers have plans – as the 'Belvedere group' had elaborated for Franz Ferdinand – to use the accession as an instrument of reform, an instrument that could only cut into the flesh of the 'Hungarian half'? If these dangers existed, there was, in Tisza's view, only one way to scotch them. The new Emperor must allow himself to be crowned in Budapest as swiftly as possible as King of Hungary, with all the sacred obligations this entailed as keeper of both the Magyar legend and the Magyar lands.

There were those in Vienna who had foreseen this Hungarian pressure – the ubiquitous and tireless Polzer, for example. That same day, he had handed in to Count Wallis, Charles's former tutor, a lengthy 'pro-memoria' * on the subject for transmission to the new ruler. In this, Polzer cogently argued the obvious. The constitutional oath required of the sovereign by the Fundamental Law of 21 December 1867 in his capacity as Emperor of Austria was incompatible with the Coronation oath as King of Hungary, since the constitutions of what were now the two halves of the Empire were themselves at odds. Furthermore, though Polzer did not add this in so many words, if Charles was really resolved to be 'a father to all his peoples', how could he swear, as Hungarian King, to keep under Magyar domination those same South Slav nations who looked to him as Austrian Emperor for their liberation?

Polzer accepted that a time factor existed. By the Hungarian Laws of 1790–91, the King of Hungary had to permit himself to be crowned within six months of his predecessor's death. But this delay, he argued, should be used (and if necessary prolonged) to enable the Austrian and Hungarian

---

* Text in Polzer, *op. cit.*, pp. 113–15.

Parliaments to reconcile their conflicting laws once and for all and so preserve their joint sovereign from swearing contradictory oaths.*

Reasonable though all this advice may seem today, on 22 November 1916 it overlooked – or perhaps consciously over-skipped – one massive reality. The two halves of the Empire were then locked together midway in a war for their joint survival. Vienna depended on the wheat, no less than on the battalions, of Hungary in order to fight on. It was a poor time to pick a quarrel. And in any case, though Polzer had correctly anticipated Hungary's move, he was not prepared for her to strike so quickly.

Around midday, the cream and gilt doors of the audience-chamber opened again and a very satisfied Count Tisza came out. He had won his point, and he now lost no time in ramming it home. He went immediately over to the private office in the palace and prepared an autograph letter for the Emperor to sign. The brief historic note was issued on the following day, 23 November. It read simply:

Dear Count Tisza!

Moved by the intention to have myself crowned as soon as possible as King of Hungary, Croatia-Slavonia and Dalmatia, I instruct you, in consultation with Parliament, to submit your relevant proposals.

That complex and ancient heritage which was the pride of the Empire and also its doom was symbolized in those three titles.

Charles knew full well what he was putting his signature to, and the audience had been long and earnest. How had Tisza done it?

This is the Empress's account:

'Count Tisza stressed to the Emperor that, according to Hungarian law, he was only *Erbkönig* or hereditary king of Hungary until he was crowned and that, as such, he could neither promulgate nor even prolong certain basic laws. Some of these laws, including economic ones vital for the war, were due to expire at the end of the year. Hence the hurry: not even the full six months could, in these special circumstances, be allowed to pass.

'The Emperor consulted on the spot his experts. They all upheld Tisza's argument and all declared the matter to be urgent. At this, the Emperor agreed, and the legal point explains the date chosen for the coronation, 30 December 1916, almost the eve of the new year.

'The Emperor knew what he was doing and he knew the formal effect

* Franz Josef, it may be remarked, avoided the dilemma by not taking the Hungarian Coronation oath until 1867 – the year of the Compromise – and by never taking the oath in Austria at all!

this would have on his reform plans. But the legal arguments were un-assailable and the need for haste was there. He agreed in order to be able to bring the war to a rapid end. The Hungarian problem he hoped to sort out after the war.

'In one sense, of course, the friction between the Hungarians and the other nationalities under them was the Empire's biggest handicap. But these – we thought – were questions which must be left for peacetime. In war, Hungary was a pillar of the Dual Monarchy, and Tisza was the man of iron who carried that pillar.'

Exactly five weeks after that audience in Schönbrunn there was enacted in Budapest Tisza's triumph and Charles's calculated gamble – the Corona-tion of the young Emperor and Empress as King and Queen of Hungary. It was the Dark Ages of Central Europe, let alone the Middle Ages, which now came with their finery out of the castles and cathedrals, out of the palace vaults and bank strong-rooms and paraded together for the last time on that December day. The streets of Budapest had been filled with triumphal arches, flags, banners, portraits and flowers for the event. This was the Magyars' day, but above all it was the day of the powerful nobility who sought protection for their own privileges as well as for their nation in the ceremony. Here is how one of this tiny closed circle described the atmosphere fifty years afterwards. The fact that the author, Countess Catherine Karolyi, was the wife of that earnest but confused Hungarian radical who was soon to help blow up the world she depicts only adds piquancy to her words:

The court robes of our grandmothers, preserved with moth-balls, were taken from the lofts and cellars where they had lain throughout the interminable reign of Franz Josef, and all our houses smelt of camphor. My robes, worn by my husband's grandmother, were of fiery red velvet, with puffed sleeves and a train embroidered in gold. The mantle had been ordered from Spitzer, the famous Viennese dress-maker, and was of pure gold brocade trimmed with sable. I shamefacedly noted in my diary that it had cost 5,000 gold gulden. . . .

At last, the great day came . . . the dawn was grey and dull when Daisy Karolyi and I started off in the century-old coach which had been stored away for decades. The grey high-steppers pranced with dignity and our advance was slow. . . . The streets were frozen and slippery. The tiara pressed painfully on my head – the spot remained sensitive for years – the tight bodice was suffocat-ing, and we could not relax by smoking. Daisy, seated beside me in silver brocade, finally lit a cigarette. At once we saw a small plump white-gloved hand from the next coach shaking at us in violent disapproval. It was Aunt Geraldine, our mother-in-law.

From the suspension bridge over the half-frozen Danube we detected the out-lines of the Royal Castle emerging from the mist, lit up like a burning torch. I wondered if those lights, so seldom seen in Budapest, would go on burning all through the reign of the new monarch, or would the palace return to its usual gloom?

Like a dark serpent, the carriages crept up the hill. For fifty years, the Hungarian nobles had longed for their sovereign to give them – and the capital – the glamour of royalty, of court life with its celebrations, titles and decorations. Franz Josef had never forgiven them the Revolution of 1848, and had never cared for the Magyars. Now there was hope that all this would change. Even the 'Second Nation' in the trenches – the soldiers barred from participating in the festivities – trusted that the peace-loving young King and Queen would have the courage to resist the German Kaiser and stop useless bloodshed.*

That eye-witness description has something else to commend it apart from its vividness. It reflects the longing of Dualist Budapest for a fuller share of the Imperial pomp and glory that was still Vienna's portion of the bargain. It reflects the hopes placed in Charles not as the new ruler of the Empire, but as the new King of the Magyar nation. And it throws an echo, even from within a scented carriage, of the universal longing for peace.

Charles and Zita, the principals of this pageant, were certainly conscious of all three factors as, shortly before nine o'clock that morning, they descended from the royal coach drawn by eight snow-white horses, and entered the Gothic Cathedral of Mathias Corvinus for their Coronation. Above all, there was this almost stifling sense of Magyar nationhood which bore down on the whole ceremony as heavily as the brocaded garments on the actors. These vestments and regalia were, indeed, its tangible symbols. The central part of the crown which the Hungarian Prince-Primate Dr Csernoch, aided by Count Tisza, now placed on Charles's head was the same one that Pope Sylvester had sent to King Stephen for his coronation in the year 1000.† The heavy coronation cloak placed round Charles's shoulders had been embroidered by Stephen's consort, Queen Gisela, in the year 1031. The sword that was buckled round Charles's waist after the anointing at the High Altar was even held to be a relic of the great Attila, King of the Huns, which centuries later Stephen had also swung in battle. In fact, the weapon was almost certainly of late Gothic origin but there was good reason why, in this case, the Hungarians bent the truth to fit their legend. 'St Stephen's sword', as we shall see in a moment, played a vital part in the unique ritual which bound the Magyar king to the Magyar people.

* Catherine Karolyi, *A Life Together*, pp. 167–8.

† The jewelled head-band on the crown is not much younger. It is believed to be a gift sent by the Byzantine Emperor in or around A.D. 1075 to Stephen's successor, King Geza.

Something of this special link can be heard in the Coronation oath which the freshly-crowned monarch had to take in the open air of the Cathedral Square.

We, Charles IV, by the grace of God perpetual Apostolic King of Hungary and her associated countries, swear by the living God, by the Virgin Mary and all God's saints that . . . we shall not alienate the boundaries of Hungary and her associated countries, nor anything belonging to those countries under any title whatever; *shall not reduce but as far as possible increase and extend their territories*; * and shall do all that we may justly do for the welfare and glory of these our countries. So help us God and his Saints.

This holy pledge to preserve above all else the integrity of 'St Stephen's lands' was now driven home by an extraordinary act of secular theatricals. After the oath, Charles mounted a magnificent iron-grey horse, whose stirrups and bridle trimmings were of pure gold, and, accompanied by a cavalcade of Hungarian notables in fur-trimmed uniforms with the white-plumed *Kalpak* on their heads, rode slowly up to the so-called *Diszter*. This was a mound close to the palace which contained piles of earth brought in from every county of Hungary. Like every Hungarian King before him, Charles, the ancient crown on his head, galloped alone up the hillock and, pausing on its peak, swung 'St Stephen's sword' to north, south, east and west – four strokes that symbolized his promise to defend the kingdom that was now his against all comers.

A foreign pantomime it may well seem to us today. But to those present on 30 December 1916, it was a living drama in which their ancient nation had been re-born again. As Charles rode down from the mound (the heavy crown, according to some accounts, askew after these exertions) all the church bells of Budapest tolled, the gun salvoes thundered out, the military bands struck up the anthem, and the crowd of nobles on the palace hill shouted their '*Eljen a Kiraly!*' ('Long live Charles!') in the winter air. The Hungarian magnates were acclaiming their new patron and partner. Charles was shouldering his inheritance as King and his burden as Emperor.

It is interesting to record what it all meant to him – and to his young wife who, as the new Queen of Hungary, had also been touched in the cathedral ceremony with St Stephen's crown, though in her case only fleetingly and on the right shoulder. Looking back on the day after fifty years, the Empress commented:

'The thing that impressed both of us most about the whole ceremony was the moving liturgical side of it all – especially the oaths that the King

* Author's italics.

took at the altar before his anointing to preserve justice for all and strive for peace. This sacred pledge given in the cathedral was exactly the political programme he wanted to carry out from the throne. We both felt this so strongly that hardly any words were necessary between us.

'My husband did not express afterwards any feeling of nervousness that, by this coronation, he had made his attitude inflexible with regard to the Monarchy as a whole. He felt he had made the position clear to Tisza that he had consented to the ceremony for legal reasons, and that reform would still have to come later.

'As for the coronation celebrations planned in Budapest, the Emperor cut them short by deciding to return to Vienna that same day. This doubtless disappointed Hungarian society, but he felt that festivities were simply not appropriate to wartime, when every day so many were dying on the battlefields.'

The Hungarians had got their new King. But, the moment the ceremony was over, he had felt and acted again as the Emperor of all his peoples.

A mountain of problems and an untried team of helpers to shift them with were awaiting Charles in the Vienna to which he had so swiftly returned. With one important exception, he had completely replaced the old guard of Franz Josef's key advisers within a month of succeeding him. These new men were still feeling their feet on a political terrain made treacherous by intrigue and resentment. It had been a decorous change-over, but a clean sweep for all that. Court, government and Army were all affected.

Of the freshly-appointed court officials, only two were of real political significance. The first of these was the new Court Chamberlain, Prince Conrad Hohenlohe, who had held high ministerial office under Franz Josef and who became an important influence behind the scenes in shaping Charles's early governments. The second was Polzer, the friend and mentor of Charles's youth, whom the Emperor now appointed at the age of forty-seven to be head of his private office. Polzer, as he showed in that accession memorandum, had diagnosed the Hungarian ailment which was draining the Empire's political strength, and he was to produce several more private prescriptions of his own for curing it. His loyalty, sincerity and ingenuity were beyond question. His greatest shortcoming as an adviser lay perhaps in his training which, up to the very moment when he took over the power-house of the Empire's affairs, had been as a civil servant with a strong taste for arm-chair political theorizing but no experience whatever of political office. Had Polzer come up the ministerial ladder of power, he might have developed into that fearless reforming Prime Minister which the Emperor Charles always sought and never found.

As it was, his talents failed to bridge the gap between the intellectual and the man of action. He was, to revert to the medical metaphor, an amateur physician – of which the Empire had too many – and not a skilled surgeon, of which the Empire had not one with the courage of his calling. Indeed, when it came to it, Polzer recoiled outright from the challenge of action. The Empress recalls that on only one occasion did he fail his beloved sovereign: but that occasion was perhaps more vital than any other. It came when the Emperor once appealed in desperation to his old adviser to take over the government and actually execute some of the reforms he was constantly proposing. Polzer declined. He was a man of blueprints, not a man of power.

Here indeed we touch on the most desolate aspect of the Viennese domestic scene in the middle of the First World War. It was a stage almost entirely devoid of any politicians worthy of the name, and completely empty of real statesmen. This was, of course, largely due to that late and artificial start to 'parliamentary life' which, as described above, Vienna had made only half a century before the war had broken out. And when war began, such rudimentary training that Schmerling's Parliament had given to the Empire's political leaders had been cut short altogether when Parliament itself was suspended as being too subversive a body to operate in such critical times.

This was a short-sighted blunder that Charles was soon to redress. But grave damage had already been done by the time of his accession. Abroad, Vienna's political image – quite unjustly – looked more reactionary than that of Budapest, which had kept its Parliament going in wartime only to use it as another instrument of Magyar repression. At home, the national spokesmen, deprived of a public sounding-box for their rivalries and discontent, only fed on their grievances in private intrigue and moved further away from the crown in the process.

This appalling scarcity of political talent was aptly expressed by the government Charles inherited as well as by the one he put in its place. The 'sitting tenant' left by Franz Josef was Dr Koerber, a cautious bureaucrat, who had never properly grasped the reins of power but always fingered them nervously as though afraid that at any minute the horse would bolt underneath him. His successor (after much intrigue in which Prince Hohenlohe played a powerful hidden role) was the exact opposite in origin, but Koerber's complement when in office. Count Clam-Martinitz, who was appointed Prime Minister on 20 December 1916, was a Bohemian nobleman of the bluest blood who – for all his decency, tact and sincerity – was incapable of thinking about the Empire's social reform needs for the same reason that he was incapable of thinking under 30,000 acres. In his fastidious eyes, politics was not quite the calling for a gentleman. And he, in turn, was to be followed by Seidler, another civil servant, if anything more pedantic than Koerber, who was to linger on in office until the closing months of the Empire's life.

Thus the best that Charles could find to serve him as Prime Ministers were civil servants, who were at heart afraid of political power, or feudal aristocrats, who at heart despised political power. In this respect too the last Habsburg was unlucky. From that first category of men the Tudors in their day had found their Wolseys, the Bourbons their Richelieus. From the second category his own House of Austria had once produced a Count Kaunitz or, as at Franz Josef's accession, a Prince Felix Schwarzenberg. Now, at Charles's accession, both layers of society failed to yield anything of note. The idea that the hour of need inevitably throws up the man was proved here to be a myth – unless we take Charles himself as history's victim in its predestined tragedy. To rebuke him for failing to select strong ministers is absurd. There were none about.

There was one partial exception to this general scarcity of talent. He was Count Ottokar Czernin, another Bohemian noble whom Charles had made his new Foreign Minister on 22 December. And, perhaps because the exception was only partial, his appointment was to become a political incubus to the Empire and an agonizing personal tragedy for the Emperor. It is worth taking a closer look at this man who was to play such a crucial and quite disastrous role in Charles's life.

Politically, Czernin was a gifted dilettante. This was no bad thing in itself. Indeed, it placed him above most of the other aristocratic amateurs at the Emperor's disposal. But he was also lazy, unstable in character, unpredictable in temperament and arrogant to a fault, even by the haughty standards of his class and times.

These defects combined to make his talents dangerous as well. His own vanity had convinced him, for example, that he was a great statesman; and his occasional flashes of brilliance – contradictory though they often were – persuaded many others to share his opinion. He was a man without measure because he was a man without respect. He lacked even that instinctive loyalty to his sovereign which alone bound the old Order together. He was convinced of the aristocracy's continued mission to rule. He failed to see – let alone carry out – its cognate duty to serve. Some of these faults might have been redeemed in office had he at least shown any consistency of policy. But because there was nothing – beyond fierce family pride – which this extraordinary man seems to have looked up to, there were no fixed stars to guide his course. He was always oscillating between the opposite poles of 'Greater Austria' and pan-Germanism in a way that not only bewildered the enemy (which was perhaps desirable in wartime) but the allied capitals of Vienna and Berlin as well. He was, in short, a Foreign Minister of Bismarckian complexes, but with only a sliver of Bismarckian talent and not even that much of Bismarckian loyalty to the crown he served. And this for the diplomatic head of a threatened Empire that needed consistency, self-effacement and moderation to survive.

These faults of Czernin's were only to develop and display themselves in office. Charles appointed him in good faith and with high hopes for two reasons. The first was that Czernin's liveliness of mind and immense self-confidence seemed to set him apart from his very uninspiring contemporaries. The second and more important reason was – according to the Empress – that of all the men around the Emperor in December 1916, Czernin appeared the most convinced of the need for an Austrian peace initiative. As this conviction was the driving force behind Charles's every action and endeavour as a ruler, it is not surprising that he should have picked for his Foreign Minister the one candidate who seemed, in those early days, to share both his policy and his resolution. Ironically, it was a European scandal over these Austrian peace moves that finally drove the Emperor and his haughty lieutenant apart, and rocked the house of Habsburg in the process.

Czernin's appointment, so full of unexpected drama for the future, seemed at the time to provide merely the successful finishing touch to the formation of Charles's first government. With both Court and Cabinet reconstituted, there remained only the Army to be brought into line with the new reign. Charles had already announced one major reform in this direction ten days after his accession. Under Franz Josef, the supreme commander of all Austro-Hungarian forces had been not the Emperor, but the Archduke Frederick. Now, under a brief Order of the Day of 2 December, Charles proclaimed that he himself, 'in the exercise of his sovereign rights', was assuming direct command over all the military and naval forces of the Empire. There was no question – as was freely rumoured at the time – of the Archduke Frederick resenting his 'dismissal'. He had himself raised the question of an eventual handover with Charles during the last weeks of the old reign and had anticipated that the young heir-apparent, who had served with distinction on both of the Empire's main battlefronts, would want to take over complete military control once the throne was his.

The only question was: would this supreme command remain the technicality it had been ever since August 1914, with the formidable Chief of Staff General Conrad continuing in real charge of the war? The question was answered on 1 March 1917 – the one key change that Charles delayed until the new year – when Conrad was replaced by General Arz. When, two months before his death, Franz Josef had asked Charles about Conrad's suitability and about suggestions for possible successors, Arz was one of the names Charles had put forward. The new Chief of Staff was thus the new Emperor's man, and he was to serve him loyally and competently until the end. But Conrad's dismissal – here the word is justified, though the General was given an Army Group on the Italian front – was not merely the removal of a brilliant but erratic autocrat with whom Charles could never have worked. It was also the culmination of a deliberate process by which all leaders of the 'Vienna war party' of 1914 (or 'hawks' as they would be called today) were now shifted from the centre of the stage to the wings. Thus the other main 'hawk' of Sarajevo, Count Berchtold, who as Austrian Foreign Minister had signed the fateful ultimatum to Serbia, had now been given the almost ludicrously insignificant post of *Oberstkämmerer* at Charles's court.

This was indeed a strange situation. The new ruler had proclaimed himself Commander-in-Chief with a speed and crispness that would have delighted the fiercest militarists among his subjects. Yet, at the same time, he had distanced himself from the war's protagonists in a manner that would have appealed to the deepest pacifists of the Empire. This was not a paradox in Charles's nature. It was a paradox in his destiny. He was forced to champion with every act and utterance in public a war that he loathed with every fibre of his soul.

Polzer at Court; Clam as Prime Minister; Czernin at the Foreign Office; Arz as Chief of Staff. This was the inner quartet on which the new reign at first rested. None was without enthusiasm or talent of sorts. Only one was without loyalty. But what of the man around whom they, and the Empire's fifty million subjects, all revolved? His character is in his life, and will unfold with the story. But this is how it appeared to the person closest of all to him – the woman who now shared his throne. The Empress Zita has given this general portrait:

'She describes him as being above all a practical man and a logical man. Because of this basic logic and because of his own fixed ideas about right and wrong he was quite unshakable on fundamental things like the search for peace and the need for reform.

Despite his good academic record and his quick mind, he was not what one would call an 'intellectual'. As his wife saw it, he got at the truth by common sense and instinct rather than by reasoning.

His tastes she describes as simple. He loved music, for example, but *Volksmusik* rather than symphonies or operas. He had little time for reading once war broke out, but when he did get the chance it was history or travel books that he read for preference.

Her portrait continues: 'He had an enormous sense of humour and always saw the funny side of anything. This was the Austrian in him. It was one of the many reasons why he had such difficulty with the Prussians.

'He was a great sportsman. His uncle, Franz Ferdinand, had the reputation, of which he was very proud, of being about the best shot in the Empire. My husband, in fact, shot even better and I remember that at big driven shoots where both men took part before the war, the Archduke Charles would always deliberately and tactfully miss a few birds so that his uncle could have the biggest bag of the day. This didn't worry him in the least. Shooting, however much he enjoyed it, was something to be indulged in with moderation as far as he was concerned.

'This same moderation was the rule of his everyday living which indeed was exceptionally plain and modest. For example, drinking. He drank at lunch and at dinner an average of one glass of *Schilcher*, which was a very ordinary *Sandwein* from the Burgenland. The Saxon Minister, Baron Tucher – who was a great wine expert – was curious to taste this special brand which the Emperor always ordered for himself. One day, when he was dining with us, the Emperor satisfied his curiosity. The man is said to have taken one horrified sip and then to have exclaimed: "If I had not Your Majesty's word for it that this was wine, I would never have believed it!"

'It was rather the same with smoking. At the beginning of our married life he used to smoke cigars; but these he gave up because they gave me "migraine". After that he smoked cigarettes, but one or two only, after meals.

'His tastes in food were so simple that I don't really think he ever cared much what he was eating. The most difficult thing about it was that he didn't even have a favourite dish – as our Bohemian cook* was always complaining to me after our wedding.

'As for relations with others, he always listened as Emperor to everyone and always tried to think himself into their ideas and see their point of view. He had the patience to listen to things that were already well-known to him, because most people thought, after all, that they were bringing their Emperor something new and interesting and he didn't want to offend them.

'He heard everybody out on every subject and had a habit at audiences

---

* A Frau Tomsa. After the collapse of 1918 she went to Prague to cook for the President of the new Czechoslovak State, Masaryk, and told astonished guests of the old regime that she always tried to imagine to herself that she was 'still cooking for her Emperor'.

of saying "*Ja, ja*" as he was listening. As he said it to people of very different views, this became commented upon, and I remember once telling him: "People are saying that you agree with everyone."

'He replied: "Yes, it may be a bad habit. But when I say it I simply mean I understand *them* and the reasons behind their views. It doesn't mean I share those views."

'Perhaps he was over-tolerant towards others and certainly very reluctant to believe the worst in them even after it came to the surface. This was simply his nature. Time and again when we discussed this – about Horthy or Czernin, for example – he would say: "One must always look for the good in people."'

One can only comment, on that final sentence, that the biblical injunction 'Seek and ye shall find' did not unfortunately apply to the Emperor Charles in his public life.

Chapter 7

THE SEARCH FOR PEACE:
THE 'SIXTUS AFFAIR'

Almost the first thing Charles had announced in public on becoming Emperor was that pledge which he specially inserted in his accession manifesto, 'to win back for my peoples the sorely-missed blessings of peace'. Almost the first thing he did in secret was to launch his own highly personal moves to the enemy side to carry out that promise. This particular independent peace bid of Charles's (there were several after it) was to be remembered in the history books as the famous 'Sixtus Affair' – named after his Bourbon brother-in-law who was the chief intermediary. By the Emperor himself, it was to be remembered as the brightest diplomatic hope of his reign which suddenly turned, as though in a nightmares into its gravest domestic scandal.

It becomes, at times, a complicated tale to follow; but it remains alway, an important one, and this for several reasons. In the first place, nothing was more typical and vital in the life of the man we are concerned with than this relentless drive to end the war. It was, in his case, a compound of hot passion and cool reason: the hatred for war as such and the realization of what it meant for his Empire. *Friedenskaiser*, the Emperor of Peace, was the only title that even his Republican successors of 1918 could not deny him. He would have wished for none better.

The Sixtus affair is interesting also as a historical museum-piece. Together with some of Charles's later ventures, it offers about the last example of dynastic diplomacy in the old Europe – the attempt to settle the supreme affairs of nations directly between their rulers on the grounds that, ideally, these are just as representative as Parliaments and, in wartime, far more effective. The fashion did not, of course, die out with the Emperors; merely the form. The secret 'summit diplomacy' of the Second World War had much in common with the secret dynastic diplomacy of the First.

But this strange episode is memorable above all for what was at stake. Had Charles's independent peace bid to the *Entente* succeeded in the first months of 1917, the whole war could have been shortened by eighteen months. This would not only have saved hundreds of thousands of lives on both sides of the barbed wire jungle; it would have prevented also that almost total economic and moral exhaustion of the European continent which the final merciless phase of the struggle brought about. Bolshevism, which was yet to erupt when Charles made his first moves, might have been contained in a continent restored to tranquillity. The Austrian Empire itself, still regarded at the time in both Paris and London as part of the natural order of things, would certainly have survived long enough to tackle its supreme test of peacetime reform. In short, Europe might well have had a different soul as well as a different body to those we know today.

Nor can these speculations be called of no account because they never became realities. Events become their own yardstick. But an individual must be measured by what he attempted, not only by what he achieved. When Anatole France, looking back on the whole vain peace-making manoeuvres of the war, wrote: 'The only honest man to emerge during this war was Charles of Austria; but he was a saint and nobody listened to him', he was perhaps indulging a little in poetic licence. But neither part of that verdict was far from wrong.

Prince Sixtus, an elder brother of Zita's, had been a friend of Charles's since childhood, and was a natural choice when the new Emperor selected an intermediary between himself and the enemy *Entente* camp. Sixtus combined discretion with a lively intelligence and Charles knew, from countless pre-war discussions in the family circle at Schwarzau * and Hetzendorff, that his brother-in-law shared his own basic political views. Like Charles, the young Bourbon prince feared and mistrusted the German hegemony which threatened continental Europe. Like Charles, he saw as the best means of countering it a revival of the eighteenth-century Kaunnitz policy that had linked Austria with France. What both men were ultimately aiming at, for peacetime even more than wartime, was a new European alignment in which Austria would ease herself out of her cramping 'vertical alliance' with Germany and join a looser and broader 'horizontal alliance' with France and Britain – a grouping that would stretch from Transylvania right across to the coasts of Ireland. To Sixtus, such a classic 'reversal of alliances' spelt protection from Germany as the

---

* Sixtus and his brother Xavier were, in fact, actually staying at Schwarzau, where they had largely grown up, when war broke out. It looked at first as though the Austrian authorities wanted to hold them as hostages; but the Emperor Franz Josef intervened personally on their behalf and they were able to leave for Switzerland on 20 August, having lived a fortnight in what was by then enemy territory.

ancient enemy. To Charles it spelt liberation from Germany as the dictatorial ally.

Sixtus, of course, was not politically neutral. He could not be. He was no Swiss nor Swede but a Frenchman to the core. Three months before war broke out, he had taken his degree as a French Doctor of Laws on the thesis that 'a Bourbon is always a Frenchman'. Two years later, when he and Xavier were both decorated with the French *Croix de Guerre* while serving at the front as Belgian artillery officers,* Sixtus wrote in an ecstatic letter about the ceremony: 'The first duty of a Bourbon, the greatest glory he can dream of winning, is the service, always and before all things, of France.'

But this glowing patriotism never ran counter to any of Charles's ideas in the negotiations that followed. Indeed, on the point dearest to any French patriot's heart – the return of Alsace-Lorraine – the Emperor, as we have seen, had already made up his own mind when still an Archduke in his teens. The way things turned out in the end, it was perhaps a pity that Charles's brother-in-law in the *Entente* camp was not a member of the ruling British House of Windsor instead of the dispossessed French House of Bourbon. But neither man can exactly be blamed for that. The way things started, Prince Sixtus was, for both Paris and Vienna, the most hopeful common factor. He was a politically-minded Bourbon without being a French official, and the Emperor's friend and relative without being an Austrian.

The Sixtus affair began not in Austria at all, as is generally assumed, but in France.

As the Empress recalls it:

'The first impetus for wartime contacts between Paris and Vienna came during the Emperor Franz Josef's reign and it came from the French side – not formal proposals but a clear interest in talks. In the second half of 1915, during periods of calm at the front, my brother – then an officer in the Belgian Army – wrote some articles for the big French review, *Le Correspondant*. In these he sought to explain how Austria was essential for the equilibrium of Europe and how misplaced therefore was the campaign of

---

* The two princes' request to be commissioned in the French Army had been turned down according to the law of 1889, which prohibited all members of France's former ruling houses from entering military service. They then tried the Red Cross, in vain; and next applied to the British Army for posts as interpreters – only to be refused by the War Office. The Belgian King, to whom they were related, finally arranged commissions for them in his Army and in August 1915 their stubborn fight to get into uniform was rewarded. It was typical of such an international family that two other brothers – Félix and René – were serving in the Austro-Hungarian Army, though by agreement they never fought on the French front.

1 Persenbeug Castle, on the banks of the Danube some fifty miles upstream from Vienna,
where Charles was born on 17 August 1887. The time was as tranquil as the scene. It was the
Indian summer of Franz Josef's long reign. The revolutions that had shaken the Empire in 1848
were nearly forty years past; those that were to destroy it under Charles in 1918 lay more than
thirty years ahead.

2 The boy Charles (standing in sailor suit) with his father ('Handsome Otto') behind. His mother, the Saxon princess Maria Josefa, holds his young brother Maximilian. The sad and rather strained air of this formal family portrait is appropriate. It was an unhappy marriage and Archduke Otto had barely turned forty when he died in 1906.

3 His first uniform: Charles as a Lieutenant in 1904, aged seventeen. He went on, in the First World War, to command an Army Corps on the Italian Front and an Army on the Russian front, before becoming automatically Commander-in-Chief on his accession to the throne in 1916. He loved his regiments and served them proudly; but he loathed war and strove from his first day of power to bring it to an end.

4 A picture-book betrothal portrait taken in January 1911. Charles and his fiancée, the beautiful Princess Zita of Bourbon-Parma, who became the focus of so much political controversy during the war. His own marriage, unlike that of his parents, was to be serene and devoted to the end. This happy family background was indeed one of the few constant comforts of a tragic life, whether on the throne or in exile.

5 The wedding on 21 October 1911 at Schwarzau, the castle in Lower Austria which belonged to Princess Zita's father, the exiled Duke Robert of Bourbon-Parma. No fewer than twenty-two children from his two marriages grew up happily here together. Behind the bride can be glimpsed the moustached face of Charles's uncle, the Archduke Franz Ferdinand. It was his murder at Sarajevo less than three years later that triggered off the First World War and made Charles Heir-Apparent to the Habsburg throne.

6 On the balcony at Schwarzau during the wedding reception. At the right is the Emperor Franz Josef. The old monarch had already then been sixty-three years on the throne and still had five years of rule ahead before his death, and Charles's accession in November 1916. The Emperor was in an unusually gay mood at the wedding which, he fondly believed, had assured the continuity of his dynasty for one or two generations to come.

hate against her in the French press. This, he maintained, should be concentrated against the true enemy, which was Germany.

'Soon after these articles appeared, he received a letter at the front from the well-known M. de Freycinet, a former diplomat and Minister of State with an influential circle of friends. The writer asked Prince Sixtus to make a point of contacting him on his next leave in order to meet several "high officials" who shared his views in Paris.

'This my brother did, and at intervals during the ensuing months he saw, through Freycinet, people like Jules Cambon, the Director-General of the French Foreign Office; Paul, his brother, who was envoy in London; and finally (through the Chief of Protocol, M. Martin), the President of the French Republic, M. Poincaré himself. All these people pressed Prince Sixtus to seek contact with his brother-in-law in Vienna who was then of course still the heir-apparent. But he always demurred, saying that there was no point until that brother-in-law had become Emperor.

'Then, immediately after Franz Josef's death on 21 November 1916, these same circles in Paris approached Prince Sixtus again and suggested that he could "render great service to Austria and to France" by getting in touch at once with his relative, who was now the new ruler.

'He asked for time to think it over. But just at this point a similar initiative came from us in Vienna. Almost immediately after his accession, the Emperor asked me to write to my brother to see if we could make contact with the French and start things up at a family level. It was agreed in advance that, if they met, not a single word would be exchanged between them about the military situation, including even things like the food position, as they were on opposing sides and this was important intelligence. This agreement was later always scrupulously adhered to. So it happened that, within a few days of Franz Josef's death, almost simultaneous feelers were put out to each other from Paris and Vienna, both passing through my brother.'

All moves to stop wars depend largely for their success or failure on the tide of battle prevailing when they are made and the future assessments of victory or defeat in the rival camps. So it was throughout with the Sixtus affair, though, in its case, politics rather than grand strategy were to doom it in the end. But at that turn of the year 1916–17, when the Empress sent off her first letter, the prospects for peace looked brighter than they ever had done – or ever were to do again until the *Entente* victory imposed its own blunt armistice two years later.

The slaughter had now lasted for twenty-nine bloody months. On the key Western front it was bogged down in Flanders mud: the German offensive against Verdun and the British attack on the Somme had both petered out with great losses sustained but no great prizes won. In the wide spaces of the Eastern front, there was more room for manoeuvre and for sweeping strokes of generalship. Even here, however, the end of the year had brought, if not a stalemate, at least a balance of victories. In June the great Russian drive under Brusilov (which, as we have seen, caused Charles to be hastily transferred from Italy up to the Galician front) had captured an entire Austrian army of 250,000 men with all its guns, and had brought about an advance of thirty-seven miles – enormous by First World War standards. But in July powerful German reinforcements had checked Brusilov's advance, and then came Mackensen's brilliant thrust across the Carpathians into Rumania, which had joined the *Entente* side in August. On 6 December 1916 Bucharest had been occupied by the Central Powers. Serbia had already been cut to pieces. These were not decisive blows. They were, however, big enough to enable Charles to make his move against a background of strength.

The estimates that both sides were then making of the prospects ahead were also hopefully sobering from the peacemaker's point of view. On the *Entente* side, the General Staff could calculate at the end of 1916 that they still had a superiority of five to three in manpower and that their own reserves for 1917 – put at another nine million men – were also substantially greater than the enemy's. Yet of that reserve, 6½ millions were Russians. There was already some doubt about their reliability and these apprehensions were to be borne out beyond belief in the New Year when revolution swept Russia right out of the war. On the other hand, that great counterbalancing stroke of history – America's entry into the conflict on the *Entente* side – still seemed as unpredictable as the Russian collapse. Exhaustion and uneasiness were common to both camps. A sincere and detailed proposal from the Central Powers side (unlike that haughty and vague joint peace note issued at Berlin's dictation on 12 December 1916) would surely fall on receptive ears in London and Paris. That confident, almost gay mood of 'Home for Christmas' in which the troops of all the nations had first marched into the war had long since evaporated. This was the third Christmas looming up. By now, the soldiers were only interested in getting home at all. Charles would have launched his peace move in any case as soon as the throne was his. It so happened that he picked an almost ideal moment.

Things started off at a brisk pace. The King of the Belgians, in whose Army the princes were serving, had agreed at Christmas to their undertaking this secret mission that both Vienna and Paris were proposing. On 29 January they made preliminary contact in Switzerland with their mother, the Duchess of Parma, who had also been writing them at Charles's behest. This good lady, who has gone down in some history books as the leader of a Parma *camarilla* of political spiders, in fact leaves the story as soon as she makes her début as an anxious messenger. She had only come to hand her sons a letter from their sister in Vienna, endorsed with a few lines by the Emperor, imploring them to help in the work of peace, and she seems to have been plunged straight out of her depth when Sixtus – who was a real political animal – took the opportunity to put on record, via his mother, his own ideas of the *Entente*'s 'fundamental and prerequisite terms'.* These comprised:

1. The restoration to France of the Alsace-Lorraine of 1914.

2. The restoration of Belgium, with the Congo.

3. The restoration of Serbia, with Albania added.

4. The cession of Constantinople to the Russians.

The first two points represented the very minimum that Sixtus, as a French subject and a Belgian officer respectively, could be expected to support. But, like the other two, these proposals were not his personal brain-children so much as the outcome of those months of exploratory talks with French politicians at all levels which had prepared for his mission.

At all events there was nothing in these requirements to dismay Charles when he received them in Vienna in the first days of February. His next envoy (this time a Hungarian childhood friend, Count Thomas Erdödy) was already back in Switzerland again on 13 February to hand the two princes his reply. This virtually accepted without argument points 1, 2 and 4, but substituted for point 3 – where the flesh of the Empire would be touched in the quick – another solution. Charles called instead for the creation of a southern Slav monarchy, to embrace Bosnia-Herzegovina and Montenegro, as well as both Serbia and Albania. Vienna meant to see that the thorn of Belgrade, which had for so long cut into its heel, would be well padded in future.

The Empress relates of this first stage of the secret contacts:

'The return of Alsace-Lorraine was of course a French interest. But it was also one of the Emperor Charles's, who was the head of the House of Lorraine. This family link of his with Lorraine was one reason why President Poincaré, who came from that province himself, had so much personal sympathy with the Emperor.

* See Manteyer-Sixtus, *Austria's Peace Offer 1916–17*, pp. 37 *et seq.*, for this and subsequent developments, as seen from the French side.

'Those four points that Count Erdödy took back to Switzerland were personally drafted by the Emperor. It was still too early in his reign for him to have formed any close circle of advisers around him. As for the South Slav kingdom idea, I remember that he had pondered on this – and discussed it with several advisers and friends including my brothers – while he was heir-apparent and even earlier, before the war. This was not the same as Archduke Franz Ferdinand's "Trialist" ideas for the South Slavs, for it was not meant as an end in itself. It was envisaged by the Emperor as part of his overall federalist solution.'

By now Count Czernin, Charles's new Foreign Minister, had been brought into the secret in Vienna. He was full of enthusiasm for the project and even, on 17 February, penned a private note to the Empress urging her and the Emperor to follow up these family approaches 'with all speed'.* This sounded positive enough. Yet Czernin's role in the affair, which was to culminate in drama and disaster fourteen months later, even began on an unhelpful note. The French, having received Erdödy's hopeful reply, now began pressing Vienna for a formal and, if possible, public declaration by the Emperor of a separate Austrian peace initiative on the lines tentatively sketched out in Switzerland. This was clearly expecting too much too soon. However, the answer which Czernin issued to Count Erdödy for his next meeting with the princes in Switzerland was far too savage a retort, starting off as it did with the unequivocal statement: 'The alliance between Austro-Hungary, Germany, Turkey and Bulgaria is absolutely indissoluble and the conclusion of a separate peace by any one of these states is permanently barred.'

The Czernin memorandum was unsigned, but its authorship was evident. Its tone as well as its contents would have made nonsense in advance of all the Emperor's endeavours had it not been moderated in some way. After some hesitation, the Emperor decided to let it go as it stood, but he attached to it a few pencilled notes in his own hand to stroke down the feathers he knew would otherwise be ruffled in Paris. The key sentence of Charles's commentary was the pledge: 'We will support France and use all the means in our power to bring pressure on Germany.' This expressed his aim exactly. It was not so much a separate Austrian peace he was after but rather an independent Austrian move to lead Germany into a general settlement between the two camps.

Why did Charles allow even this first unhelpful intervention of his Foreign Minister to take place at all? In fact further 'dual notes' were to follow, with Czernin always behaving as though he were the lofty

* Unlike much of the private correspondence of that period, this letter, which is important in regard to later events, has survived.

sovereign and Charles as though he were the pliable Foreign Minister. The Empress sums up her husband's reasoning as follows:

'The Emperor took pride in being a constitutional monarch and he was determined to stay one too – even in wartime. He therefore was obliged to bring his Foreign Minister in on this. In any case, Poincaré would have asked: "What does your Government and your Foreign Office think of your views?"'

'Moreover, Czernin at this time was the only one of the Emperor's ministers and senior officials who had said he was ready to support him in launching a peace move alone. The Emperor told me he had asked them all. Not one of them, apart from Czernin, had wanted to touch any separate Austrian initiative: they all had such a blind faith in German victory.

'As for the practice of dual notes, the Emperor wanted his own personal messages to go out to show that the Crown and he himself were behind the move and to get into direct touch with Poincaré. But the Foreign Minister had to show his hand too, to prove that the Emperor was not working behind the backs of his ministers.

'Unlike the Emperor, Czernin never signed these notes of his. My husband often pressed him to do so and also to make plain in them his unqualified support for the policy. But Czernin always refused point-blank. Whatever the reason, these unsigned notes were the best that the Emperor could extract out of his Foreign Minister.'

The Emperor had judged the French mood correctly. Those pencilled comments of his saved the day. When Prince Sixtus saw Poincaré again (on 5 March and 18 March) to hand over his messages, the French President's reaction was that Count Czernin's note was 'wholly inadequate and might be disregarded', but that the Emperor's additions to it were quite another matter 'and made an exchange of views necessary'. The Austrian initiative now took two great steps forward. In the first place Poincaré undertook to write about it to the Tsar of Russia and to King George v and Mr Lloyd George, the new Prime Minister in England. In the second place Prince Sixtus himself, at Charles's urging and with the approval of the French Government, prepared to make a secret journey to Vienna. The Sixtus affair had now moved from the family chronicles to the history books.

As regards the next episode, one might almost add that the affair had moved into the world of film scenarios as well. For the scene now shifts on 23 March 1917 to the outer courtyard of the Habsburg castle of Laxenburg in the plains south-east of Vienna and not far from the river boundary with the 'Hungarian half' of the Empire. It is seven in the morning, still pitch dark, and the weather is wild. Indeed, for two days the castle has been buffeted and blanketed by a continuous snowstorm. Four men, muffled against the wind, get out of a car and give a pre-arranged password to the elderly Captain of the Guard, who is in his Emperor's confidence. On receiving it, the officer leads them to a small doorway in the castle walls which opens on to a staircase leading directly to the sovereign's private apartments. The four pre-dawn visitors are Count Erdödy, the messenger; the Colonel in command of the Austrian police on the Swiss border and, of course, the Princes Sixtus and Xavier of Bourbon-Parma – now deep, in mid-war and mid-winter, on soil that was enemy yet friendly.

The reunion, as can be imagined, was charged with emotion. The two families that had played together as children, the two dynasties that had been linked by marriage, now met in a technical sense as foes, but in an attempt to end the conflict that had driven them apart. The Empress stayed only for the first quarter of an hour or so, greeting her brothers again after a gap of over eighteen months which must have seemed like eighteen years. Then – still before dawn – Count Czernin arrived at the castle and the Empress withdrew as the real talks began.

They followed the same strange dual pattern as all the secret exchanges which had preceded them. The Emperor stressed the need for peace before the whole continent destroyed itself in the vain quest for total victory. He repeated that, as head of the House of Lorraine and a descendant of the Counts of Alsace, he would support the return of those provinces to France as the basis of restoring that peace. Czernin – who stayed one and a half hours, not twenty minutes as has been stated – was throughout cold, reserved and vague, even questioning certain aspects of the Alsace transfer already accepted by his sovereign.*

However, the other main points – the restoration of Belgium and the reconstitution of a Serbian kingdom with an outlet to the sea – were agreed without any further reservations by the Foreign Minister; and he certainly did not demur when the Emperor stressed that there could be no question for the moment of territorial concessions to Italy, Austria's only 'popular enemy'. This, for Charles, was something which might follow but should not precede an agreement on general peace terms with Italy's *Entente* partners. As for the Tsarist claim to Constantinople, which

* Though the Empress was told afterwards by the Emperor of what had transpired after she left the company, there is only one surviving participant of the whole talks from start to finish – in Laxenburg and later in Vienna. He is Prince Xavier, now aged seventy-eight, and I am greatly indebted to him for providing me, through the Empress, with a detailed memoir which contains some points additional to the account released by the late Prince Sixtus just after the First World War.

Paris had sponsored in the earlier exchanges, it was accepted that this might also be shelved for the time being, in view of the revolution that had just erupted in Russia, throwing the whole future of the eastern colossus into doubt.

When the princes returned to Count Erdödy's house in Vienna that night they both felt that an excellent start had been made. But a question mark still hung over Czernin's personal enthusiasm for the whole venture. In an attempt to remove it, the two princes asked him to call on them early the following morning. Though Czernin again began by being reticent, a pledge of unconditional support for all that had been discussed at Laxenburg was extracted from him at the end.

According to Prince Xavier's notes of the French conversation, this final exchange went as follows:

Sixtus: 'Do you accept – yes or no – the basic proposals, because without your support I can get nowhere in Paris or London?'

Czernin: 'But of course I agree with His Majesty. We must not lose this first and perhaps decisive chance. But I beg you to be extremely prudent. Think of the might of Germany and of my own responsibility.'

Sixtus: 'I guarantee the prudence. But are you really behind your sovereign? (*Couvrez-vous réellement la responsabilité de votre souverain?*)'

Czernin (as though surprised): 'But of course. I am his Minister of Foreign Affairs.'

Though it betrayed Czernin's nervousness of Berlin and his concern for his own interest, that pledge was unequivocal. It is of importance in judging the minister's attempts, little more than a year later, to deny his complete involvement in the affair.

While his brothers-in-law were pressing Czernin in Vienna, Charles was meanwhile busy at Laxenburg. Well before their reunion, Sixtus had been urging Charles to commit himself in person and on paper to the basic principles agreed between them so that both the authenticity and the supreme sponsorship of the Austrian peace move would be placed beyond question. He had even submitted draft statements for the Emperor's signature.

Charles now took the plunge. He spent virtually the whole of that day – 24 March – composing a letter in French which, though nominally addressed to Prince Sixtus, was in fact intended for President Poincaré and, through him, for the leaders of the entire enemy camp. The Empress recalls that several drafts were made, all by the Emperor himself, who wrote perfect French. Ob several technical points, however, and on the correct turn of certain diplomatic phrases, he consulted Czernin through his direct private telephone line to the minister. Thus, though Czernin never seems to have read the letter, he knew its contents – both by taking part in the exhaustive discussions which had preceded it and by advising the Emperor while it was actually being drafted. This again is important testimony in judging the public uproar and the bitter confrontation between the Emperor and his minister in April 1918.

When the princes came out to Laxenburg again later that day to take their leave, Charles handed over to Sixtus the result of his labours. The final text of this famous letter, which was to bring scandal instead of peace in its train, was as follows:

Laxenburg, 24 March 1917

My dear Sixtus,

The third anniversary of a war which has plunged the world into mourning is now drawing near. All the peoples of my Empire are united more firmly than ever in the determination to preserve the integrity of the Monarchy, even at the cost of the greatest sacrifices. By virtue of their unity, of the generous collaboration of all the races of the Empire, we have been able to hold out, for nearly three years, against the fiercest attacks. No one can deny the success of my troops in the field, especially in the Balkan theatre.

France too has shown the greatest strength in resisting invasion and a magnificent vitality. We are all bound to admire without reserve the traditional valour of her gallant army and the willing spirit of sacrifice shown by the whole French people. I am especially gratified to note that, although for the time being we are in opposite camps, my Empire is not divided from France by any real differences of outlook or of aspirations; and I am justified in hoping that my own warm sympathy for France, supported by the affection which she inspires throughout the Monarchy, will prevent the recurrence, ever again in the future, of a state of war for which I can disclaim all personal responsibility.

For these reasons, and in order to demonstrate in a precise fashion the reality of these sentiments I beg you to convey, secretly and unofficially to M. Poincaré, President of the French Republic, that I will support the just claims of France concerning Alsace-Lorraine with all means at my disposal and exert all my personal influence with my allies to this end.

As for Belgium, she must be restored in her entirety as a sovereign state, with the whole of her African possessions and without prejudice to any compensation she may receive for the losses she has already suffered. Serbia too shall be restored in her sovereignty and, as an earnest of our goodwill towards her, we are prepared to allow her just and natural access to the Adriatic, as well as liberal economic concessions. For her part, Austro-Hungary insists, as an absolute and primordial condition, that in future the kingdom of Serbia abandons all relations with, and suppresses all groups and societies whose political aim is the disintegration of the monarchy – and especially the society called *Narodna Obrana*.* Furthermore she must take all steps in her power genuinely to prevent

72

THE SEARCH FOR PEACE: THE 'SIXTUS AFFAIR'

all such forms of political agitation, whether within her borders or without, giving us her assurance of this under a guarantee from the *Entente* Powers.

The events that have taken place in Russia make it desirable for me to withhold my views about her until such time as a stable and legal government is established there.

Now that I have set out my views, I request you in turn to tell me yours, after consulting with France and England, so that we may prepare a common ground of mutual understanding on which official negotiations may be started up and concluded to the satisfaction of all.

Trusting that we may soon on both sides be able to put an end to the sufferings of all the millions of men and all the families now in sorrow and anxiety, I beg you to rest assured of my most warm and brotherly affection.

Charles.

This remarkable document met the basic demands of all the Emperor's foes except for Russia, whose case he could safely ignore for the time being, and Italy, of whose secret hold on the *Entente* through the bribes of the 1915 London Treaty he was then totally unaware. It seemed both generous and realistic as a starting bid and was soon on its way to Paris, carried by the two princes who were now spirited out of Austria again as swiftly and secretly as they had been smuggled in forty-eight hours before.

The most momentous sentence in that letter was the passage where Charles had committed himself to work for the return to France of Alsace-Lorraine – Habsburg by ancient family links but for the past fifty years under the Hohenzollern crown. Charles realized he must waste no time in trying to soften up his prickly German allies, of whose property, after all, he was disposing. On 28 March therefore, three days after his Bourbon brothers-in-law had left his capital, he telegraphed the Emperor William suggesting a meeting at the German GHQ Homburg vor der Höhe on 3 April. The pretext Charles used – to introduce his wife to the German Empress (the two ladies had never met) – did not sound quite so thin in that age of dynastic courtliness as it would today. But it was made clear that Charles intended to use the occasion for far-ranging political talks. He informed William that he would be bringing Czernin with him and asked the German Emperor to summon his own Chancellor and Foreign Minister to the Supreme Headquarters where the real military rulers of Germany anyway resided. William agreed with all these proposals in a reply sent the following day. At 9 A.M. on 3 April the Austrian imperial couple with their suite duly arrived in the royal train at Homburg.

* Heavily implicated in the preparations for the assassination of the Archduke Franz Ferdinand.

The following recollections and general comments of the Empress Zita are of interest here:

'The purpose of the Homburg meeting was not to break the news to the German Emperor that we had made a move to the other side, for this *we had already told him*. When Emperor William was in Vienna in February 1917 my husband had confided to him that he had taken an opportunity to make contact with the *Entente* to find a possible solution to the war.

'The German Emperor immediately asked for the name of the intermediary. My husband replied firmly: "That's something I cannot tell you, but I can guarantee his discretion." Emperor William accepted this and said: "All right, go ahead. I agree."

'If we had a friend in Germany it was the Emperor William. But he was completely under the thumb of his generals. This, I think, was largely because he was such a dreamer. He believed in his dreams and one of them, unfortunately, was that of final victory. And so he handed over everything to Hindenburg and Ludendorff.

'I remember that, on one of our visits to him – when, as usual, he was being a charming and attentive host – I protested: "Really I'm taking up too much of your time. You must have far more important things to do than look after me." And he replied: "No, this is just when I do have time because it's war. There are no civil problems any longer and, as for the military side, my generals look after that and report to me every night what has happened!"

'And on this April visit to Homburg, I remember how I first met Hindenburg. This again was so typical. We came into the salon for lunch and the Field-Marshal was already there, standing in the middle of the room alone almost in a Napoleonic stance. "*This* is Hindenburg", said the Emperor William as he introduced us – in a proud and dramatic tone of voice.

'I had in fact a private matter to bring up with him. We had heard in Vienna that German Air Force planes had bombed the home of the King and Queen of the Belgians, choosing their name-day [15 and 19 November] each year for the attack. I resolved to try and raise the question in some natural way at the Homburg Conference.

'The moment occurred when I was standing with the German Empress looking at the collection of all our notabilities gathered in the salon for a reception – sovereigns, generals, ministers and so on. I said to her: "Just imagine if France and England knew this meeting was taking place and bombed the building!" She was horrified at the mere thought, so I passed it off by saying lightly: "Don't worry. I am sure the English would not bomb because they would know there are ladies present." And then I added the remark I had been leading up to: "But I am told that the Queen of the Belgians *is* being bombed by German pilots."

'The Empress was incredulous and, to my delight, called over Hindenburg to whom, at her request, I repeated the charge. Hindenburg also expressed disbelief and said he had never heard of these attacks, but that he would go into the matter immediately. And the fact was that, from that time on, the bombings stopped.

'That was my only "political" activity at Homburg. I was not, of course, present at any of the discussions. But it was clear from the remarks the Emperor made afterwards when we were travelling back to Vienna that things had not gone well over the peace moves. He said to me in a rather dejected way: "There are frightful difficulties with the Germans because they simply cannot be brought to reason. In the end, we may have to go our own way, even at the risk of being swallowed up by them. But before that we must try everything. Perhaps it will work after all."'

An account given of these Homburg discussions by Baron Werkmann, one of the Emperor's staff,* shows that Charles had good reason to feel depressed. At no point now or later did he reveal to William the details of the proposals he had made to France. But the Germans would have been abominably bad at putting two and two together had they not sensed what was in Charles's mind. According to Werkmann, the critical talks on a peace settlement began at 5.30 in the afternoon, after a series of separate discussions which had continued all day between the two sovereigns and their ministers. At this final joint session Charles sought to convince his allies that unless they were ready to give up Alsace-Lorraine to France there was no hope of a general peace. So that there should be no question of a one-sided sacrifice, Charles authorized his ministers to abandon Vienna's cherished 'Austro-Polish' policy in the same cause and to work instead for attachment of the proposed Polish kingdom to Germany, and even to give up the Austrian province of Galicia to this new Berlin-orientated state. It was an Austrian sacrifice in the East which outweighed in everything except prestige the cost of the proposed German sacrifice in the West. The suggestion was not rejected; but neither was it accepted.

Charles left his German allies knowing that he would have to go forward alone. Yet still there was no thought in his mind either of a public breach with them or of a private betrayal. His aim continued to be to prepare for a general peace settlement, not to conclude a separate one. Only as a last resort – with Germany refusing to join peace talks whose outlines he had agreed in advance with the *Entente* – was Charles prepared to consider denouncing the alliance with Berlin outright and taking

* See Werkmann, *Deutschland als Verbündete*, pp. 222–3.

Austria out of the war by herself. And not until the House of Habsburg was falling down over his head did he consent in the end to this drastic step.

Barely had Charles got back to Vienna than a new menace erupted – both to his alliance and to his secret peace moves. On 6 April 1917, the United States, driven to the brink of neutrality and beyond by the all-out U-boat campaign which Berlin had launched in January, finally declared war against Germany. Not, for the time being, against Austro-Hungary. Indeed, the strange situation now arose whereby, for most of 1917, Charles continued to maintain an envoy in Washington, a city which was an enemy capital to his own German allies. There were several reasons why President Wilson allowed this distinction to be made. As regards the immediate issue of U-boat warfare itself, the Austro-Hungarian submarine fleet had played no direct part in the attacks against American ships. Furthermore, the Americans were aware of the extreme reluctance with which, in Vienna, Charles himself had fallen in behind Berlin in this fateful 'escalation' of the conflict.

It would be truer to say that Charles had not fallen in at all so much as been dragged along kicking by the German General Staff. The end of 1916 had brought, as we have seen, a stalemate on the battlefronts, while the only public diplomatic exchange between the rival camps – the joint Peace Note of Central Powers drawn up on Germany's terms – had predictably turned into a dialogue of the deaf. Nothing could be more typical of the contrast between Vienna and Berlin than the way the two allies responded to this all-round deadlock. Charles sought to break it by a one-sided peace move to end the war. William, mesmerized by his generals and admirals, sought to break it by a one-sided strategic move to intensify the war.

It is interesting to note that Charles's own top military and naval advisers supported the Germans on this issue. To a man, they had succumbed to Berlin's siren song that only on the high seas could mobility be regained and victory won. England, they repeated after the Germans, would be conquered by starvation in a matter of months, if not weeks. Charles, supported by several of his civilian ministers, including Czernin, stood out against both General Staffs. It was one of several examples in his reign where the Emperor saw clearer than his experts because he was looking further ahead. He used military logic against them – the fact that, for example, every offensive move in war produced a defensive answer. But his main case was political. The Empress recalls a series of heated arguments of this sort in the months that led up to the German declaration:

'Every time the Emperor Charles saw Emperor William in Vienna or at their headquarters in the field he tried his utmost to persuade his ally that if an all-out U-boat campaign was launched, America would come into the war and then the last hope of victory would be gone. The German Emperor's reply was: "It will work so quickly that England will be brought to her knees before America can do anything!" It was hopeless!

'Then, on 20 January, the Chief of the German Naval Staff, Admiral Holtzendorf, came to Baden himself to argue the German case before an expanded meeting of our Crown Council. It was presided over by the Emperor Charles, who still remained opposed afterwards despite the combined arguments of his own advisers and his guests. Holtzendorf had "personally guaranteed" the meeting that his U-boats would make England sue for peace in four months!

'Finally, when the German Admiral was debating the issue alone with the Emperor, the truth came out. "It is anyway too late for arguments," he announced. "Our U-boats are already out at sea with their new orders and a countermand can no longer reach them in time."

'The Emperor, who was absolutely shattered as well as angry at this, said to me afterwards: "Now it's the end. If America comes in we are finished for good. The Empire will be cut off from the outside world."' *

Now, at the beginning of April 1917, that American entry into the war which Charles had feared and foreseen was an accomplished fact. The blow had come just when his own offensive on the peace front was off to a seemingly promising start. Charles had no illusions that, before long, the *Entente* would begin to gain even more in strength from America's vast reserves of men and money than it would lose through the death-throes of its Russian ally. Speed was more essential than ever if a diplomatic break-through were to be made in time. He resolved on one further drastic attempt to din some sense into William's ears. The result was one of the most extraordinary documents of this or any war.

Less than ten days after Charles had left Homburg, one of his aides

---

* The atmosphere for the rest of the German visit was distinctly frosty, as the following episode shows. (Recounted in Werkmann, *Deutschland als Verbündete*, pp. 124–5, and confirmed by the Empress to the present author.)

'While defending his plan at table during an official dinner, Admiral Holtzendorf snapped at the Empress: "I know you are an opponent of U-boat warfare. You are against war altogether."

'The Empress replied: "I am against war as every woman is who would rather see people live in joy than in suffering."

'Her calm words seemed to arouse the Admiral even more. "Suffering, what does that matter?" he burst out. "I work best when I have an empty stomach. Then it's a case of tightening your belt and sticking it out."

'The Empress finally cut short the unpleasant scene with the remark: "I don't like hearing people talk of sticking it out when they are sitting at a fully-laden table."'

suddenly reappeared at the German GHQ bearing a special despatch for the Emperor William. This consisted of a lengthy memorandum setting out Austria's views on the war, signed by Czernin and addressed to Charles. The Austrian Emperor had urgently forwarded the report 'for information' to his German ally with a brief covering note. The minister's memorandum to his sovereign was generally disquieting but by far its most alarming passage read as follows:

It is absolutely plain that our military strength is nearing its end. It would only waste Your Majesty's time if I were to elaborate all the details. I need refer only to the shortage of raw materials for munitions production; our completely exhausted manpower reserves; and, above all, the mood of deadening desperation which under-nourishment produces among all sections of the people and which makes it impossible for us to go on shouldering any longer the burden of war. . . . *We must make an end at any price by the late summer or autumn of 1917.*

There was a great deal more, especially on the dangers which the unrest caused by the Russian Revolution represented to the dynasties and empires of both Austro-Hungary and Germany. This section culminated in the blunt (and prophetic) advice: 'If the monarchs of the Central Powers are not capable of concluding peace within the next few months, then their peoples will do it for them over their heads.' This too was stern stuff. But the most startling part of the whole document was still that passage in which Austro-Hungary in effect gave a maximum of six months' notice to her allies to quit the war altogether.

William and his advisers might have been even more startled had they known the truth about this memorandum. It was not Czernin's work at all. It had been inspired and largely drafted by the Austrian Emperor himself.

The Empress Zita relates of this episode:

'After the Homburg Conference, the Emperor had the idea of composing a memorandum to impress on the Germans how desperate the situation was getting. He wrote it mostly himself but, by agreement of course with Count Czernin, used his name to make it appear like a report of the Foreign Minister's. He calculated that in this way the memorandum would have far more effect on the Emperor William, since the Germans were well-disposed to Czernin and regarded him as less of a "pessimist" than his sovereign. Had my husband signed the document himself it would have been regarded at Homburg as just another gloomy personal outburst from the Austrian Emperor.

'The handling of the affair at Homburg incidentally gave us a pretty grim insight into German military security, which was supposed to be so good. The document had been handed over marked strictly secret and for the Emperor William's eyes only. That very same evening, Count Ledochowski, our officer who had taken it to Homburg, heard its contents being freely discussed at the Imperial table by the German General Staff, in front of all the servants. Even we were careful on visits about those German mess servants. We used to call them the "gold-rimmed waiters". Several of them had gold-rimmed spectacles and high foreheads and looked more like professors than ordinary soldiers. Indeed we had good reason to suspect that they included enemy agents specially picked for their intelligence so that they would understand the significance of what they heard.'

In the event, it did not seem to matter how many people at Homburg had learned the secret of Count Ledochowski's mission. The German reaction, when it came in a reply from the Emperor William two days later, was one of routine expressions of faith in final victory. Thanks to the U-boat sinkings, William crowed, potatoes were already 'not to be had for love or money in London'. Soon England would be forced to ration herself 'like a beleaguered fortress'. Everywhere, 'time is working for us'. Charles had sent out an s.o.s. and had got back a parrot-cry.

His only hope after this rested in Paris and London, where we must now follow Prince Sixtus.

Chapter 8

A SEARCH FOR PEACE:
THE FADING LIGHT

On 31 March 1917 Prince Sixtus, back in Paris, handed Charles's Laxenburg letter to the man for whom it had really been written – President Poincaré of the French Republic. It was, as can be imagined, well-received by the statesman who had helped to launch the whole affair, and steps were now taken to spread the peace move across the Channel. The President undertook to write straight away himself to King George v, giving the gist of the Austrian Emperor's letter, and ministerial visits to England were agreed for more detailed discussions later.

But though Poincaré was still at his desk in the Elysée Palace, the French Government had changed while Sixtus had been away, and the change was to turn out very much for the worse from Charles's point of view. The Cabinet of M. Briand – who during the war and after it proved himself a strong personal supporter both of Austria and her Imperial House – had broken up. On 19 March a new administration headed by M. Alexandre Ribot took its place. Compared with Briand, Ribot was a weak and unimaginative figure and he shared little of his predecessor's enthusiasm for wooing Vienna in order to weaken Berlin. From the moment he steps into the driver's seat in Paris, a touch of the French hand-brake can be felt on the Austrian peace move, and this backward pull was to increase as the weeks passed.

To begin with, however, Ribot had no option but to explore further the policy he had inherited. At dawn on 11 April he slipped across to Folkestone for a secret discussion with Lloyd George at the British Channel port. According to one account, Ribot, full of his own importance, greeted the British Prime Minister on the quayside with the dramatic words: 'Do you know why I have come? I am bringing you a letter from the Emperor of Austria.' 'But that means peace!' Lloyd George burst out. 'Not so quick! Let's first of all read the Emperor's letter in the hotel,' Ribot replied, caution returning once his resounding entry on stage had been made.

Not so quick indeed. When the two men emerged from the hotel after three hours of talks they were agreed that no immediate response to Vienna was possible. Italy, whom their two countries had bought over by secret bribes exactly two years before, would have to be consulted first, since those promises had consisted largely of territorial gains at Austria's expense. The interests of the ally they had had to pay dearly for thus clashed with those of this new would-be friend who was offering herself for nothing.

The size of the problem could be measured by the size of the bribes. In the Treaty of London of April 1915 Italy had been promised (besides the twelve Dodecanese islands from Turkey and some pickings in Africa) the following territory, all from Austria, as the price of her defection: the Trentino right up to the Brenner Pass with a quarter of a million German-Austrian inhabitants; the great Austro-Hungarian port of Trieste ('the lung of the Empire', as it was called in Vienna), together with all Istria as far as the Quarnero and a handful of offshore islands; and finally about half of the Austrian province of Dalmatia with another string of islands along the coast. It would have been a savage demand for a victorious Italy to have made with her foot on the Empire's chest. With not a single Italian soldier standing anywhere on these territories it looked, in April 1917, a somewhat ludicrous demand as well. But savage or not, ludicrous or not, Britain and France were pledged to this arrangement and it overshadowed all their calculations in that Folkestone hotel. The Italian hurdle had to be taken and it was agreed it should be faced at once. The outcome was a meeting between the two Prime Ministers and Baron Sonnino, the Italian Foreign Minister, held in a railway carriage at the little French Alpine resort of Saint-Jean-de-Maurienne on 19 April.

Sonnino was an unavoidable partner for the discussions. He was also an unhopeful one, for it was he who had largely negotiated the 1915 treaty from which his country stood to gain so much for so little. On top of this, Lloyd George and Ribot were to some extent handicapped in broaching the matter at all by the oath of secrecy Prince Sixtus had extracted from each of them not to divulge even the existence of the Emperor's letter – let alone its details – to anyone outside the chosen few in London and Paris. Discussion of a separate peace with Austria had therefore to be introduced in a general way at the conference, Lloyd George using recent rumours of Russian overtures to Vienna as a means of raising the whole subject. Though at the time he regarded this roundabout approach as a disadvantage, it is doubtful whether he would have got a different reaction from Sonnino had he been able to read the whole of the Laxenburg letter out aloud in the railway carriage. The inescapable fact was that Italy could win far more by standing pat on the 1915 secret pledges than by any separate compromise now with Austria – who at that time was in a strong military position all along the entire southern front.

Sonnino as good as vetoed the whole idea outright. He even employed the argument that, if a separate peace were made with the traditional enemy, Austria, it would be difficult to persuade the Italian people to carry on the war at all. He thus, in effect, used the threat of defection from the *Entente* camp to make sure of those bribes he had got two years before for deserting the opposite camp! It was not a pretty diplomatic spectacle but Lloyd George had to face it, especially as he could not press the matter too hard at this stage without arousing the wily Sonnino's suspicions.*

At the suggestion of M. Ribot therefore – who was already beginning to slide on to Italy's side – the following very negative formula was adopted to sum up the talks:

Mr Lloyd George, M. Ribot and Baron Sonnino had a discussion about the approaches which Austria might be inclined to make to one or more of the Allied Powers with a view to securing a separate peace.

They reached an agreement that it would not be opportune to enter on a conversation which, in present circumstances, would be particularly dangerous and would risk weakening that close unity between the Allies which is more necessary than ever.

With that the statesmen parted and Saint-Jean-de-Maurienne's brief moment of glory was over.

Lloyd George had already met Prince Sixtus for an hour's preliminary talk in Paris on 18 April, on his way down to Saint-Jean, and he now had a second and more substantial meeting with the Prince on his way back to London. The British statesman has given a general account of their conversations in his *War Memoirs* and Prince Sixtus a far more detailed one in his writings. Here is an extract, from the Frenchman's full record, of their second meeting on 20 April. It reveals, far better than the formal reports, the extent of the Italian obstacle. It also demonstrates Lloyd George's own personal sympathy for the Austrian position and for Charles's reluctance to yield up large tracts of his Empire gratuitously to a treacherous ex-ally who had not even managed to occupy them by force. This second talk, like the first, took place in the British Prime Minister's suite at the Hôtel Crillon in Paris.

Mr Lloyd George: 'Signor Sonnino told me that Italy . . . could not

---

* According to British information the Italian Foreign Minister only learned of the existence of the Sixtus letter several months later in July 1917.

possibly make peace terms with Austria in which her own war aims were not realized. Moreover, no [Italian] Government could remain a single day in office which proposed a peace without compensation. It would be swept away by the people who would rise up in revolution; banish the King and set up a Republic dedicated to a fight to the finish.'

Prince Sixtus: 'What does Italy demand?'

Mr Lloyd George: 'A great deal. The Trentino, Dalmatia and all the coastal islands.'

Prince Sixtus: 'And Trieste?'

Mr Lloyd George: 'Trieste might perhaps be subject to discussion, though the Italians are very keen to get the town.'

Prince Sixtus: 'And are all these conditions to be regarded as *sine qua non*?'

Mr Lloyd George: 'Yes.'

Prince Sixtus: 'Then on what conditions do you think we can make a peace to include Italy?'

Mr Lloyd George: 'It is essential that Austria give up something to Italy. Italy is our ally and we cannot make a peace without her.'

Prince Sixtus: 'In that case, why does Italy not take the territory she covets by force of arms?'

Mr Lloyd George: 'So far as we are concerned, we ask nothing more than to make peace with Austria. We have no feeling of hatred towards her, any more than you have in France. If she really wants peace she must make these concessions. . . . I fully understand what the feeling in Austria is – that Italy, who was her ally, has deserted her and joined forces with us; but on the other hand Austria will be obliged to come to terms. . . . We are quite ready to welcome her; but, once again, she must sacrifice something to Italy. . . . The day that Austria shows herself willing to cede the Trentino and the Dalmatian islands we can begin to arrange terms for her.'

Prince Sixtus: 'All right. I shall tell that to the Emperor's envoy and shall let you have his answer.'

The Prince then took his leave, having arranged to come over to London later for another man-to-man discussion with the Prime Minister. It looked, on the face of it, a dim prospect. But there were two quite unconnected rays of light which made the horizon not entirely dark. The first was the dogged personal enthusiasm with which Lloyd George, now let into the secret of the Sixtus letter, pursued the policy of a separate peace with Austria. His Celtic imagination had been stirred by the thought of a bold unorthodox stroke to cut the deadlock of the military conflict with a diplomatic knife. As we shall see, he was eventually to argue for a reversal of the *Entente*'s entire war strategy in a bid to divide the Central Powers – and, incidentally, circumvent the Italian veto on a separate peace. All this was to develop later that summer in the secrecy of the War Cabinet room and quite unbeknown to the Emperor Charles. But Vienna's second ground for hope was both immediate and tangible. It was nothing less than a spontaneous peace-feeler from Italy.

Needless to say this came neither from Baron Sonnino nor from his political entourage. The driving force behind it was the Italian Army Commander, General Cadorna, and his own motives were those of a plain soldier: the morale of his troops was already low and might crack altogether under the pressure of the major Austrian offensive expected that spring. The general was not acting by himself. Some of Sonnino's political rivals like Giolotti and Tittoni appear to have agreed with the move and King Victor Emmanuel himself was believed to support it. But the Italian Army made itself the spokesman and the terms it offered were, compared with Sonnino's rapacious standards, dirt cheap. In the early part of April – before, that is, the Saint-Jean meeting took place – a staff officer from the Italian GHQ arrived in Berne and called first on the Military Attaché of the German Embassy. Italy, he was authorized to state, desired to make immediate peace with Austria and asked only for the cession of Trento and Aquilea in return. Would the Germans please press their Austrian allies to accept?

This last request was unconsciously ironic. But it was an awkward complication that, for some strange reason, Cadorna had chosen to go to Germany first. It was also an unfortunate circumstance that this important Italian peace bid – the only one of its kind – should have reached Vienna at the very time when optimism was at its height over the Emperor's own peace initiative. With the benefit of hindsight one can say it was a pity that the Cadorna offer was not energetically followed up by Austria – if only to find out what was really behind it. But in the context of that hopeful Viennese spring of 1917, the first and last Charles was to experience, one can see the reasons why he held his hand.

As the Empress has said, discussing this mysterious episode: 'The Emperor did not at this stage want to get into complications with Italy before a final answer arrived from the *Entente* to his soundings through Sixtus. He wanted to play a straight game. His attitude was: "France and England would only get suspicious if we start up with Italy behind their backs." We did not know then of course that Ribot in Paris was already determined to block progress.'

Whatever the motives, or the consequences of this attitude, the Cadorna

offer was not pursued; indeed, a pencilled note by Czernin which has survived in the Vienna archives describes it as 'rejected'. The main effect of
the affair at the time seems to have been to increase the Emperor's conviction (if that were possible) that he was acting on the right lines and
certainly to have strengthened his hopes for the outcome. Italy, the barrier,
was now offering herself almost as a stepping-stone.

One thing the whole episode did underline for Charles was the need for
another early face-to-face talk with his brother-in-law. No time was lost.
It was not until the end of April that he had received Prince Sixtus's
report of his latest talks in Paris, stressing the insistence of both Lloyd
George and the French leaders on territorial sacrifices to Italy. On 4 May
Count Erdödy, the Emperor's faithful postman, was already back in
Switzerland again with two more letters for the prince. The first was a
brief note in German from Charles saying it was 'absolutely essential' for
Sixtus to come to Vienna again to clear up 'two points which are still not
clear'. The second was an even shorter message in French from the
Empress, which is of interest because it refers obliquely to the Cadorna
affair and marks her only political contribution to the Sixtus correspondence. It reads simply:

'There are fresh developments which are not clear. Italy is trying
to secure more through you than she has asked us for directly. Come
to us.'

Come he did, reaching Count Erdödy's house in Vienna in the evening
of 7 May and going out to Laxenburg again the following day. The
sequence was identical with the first visit but everything else seemed to
have changed for the better. Even the weather played its part. Instead of
being wrapped in a bitter snowstorm, as it had been on that March night,
the yellow castle now sparkled in the spring sunshine and the Emperor
was able to receive his brother-in-law out of doors in a special part of the
park he always reserved for open-air audiences.

The prince began by repeating some points Lloyd George had rubbed
home – that the German submarine offensive would fail in its object and
that American intervention on the *Entente* side would, on the other hand,
prove decisive. Here he was pushing at an open door, for Charles had
predicted both developments months before. The nub of the discussion
centred naturally on Italy's claims, as relayed through London and Paris,
and on the need for an Austrian 'sacrifice'. The Emperor now took an
important step forward, and a bold one considering how explosive an
issue the Italian one was for his own subjects of all races. According to
Prince Sixtus's account:

'The Emperor stated that he was prepared to make the necessary sacrifices to Italy, but that these must be no more than was strictly fair, confined, that was, to territories Italian in speech and sentiment. Popular feeling must be taken into account in dealing with all these districts, and it would not do to trace arbitrary frontiers on the map for countries of which one had no first-hand knowledge.' Charles went on to indicate that even South Tyrol (Trentino) could be ceded to Italy in the interests of a peace, though the gallantry which his troops had shown in defending this coveted Austrian territory from invasion made it essential that the Monarchy should be given some compensation in return. There was a wide-ranging discussion as to where this compensation might be found: Silesia, or one of the German overseas possessions? The Prince suggested that one of Italy's African colonies like Somaliland might even fit the bill, and he added, in blissful ignorance of the twentieth century's later problems, that 'a negro is better value than an irredentist'.

But whatever the compensation, it was clear that the Emperor was now ready to make the vital and, for him, painful concession of handing over the Trentino, which he had himself helped to defend in battle. Sixtus quotes Charles as saying that he was 'unreservedly taking this first step towards a settlement and with a ruthless sacrifice of his own personal pride'. The road to peace seemed to the Austrian ruler – ignorant of the secret London treaty and with Cadorna's offer still ringing in his ears – to have been finally opened up by this gesture.

Even Czernin, who joined the open-air discussion at this point, seems to have caught the spirit of the occasion. He was much more amicable to the prince than in March and also much more forthcoming. He raised no objections to anything that had passed, emphasizing only that Italy should herself provide the *quid pro quo* for whatever Austria had to cede her and should not be allowed to pay Vienna in someone else's coin. He also added an earnest plea that the 'next and final interview' should take place between professional diplomatists. The belief all round was that the dove of peace had been put in its cage at last on that sunny afternoon in a quiet corner of Laxenburg Park. The Emperor promised Prince Sixtus a second letter for the *Entente* on the Italian question and an early meeting for formal negotiations was envisaged in Switzerland. 'And so,' the prince commented when describing the farewell scene, 'everyone was delighted, hoping to see an early and propitious end to the war.' To Charles the peacemaker this moment must have seemed as golden as the day. Like the day, alas, it was doomed to fade.

Charles's second autograph letter from Laxenburg, which Sixtus took home with him the next day, was much shorter than the March epistle, and only the first part of it need concern us here. This reads:

My dear Sixtus,

I note with satisfaction that France and England are in agreement with me upon what I hold to be the essential basis of a European peace. At the same time they express their opposition to any form of peace in which Italy does not participate. As it happens, Italy has just approached me with a demand for peace between herself and the Monarchy in which she abandons all the inadmissible claims of annexation she has hitherto maintained in regard to the Slavonic states on the Adriatic. She has limited her claim to the Italian-speaking portion of the Tyrol. I have myself postponed the examination of her demands until I hear from you what answer France and England may make to my offer of peace. . . .

The understanding which the Monarchy has reached with France and England on so many essential points will enable us, we feel sure, to overcome whatever obstacles may remain in the way of an honourable peace. . . .

At the last minute Czernin put in his oar again. He added to the Emperor's letter a brief note of his own scribbled in German – unsigned as usual and peremptory in tone as usual. One of its four points was a vital one which Charles might have touched on himself at this stage of the contacts and which he would certainly have raised later had full-blown negotiations resulted. What guarantees, Czernin asked, would be forthcoming that the integrity of the Monarchy with the border adjustments now under discussion would be preserved at any eventual peace conference? But the general tone of Czernin's memorandum was far from conciliatory – stressing, for example, Austria's absolute rejection of any 'one-sided territorial concessions'.

Czernin may well have been stirred to write in this way out of wounded vanity that this major diplomatic adventure was not being launched in his name. To give him maximum credit for his motives, he may also have been genuinely anxious that his young sovereign was going too far too fast. Yet that was precisely what Charles intended. With every day that passed, the propitious time for a peace initiative drained away like sand out of an hourglass. To go too far too fast was, in May 1917, the only way to get anywhere.

From here onwards, the Sixtus affair – launched by Charles in Paris through a Frenchman to French leaders – is virtually taken over by the Prime Minister of Britain. As Ribot slides deliberately out of the picture, Lloyd George comes more and more to the forefront – nagging his allies, prodding his Cabinet colleagues, and urging his own sovereign to make something of Charles's offer, despite the Italian obstacle, while there was still time. Prince Sixtus himself must have sensed this marked difference of atmosphere when, armed with the second Laxenburg letter, he now visited both Western capitals to get that final 'yes' from the *Entente*.

The talk he had in Paris on the evening of 20 May with President Poincaré and M. Ribot was, on the whole, a dampening experience. The President, while admitting that the compensation problem for the Trentino was 'not so simple', at least talked as though he wanted to continue along the same road of negotiations and saw hopes of a settlement at the end of it. Ribot, on the other hand, talked as though France were being lured into a dangerous *cul-de-sac* and he must therefore put down all the obstacles he could to save her. Thus he even raised question marks over the three issues already basically agreed in the secret contacts: Alsace-Lorraine, Belgium and Serbia. He dragged in the complication of Rumania's future claims and, on the cardinal point of Italy, refused to do anything to oppose Sonnino's uncompromising stand at Saint-Jean. His only positive suggestion was that the King of Italy should be approached in person, a proposal that later developed into a project for a meeting between all three Heads of State – President Poincaré, King George v and King Victor Emmanuel. Even this turned out to be a delaying move, and may have been intended as one.

As he took his leave to go on to London, Prince Sixtus noted these impressions of the talk:

President Poincaré – Very quick-witted and clear-sighted. Very well informed of the European situation and keenly patriotic.
Premier Ribot – Aged and worn-out. Kept taking off and putting on again his tinted spectacles. Could see all the difficulties of the situation but nothing more. Not a man of action. . . .

The same rebuke could not be applied to Lloyd George, whom the Head of the French Foreign Office, M. Jules Cambon, was to describe indeed as 'an impetuous Celt' for his zeal in trying to get these Austrian talks off the ground. Sixtus's account of his first London talk with the British statesman recaptures the flavour of this impatience. They met on 23 May at No. 10 Downing Street, which the Bourbon prince evidently found a little drab and workaday after the chandeliers of Laxenburg and the Elysée:

The house in which the British Government has installed its Premiers for three centuries is quite small and rather old-fashioned. I was shown into an ante-room decorated with all sorts of horns from the Colonies. Mr Davies (the Prime Minister's secretary) took me to the Premier's study, where I waited a few minutes. It was in great disorder: a large desk – quite commonplace – with several tables, vases of flowers, a typewriter, books and reports. I could see that I was in the house of a 'man of business'.

When the talk began, Lloyd George, who had received a copy of the second Laxenburg letter, described it as 'very kind', and asked straight away how compensation could be found for the Emperor Charles if he ceded the Trentino. A transfer to Austria of either a German or an Italian colony was discussed and more or less discarded. Unlike Ribot, however, Lloyd George saw the prize ahead as well as the difficulties ahead and he wasted no time in pursuing it.

When the question of a Heads of State meeting cropped up, for example, he declared: 'We ought to see the King at once. I will telephone now and ask for an audience.' And while that was being arranged he started making tentative plans for the formal peace talks with Austria. According to Prince Sixtus's account:

> Mr Lloyd George said he wanted no diplomats. Diplomats were invented to waste time. . . . Why could not M. Ribot and himself meet Count Czernin? . . . Only those men who were at the Head of Government of each country and had authority in their Parliaments could meet together to discuss questions of such grave importance.

Prince Sixtus's audience with King George v took place only two hours later at three o'clock that afternoon. Neither Lloyd George nor the prince himself in his otherwise very full account of his activities records anything of what transpired. Not even his relatives in Vienna were given any details. The Empress Zita later learned merely that the British monarch was 'very favourably disposed' towards the Austrian peace project. This impression is supported by the following extract from the King's own diary:

Wednesday 23 May 1917 – Buckingham Palace
. . . At 3.0 the Prime Minister brought Prince Sixt [*sic*] of Bourbon – brother of the Empress of Austria who is serving in the Belgian Army. He came to inform us that the Emperor of Austria had written to him to try and arrange for a separate peace with the *Entente*; the difficulty will be Italy; it is of course very secret only M. Poincaré and M. Ribot know. It would be a great thing if it could be brought about. . . .*

Any hopes that the prince may have entertained at this stage were now to be dashed slowly on the rocks of Sonnino's intransigence in Rome. But it was the French Premier, M. Ribot (influenced strongly by the Permanent Head of his Foreign Office, Jules Cambon), who steered them on to those

* From the Royal Archives, Windsor Castle. Published by Gracious Permission of Her Majesty The Queen.

rocks, for all Lloyd George's efforts to reach clear water. Ribot and Cambon had somehow convinced themselves that if Austria and Italy made a separate peace, Italy would promptly back out of the war carrying her Tyrolean prize with her, and that the harm done to France by this would more than balance the fact that Germany had lost her chief ally. It was a classic example of diplomatists becoming so subtle that they forsook common-sense. As Lloyd George himself commented on this French position:

To hold that the possible defection of Italy would not be compensated ten-fold if the millions of Austrian troops were withdrawn from the ranks of our enemies; if Turkey and Bulgaria were cut off from Germany and forced to make terms; if the Austrian submarines were withdrawn from the Mediterranean and the submarine bases there closed; if our armies in Salonika, Egypt, Palestine and Mesopotamia could be reduced to garrisons; if the corn of Russia and the Danube could be brought to France and if, on the other hand, the food, petroleum and other supplies of the Dual Monarchy and Rumania were with-held from Germany; if Prussian militarism, deserted as it would be by all its allies and opposed by the most powerful nations in the world, were forced into a position of foredoomed defeat – to ignore all these advantages which must follow from a separate peace with Austria and be prepared to forgo them all . . . appears an unbalanced attitude of mind.*

Unbalanced or not, the French stand was decisive. Had Paris shared the enthusiasm of London for negotiations with Austria, Sonnino, surrounded in his own camp by so many protagonists of peace, would have been brought growling to heel. Instead it was England who faced the opposition of two allies, and Sonnino accordingly barked defiance at will. On 30 May he produced three irrelevant pretexts for avoiding the Heads of State meeting.† Lloyd George promptly retorted by suggesting instead a meeting of the Italian, French and British Prime Ministers,‡ only to have this idea held up by Sonnino and finally converted in a general conference in Paris at which the Austrian question was swamped under a broad agenda. At this meeting, incidentally, Ribot added a positive breach of faith to all his sins of omission by showing Sonnino the entire Sixtus correspondence – despite his solemn pledge to the prince, which was in effect to Charles, to keep the secret.

By now, however, the prince had anyway given up. As late as 5 June, he

* *War Memoirs*, IV, p. 2028.

† British Foreign Office telegram 108183/17, Sir Rennell Rodd to Foreign Office, 30 May 1917.

‡ Foreign Office to Paris No. 1537 of 9 June 1917, and to Rome No. 1108 of 13 June 1917.

was still hanging around in Westminster, waiting for some positive reaction from Rome; and Lloyd George, though exasperated himself at the delay, was still offering encouragement. He told the prince at their final talk that day:

Italy owes us an answer and she shall give us one, I assure you. It is just because Signor Sonnino is so obstinate and difficult and troublesome that I want the King of Italy to have a say. His influence will balance Sonnino's. The chance of peace with Austria is too important to us to let it slip. . . .

The next day the prince left London for Paris where he spent another three weeks trying to talk some action into the devious M. Cambon and the cautious M. Ribot. It was no use. They refused to join London in prodding Sonnino because of their conviction that France would somehow be wounded in the process. On 25 June 1917, Sixtus finally gave up. He left Paris to rejoin his regiment so as not to miss the forthcoming offensive on the Belgian front. He must have felt, as he got back to the battlefield again, that even trench warfare was a mobile thing compared with diplomacy. On paper, the Sixtus affair begins to fade out at this point. Charles never received a direct answer* to that second Laxenburg letter he had penned with such hope.

But it was only on paper that his ideas died. Unbeknown to Charles, they were now to be taken up in a totally different and far broader context by the 'impetuous Celt' in London, who continued to fight for them among his colleagues throughout that summer. Lloyd George's aim in this controversy – and indeed his whole restless and far-ranging approach to the problem – was almost a replica of Churchill's a generation later. Like Churchill in the middle of the Second World War, Lloyd George in the middle of the First argued for a blow at what his successor called the 'soft underbelly' of the enemy's Southern front in order to weaken resistance on the iron-hard Western front. Like Churchill he was overruled. The result, for the peoples of the Danube Basin, was far-reaching on both occasions. An Allied victory in the south in 1917 could have saved the Austro-Hungarian Empire; an Allied victory there in 1944 could have saved most of those same lands from Soviet Communism.

We are fortunate in having available an expertly annotated survey of all Lloyd George's efforts to draw or knock Austria out of the war, a record compiled by no less an authority than the Secretary to the Cabinet, Sir Maurice Hankey. It was drawn up in interesting circumstances.

* An indirect rejection was finally given in a statement to the French Chamber by M. Ribot on 12 October 1917.

In the spring of 1918, when the public show-down over the Sixtus affair between the Emperor Charles and his Foreign Minister Czernin was rocking Europe, Lloyd George faced criticism in his own Parliament for action behind his colleagues' backs over the Austrian move the year before. To give him ammunition to meet this charge, he ordered Hankey to compile, from all the War Cabinet minutes and Whitehall telegrams of 1917, a complete account of the episode. Hankey laboured away and the outcome was three long memoranda to the Prime Minister of 11 May, 13 May and 15 May 1918 – marked 'Very Secret', 'Secret and Personal', and plain 'Secret', respectively. It is from these memoranda that the following final phase of the 1917 affair is reconstructed.*

The first two of these memoranda have been drawn on already in compiling the general account of the Sixtus affair given above. They are mainly interesting in showing how, from the very start of the episode, Lloyd George tried to instil enthusiasm into his Cabinet colleagues and his generals. On 9 May 1917, for example, soon after Lloyd George's return from the abortive meeting with Sonnino at Saint-Jean, the War Cabinet held an important discussion on the question of separate peaces in general – prompted by the fear that Russia, now in the grip of revolution, might defect from the *Entente* side. Hankey records the following intervention of the Prime Minister, who was of course unable to tell his Cabinet of the Sixtus letters:†

In such circumstances [a Russian defection] the best chance for the Allies would appear to be in a separate peace with Austria, *in which Italy might have to be compelled to acquiesce.* [Author's italic] If we failed to induce Austria to make a separate peace, he could see no hope of the sort of victory in the War that we desired. . . . If it should prove impossible to persuade Austria to make a separate peace, he inclined to the view that it would be a mistaken policy to sacrifice hundreds of thousands of lives in attacks on the Western front.‡

The official minutes of the meeting included a reference to this point.

The subject, Hankey records, next came before the British War Cabinet on 8 June 1917, and here the context was not the threatened Eastern front but the deadlocked Western front. General Nivelle's French offensive had petered out without any commensurate gain. The British Commander Sir

* All three documents in the London Beaverbrook Library of Lloyd George's papers and made available by kind permission of the Trustees. (F23/2/33; F23/2/34; F23/2/35.)
† Hankey, who had accompanied Lloyd George to the St Jean conference, *was* told of the existence of the Austrian Emperor's letters, though without their details, under the strictest pledge of secrecy. The Prime Minister, he records, did this on their journey down 'in case anything happened to him'.
‡ Hankey Memorandum, F23/2/34 of 13 May 1918, p. 7.

Douglas Haig was pressing for authority to launch another attack of his own in Flanders. General Sir Henry Wilson, Head of the British Mission at French GHQ, had been called to London to inform the Cabinet about the true state of the French Army and nation, which were both showing alarming signs of cracking. In an unvarnished report, the General told the Cabinet that 'it would be difficult to hold the French Army together for another winter without some real success, military or diplomatic'.*

This touched off Lloyd George again. Immediately, those Laxenburg letters he was unable to show his colleagues seem to have flashed into his mind. Hankey, who, for greater secrecy, was ordered to make only one record† of this meeting in his own strangely schoolboyish handwriting, goes on:

The Prime Minister then adverted to the possibility of a separate peace with Austria, which he had no doubt we could secure on terms. The difficulty was that Baron Sonnino had succeeded in manoeuvring the King of Italy out of the proposed conference between our King, the King of Italy and the French President. Baron Sonnino had probably suspected that the real object of the conference was to discuss the possibility of peace with Austria and had burked it, owing to the fact that he himself was, for political reasons, not in a position to make peace on the Austrian terms. The latter included the cession of the Trentino (but not of Trieste, nor Gorizia, nor Dalmatia) in return for the cession by Italy or the Allies of Erythrea or some colony, and the independence of Serbia was also provided for. Hence Baron Sonnino's political difficulties.

The Prime Minister felt that we ought not to let Baron Sonnino stand in the way of a separate peace with Austria [author's italic] and we ought to insist on seeing him, even if we could not get the King of Italy to a conference. . . .‡

There followed a curious 'round-the-bushes' discussion of the 'Austrian negotiations' in which Lloyd George's Cabinet colleagues were clearly handicapped – and perhaps mystified – by not knowing precisely what it was their Prime Minister had in mind. But the end of Hankey's 'Most Secret' handwritten account is significant.

The Prime Minister insisted that Austria was at least entitled to a reply.

It was generally agreed that the Austrian approach was to be pursued . . . the War Cabinet were of the opinion that, if properly handled, these negotiations might result in the isolation of Germany and a general peace on the terms sought by the *Entente* powers and that, while great caution was necessary, the opportunity ought not to be let slip.

* *Ibid.*, p. 11.
† Appendix 2.
‡ F23/2/34, *op. cit.*, p. 11 and CAB 23/16 (Public Records Office).

The War Cabinet decided:

(*a*) That the Acting Secretary of State for Foreign Affairs should send a telegram to Rome asking Baron Sonnino to meet the representatives of the British and French Governments at some French town or, if preferred, at some English town;

(*b*) That a Committee on war policy should be set up.

As we have seen, Baron Sonnino managed effectively to block the first resolution. The full scope of the second resolution is described in the last of Hankey's special memoranda on the Austrian peace issue.* It was nothing less than an attempt by Lloyd George in the second half of 1917 to help Austria out of the war by knocking her out by herself – even if it meant standing the conventional grand strategy of the *Entente* on its head in the process.

Hankey begins by noting that the special Cabinet Committee on War Policy set up at the meeting of 8 June 1917 sat during the greater part of the following seven weeks. He continues:

By far the most important question it discussed was as to whether the then forthcoming offensive of the Allies should be conducted in Flanders, as Field-Marshal Haig, with General Robertson's [Chief of Imperial General Staff] support, urged, or whether the Allies should adopt a defensive attitude on the Western front and concentrate their artillery on the Italian front, with a view to a stroke against Austria, designed with the object of compelling that country to make a separate peace. Apart from no less than 21 formal meetings . . . at which a large amount of naval and military evidence was taken, the Committee dined together on two occasions, at both of which this question was the main topic of conversation.

It was at the tenth meeting of this Cabinet Committee that Lloyd George, having voiced all his misgivings about the ruinous cost and problematical dividends of the Flanders offensive, came out with all the force and persuasiveness he could muster (and they were considerable) for the second alternative: the knock-out blow against Austria on the southern front. Hankey's account of his argument shows how deeply the secret peace moves of the Austrian Emperor had influenced the British Prime Minister's thinking, even to its battlefield application. In the Cabinet Secretary's version:

He felt that the fatal error which had been committed in the present war had

* This final memorandum of Hankey's to his Prime Minister of 15 May 1918 (Beaverbrook Library, Reference F23/2/35), contains some detail and much comment not covered in the full account of the controversy which Lloyd George himself gave in his *Memoirs*, IV, pp. 2149–204.

been continually to attack where the enemy was strongest. Surely, it was a mistake to strike with the sword at the thickest part of the enemy's armour. If we had made efforts earlier in the war to knock out Austria, we should be in a far better position now. He felt, however, that we had another chance of effecting this.

There was not the smallest doubt that Austria was anxious to be out of the war. This was not a matter of conjecture but of absolute knowledge. Austria, however, would not be willing to pay the price demanded by the Allies, although if another heavy blow were struck against her she might be brought to accept our terms. . . . The prize was by far the biggest in sight. If Austria could be forced out of the war, Bulgaria and Turkey would automatically have to go out. The umbilical cord of the Central Alliance would be cut. . . .

How then was this result to be accomplished? It was his belief that Trieste was the only thing which stood between Italy and a separate peace with Austria. He had reason to believe that Austria would be willing to cede the Trentino now, but not Trieste. If Trieste were captured,* Austria would have to appeal to a population that was half-Slav to recapture it. They would refuse. . . .

Hankey describes how Lloyd George then painted to his assembled ministers and generals the grim picture if Russia were to go out of the war with Austria still in. Germany could throw $1\frac{1}{2}$ million men into the Western front, a mass of troops that not even the now certain American reinforcements could balance in time. And he concluded: 'Hence the vital necessity of the hour was to get Austria out of the war in order to give Sir Douglas Haig a chance of victory next year.'

But Britain's generals – mesmerized, precisely as their German counterparts were, by that bloody will-o'-the-wisp of 'final victory' in the West – were not to be done out of their Flanders offensive. They ignored all Lloyd George's pleas to them to see the whole European battlefield as 'one and indivisible'. Their eyes were fixed on that single arena of mud and barbed wire across the Channel which had already claimed such mountains of human sacrifice, on which they were now to heap mountains more. Lloyd George, the civilian with a broad vision, had no option but to bow to the verdict of these eminent experts in blinkers. As Hankey tersely records this momentous decision:

Owing to the very strong views expressed by Field-Marshal Haig and General Robertson, which were supported on naval grounds by Admiral Jellicoe, who laid the utmost stress on the danger to the Navy of allowing Ostend and

---

* In a memorandum on the subject quoted in his *Memoirs*, IV, pp. 2169–75, Lloyd George was more specific about Trieste. The Italian lines were already only eight miles from the city. Surely, he argued, if the Allies could provide the equivalent of a bombardment by 300 extra howitzers, the port could be taken.

Zeebrugge to remain in the enemy's hands, the Committee decided to sanction the Flanders offensive, keeping the Italian offensive in reserve as a second string.

One can only surmise, of course, what would have happened if Lloyd George's plea had been heard and General Cadorna's Italian armies had been helped that eight miles into Trieste during the summer and autumn of 1917. There is no need to surmise about the results of the alternative actually chosen. On 20 July Haig was duly authorized by the full War Cabinet to 'carry out the plans for which he has prepared'. At the end of his long offensive, which began with the 'folly of Passchendaele', the British Army in Flanders had lost 400,000 men compared with 250,000 of the enemy and was – in the view of many observers – even worse placed at the end of this muddy slaughter than at the beginning.

Still Lloyd George did not give up. On 25 and 26 July, nearly a week after the Flanders offensive had finally been authorized in London, the long-deferred inter-Allied Conference between Britain, France and Italy took place in Paris. Baron Sonnino had managed both to delay this meeting and then to enlarge its agenda to such an extent that no detailed discussion of the Austrian peace move was possible. But Hankey, who was present as Cabinet Secretary throughout the final session, shows in his memorandum how Lloyd George dragged up his pet project into the conversation again and again, like a dog returning to dig up its favourite bone. Moreover, he explicitly referred to his Austrian solution as one which would preserve the multi-lingual Empire in existence. In Hankey's words:*

Mr Lloyd George pointed out that if the whole of the Russian, Roumanian and Serbian claims against Austria were realized in their entirety, the break-up of the Austrian Empire was involved, but that the Italian claims could be exacted without any such break-up. . . . *If Austria received a sufficiently severe blow she might find herself in a position to justify her Government acceding to the major part of the Italian claims.*

And he continued, in tones very reminiscent of Churchill arguing a similar strategic proposition with Roosevelt a generation later:

Hitherto, the *Entente* powers have shown too little anticipation. They have been too slow footed. This was one of the opportunities, by taking swift action, to convert a possible defeat into a victory. . . . Merely to hold on [in the West] was to face a disastrous peace. To get Turkey out of the war was important, but to get Austria out infinitely more so. . . .

* Hankey Memorandum of 15 May 1918 (Beaverbrook Library, F23/2/25), pp. 21 and 22.

It was now the turn of the French generals present, Pétain and Foch, to echo the language their British counterparts had used in the London Cabinet discussion the month before. As Hankey records it:

French military opinion however was dead against the proposal. . . . General Pétain pointed out that the British attack now to be developed was to be followed by a big French attack. Very large quantities of artillery were committed to these offensive operations. It would be impossible to disengage them at present and to concentrate them on the Italian front.

And thus, as the Cabinet Secretary sums up, 'no immediate result, so far as any operation connected with a separate peace with Austria is concerned, followed the Conference'.

There was a final and very lengthy discussion of a separate blow at Austria, expressly designed to get a separate peace, at the next Allied Conference in London, held on 7–8 August 1917. A tone of weary stubbornness has crept into Lloyd George's pleas by now. In Hankey's words:

Mr Lloyd George observed that he had always thought himself that the best policy was for the Allies to try really to crush Austria. He had made the suggestion in Rome and it was then considered too early. He made it now and it was apparently considered too late. He contrasted the method of the Central Powers in pooling their resources . . . with the Allies' efforts which, gallant though they were, only chipped a few bits off a granite rock. . . .

The Italians, who were just mounting an attack of their own against the Austrian armies for which they needed all the Allied help they could get, now ranged themselves, for military reasons, behind Lloyd George's appeal. And though the British and French High Commands (represented on this occasion by Robertson and Foch) again successfully insisted that Austria could only be knocked out of the war by the defeat of Germany in the West, those same generals were soon forced to think again. The Italian attack was duly launched on the Carso with the resources Cadorna had at his disposal and by 25 August unexpectedly good progress was reported. At the same time, the British offensive in Flanders, which had by now been hopefully despatched like a steam-roller into a swamp, was predictably beginning to get bogged down. The contrast was crass enough to impress even that single-minded quartet of Haig, Robertson, Petain and Foch. Hankey describes how, after initial reluctance on the part of the General Staffs, it was decided early in September to detach 100 heavy guns from the First French Army in Flanders and send them to the Italian front to support General Cadorna's decisive thrust.*

* See also Lloyd George, *Memoirs*, IV, p. 2285, for a fuller account of the episode.

Then came the last twist of the knife. Barely had the guns arrived in Italy than the British War Cabinet was told, on 21 September, that Cadorna had abruptly and unexpectedly called off his entire offensive for 1917, and was preparing instead to sit down, still outside Trieste, and wait for the Austrians to move. This military about-face of the Italians was as fateful as their various diplomatic somersaults. At an Allied Conference held at Boulogne on 25 September 1917, it was decided that the British and French heavy artillery should be brought back again from the Italian front. The enemy move, when it came, was the German-led offensive of October, which led to the staggering Italian defeat of Caporetto. Cadorna's passivity also had a major political outcome. As Hankey writes in the last paragraph of his final memorandum:

'General Cadorna's decision not to attack put an abrupt end to the policy of striking a combined blow at Austria as a preliminary to a separate peace.'

The guns that might have been used to tear a hole in the enemy's vulnerable southern front were now put back on their job of churning up more fountains of Flanders mud. And under it all there lay by the end of the year not only the 625,000 dead of the Passchendaele offensive and its off-shoots. Buried as well, and equally without hope of resuscitation, were all the Emperor Charles's dreams of an early and honourable end to the slaughter, and all Lloyd George's plans to help him realize those dreams in a way that would also serve the Allied cause.

Though there were to be important side-effects in the year of catastrophe ahead, the Sixtus affair in the form Charles launched it may be said to have finally flickered out with the abandonment of Cadorna's Italian offensive in September 1917.* Why did it fail, this remarkable peace-making venture with which the name of the last Austrian Emperor will always be linked?

Looking back, there seem half-a-dozen good reasons why it could never have succeeded. Yet this is the false perspective of hindsight. None of the

---

* In August 1917 another secret Austrian dialogue with the *Entente* had also fizzled out. This was the so-called Armand–Revertera talks between a French Army major and an Austrian diplomat meeting in Switzerland. The initiative came, on the French side, from the General Staff, who made a curious foray into diplomacy by suggesting that, if Austria withdrew from the war and ceded both Trieste and the Trentino to Italy, she might be 'rewarded' at Germany's expense by having the whole of pre-1772 Poland, as well as Silesia and Bosnia, added to the Habsburg crown. On the Austrian side, these rather unrealistic contacts were handled by Count Czernin, and the Emperor concerned himself but little with them. The intermediaries, who were both junior in status, had no knowledge of the Sixtus talks going on over their heads. The episode was an interesting *ballon d'essai* of the French military but never gained any political height.

complications was in itself insuperable. It was the unpredictable way they combined that counted.

Italy's claims under the Treaty of London – the secret obstacle which was hidden from Charles when he launched his move – certainly formed the biggest diplomatic barrier. Yet even that could have been surmounted by political pressure had France been prepared to follow England's lead in the early summer of 1917. Equally, it could have been removed by military pressure had the generals of the *Entente* camp – British, French and Italian alike – responded to Lloyd George's constant pleas for a 'knock-out blow' in the south. Indeed on the political front, the change of government in Paris in March of 1917, with Ribot succeeding Briand, was to prove an even greater blow to Charles's hopes than the intransigence of Sonnino in Rome. Henceforth France helped to stiffen that intransigence instead of combining with England to reduce it.

The ever-changing tide of battle was an elemental and uncontrollable factor which muddied all these diplomatic problems further. Charles, as we have seen, had launched his peace moves at the end of 1916 into a situation of propitious deadlock. But with every offensive either planned or feared or executed by the generals on either side, this situation shifted – always enough to complicate his peace project, yet never sufficiently far to impose it. As Musulin, the Austrian Minister in Berne, complained in the spring of 1917: 'We are in a vicious circle. If things go well for the *Entente*, they don't want to hear of peace. If things go well for us the Germans exclaim "Don't hurry".'

This swing of the battle pendulum continued, of course, until the very end of the war, making temporary peacemakers out of the generals as it moved. As late as 10 June 1918, for example, when Hindenburg's last great gamble in the West had brought German troops to within forty miles of Paris, Marshal Joffre could exclaim in the deepest gloom: 'We ought to have made terms with Austria last year . . . then Germany would have had to give in.'* Yet the very next day the counter-attack began which was to save Rheims and – with the help of hundreds of thousands of fresh American troops – go on to crush the German Army in final defeat. It was this full-blooded American commitment in the war that by the summer of 1918 had made all talk of a compromise peace sound rather hollow. Yet this background was not there in the summer of 1917 when the balance of advantage between Russia's defection and America's entry was still being finely calculated in the *Entente*'s books. 1917 was, as Charles well knew, the last year in which a settlement, as opposed to a capitulation, was possible. It was symbolic that one of its closing events was America's

* Quoted in Sixtus-Manteyer, *op. cit.*, p. 302.

long-deferred declaration of war against Austro-Hungary on 7 December. That act, which the Emperor had so dreaded, not only sealed the fate of his peace plans but also the fate of his Empire.

On the side of the Central Powers, it is unquestionable that the biggest single factor which blocked the Sixtus affair, and all other peace moves of Charles, was the blind faith of his German allies in ultimate victory. Hindenburg and Ludendorff had to have the sword broken in their hands before they would believe that it was not invincible. Faced with this knowledge, why did Charles not 'go it alone' and declare a public breach with Berlin in order to force both sides to the conference table?

The Empress Zita recalls many discussions that her husband held on this point.

'The Emperor always felt that – except as a last emergency – he simply could not risk an open break with Germany because of the situation at the front. After 1916 the combined armies were at the last instance and in the event of a policy deadlock under German overall direction. Our troops were so mixed up with German divisions in all the commands that a separate withdrawal would have been as good as impossible. The Germans in any case would have resisted it and there would have been fighting – with many of our Hungarian units, who were traditionally pro-German, in a very difficult position.

'We knew that the Germans had already made their detailed plans to occupy Austria – and presumably put the Emperor and myself under arrest – should the need arise in their eyes. In these circumstances, the Emperor could only have made an open breach if guarantees had been forthcoming from the *Entente* that they would render us the necessary support in time, and such guarantees were never given.

'So the Emperor always went back to his hope of trying to prepare for a general peace through separate peace-feelers of his own. His aim was to get things to a stage where he could say to Berlin: "Look, I have already reached this point in talks with the *Entente*. Now join in with me so that we can bring the whole thing to an end." He always realized that, if this stage were ever reached and the Germans still refused to join, he might have to go on alone. But this was to be the ultimate, desperate step. He always prayed it could be avoided.'

Charles was in fact to be driven to this 'ultimate desperate step', but only in the autumn of 1918, when it came too late to stop anything or to save anything. As for 1917, he might well have echoed Pindar's saying that 'The favourable moment is the sovereign of all things'; and added, for the Greek poet's benefit, that even a favourable moment needs favourable men to exploit it. For in the last analysis it was personalities perhaps even more than policies which defeated the Sixtus affair. In Charles's camp there were too many people, like Ludendorff, prepared to gamble everything for victory. And in the *Entente* camp, with the notable exception of Lloyd George, there were too few people prepared to gamble enough for peace.

For all this, there were times, early in 1917, when the Emperor's peace moves seemed to have an almost even chance of success. Many far less noble ventures in history have succeeded against far greater odds.

Chapter 9

1917: THE SEARCH FOR HARMONY

꙳꙳꙳

The last six weeks of 1916 had been barely enough for Charles to get the feel of the crown on his head. In the ten and a half months of 1918 that were to be his final span of rule, he was kept too busy trying to hold that crown on to indulge in much long-term meditation about the Empire's future. 1917 was his only full year of power. It was also the only year when, in some measure, he could hope to control events around him. He spent it abroad in the search for peace already described. He spent it at home in the search for harmony between the quarrelsome nations under his sceptre.

The two quests were, in fact, part and parcel of the same programme, the same policy, the same dream. Unique in so many ways among all the warring powers, Austria-Hungary was unique also in this. Her diplomacy and her domestic affairs were intertwined to a degree that no other belligerent could even have envisaged in its own affairs. Yet the link between the two was not so much a neat knot as a hopeless tangle. Domestic reform – the need to present the venerable Empire in a more modern and democratic 'image' – became the *sine qua non* of any successful negotiations with an *Entente* camp increasingly dominated by Wilsonian philosophies. But the more desperate the war got, the more hazardous it became to risk drastic surgery at home on a multi-racial state that needed every ounce of its combined strength to fight on in the trenches. Charles needed reforms to get his peace. He needed peace to get his reforms. The riddle proved insoluble.

Before 1917 was far spent, however, an event took place which convinced even the most conservative of his advisers that Austrian political life would have to be brought out of the anaesthetic administered by the military doctors ever since August 1914. That event, of course, was the Russian Revolution of March which, as has been noted above, first gave all the national and racial tensions of the Habsburg Empire a lethal quality by adding to them the new and explosive ingredients of class war and ideology. Charles's own reaction to the revolution was typically clear-sighted. He recognized the long-term dangers of the situation and, because of them, he opposed any short-term exploitation. The main point at issue here was the German plan to smuggle Lenin back into Russia from his Swiss exile in order to spread unrest and complete the destruction of the Slav colossus on the Eastern front. In this, the Emperor William and his generals saw only the enemy army that they now had the chance to cripple. Charles saw beyond the trenches to the menace that Bolshevism posed for the peoples as well as the dynasties of Europe as a whole.

The Empress Zita recounts: 'He tried to oppose the idea of smuggling Lenin into Russia in the German sealed train and tried to talk the German Government out of the scheme on three grounds. First, that this was an unfair and irresponsible thing to do to the Russian people. Second that the more chaos was caused in Russia the more difficult it would be to find anyone to talk peace with. And third, that once Communism got established in Russia, it wouldn't stop there but would spread and both Germany and Austro-Hungary could become engulfed. Evil, he was convinced, could only breed evil. He put these arguments personally to the German Emperor and also through Government channels. And it was for these reasons that he refused point-blank to consent to the original German proposal, which was that Lenin's sealed train should cross via *Austrian* territory to the East.'

The last of the three arguments Charles had developed eloquently in that long memorandum which he had inspired himself during the Sixtus moves but which had gone out to the Emperor William over Czernin's signature on 10 April 1917.*

Five monarchs [he had warned his fellow-German sovereign] have been dethroned in this war, and the amazing facility with which the strongest Monarchy in the world was overthrown may well cause us anxiety and call to mind the saying: *Exemplae trahunt*. Let it not be said that in Germany or Austro-Hungary the conditions are different. Let it not be argued that the deep-rooted monarchist feelings in both Berlin and Vienna rule out the possibility of such a development. This war has opened a new era in the history of the world. It is without example and without precedent. The world is no longer what it was three years ago and it would be vain to seek a historical parallel for the happenings which have now become daily occurrences.

And then had come a sentence which revealed the vulnerability of his multi-racial Empire compared with the single-nation state of the Hohenzollerns:

The Russian Revolution affects our Slavs more than it does the Germans [i.e. the German Reich] and the responsibility for continuing the war is a far graver

* See p. 78.

one for the Monarch whose country is united only through the dynasty than for one where the people are fighting for their national independence.

The menace of the March Revolution to Austria was thus crystal-clear. So in theory was the solution. It was to restore to the Habsburg Empire that rule of law which had been abruptly suspended ever since the outbreak of hostilities. This was now doubly urgent, for the wartime political system which Charles had inherited appeared to the outside world in some ways even more archaic than the Tsarist structure that had just been toppled in Russia. Vienna was the only one of the warring capitals to rule without even the outward trappings of democracy. Parliament had not met once since 1914 and, potentially more sinister, its powers had been supplanted by re-invoking the notorious Paragraph Fourteen of the 1867 Constitution. This paragraph, which enabled the Emperor to govern by direct edict in any emergency, put Charles, like his great-uncle before him, within a pen-stroke of dictatorship. Already in the first months of his reign there had been voices urging him to take up that pen and sign his way to absolutism. Some of the Austro-German landowners and industrialists of Bohemia, for example, would have liked Paragraph Fourteen employed to guarantee at one blow their political supremacy over the Czechs. At the other end of the spectrum stood the anti-Magyar reforming radicals who contemplated using the same emergency powers to end the whole Dualist system, and with it Budapest's hold over the South Slavs, by an imperial decree.

There was never much prospect of Charles being tempted into these extreme steps which he would have regarded as leading indirectly to the Devil as well as straight back to the Middle Ages. He was determined to be a constitutional monarch and, when peace came, to remove Paragraph Fourteen altogether. This was the simple explanation for his refusal, after his accession, to take the oath to the Austrian constitution he had inherited. As he commented once to the Empress: 'I wouldn't even dream of swearing to uphold a constitution which I am determined to reform from the bottom up.' And since, unlike Hungary, Austria possessed no crown of her own – sacred or otherwise – which had to be placed on his head,* Charles could persist with his refusal.

Yet these safeguards were the purely accidental ones of the new ruler's own character and intentions. In practice, as well as in appearance, the Austrian half of the wartime Empire now seemed too reactionary for comfort. One immediate result of the March Revolution, therefore, was

* A Bohemian Crown did duty for the Austrian State Crown when required. This was the oddity of oddities. The Habsburgs were Kings of Hungary and Bohemia but only Archdukes of their own Austria.

the recall of the Vienna Parliament in order to give Austria at least the semblance of democratic respectability. On 16 April, little more than a month after the upheaval in Russia, the Austrian Government discussed plans for the first wartime parliamentary session, which was finally fixed for the end of May.

This would restore the shell of democracy. But the real question throughout that April and May was: what kernel of reform, if any, would now be placed inside it? During these weeks, that stubborn idealist and tireless manufacturer of blue-prints, Arthur von Polzer, again played a vital if hidden role at the Emperor's elbow. Polzer had pondered long on the lessons of the Russian Revolution, on the growing championship of the 'little nations' from the *Entente* camp abroad, and on the ugly pressure from the Austro-German magnates at home to have their privileges in Bohemia perpetuated by Imperial ordinance before the new Parliament had a chance to tinker with them. He had concluded that there was only one way to meet all three problems – and at the same time realize his old aim of reducing Magyar hegemony. This was for the Government to announce, in general but unequivocal terms, its intention to grant national autonomy to all peoples of the Empire, within the limits imposed by the state's interests as a whole. Such an announcement should be made before the Vienna Parliament re-assembled at the end of May. If possible, that Parliament should then be made one of the chief instruments of the proposed reform.

Polzer must have blessed the Court train and the frequent journeys the Emperor made in it. Far away from Schönbrunn and the Hofburg, clattering peacefully hour after hour across the ever-changing and always beautiful landscape of his Empire and with only a handful of chosen intimates around him, Charles on these occasions had time to breathe and time to think. Polzer, as the private secretary, was usually aboard and seated closest to the receptive ear of his master. One such golden opportunity presented itself now. The Emperor, returning from the South-West front, ordered Polzer to meet his train at Marburg on 11 April and give him a detailed political report during the journey back to Vienna. For close on five hours, Polzer was able to put his case without interruption. The Emperor, in principle, approved – not surprisingly, for universal autonomy within the Empire was simply his own dream of federation put into different words. Polzer was told to draw up his draft manifesto with two conditions. The first was that it should be submitted to Count Clam-Martinitz who, as the Prime Minister in Vienna, was the Head of the Austrian Government which would have to promulgate it. The second was that the manifesto 'should in no way reflect upon Hungary'. Both were conditions which the constitutional head of a Dual Monarchy felt bound to impose. They proved enough to shelve the whole scheme. Clam was polite but non-committal when receiving Polzer but, backed up by Czernin and others, was implacably opposed to such a radical step when consulted privately by the Emperor. The political leaders in Budapest, where the Emperor went for a one-day visit on 14 April, were equally hostile. On his return from the Hungarian capital, Charles had to tell his secretary that the manifesto would have to be dropped.

Polzer, whose tenacity was worthy of those Magyars he so heartily dis-liked, waited patiently for the next trip in the special train. Sure enough, another one came just in time. On 15 May, a bare fortnight before the new Parliament was due to assemble, he found himself again discussing the Empire's future on a return journey to Vienna from Trient in the South Tyrol. Once more, Polzer argued the case for his autonomy programme as the *vade mecum* for all the Empire's ills. This time the Emperor slept on it as the train travelled northwards through the night. In the morning Polzer thought that victory was his at last. He was summoned by Charles and told to ring Count Clam immediately with orders to insert a passage on national autonomy in the forthcoming Speech from the Throne. It must have been a jubilant private secretary who ordered the royal train to stop at the next station and then leaped out to call up the Prime Minister and so launch the reform of an empire from a country station-master's telephone.

It was indeed too good to be true. Clam in Vienna was quite unmoved. The proposal, he retorted, would upset his own draft speech entirely; he would have to speak to the Emperor himself about it. The final outcome, when Vienna was reached, was that, though a special study commission on the matter was set up as a consolation prize for the wretched Polzer, his autonomy plan as such was again dropped. This time it went into a longer sleep. Indeed it only stirred again in October 1918 during the last weeks of the Empire's existence, when Charles proclaimed federalism in the Austrian half of his kingdom in a last vain bid to save the whole Habsburg sand-castle from the incoming tide.

Could it and should it have been announced eighteen months earlier in the spring of 1917, as Polzer urged, at a time when the balance of war was not unfavourable; when great things were expected of the popular new monarch; and when hardly a soul, inside Austro-Hungary or in the world outside, even contemplated the Empire's early and total collapse?

On the face of things, the answer is yes, and Charles's apparent four-fold change of direction within as many weeks looks like the vacillation of an irresolute man. Yet those original instructions of his to Polzer should be recalled. Charles had already rejected rule by arbitrary decree, on both moral and political grounds. That meant that the announcement of radical reforms in wartime could only be made with the agreement of the Vienna government which, under him, would have to promulgate them. He had also sworn at his Budapest Coronation to maintain 'the lands of St Stephen's Crown'. That meant that changes in Hungary could not be imposed by him but only introduced with the consent of those who ruled St Stephen's lands in his name. And the harsh truth was that the Cabinets of both Vienna and Budapest did not contain a single minister prepared to back the plan when Polzer put it forward. In a sense, of course, both they and he were right – they to sustain the wartime present; he to safeguard a peaceful future. It was the old time riddle again, and how little confidence even Polzer himself had of solving it in practice, rather than on paper, he was now to demonstrate. Six weeks after the second defeat of the autonomy project, Charles asked his private secretary point-blank (again on one of those train journeys) whether he would be prepared, as Prime Minister, to lead a reform Government of his own into action with the Emperor behind him. Polzer refused. It was not simply moral cowardice. It was also a recognition of the formidable arguments of his opponents.

Yet, having said all this, the fact remains that when, on 31 May 1917, the young Emperor rose to make his eagerly-awaited address to Vienna's first wartime Parliament, a unique opportunity was sadly missed. The ears of the world, as well as those of his fifty million subjects, were cocked for his words. He had to disappoint them all. A reference to ruling 'in the spirit of true democracy' echoed, it is true, the new mood and language of the day. Yet on the crucial issue – political reforms within the Empire – there was silence wrapped in resonant generalities. The Emperor merely expressed his confidence that the new Parliament, in conjunction with the throne, would create the necessary preliminary conditions 'in order, within the framework of the unity of the State, and with its functions assured, to guarantee the free national and cultural development of nations possessing equal rights'. This was a far cry indeed from that proclamation of national autonomy which Polzer had pressed for and which Charles itched to make. But there was little point in the Emperor sounding a bugle-call when he knew that not a single officer would line up behind him for the charge. For a monarch who had just proclaimed in that same speech his fidelity to constitutional rule, the combined opposition to reform of the Vienna and Budapest Governments was an insuperable obstacle.

The anodyne quality of the royal address showed up all the more painfully against the declarations of the principal national delegations – themselves also the product of weeks of political haggling – which the new

Parliament had heard at its opening the day before. Loyalty to the Habsburg Monarchy was still their prevailing note. But beneath this an undertone of impatience was creeping in. Here and there concessions could even be detected to that tiny but strident minority of radicals who questioned the whole validity of the Empire and sought their political salvation outside it. Typical of this slight but very significant shift of emphasis was the performance of the Czechs.*

Masaryk, Benes and the other Czech exiles who were working hard for their recognition as a separate Government in the West naturally regarded the reconvening of a Parliament of reconciliation in Vienna with concern and misgiving. In April 1917, they sent messages to their former colleagues in Prague pleading with them not to send a full delegation to Vienna and to take a very tough line when they got there. Unlike the exiles, the overwhelming mass of the political parties in Prague, who had by now merged into the so-called Czech Union, still did not even envisage life outside the Habsburg Monarchy.† Indeed they regarded the crown, especially now Charles was wearing it, as their best protection against the German magnates of Bohemia, whom the new Emperor had conspicuously failed to support. On the other hand, there was the revolutionary example just given by their great Slav blood-brothers in the North to be taken into account. There was also America's entry into the war to be considered and President Wilson's talk of self-determination.

Finally, just before Parliament met, the pressure from the politicians in exile had been matched by a remarkable outburst of 'progressive' thinking in Prague itself. In the middle of May, 222 Czech authors signed a Manifesto addressed to the professional politicians. It was vague enough yet also ominous enough in tone. It called on the nation's deputies to insist on unspecified 'Czech rights' when in Vienna and, though there was no Slovak author among the signatories, the Manifesto made the first passing reference in print to the 'Czechoslovak nation'. Without actually crying '*Austria delenda est*', the appeal concluded: 'A democratic Europe, consisting of free and autonomous states, is the Europe of the future.' It was a victory for radical thinking though not yet for radical policy. The issues raised by the authors – especially the strange concept of Czechoslovakia – kept the Czech deputies arguing over the final draft of their declaration for

---

* See Zeman, *The Break-Up of the Habsburg Empire*, pp. 115–27. This admirably concise account of the process of political disintegration is particularly strong on Czech events.

† Only the tiny Progressive Party, which had two deputies, and the Realist Party of the exiled Masaryk, which had no deputies at all apart from him, took an anti-Habsburg stand. In the spring of 1917 they could still be regarded on all sides as a lunatic fringe.

the rest of the month. Indeed, they only managed to complete it the day before it was read out. The key passage ran as follows:

The representatives of the Czech nation are deeply convinced that the present dualist form of government has led to the emergence of ruling and subject nationalities which is harmful to the interests of the whole. The transformation of the Habsburg monarchy into a federal state consisting of free and equal national states is necessary if all national privileges are to be abolished and if the general development of nationalities in the interest of the Empire is to be secured. Relying at this historic moment on the natural rights of nations, on self-determination and free development, reinforced in our case by inalienable historical rights, we shall demand the unification of all the branches of the Czechoslovak nation into one democratic state. We must not forget the Slovak branch, which forms a close historical unity with the Czech lands.

It was all there, the whole increasingly muddled, increasingly contradictory mixture. Appeals to the deep roots of the past combined with echoes of the new catchwords of the present; and, running through both, the hope that the young Emperor wearing that ancient crown could somehow link the two and save his own heritage in the process. In many ways they were so close, the Czech delegation and their monarch. Both realized Dualism had to go. Both looked to genuine federalism to take its place. The problem was how, when and with whom to effect that mighty transformation.

Though this Czech declaration stole the limelight, the other Austrian delegations showed that their minds, too, had been moving in the same direction. As regards the most important of these, the South Slavs, there had been the same marked tendency towards burying inter-racial and inter-party rivalries, again accelerated by the galvanic shock of the March Revolution. The so-called South Slav Committee, though looser-knit than the Czech Union, also came to Vienna with a united constitutional programme. And this too, though loyal to the crown, demanded a federal-type reform and thus declared formal war on Dualism and the hold it gave Budapest on part of the South Slav lands. As the Slovene leader Korosec, speaking for all his colleagues, told Parliament on 30 May:

We demand the unification of all the lands inhabited by the Slovenes, Croats and Serbs of the monarchy into one autonomous state, free from all foreign domination and to be ruled democratically under the sceptre of the Habsburg dynasty.*

This chorus of the Empire's North and South Slavs for autonomy did not, of course, go unanswered. Quite apart from the hostile reaction of

* *Parliamentarische Chronik*, Vienna, May 1917.

Budapest, the Austro-German groups in Vienna's Parliament had their emphatic say. Their spokesman, the right-wing deputy Pacher, attacked the Czech demands for autonomy in Bohemia, which he claimed – in a flash of prophecy that Adolf Hitler was to make true twenty years later – 'would force the millions of Germans in the Sudeten lands into unifying against their will in a new state'. For good measure, Pacher declared the Austro-Germans' opposition to the South Slav demands as well and he added a sentence that would have made any Austrian Emperor think: 'The Germans declare their loyalty to the unity of the state and expect this loyalty from the others, especially in wartime.'

Here was the power dilemma built into the time dilemma surrounding all reform. It was the Austro-Germans and the Magyars who, as the pillars of the Empire, carried the main burden of that Empire in war. How could the Dualism that this preponderance constitutionally embodied be undermined without these pillars collapsing militarily, and the whole roof they supported falling down over the Emperor's head?

Whatever the answer to all these riddles, it was not the one finally read out to Parliament on 12 June by the Prime Minister, Count Clam-Martinitz. This combined ringing appeals for loyalty with a total absence of any concessions that might have made such loyalty seem, to the restless Slavs of the Empire, at all worthwhile. Because the various programmes Parliament had heard were contradictory, they could, Clam implied, be ruled out now and for all time. There was no hint even of peacetime reforms in his speech and, for that matter, no hint of peace itself. 'My programme,' he declared, 'is Austria.' This meant nothing because it could mean anything; and, without action to follow it up, it offended everybody. Clam's end, which was swift, could not have been more constitutional. He had somehow to get his budget passed by the reconvened Parliament and, as both the Slav and Austro-German groups were sulky over his hollow speech, the vote of the Polish deputies became decisive. They demanded an exorbitant political price in return. Clam rejected the blackmail and on 21 June was thus forced by the budget *impasse* to resign.

Charles had appointed him, six months before almost to the day, in the hope that he had found his 'reforming Prime Minister'. Like all who were to follow Clam in that office, he proved a sad disappointment. Honourable and loyal though he was, the seeds of his failure were inborn. As the bearer of an ancient Bohemian name, he might have been expected to support the cause of the Czech race whose blood he shared. But as a great feudal landlord he shared something even more powerful with the Austro-German magnates settled by the Habsburgs since the mid-seventeenth century all over his homeland: the common interest of preserving a privileged way of life. And so the reformer turned out, perhaps predictably, to be a cautious conservative.

What happened next revealed all the barrenness of the Viennese political landscape. Thanks to that woeful shortage of talent already described, there was no obvious candidate for Clam's position – neither any elder statesman of unchallenged authority to be brought back from retirement nor any up-and-coming young politician on whom it seemed worth taking a gamble. To be fair, these gaps in the younger generation were partly to be traced back to Franz Josef's decision to govern his wartime Empire without a Parliament. Had a vigorous parliamentary life continued in Vienna after 1914, the same rising men who were soon to run the Austrian Republic – pragmatic Socialists like Karl Renner and pragmatic Catholics like Prelate Seipel – might have been harnessed already by 1917 to the running of the Empire. But whatever the reason, the stage after Clam's departure looked very empty, and Charles was forced to bring on a caretaker to fill it.

After vain attempts to get the distinguished jurist Dr Lammasch for the post, on 23 June Dr Ernst von Seidler, whose public life had been spent almost entirely as a civil servant in the Ministry of Agriculture, was appointed Austrian Prime Minister. His mandate was the strictly limited one of getting the Budget passed. To stress its provisional nature, the majority of his Cabinet members were not even given ministerial status. But the caretaker turned into a tenant. Seidler remained in office for more than a year. For thirteen months, with the best of intentions but not the best of talents, he administered the heart of the Empire like the bureaucrat he was instead of the statesman that he ought to have been. And when Charles finally dropped him, in July 1918, Austria's case was rapidly growing too grave even for a statesman to save.

By a strange coincidence, Tisza in Budapest had fallen only a month before Clam in Vienna. Though in Austria the Emperor had been inclined to let developments find their own level for a while, in Hungary he had deliberately forced matters to a head. Indeed, Tisza's resignation on 23 May 1917 was the climax to a personal struggle between the Hungarian Prime Minister and his sovereign that had been growing in intensity all the year. Inhibited by his Budapest Coronation oath against reforming 'St Stephen's lands' from above, Charles became resolved to try to reform them from below through the introduction, stage by stage, of universal suffrage into the Hungarian half of his Empire.* Perhaps, he reasoned, democracy could break the Magyar spell where diplomacy had failed. A

* For Hungary's archaic voting pattern at this time see p. 37. Universal suffrage had been introduced in Austria, largely at the crown's insistence, in 1905.

Budapest Parliament which genuinely represented all classes as well as all races of the Hungarian kingdom might indeed have blunted South Slav agitation without toppling at one blow the Empire's Dualist structure.

But Tisza, that resplendent figure of the Middle Ages, was not to be persuaded, even by his beloved sovereign, that Hungary was yet ready for the twentieth century. Indeed, he saw in what he called 'voting rights radicalism' a threat to the mystical historic qualities of the Magyar state and *therefore* a threat to its existence. To Hungarians of Tisza's stamp, it was the past which lived, not the present, which was there only to justify the past. The King-Emperor in Vienna and the opposition leaders in Budapest – the Counts Apponyi, Andrassy, Zichy and the ultra-radical Michael Karolyi, of whom we shall hear more later – all pressed Tisza to change his stand. In vain. The most this atavistic idealist would agree to was to give the vote to any Hungarian soldier, irrespective of age, rank or race, who had won the Silver Medal for bravery in action. He even resisted the Emperor's attempts to extend this 'medal democracy' by granting the franchise to any bearer of the Charles Cross, a much commoner decoration awarded simply for twelve weeks' front-line service. So the existing system, whereby less than twelve per cent of Hungary's twenty millions had the right to vote, stayed unchanged even in the dawn of the Wilsonian era.

But Tisza himself had to go. On 23 May 1917, after some political manoeuvring in Budapest – complicated as always – he was virtually forced by his Emperor to resign. Hungary's 'man of iron', and perhaps the most formidable political figure in the whole Empire, had gone. His fall led to pledges of electoral reform in plenty, but universal suffrage was never introduced in practice. On the other hand, once Tisza had handed over power, there was a vacuum of integrity combined with authority in the Budapest Government that was never filled again. His immediate successor, Count Moritz Esterhazy – a surprise selection of Charles's from the younger generation – proved earnest but weak. He lasted barely three months, to be succeeded in August 1917 by a return to the older generation in the person of Alexander Wekerle. Wekerle's main strength lay in his shiftiness which had been apocryphal in Vienna even in Franz Josef's day.* Charles perhaps felt he needed such a political 'fixer' to hold the incredible tangle of Budapest politics together until another clear leader of Tisza's stature emerged or until Tisza himself repented of his medieval ways (which he began to do in October 1918: too late).

---

* One story had it that, during an audience, Franz Josef asked Wekerle whether it was raining. When the minister said it was, the Emperor walked over to the window, looked out and replied: 'You have made a mistake, Wekerle, it really *is* raining.'

But, like the caretaker in Vienna, the fixer in Budapest was to linger on as Prime Minister until the last phase of the Empire's life. Charles had hoped that this man of elastic might at least be able to keep to a liberal middle course in both the Empire's politics and those of Hungary. In fact, when the final crisis came in the autumn of 1918, Wekerle presented his master with the worst of both worlds. He blocked Imperial reform in Vienna and handed over the crown to the revolutionaries in Budapest.

Progress by constitutional changes had been shelved. Progress by electoral reform had been blocked. But one channel remained by which Charles could breathe some fresh air of tolerance and conciliation into the stifling scene. It was a highly personal method – indeed, the unchallenged prerogative of the sovereign: amnesty. Just as in foreign affairs the year 1917 was marked by his peace offensive of the spring, so in domestic affairs it was stamped by his amnesty proclamation of the summer. As with the Sixtus affair, its roots went back to his time as Archduke and heir-apparent and were embedded in his own character. The Empress Zita relates:

'Long before his accession, the Emperor grew very concerned about the sentences passed by some of the Army's courts martial – about their severity and also about the way in which the verdicts had been reached. As he was always travelling about between the various war fronts he had plenty of opportunity to see and compare what was going on. He was particularly worried about the summary trials of political agitators – above all the Czechs – by Austrian military courts. He considered many of them plain acts of injustice and, even as heir-apparent, pleaded with the Emperor Franz Josef to commute the death sentences passed into terms of imprisonment.

'When he succeeded to the throne he soon took steps to have these trials reviewed – above all as a plain matter of justice which he, as sovereign, was pledged to uphold. He reasoned that if these sentences were left to Parliament to debate there would simply be an uproar and we should get nowhere. They must therefore be settled by an amnesty.

'That was the first consideration. But also, of course, as the amnesty was a step towards internal peace in the Empire it was a step also towards internal reform, and the Emperor saw it in this light as well.'

It was the problem of the Czech agitators which made the amnesty such a politically explosive issue for the whole Empire. The radical leader Dr Karl Kramar and his associates Raslin, Cervinka and Zamazal had all been sentenced to death by military tribunals in Franz Josef's reign on charges which sounded grave enough in a country at war. They had been accused of furthering in word and deed the dismemberment of the Empire and the weakening of its military capacity – in word by pan-Slav propaganda calling for a separate Czech state, and in deed by helping recruitment to the Czech 'freedom legions' which were forming to fight against their own Empire in the *Entente* armies. There could be no shadow of doubt that, if the charges were proven, they constituted high treason for which the death penalty applied. Charles's objection on the legal side was that the trials had not been fair ones since the examining magistrates and judges had virtually taken their instructions from the War Office. On the political side, he reasoned that the way to meet the growing challenge of separatism was not to execute the agitators but to win them over. The death sentences on the four leaders had already been suspended in 1916. Early in 1917, as a first step to meet both these points, Charles as Emperor commuted all of them to prison terms ranging from six to fifteen years.

His general amnesty was the natural extension of this policy. It was also a hazardous one. Ranged against it were not only the Austro-German and Magyar conservatives who saw any concession to Slav radicalism as a threat to their dual supremacy. The military leadership, arguing on purely military grounds, feared any step which might only encourage agitation among the Army's Slav troops by appearing to condone it.

This was not the first such conflict of interests the young Emperor had had with his generals over his humanitarian measures. Charles's Orders of the Day of 2 March and 19 July 1917, which forbade certain traditional military punishments, caused much head-shaking among the commanders fearful for troop discipline. The Emperor's ban on the bombing of open cities by his own planes also caused a great deal of muttering among the General Staff. (He had been prompted to it by the experience of Karlsruhe, which had been bombed by the enemy while a Corpus Christi church procession was moving through the streets.) Though the generals easily managed to get arsenals and other military targets exempted from the ban, strict instructions to avoid churches and art monuments were issued for all future air operations. Charles's argument that the destruction of Europe's cities and centres of culture constituted an act of barbarism that would not end the war but would always be condemned by the civilized world was a good twenty years ahead of his time. It certainly sounded odd talk to some of his generals in 1917.

But the proposed amnesty to cover Czech agitators was the Emperor's biggest challenge of them all, both to conservative military and political opinion at home and, needless to say, to the stern views of his German allies abroad. That he pressed on with it regardless of the criticism and misgivings all around* him is a tribute to that moral courage and tenacity with which he pursued any aim that his conscience compelled and his constitutional powers permitted. On 1 June the indefatigable Polzer was given the task of wading through all the documents relating to the early wartime Czech trials. He discovered, as the Emperor had expected, abundant evidence of bias. On 29 June, without consulting Polzer further about his decision, Charles announced to his new Prime Minister Seidler that an amnesty would be granted. On 2 July – six weeks earlier than planned – this was duly issued.† It freed all persons 'sentenced by military or civil courts . . . on charges of high treason, insults to the Royal Family, disturbance of the public peace, rebellion, and agitation', and excepted only those who had 'fled abroad to escape persecution; had deserted to the enemy or who had not returned to the Monarchy at the outbreak of war'.

The final clause left both *émigré* political leaders like Masaryk and military deserters of all races classified as potential traitors. Otherwise the pardon was complete and sweeping. Before the month was over, 2,593 prisoners had benefited by it. The amnesty produced those touches of irony that seem inseparable from the Austrian scene. The star prisoners, Kramar and his group, were released almost on the same day as the Czechoslovak Brigade they had been accused of helping penetrated the Austrian lines at Zborow in Galicia, fighting side by side with the enemy Russian forces. Ten weeks later, a Slovene officer deserted to the Italians on the Trentino front and betrayed the positions of the Austrian troops in that sector. Such incidents only strengthened the critics who accused Charles of undermining, by his very benevolence, the foundations of the Empire's strength.

But Charles remained convinced that his Empire must be saved not only on the battleground but also, and perhaps even more so, in the political arena. It was harmony at home that was needed to bring about peace and security abroad. A remark made by Masaryk himself, when the news of the amnesty reached him abroad, seemed to bear the Emperor out. 'One

---

* Even the Empress, who rarely failed to share his views and who certainly did not lag behind him where humanitarian issues were concerned, needed convincing that the amnesty was a gamble worth taking. Czernin and General Arz were not even told that an amnesty was being prepared, on the grounds that each would try to oppose it in his own sphere. Charles's secretive tactics here were politically debatable, though technically defensible.

† The original intention had been to announce the amnesty on 17 August, the Emperor's birthday. Seidler, for parliamentary reasons, suddenly called for it immediately on 1 July, when the Emperor was on a state visit to Bavaria and Württemberg. It was issued the following day, which happened to be the name-day of the Crown Prince Otto.

more step like that', the leader of the Czech exiles is said to have exclaimed, 'and we are finished!'

Happily for Masaryk, unhappily for Charles, that vital 'one step more' was not to come. In the amnesty affair, the Emperor had been able to follow his own set course because that course was unchallengeable within the bounds of his own prerogative. When he attempted to build on it politically, however, in pursuit of his wider objectives, ministerial opposition could not be by-passed in the same sovereign fashion. Two such attempts were launched within a week of the amnesty being proclaimed.

The first was the Emperor's approach to Dr Josef Redlich, an Austrian professor of international repute in constitutional law, to head a 'Reform Cabinet' to relieve Seidler's caretaker administration. Redlich, who had keen political as well as academic ambitions, accepted the offer on 5 July * and agreed to try and form a government to carry out the three-point programme Charles outlined: national autonomy within a unitary state; self-determination of the Empire's peoples within this framework and that of the historic 'crownlands'; and finally, if agreement could be reached with Hungary, some reference to peace.

All this unfolded as the professor and his young Emperor strolled that day in the early evening sunshine under the chestnut trees of Laxenburg Park. Time and again the Emperor came back to his amnesty as the spring-board for this great reforming leap. Time and again he stressed the need for genuine 'constitutional democracy' within the Empire as the pre-condition for any peace settlement with the *Entente*. He knew full well where the chief danger of opposition lay – with the Austro-German and Hungarian conservatives – but seemed determined to meet it head on. As he had remarked to Redlich in a preliminary talk the day before: 'Bohemia is admittedly the weather-cock of Austria. The Germans in Bohemia are very important, but the whole of Austria cannot dance to their tune.'

Brave words, yet that was precisely what happened when Redlich moved from Laxenburg back to the *salons* and parliamentary corridors of Vienna and tried to form his Government. The German parties refused him their support outright and the whole pan-German opposition to these 'centrifugal tendencies' in the Empire received powerful moral backing from an unfortunately-timed visit which the German Emperor and Empress paid at this juncture to Vienna. The 'king-makers' like Konrad Hohenlohe and Czernin, who had at first seemed to support Redlich, now veered away from him. By the time the politicians (including Redlich) dispersed for their August holidays, it was clear that the 'Reform

* See Josef Redlich, *Tagebuch II*, pp. 216 *et seq.*

Cabinet' had again been blocked – by parliamentary obstacles which Charles had no power to remove.

The same fate overtook another reforming project launched parallel with Redlich's effort in that hectic first week of July 1917. This was a scheme to entrust the task of revising Austria's constitution to a special State Conference composed of fifteen to twenty members, all of ministerial rank. Polzer and his master leaped on the idea with joy, and terms of reference were hopefully drafted. But, despite the fact that it had been a German deputy, Dr Urban, who had proposed the idea, it was again the German parties – helped by a premature press disclosure – who took the lead in vetoing it. Within a week the project had been dropped on the grounds that the proposed State Committee would 'infringe the rights of Parliament'.

Thus though Charles's amnesty could stand on its own as a royal act of humanity and justice, it did not produce the political fruits he had hoped. For the Slav radicals, mere pardon, as the Emperor had foreseen, was not enough. For the Magyar and German conservatives, as he had feared, it was already too much. These seeds of mercy were eventually to yield a late harvest. Thanks to measures like the July amnesty, which restored to wartime Austria the qualified rule of law, tyranny could no longer be used to suppress the thrust of the new political movements. And when, in the autumn of 1918, the Monarchy began to fall apart, nobody could use the hangman's noose in an effort to hold it together. If this benefit came too late to save the Empire, it still came in time to save bloodshed. It was therefore something over which in retrospect the amnesty's author could and did rejoice.

There was little for him to rejoice about at the time. The released Kramar entered Prague in triumph on 15 October 1917, the crowds greeting him like a victorious Roman general returning from the battle-field. With his return to the arena, that rising tone of intransigence which had been heard in Czech politics ever since the spring became louder than ever. Despite all Charles's efforts to secure stability, the year thus ended in Prague – as in Vienna and Budapest – on a note of temporizing, unrest and trepidation. But there were other consolations.

It was on the battlefronts rather than on the domestic scene that, unexpectedly, a stability of sorts seemed to emerge in the closing months of 1917. In the East, the call of the new Bolshevik leaders in November for peace talks led to the opening of armistice negotiations and a lull in the fighting. In the South, the fighting had flared up more fiercely than ever, but at last it went Austria's way. All that year, the Austro-Hungarian troops facing the Italians along the Isonzo had shown that, though the

Empire's politicians were quarrelling in all its capitals, the multi-racial army was still united in war. The great enemy offensives of the spring and summer (the so-called 10th and 11th Isonzo battles) had been held, though with heavy losses, by an Imperial army which consisted of sixty per cent of Slav troops, sixteen per cent of Magyars and only thirteen per cent of Austro-Germans, with eleven per cent of Rumanians making up the rest.

Now it was the turn of the Italians to be hammered. By the autumn – thanks to pressure by the Austrian Chief of Staff General Arz* on Charles, and Charles's subsequent pressure on the German High Command through the Emperor William – a special new assault Army, the Four-teenth, had been secretly formed behind the Austrian lines. It consisted of six German divisions moved in specially from other war theatres and three Austro-Hungarian formations, all under the command of the experienced Prussian General Otto von Below. On 24 October, after a heavy artillery and gas bombardment, this spearhead force struck and broke through the Italian lines at Tolmein, and the other Austro-Hungarian Armies to the left and right of it † joined in a general advance all along the front.

The success of the operation matched the fondest dreams of its planners. Within a few days every inch of Austrian soil that the Italians had won in eleven successive campaigns had been regained and the attack carried on to Italian territory. By the end of the month, the troops of the Central Powers entered Udine, the capital of Friul Province; in early November the Tagliamento river defences were stormed and the Italians streamed still farther south to the line of the Piave. When a halt was called after some four weeks of fighting, the Italians had lost (according to the official Austrian figures) nearly 294,000 men taken prisoner, with a further 30,000 wounded and 10,000 killed. Their losses in equipment were commensurate: 3,152 guns, 3,000 machine-guns and some 300,000 rifles. Even more precious to the Austrians was the narrowing of their dangerously extended southern war front as they had advanced on the waist of Italy. When the attack began this had stretched from Astico in the West to Duino on the Adriatic Sea in the East, a distance of 240 miles. When it ended on the Piave a month later, the line had been reduced by nearly two-thirds to a mere eighty-seven miles. The Southern front was, for the time being at least, triumphantly secure.

A political price had to be paid. The operation as a whole had been on an Austrian front and under Austrian control. The field command over all

---

* For a detailed account of the planning and of the battle itself, see Arz, *op. cit.*, pp. 170–85.

† The First and Second Isonzo Armies; the Tenth Army and the so-called *Kraus-Korps*.

the Allied forces involved was in the hands of Charles's uncle, the Arch-duke Eugene. Charles himself held the supreme command, moving from sector to sector of the front and following hard on the heels of his advancing troops.* It was true also that, taking the entire Allied forces in action, Austro-Hungarian formations outnumbered German ones by nearly three to one. Yet it was equally undeniable that the decisive opening blow had been struck by the Fourteenth Army and that this army had consisted mainly of borrowed German divisions under a borrowed Prussian general. Whether the victory would ever have been scored without this infusion of German strength (valued by Arz because of the superior artillery equipment and air arm of the divisions rather than because of their actual numbers) is a moot point. What is certain is that Charles's initial misgivings about asking for German help in the attack now proved well-founded.

The Emperor William, who had come South to visit his German troops engaged, met Charles near Trieste on 11 November for a celebration conference. Inevitably, the Germans used this joint triumph on the battlefield to try to press the reluctant Austrian ruler closer to their iron breasts politically. There was little Charles could do to escape their embrace despite the fact that, once the Piave was reached, the German divisions engaged were pulled out one by one from this 'secondary front' and moved back to the West. It was the hour of Czernin and the Berlin faction. A few days after the Isonzo breakthrough, Charles had felt obliged to thank his Foreign Minister publicly for his 'systematic policy of broadening and deepening' the German alliance. On 21 November, the day after the official end of the offensive, Czernin's great opponent Polzer resigned from his key post as head of the Emperor's private office, and Charles thus lost the principal ally in his struggle against German and Magyar conservatism.†

Finally, on 6 December 1917, Czernin himself put the seal on this new emotional tie between the two Empires. He declared, in a major policy speech:

We are fighting for the defence of Germany just as Germany fights to defend us. In this respect I accept no territorial distinctions. If anyone asks me whether

---

* He had an unpleasant moment when, crossing the swollen River Torre, he left his stranded car and was carried off by the current. Accounts that he almost drowned seem, however, to owe something to the telling (not by himself).

† The immediate cause, according to the Empress, was a deliberately provoked anti-Hungarian outburst of Polzer's in front of Hungarian leaders which had compromised the Emperor too deeply as King of Hungary. But the upsurge of pan-German feeling over the Isonzo victory also helped to weaken Polzer's position.

we are fighting for Alsace-Lorraine I reply – yes indeed, we fight for Alsace-Lorraine just as Germany has fought for us at Lemberg and Trieste. I make no distinction here between Strasbourg and Trieste. . . .

It was stirring stuff, and these were impeccable sentiments to come from an Austrian leader in the after-glow of an Allied victory. But if Czernin was still the loyal servant of his master, they were also dangerous and somewhat dishonest sentiments. Dangerous because President Wilson had just publicly repeated the familiar – and sincerely based – reproach of the *Entente* powers that Austria was acting as a passive satellite of Germany, who was considered the real menace to European peace. Czernin's words, it seemed, were Vienna's uncompromising answer, an answer which could only strengthen the *Entente*'s growing belief that both of its main enemies would have to be crushed together. And somewhat dishonest because, as we have seen, Czernin had connived only that spring and summer in his Emperor's secret attempts to end the war – at the cost, to Germany, of those same provinces of Alsace-Lorraine.

The full reckoning for this contradiction was to be presented before many months of the new year were out. Meanwhile, as the old year ended, Charles could ruefully reflect that all his efforts to secure stability at home had done little more than hold the structure from slipping further, while even his new stability on the battlefront had been won at an awkward political price. Taken together with the collapse of the Sixtus peace moves, it was a depressing balance-sheet for his first and last full year of power. And the worst was only starting.

Chapter 10

ROPES AND QUICKSANDS

The year of catastrophe began as it was to go on. The cold, hunger and sheer weariness of a fourth winter in uniform now started to gnaw at the body of an Empire already stretched out almost beyond endurance on the rack of war. In January 1918 its joints began audibly to crack.

The December had been a bitter one, even worse than that of 1916, with freezing temperatures and heavy snowfalls setting in long before Christmas. For months, the Monarchy's food position had been growing increasingly desperate – so bad that, in the words of one eye-witness, 'Many workers seemed to be living mainly off sour cucumbers'.* Now a poor autumn harvest had produced the second successive New Year crisis. There was nothing for it but to slice the loaf even thinner. On 14 January 1918, the flour ration was further reduced in the Austrian half of the Empire from 200 to 165 grammes per day.

The workers, hit in their stomachs, struck back hard. That same day, all the employees at a war plant near Wiener-Neustadt, twenty-five miles south-west of the capital, walked out of their factory and besieged the town hall. It was only the beginning of trouble. Hunger protests ran on like a fuse through the Empire's industrial centres. Within forty-eight hours, nearly 100,000 men were out on strike in Lower Austria alone. Before the week was out, the movement had spread to the provinces of Upper Austria, Styria and Tyrol; to Brno, the capital of Moravia; and even down the Danube to Budapest, though the food position in the Hungarian half of the Empire was incomparably better.

One reason for this alarming chain reaction was to be found in the tone of the protests. For the first time, they were political as well as economic. The Wiener-Neustadt strikers, for example, attacked not only the cut in flour rations and the doubling of tobacco prices; they demanded also the immediate conclusion of the peace talks already under way on the Eastern front with the Bolshevik emissaries at Brest-Litovsk. Nor was this first

* Josef Redlich, *Tagebuch*.

excursion of the Austrian factory bench into high diplomacy prompted merely by the hope that a settlement in the East meant bread from the granaries of the Ukraine. Ideological appetites had been whetted beside physical ones. As in Hungary, where workers' Soviets had sprouted into brief life at a number of factories, so in the affected areas of Austria, workers' committees were formed which began to use Bolshevik slogans, though they shrank from Bolshevik action. Indeed, the Danubian omens looked so bright to the new rulers of Moscow that, on 22 January 1918, *Pravda* headed its report of the strike events with the words: 'On the Eve of the Austrian Revolution'.

For a hard-pressed Empire which had only just won itself a breathing-space on the battlefronts, the threat was as intolerable as it was dangerous. Yet, as the Communists were soon to discover (and the Nazis twenty years after them), there is in the Austrian character a mixture of caution, softness and common-sense which leads almost invariably to 'half-and-halfness' of action and blurs the edges of all extremism. This acted as a natural dampener now. Government policy towards the strikers' leaders, which was a shrewd mixture of force and flattery, also helped to stabilize the position. Seven full-strength Austro-Hungarian combat divisions were pulled back hastily from the now still Eastern front and marched into troubled industrial areas of the homeland. Their mere presence gave Austria's ever-reluctant revolutionaries all the pretext they were at heart seeking for not mounting the barricades.

And on 19 January special balm was offered to their pride. A declaration by Count Czernin himself was handed over to their representatives, in which the Foreign Minister solemnly assured the workers' council that he would not allow the Brest-Litovsk negotiations to be held up. For good measure (and well outside his province) he also promised reforms in the system of military control over arms industries and food rationing. Given Czernin's haughty character, these assurances may well have been drafted with supercilious contempt, for diplomacy was something he did not even like his Emperor meddling with, let alone a horde of factory hands. But sincere or not, this conciliatory gesture, coupled with the Army's show of force, took all immediate heat out of the crisis. The next day, the Vienna Socialist organ *Arbeiterzeitung* recorded a decision by the strike leadership to call for a return to work in view of the Government's 'accommodating attitude'. Within a week, just as *Pravda* was starting to proclaim Austria's revolution, everything had returned temporarily to normal.

However, for all those who dared to look at it and read it, the writing was now on the wall. The ideological struggle, eloquently preached and triumphantly exemplified by the Bolsheviks, had given a new dimension to all the existing racial rivalries and economic strains of the Empire. That warning, which Charles had been for months trying to din into the ears of both his German allies and his own ministers, was now more urgent than ever: 'If the warring governments will not make peace, the peoples will make it for them over their heads.'

Throughout this winter of hardship and unrest, Charles did what he could to limit repressive measures. The Empress remembers one occasion when the Army Commander in Lemberg, who happened to be a single man, ordered his troops to fire on women hunger demonstrators. The incensed Emperor ordered his instant recall, commenting: 'I'll send a Commanding Officer there with a family, who knows what hunger is.' The Emperor also did what he could to ensure that the Court cut out all luxury and tightened its belt as far as was feasible for any royal household which was expected, even in war, to entertain a constant stream of visitors from its own provinces and abroad.

Charles's personal tastes have already been described. They were so simple as to set an example in themselves. The Empress recalls that during the war years he only regularly ate one solid meal a day and that was at breakfast, when he would have warm meat and vegetables and a glass of warm mineral water drunk on his doctor's advice for his heart. On a normal working day he then ate practically nothing until the evening – little or no lunch and never tea – while the evening meal itself was a frugal one. White bread or pastries made with white flour they never saw, except on the periodic visits to Budapest, which was not the capital city of the Empire granary for nothing.

Hungary indeed held the key to the Monarchy's food plight. It provided almost all of the 100,000 railway wagon-loads of wheat that the Army needed each year to feed itself on; the bulk of the 45,000 tons of fodder required annually for the Army's half-million horses; and most of its meat supplies.* And when these priority demands had been met, the civilian population of the Empire then depended on what extra supplies could be squeezed out of the Hungarian plains to keep it going at subsistence levels.

Charles, shaken by the food riots, now tried to turn this key. On 25 January, after another re-shuffle of the Hungarian Cabinet (still headed, of course, by the indestructible Wekerle), Prince Louis Windischgraetz became Food Minister with a brief from his Emperor to increase Hungary's food contribution by any appropriate means, including requisitioning. Windischgraetz, a political soldier of fortune who was soon to earn himself the label of 'Red Prince' for his radical views, was the wrong man

* Arz, *op. cit.*, pp. 195–6. See also Zeman, pp. 141–2, and Lorenz, pp. 430–2.

for many jobs he undertook but the right man for this. Yet all the energy of this aristocratic *beau sabreur* could not conjure those extra grain sacks out of the kulaks – Hungary's peasant farmers whose stubbornness was still proving the despair of the country's real Red Princes half a century later. Particularly in the Austrian half of the Empire, the Government went on steadily retreating in the battle against hunger. In this battle, the people were already taking matters into their hands. Barter, black market, plunder and pilfering, all on a mass scale, helped out the meagre ration cards.* On the first two operations, at least, the rich did far better than the poor. The result was to sharpen further this new Austrian phenomenon of class hostility as well as to reduce the prestige of all authority as such.

Charles soon had something even more deadly to worry about than the food crisis. If January had been the month of strikes, February was to be the month of mutinies. At midday on 1 February a shot sounded out from the flagship of the Fifth Fleet of the Austro-Hungarian Navy, anchored in the peaceful Gulf of Kotor. It was a signal, not a salute. Sailors ran up a red flag on Admiral Hansa's battleship and the ship's band, which normally played light music at lunchtime to entertain the officers at their meal, struck up the 'Marseillaise' instead. Within the hour, red flags were fluttering from the lanyards of every one of the forty men-of-war anchored in the bay. The Imperial Fifth Fleet had mutinied. It was the first such case in any of the Empire's armed forces during three and a half years of fighting.

Significantly, the principal ringleaders were Croats and Czechs – the race which for months past had been setting the pace in general defiance of the crown. Only three weeks before, this defiance had reached a new political pitch back in Prague when some 150 deputies from Bohemia, Moravia and Silesia met under Socialist inspiration to produce a resolution declaring the so-called 'Czechoslovak nation' free from all obligations 'both towards the Dualist Monarchy and towards the dynasty'. The Kotor mutiny was the uniformed counterpart to this. The sailor who had largely planned it, Frantisek Ras (and who now 'took command' of the flagship), was himself a member of the Czech Social Democratic Party. Another Czech, Stonavsky, was elected Chairman of the 'Central Council of Sailors' which was set up to administer the paralysed fleet.

The mutiny was short-lived, mainly because the rebels neglected that first principle of revolt, which is to seize and hold the communications system. Instead, the officers – who were nearly all Austro-German and Hungarian and the professional representatives therefore of that con-

---

* Even the dead were touched by the acute shortages. To save textiles, the Government recommended that corpses should be buried naked.

servative Dualism which was under fire – managed to transmit calls for help. On 3 February the Third Fleet steamed into Kotor to restore discipline and the rebellion crumbled. The amateur rebels paid a professional price. Of the forty defendants (predominantly Slav and Italian) who were now court-martialled, five, including Frantisek Ras, were sentenced to death and executed.

The Empress has the following recollections of this episode:

'The Emperor was not really surprised by the Kotor mutiny. He told me that he had for a long time feared that something of the sort might happen. Our navy had been forced into idleness by the *Entente* blockade of the high seas and the Fifth Fleet, who were relatively well fed, had been cooped up for months in the same harbour.

'Though he fully realized the seriousness of the mutiny, he was not in favour of draconic punishment. Indeed, if he had had his way the five death sentences would have been commuted into prison terms. He was travelling when the appeals of the condemned men for pardon were sent to him. They reached the Emperor's suite late in the night and, by a mistake, were only handed to him in the morning when the executions had already been carried out. He was very distressed at this.

'He ordered an immediate review of the whole navy position. As a result the command structure was changed and many older officers had to hand over to their younger colleagues and serve under them, which they did loyally. One of the younger officers who came into greater prominence now was Horthy, who had distinguished himself as the dashing commander of the *Novarra*.'

So reorganized, and with Horthy playing an ever bigger role, the Austro-Hungarian Navy sailed on, or rather idled on, until the final collapse nine months later. But as with the strikes on the home front, this first serious disturbance on the battlefront opened a new chapter in the Empire's decline. Parallel trouble in the Army did not start until May, when a series of mutinies started up from the Styrian garrisons. But already in that first week of February, no one in authority could be unaware of what the Kotor episode meant. Hitherto, as the Italian campaigns of the previous autumn had shown, the armed services had remained both the citadel of the Empire's loyalty and its outer walls. They symbolized both the vast multi-racial spread of the Monarchy and its centralized power. Indeed, it was only in uniform that the conglomerate Empire was still united in both appearance and deed. Now the first breach in the centre and the perimeter had been made. The omen of Kotor seemed all the more chilling because it was also with a naval mutiny – that of the Russian sailors at Kronstadt – that the collapse of another empire had started, while the signal for the final assault on the Winter Palace only four months before had also been a shot from a Russian ship.

Now more than ever, only a rapid peace could save Austria-Hungary. The Emperor was soon to make another attempt to achieve it through the dynasties. But first, he was to be approached himself, by the very destroyers of the dynasties. By the end of 1917, Charles wanted peace to fight Bolshevism as much as to fight Prussianism. Ironically it was the Bolsheviks who, on 28 November, now offered peace to him and his allies. The Empress has confirmed the personal repugnance with which the Emperor entered into negotiations with men who had already dynamited the old order in Russia and who threatened to destroy it everywhere else. But he knew he had no choice. The prizes at stake – the final liquidation of the great Eastern battlefront and the promise of Russian grain for the homeland – were too great. And, quite apart from all material dividends, the word 'peace' kept its sanctified ring for Charles even when uttered by a Bolshevik.

The confused tale of these negotiations, which dragged on throughout January and February of the new year, need not long delay us here. It is significant that the place where they were held, Brest-Litovsk, was the German Supreme Headquarters on the Eastern front. Throughout the whole conference, Czernin, who headed the Austrian delegation, sat under the German military shadow, represented by the formidable General Max Hoffman.

The first peace treaty to be concluded in the war was that reached on 9 February 1918, between the Central Powers and the breakaway Russian Republic of the Ukraine. Czernin, who signed for his Emperor, hailed it as the 'bread peace'. So, to a limited extent, it was, though far less wheat was to move south than the Austrians had hoped. (The 12,000 or so wagons of Ukrainian food which ultimately reached the Empire represented a small fraction of Czernin's expectations.) Even these grain-sacks were bought at a heavy political price to the Dual Monarchy. The Germans had always been uncompromising in their support of the Ukrainian independence movement which they treated, logically, as another weapon to reduce the Tsar's fighting strength. The Austrians could not afford the luxury of such simple logic, as usual for domestic reasons. If they were to preserve the loyalty of the Poles within their own multi-racial Empire and, even more, if they were to win the heart of the new Poland looming up just outside that Empire, they dared not favour the rival cause of the Ukrainians unduly.

Yet at Brest-Litovsk they were now hustled by the agents of the almost

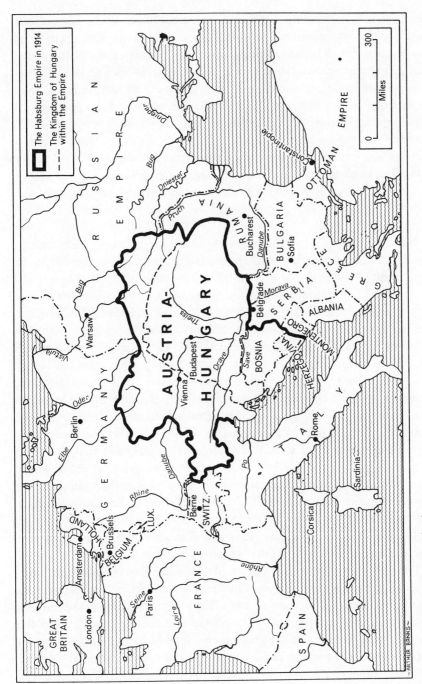

The Austro-Hungarian Empire in 1914.

omnipotent Ludendorff not only into full recognition of the Ukraine but into ceding to that state the Russian-Polish area of Kholm and the Podlasie district. A tumult of protest broke out among Poles both outside and inside the Empire. In Warsaw, relations were broken off with the Austro-Hungarian representatives. In the Monarchy's own Polish crown-land of Galicia, the black double-headed eagle was torn down from official buildings and dogs were paraded in the streets with the Emperor's military decorations hanging from their collars. This first peace of Brest-Litovsk marked not only the end of any successful 'Austro-Polish' policy abroad. It marked the beginning of the end of Polish loyalty to the crown at home. Not without justice has it been called 'the highest price the Austro-Hungarian Government had to pay for its alliance with Germany'.*

But the German General Staff, without having to weigh such complicated calculations on their own home front, could count their gains in purely military coinage. It was an impressive reckoning. To begin with, an extraordinary vacuum now set in for nearly a month after the Ukraine treaty, during which, thanks to a Soviet walk-out at Brest-Litovsk, the Central Powers were technically neither at war nor at peace with the new rulers of Russia. The Germans promptly filled this vacuum (their Austrian allies, after some hesitation, falling in as a strictly 'protective operation' behind them) with a gigantic new offensive eastwards. This brought them, against negligible opposition, to a new line stretching from Dorpat in Estonia to Odessa on the Black Sea. And when, on 3 March 1918, the Petrograd Bolsheviks hurried down to sign the second peace of Brest-Litovsk in the name of Russia, the Central Powers could really begin to rub their hands. According to one authoritative estimate made at the time,† the Germans and their allies then had no fewer than 120 divisions engaged on the Eastern front. Of these, forty had to be earmarked after the two treaties for home or occupation duties. But this still left another eighty divisions, or a fighting strength of about half a million men, for transfer to the Western and other fronts.

The effect was immediate. On 21 March 1918, after a 6,000-gun bombardment, the German Army launched its *Kaiserschlacht* or 'Emperor's Battle' in France. The scale of the offensive matched its grandiloquent label. It was, indeed, the greatest of all the vast military operations of the war, and that made it also the greatest to date in history. Though it was to crumble with astonishing suddenness in August, throughout the spring and early summer of 1918 the German advance continued remorselessly, inflicting nearly a million casualties on the Western allies and bringing

* Zeman, *op. cit.*, p. 155.   † General Arz, *op. cit.*, pp. 201–2.

Paris itself within the range of enemy guns. Only six American divisions, and these untried in battle, were already on French soil as the advance guard of those vast reinforcements promised. Would the rest arrive in time?

That fateful link between diplomacy and the battlefield – fateful above all for Austria – now showed itself again. Just as the treaties of Brest-Litovsk had made this gigantic military gamble possible, so now Germany's *Kaiserschlacht* went on to crush in its path the last political hopes of her Austrian ally as well as the resistance of the enemy armies. The damage to Vienna was two-fold.

First, the German advance caused all those in the besieged *Entente* camp to sharpen whatever weapons they could lay their hands on with which to strike back at the Central Powers. One result was extra support for those exile military forces like the Czech Legion who were fighting with them; and this support led inexorably, before the summer was out, to political recognition of the Paris-based Czech National Council itself. Temporary German victories at the front were thus won at the price of another deadly blow to the cohesion of the Austrian Empire at home.

The second effect of Ludendorff's great spring offensive was felt in the camp of the Central Powers themselves, and for Austria this internal impact was almost as serious. During four critical months of the Emperor's struggle to survive by peace policies and domestic reform, the stream of German triumphs in the West, coming on top of the German-led successes in northern Italy, poured new confidence into all who believed the Berlin dream of 'final victory'. This was their hour, if their last hour. Even those few souls in Vienna, like Charles himself, who stayed convinced that it was all a military pipe-dream, had to cover up their scepticism before the flood of exultant war communiqués. In this way, the last very slender chances that Austria still had of making a diplomatic breakthrough to the West were compromised.

The domestic impact inside the Dual Monarchy of this last German offensive will be dealt with again later, when we come to the final months of the Empire's life. The diplomatic impact is best described now, in bringing Charles's own tireless search for peace up to date.

We left this search in September 1917, after the failure of Prince Sixtus's missions to Paris and London, and after all Lloyd George's subsequent attempts to detach Austria from Germany through a switch of *Entente* military strategy had been finally blocked on the Italian front. It is Lloyd George and England who continue to set the peacemakers' pace in the *Entente* camp in the next set of high-level contacts between the two sides.

These were the secret meetings in Switzerland between the South African leader General Smuts and the Austrian diplomatist Count Mensdorff which stretched between mid-December 1917 and mid-March of the following year.

Like the probe put out by the French General Staff a few months earlier,* this was handled from the Vienna end almost entirely by Czernin, who, as Foreign Minister, was anxious to substitute his own brand of professional diplomacy for the personal dynastic excursions of his sovereign. Unlike those French feelers, however – which had been tentative, low-level and unrealistic – these English talks represented a serious attempt, made with the full authority of the British Cabinet, to get Austria out of the war. This was clear by the choice of envoy that London made in response to the roundabout overtures from Vienna. General Smuts was a statesman of world repute as well as a minister of the British Government and fully empowered to speak on its behalf.

Unhappily, the two emissaries set out from London and Vienna for their rendezvous in Geneva with totally incompatible briefs. Smuts's instructions, in Lloyd George's words, were to confine himself 'to the discussion of a separate peace with Austria and not to be drawn into any conversations as to the terms of a general peace'.† Mensdorff (a former Ambassador in London and still highly regarded there) had been ordered by Czernin to reject any suggestion of a separate agreement as 'treacherous and dishonourable' and to work solely towards a general peace settlement which would include Germany. In this, of course, Czernin was reflecting the ultimate aim of his Emperor. But the unsubtle and uncompromising way in which he approached it reflected something else – the magnetic hold that Ludendorff and the 'Berlin course' had by now established over the Austrian Foreign Minister. This, it will be remembered, was the month of Czernin's famous speech of homage to the German alliance, culminating in the words: 'I know no difference between Strasbourg and Trieste.'‡ And, at that time, the German victories in the West were still to come.

It was not quite a dialogue of the deaf when Smuts and Mensdorff held their first secret meeting in Geneva on 18 and 19 December 1917. But in view of their contradictory instructions, it was not surprising that for much of the time the two men talked eloquently over each other's shoulders. What Smuts said, however, was remarkable enough, given the authority he possessed, to have made Czernin sit up and think again.

* The so-called Armand–Revertera talks. See footnote to p. 98.
† Lloyd George, *War Memoirs*, V, pp. 2461–504.
‡ See p. 118.

According to Smuts's own report (described by Lloyd George as 'an historical document of the first importance') he began the conversations by stating that, because of the downfall of Russia, a new counterweight to Germany was needed on the European continent. He then went on:

From this point of view it was a matter of grave concern that Austria . . . should be emancipated from German domination and should, with the assistance of the *Entente*, and specially of the British Empire, make a fresh start of complete independence *vis-à-vis* the German Empire. If Austria was prepared to play that role and break with Germany she would have not only our sympathy but our active support, and we would do everything in our power to uphold and strengthen her and to assist her economic reconstruction.

When a delighted Mensdorff asked whether this meant that the break-up of the Austro-Hungarian Empire was not a British war aim, Smuts assured him that England had never harboured such thoughts. Lloyd George's envoy continued, to quote his report again:

We had no intention of interfering in her internal affairs, but we recognized that if Austria could become a really liberal Empire in which her subject peoples would, as far as possible, be satisfied and content, she would become for Central Europe very much what the British Empire had become for the rest of the world . . . and she would have a mission in the future even greater than her mission in the past.

This was getting above an ex-Ambassador's head. Mensdorff appears to have been in urgent communication with Vienna that night for, before he left Geneva, he was able to suggest to Smuts that Czernin himself might want to speak for Austria at subsequent discussions. These could, if need be, 'again be confined to the Austrian aspect of the peace'. On this note, which Smuts described as 'hopeful', the two envoys returned to their capitals.

Back in London, however, Lloyd George and the British Cabinet both took a much gloomier view when they had heard and debated Smuts's report. They felt indeed that Mensdorff's rigid refusal to 'betray' Germany had, for the moment, ruled out any separate peace with Austria. And King George v, writing from Sandringham on Christmas Day, shared the view of his ministers. A personal letter to Lloyd George began:*

My dear Prime Minister,

I am returning you the very interesting report by Genl Smuts on his mission to Switzerland. I consider that he has carried out his difficult task with great tact and has gained useful information from Count Mensdorff without giving anything away.

* Beaverbrook Library: F29/1/52.

I fear it will be impossible to get Austria to make a separate peace as at present she is entirely in the hands of Germany. . . .

With every good wish for Xmas and we must pray that 1918 may bring us an honourable peace.

Believe me

very sincerely yours

George RI

Nonetheless, with his eyes on the future, Lloyd George decided to repeat in public that pledge of support for a revitalized Austrian Empire which he had given at Geneva in secret. The Cabinet papers of the period make it clear that this was the British Prime Minister's own idea. In Britain, as in the enemy camp, labour unrest was growing over the seemingly endless bloodshed and sacrifices of the war. Lloyd George now tried, at a speech to the Trades Union Congress on 5 January 1918, to rally the workers' patriotism by re-stating what the country was fighting for. A lengthy Cabinet meeting was held at Downing Street the day before to approve the speech passage by passage. This is the Cabinet Secretary's record of how Lloyd George presented the Austrian problem to his colleagues:

There was some discussion as to the manner in which Austria should be alluded to in the statement. After referring to the legitimate claims of Italy, Serbia and Roumania, the Prime Minister had proposed to insert a phrase indicating that, subject to the fulfilment of our war aims in regard to these countries *we considered the existence of a strong Austria to he desirable* [author's italic]. His main object was to give a clear indication to Austria that we did not wish to destroy her and to make her people lukewarm in the war, thus deterring her from using her strength actively against us. Against this, it was argued that our Allies on the borders of Austria-Hungary might be discouraged. It was decided to include some milder phrase than that used in the original draft in the sense that, subject to the fulfilment of the legitimate claims of our Allies, we felt that Austria-Hungary should be in a position to exercise a powerful influence in South-East Europe.*

Even the watered-down assurances to Vienna that Lloyd George was persuaded to adopt in his 5 January speech were categoric enough. One passage began with the words: 'Nor are we fighting to destroy Austro-Hungary. . . .' Later on this was repeated, though with the cautionary comment:

---

* Public Records Office, London. CAB 23/5, 4 January 1918. At the same debate it was agreed that the principle of self-determination should be modified to apply, 'not to all races indiscriminately but merely to the settlement of the New Europe' – an interesting touch of Colonial Office caution.

Though we agree with President Wilson that the break-up of Austria-Hungary is no part of our war aims, we feel that, unless genuine self-government on true democratic principles is granted to those Austro-Hungarian nationalities who have long desired it, it is impossible to hope for the removal of those causes of unrest in that part of Europe which have so long threatened its general peace.*

A few days after this, President Wilson, while uttering his famous Fourteen Points, described Lloyd George's speech as being 'in admirable spirit'. A declaration of French support for the British statement was also made. Almost the whole pack of *Entente* cards was now laid on the table, even if the Allies were in fact playing somewhat different hands.

As far as Germany was concerned, it was Hindenburg and Ludendorff who persuaded the Emperor William to sweep them on to the floor. In his well-known letter to the Emperor of 7 January 1918 (two days after Lloyd George's speech) Hindenburg stressed that protected frontiers were 'a vital interest for Germany'. He added, in a passage which his Emperor underlined on reading it: 'In order to secure for ourselves the political and economic position which we need, we must beat the Western Powers. For this reason Your Majesty has ordered the attack in the West.'

After arguing, in effect, that talk of peace should be met only by new acts of war, the letter ended with the unctuous words:

I am definitely convinced that the policy advocated by us leads to a strengthening of the monarchy and an extended predominance of Germany, whilst the opposite policy can only bring Germany down from the height to which Your Majesty and the ancestors of Your All-Highest led her.

It was the old siren song of final victory. With the great offensive in the West already under preparation, Hindenburg could sing it louder than ever, knowing it would sound still sweeter in his Emperor's ears. The entirely predictable result of this pressure from the generals was a speech on 24 January 1918, by Count Hertling, the German Chancellor, which rejected the entire crop of *Entente* peace statements both in their spirit and in their substance.

The reaction in Vienna was more complex. While still stoutly supporting the German stand in public, Czernin seems to have become momentarily fascinated at this point by the thought of a personal meeting between himself and Lloyd George. Settling the problems of the East at Brest-Litovsk with one hand and those of the West at Geneva with the other – this was the grand Bismarckian diplomacy of which he dreamed.

* Full text in Lloyd George, *War Memoirs*, V, pp. 2515 *et seq.*

At all events, by mid-January, feelers for such a meeting had been put out. His new intermediary was another Austrian diplomat called Skrzynski, who seems to have been a good choice in all respects, except perhaps that his name was virtually unpronounceable by any Anglo-Saxon.

Throughout January and February the labyrinthine preliminary contacts were begun between London and Vienna. The British Cabinet opposed outright any idea of Lloyd George taking part himself in further talks at this nebulous stage. The Foreign Office, in particular, seemed sceptical of Czernin's motives and suspected him of playing a purely diversionary game for Germany. Finally it was agreed that General Smuts should again set out for Switzerland, and between 9 and 14 March 1918, the South African leader had another series of talks with the eager Skrzynski. Czernin, who continued to direct these in person from Vienna, now showed further signs of that unpredictable vacillation which was the worst of all his political faults. To begin with, his spokesman talked as though there had been 'a complete change in the Austrian attitude'.* Austria, it was indicated, was now determined to extricate herself from the Prussian orbit and remodel her liberated Empire on federal lines. To this end, she was willing to enter into separate peace negotiations. But no sooner had Smuts gladly accepted this (it was, after all, precisely the approach he had made himself before Christmas) than the Austrian envoy became evasive. The Austrians could be pinned down neither to dates nor to details. The talks were left hanging in the air on 14 March 1918, and were never resumed again.

The date is significant. It was exactly a week before the launching of the great German offensive on the Western front. Either Czernin had become spellbound again by the myth of 'final victory', or, just as likely, he had decided that, so long as the impending offensive lasted, it would be prudent to suspend any separate peace negotiations, *for which he himself carried the full responsibility*. Whatever the explanation (and Czernin in his own Memoirs gives us no enlightenment),† one thing is clear. Once again, the tide of war had surged back to check the tide of peace.

One other factor may have influenced this confused and confusing man. By now, his own sovereign was deep in another secret exchange of views with none less than President Wilson himself. This alternative had many advantages, some for Austria, some for Czernin. Unlike France and England, the United States was not committed by any pact with Rome to

* Lloyd George, *op. cit.*, V, pp. 2499–51.

† *Im Weltkrieg.* One of the many huge gaps in this rather muddled book is any proper description of the Anglo-Austrian peace talks which were Czernin's own creation. In fairness, he may have been inhibited by the closeness of the events; his book appeared in 1919.

hand over large segments of the Austrian Empire to Italy. Furthermore, Wilson was both the apostle of 'self-determination' and the head of the world's richest nation. He was thus the statesman from whom Austria had most to fear politically and most to hope economically. Finally, Charles's direct approach to President Wilson, like his earlier overtures to President Poincaré, offered Czernin the chance to use his influence without risking his neck. The responsibility was the Emperor's if all went wrong. The glory could be shared, if all went right. This wartime exchange between the sinking Vienna of the Old World and the rising Washington of the New was in fact to be Czernin's swan-song.

It had all begun, of course, with that political Sermon on the Mount which was to set so much else in motion across the Atlantic – President Wilson's famous Fourteen Points, enunciated on 8 January 1918, and designed to set the universe at rights. These represented American (or rather Wilsonian) thinking and were far from reflecting any jointly agreed programme of the Allies. Indeed there were some aspects of Wilson's speech that alarmed the *Entente* camp in Europe almost as much as the common enemy. Thus the plan for 'open' diplomacy (Point I) aroused as much scepticism in Paris as it did in Berlin. The call for 'absolute freedom of navigation upon the seas' (Point II) aroused more suspicion in London than in any other warring capital, for fear it should lead to a demand for the renunciation of British naval bases like Hong Kong and Gibraltar. Similar misgivings were awakened in British imperial breasts by Wilson's Point V, which appealed for 'a free, open-minded and absolutely impartial adjustment of all colonial claims'. On the future of Turkey, Poland and even Alsace-Lorraine (Points III, XIII and VIII) there were other important nuances of difference between Wilson and his European partners, while their views about post-war peace organizations (Point XIV) were still very far apart.*

It was ironical indeed that this peace platform now offered to the Central Powers should contain so much unmatured American timber that the other Allies were anxious to knock into shape. But Berlin and Vienna could only guess at the real extent of these differences. The Fourteen Points, as later elaborated by Wilson's so-called Four Points of 11 February, had to be taken as a synthesis of *Entente* diplomacy and, as regards the Austrian capital, they contained one direct challenge. This was in Point X which declared: 'The peoples of Austria-Hungary, whose place among the nations we wish to see safeguarded and assured, should be

---

* The differences are well summarized in *The Troubled Giant* by F. S. Northedge, pp. 33–7; and in *The Intimate Papers of Colonel House*, vol. iii.

accorded the first opportunity of autonomous development.' It was a delphic utterance indeed. Charles would rather have heard assurances for his Empire as a whole than for those separate peoples who made it up. On the other hand, 'autonomous development', provided it was within a common realm, exactly echoed his own programme.

It was vital to find out exactly what was in President Wilson's mind. Charles decided to do so by the simple process of writing to him. This new secret approach at the highest level was, the Empress states, entirely the Emperor's idea.* Czernin, who this time was brought in at the very beginning, showed every sign of initial enthusiasm and was consulted over every step. As during the Sixtus affair, however, his influence on the actual text and tone of the exchanges was always to lean more and more towards harshness rather than to conciliation and to vagueness rather than precision. But there was no quarrel over the new intermediary the Emperor chose. It was his kinsman, King Alfonso of Spain, the ruler of a country part-Habsburg in its history yet neutral in the present conflict.

The Austrian Ambassador in Madrid was Prince Emil Fürstenberg. He appears up to this point to have had a lean time of it at his post. His telegrams home throughout 1917 are peppered with complaints over lack of staff and cypher facilities and underlying them all is the querulous reproach that Vienna is neglecting him. But the isolated envoy must have forgiven his masters everything for that long telegram from them which landed on his desk around 19 February 1918.† In it Czernin instructed him 'in the name of the All-Highest', to open up peace talks with President Wilson through the good offices of the Spanish crown. It was a frustrated diplomat's dream of paradise.‡

The Emperor's telegram to the King of Spain began by saying that the recent public statement by President Wilson on the one hand and Count Czernin on the other had 'greatly cleared up the European situation and

---

* A low-level reconnaissance over the same ground had been made at the beginning of February with the 'conference of the Professors' in Switzerland. Charles's informal spokesman was the Austrian international jurist Professor Lammasch (who was to be the Empire's last Prime Minister). The American 'representative' (in fact little more than a pair of American ears) was the ambitious ex-professor and would-be diplomatist George D. Herron. Lammasch suggested President Wilson might start the peace-ball rolling by a public declaration that recent Austrian pronouncements had shown the Dual Monarchy to be on the right road towards 'self-determination'. Herron thought the first step ought to come from Vienna with the launching of a formal programme of national autonomy. The encounter was thus as fruitless as it was unofficial.

† Austrian State Archives, PA Rot 964 Krieg 25/29.

‡ The author knew Prince Furstenberg well as an old but still clear-headed man in post-1945 Austria. He still looked back with nostalgia to this brief moment of glory.

reduced the major controversial points to a certain minimum'. In view of this, the Emperor felt the moment had arrived for direct talks between a spokesman of his and one nominated by the American President in order to clarify the position to such a point 'that nothing further might stand in the way of a world peace conference'.* A long message then followed which King Alfonso was bidden to convey by some 'strictly secret means' to the White House.

This message concentrated on the Four Points of 11 February which Wilson had put forward as a sort of philosophical commentary to his more detailed Fourteen Points set out the month before. The additional points had been so general as to allow of almost any practical application and Charles began by keeping the argument on this safe plane. It was easy, for example, to welcome the President's opening statement that settlements should be based 'on justice in each individual case', and that the solutions found must be those 'most conducive to a lasting peace'. Even the next two of the Four Points, which declared that peoples and provinces should not simply be moved about like pawns in a game but should have their own interests safeguarded in any territorial agreement, could be gladly accepted by Charles, provided they were adpated to the Empire's complicated structure. And the fourth point – which preserved a balance between giving the maximum satisfaction to all 'clearly defined national aspirations' on the one hand without, on the other hand, introducing new elements of discord into the European scene – might have been written with a reformed Empire in mind. All this Charles therefore welcomed in his message.

But what the President was waiting for from the Central Powers was not answer to his Four Points but an answer to his Fourteen. That had partly been his purpose in speaking again, and he now wanted hard political detail as to what terms the enemy offered, not vague philosophical dialogue about the Rights of Man. Charles's message, as was perhaps understandable in an opening move, skirted delicately round this. The old Sixtus affair pledge to restore Belgium's sovereignty was repeated and it was hinted that no great difficulties would be raised by Vienna over the territorial claims of Serbia and Bulgaria (again, an echo of the 1917 Laxenburg letters). But on the far trickier problem of Italy's ambitions, Charles turned the Four Points his own way. Italian claims on Austrian territory, he argued, neither represented the wish of the population concerned nor would they contribute towards a stable peace in the future. The argument was certainly a strong one, in ethics if not in politics. But it was an argument against Washington as well as against Rome.

Fürstenberg handed over his Emperor's message to King Alfonso on 21 February. It is clear from his report on this special audience* that the Spanish sovereign had no previous inkling that he was being selected to play the part of a royal peace dove. Indeed Fürstenberg describes the King as being 'somewhat disconcerted' at hearing the news. Alfonso's only question was the very pertinent one: did the German Emperor and German Government know about and support the approach? Fürstenberg, reduced to guesswork, hinted that they did. The guess was wrong but the result was right. The Emperor's message was promptly translated into Spanish in the King's private office and was soon on its way to Washington. On 25 February it was handed over in person by the Spanish Ambassador there to President Wilson.

Vienna was not kept waiting long. A week later, on 2 March, Charles received from Alfonso a preliminary report of his Ambassador's impressions. Mr Wilson, he reported, had described Charles's letter as 'transcendental' on a first perusal, but had withheld further comment until he could study it. The President had added ruefully that the Austrian Emperor's message 'had brought him into a somewhat difficult situation because he had declared himself on various occasions to be no friend of secret diplomacy'. Charles, it seemed, had punctured the first of the Fourteen Points, even if he was to puncture no others.

Wilson's considered reply reached Vienna four days later. It amounted to one long insistent plea to the Austrian Emperor for detailed peace proposals. To Charles's suggestion for a personal meeting, Wilson replied:

I assume that the Emperor of Austria is in possession of my message of 8 January and is informed of the details of the programme which, in my opinion, should form the basis of a general peace – details which I set out in such clear and pregnant words that they could not be more clearly expressed by any representative I appointed.

On the crucial point of satisfying Italy's demands, the President noted Charles's argument that some of these claims might not be 'acceptable to the peoples directly concerned'. He went on, addressing the Emperor indirectly: 'But he has not obliged with that which I wish to receive point by point and in the most precise terms – the favour of his positive proposals.' In particular, Wilson added, he wanted to have the Emperor's concrete suggestions for 'satisfying the national aspirations of the Slav peoples on his borders'; for the future of the Adriatic Coast; and (of course) for 'definite concessions to Italy'. In other words, where, for

* Austrian State Archives, PA I Rot 964 Krieg 25/29.

example, was Serbia's proposed outlet to the sea to be? How would Bulgaria's new boundaries be drawn? And would Austria formally renounce the whole of the Trentino to Italy even if she still disputed Trieste?

This urgent, almost impatient letter of President Wilson's was, as it turned out, Austria-Hungary's last chance to end the war as an Empire. Six months later, Charles would have leaped at the same chance, meeting all the President's unspoken demands (even those concerning Italy) in return for the opportunity of direct and separate peace talks with America. Six months later, indeed, he was reduced to pleading for just such talks at almost any price that still included the mere recognition of his crown.

But March 1918 was not October 1918. Indeed, for *both* sides, the events of the autumn were not only indiscernible in the spring. They were as good as inconceivable. The lengthy reply over which Charles now laboured with Czernin for nearly a fortnight reflected the hopes and realities of the day. These were substantial. The Central Powers had torn the armies of Serbia to shreds; Rumania had just signed a separate peace with them, knocking herself out of the war; the Italian front had never been so stable, nor pushed so far South and away from Austria's own borders; the Eastern front was liquidated for good and the great attack in the West about to begin. It is this battle situation – as in the case of the parallel Anglo-Austrian talks – that can be read into the temporizing, the confidence, even the occasional haughtiness of Vienna's response. It accounts for the influence Czernin exerted in the drafting of this crucial second message. It also partly explains why Charles decided to submit to that influence.

That there was, however, a constant tug-of-war between the Emperor and his minister over the Wilson exchanges is confirmed by the Empress, who often heard her husband's comments and complaints on the subject at the time.

'The Emperor started searching for new peace links as fast as the existing ones snapped off and Wilson's speeches seemed to him to provide another chance. To begin with, Czernin fell in smoothly enough. But he soon tried to keep the exchanges under his control, like the Armand-Revertera talks and the Smuts contacts, and the usual trouble cropped up between him and my husband. All the original letters to President Wilson were drafted by the Emperor himself. But when they were passed to Czernin he always sharpened them up. I remember, for example, that he deleted one of the Emperor's references about "willingness for certain frontier rectifications". In one or two cases, the Emperor's text was altered just before the messages were sent off and while the Emperor himself was away from Vienna. He was always on the move and at the front. The rows came afterwards, but they came too late.

'As for that evasive reply about the South Slavs, an enormous struggle was still going on between the Emperor and Budapest about the project for South Slav autonomy. No agreement was in sight. How could the Emperor announce anything concrete to President Wilson when it had not yet been thrashed out with the other half of the Monarchy, and the half most concerned?'

Whatever the explanation, the Austrian reply which was finally despatched to Wilson towards the end of March might almost have been designed to break negotiations off. It repeated constantly and at great length the request for a personal meeting which the American President had just declined. Yet, for the most part, it withheld the one thing Wilson had insisted upon as a condition of progress: precise answers. The only exception to this vagueness was over Italy and here the precision was negative. Italy's claims to the Trentino, together with those on Gorizia and Trieste, were all rejected as being incompatible with Wilson's own Four Points as well as with the vital interests of the Empire. The Emperor's offer to cede the Trentino to Italy to get peace talks started, made to Prince Sixtus at Laxenburg nine months before, now seemed to have been abruptly dropped. Indeed, when one thinks back to the Sixtus affair and the Emperor's personal stand over Alsace-Lorraine, the anti-French note which creeps into this second message is quite unreal. The final draft ends with the (for Charles) incredible passage:

'There is only one hindrance to peace . . . and that is the lust for conquest of Italy and France.' This was the language of the German Emperor rather than the Austrian; it was Czernin's equation of Strasbourg with Trieste.

It was just as well that this reply never reached Washington, at least not through official channels. King Alfonso and his advisers took one look at it, disliked what they saw, and decided to play for time. Nearly a month later the luckless Fürstenberg was obliged to report from Madrid that the 'despatch of the All-Highest's message to Washington by special courier is still not possible since Spanish transatlantic steamers have cancelled their America sailings because of the U-boat danger'.*

By this time, however, two excuses for delay, each more solid than shipping hazards, had presented themselves to the Spaniards. The first was the great German attack already rolling through France which had silenced all talk of peace with its thunder. The second was conveyed in a delicate question which the Spanish Foreign Minister could now put to the Austrian envoy when pressed yet again for action. Had Vienna no

* Austrian State Archives, as above, No. 6792, dated 21 April 1918.

reservations at all about sending the message off, he asked, 'in view of the recent incident with the French Prime Minister'? *

Fürstenberg cabled home for instructions. But it was no longer Count Czernin who read his telegram at the Ballhausplatz. A week before, the almost inevitable rupture between the Emperor and his Foreign Minister had come at last. Czernin had been swept from office by a tidal wave of political scandal. Much of the good repute of Austria, and of Charles himself, had been swept away with him.

* *Ibid.*

Chapter 11

THE PRICE OF HONOUR

It was a typical Austrian irony that the ghost of the Sixtus affair should now rise up from the dead files of 1917 and smite Charles with twice the impact that the negotiations themselves had ever had in real life. The great scandal started rolling on 2 April 1918, when Czernin delivered himself of a major speech in reply to a humble address of thanks for his Ukrainian 'bread-peace' made by the Vienna Burgomaster, Dr Weisskirchner. This period marked, of course, the very flood-tide of Czernin's confidence both in himself and in a German victory. His speech was borne along by both.

Referring to Wilson's attempts 'to use Vienna as a propitious ground in which to sow the seeds of general peace', Czernin retorted that, despite the Emperor's love of peace, his monarch could nonetheless 'never commit a breach of faith, never conclude a shameful peace; and fifty-five millions stand behind their king and emperor'. Then came the sort of statement that drove Austria's well-wishers in the *Entente* camp to despair. 'Whatever happens,' Czernin declared, 'we shall never abandon German interests just as Germany will never leave us in the lurch.'

Damaging though this sort of declaration was to everything but the German alliance, it was at least within Czernin's diplomatic province. But he then left these preserves altogether and started laying down the law in home policy. Again, the tone was rabidly pan-German in that it was rabidly anti-Slav. He particularly attacked the Czech leadership within the Empire, remarking: 'The wretched Masaryk is not the only one of his sort. There are Masaryks within the frontiers of the Monarchy as well.' (This to a warring Empire whose fronts could only be held with the loyalty of its many Slav regiments.)

All these remarks, however, were put in the shade by the following passage which came towards the middle of the Foreign Minister's speech. Stressing that the Central Powers had done all they could to spare France from the new slaughter just engaged on the Western front, he went on:

A little while before the offensive in the West was started, Clemenceau enquired of me whether I was prepared for negotiations and, if so, on what basis. In agreement with Berlin, I immediately replied that I was prepared for talks and that, so far as France was concerned, I saw no other obstacle to peace except France's desire for Alsace-Lorraine. The reply came from Paris that no negotiations were possible on this basis. After that we had no further choice and the mighty battle broke out.

Czernin almost certainly had in mind at this point those low-level and inconclusive contacts with Major Armand of the French General Staff which he had himself conducted from the previous summer onwards. But whatever he was thinking of, this personal jibe at a man of 'Tiger' Clemenceau's hot temperament showed appalling judgement. Charles always allowed his Foreign Minister a fairly free rein in drafting secret telegrams. But a public pronouncement before the whole world was something very different. The first of the many mysteries of the scandal is, therefore, why did the Emperor ever allow Czernin to make this speech to begin with? The answer is that he tried in vain to correct it. The Empress relates:

'It was late at night on 1 April when Czernin, or a messenger of his, I forget which, came from Vienna to meet the Emperor, who was travelling on the Court train, and handed him a copy of his long speech to read, saying he proposed to deliver it *the following evening*.

'The Emperor read the document through before going to sleep and had several misgivings about its contents, particularly the passages where Czernin had intruded on the preserves of other ministers. As to the reference to Clemenceau, the Emperor's first impression was that Czernin was referring to something new that he had just been discussing with the French, and the Emperor's reaction was "Good heavens, these are Bolshevik methods, revealing secrets like this!" The Sixtus letters, which had been laid *ad acta* for nearly a year, never entered his head.

'At all events, the Emperor marked all his amendments on what had been submitted to him as a draft and determined to deal with the whole matter in the morning. But conceivably due to a genuine misunderstanding, when the royal train reached Vienna the next day Czernin, who had told the Emperor he would be speaking that same evening, had already delivered his speech.'*

---

* There is a rich literature on and around the April 1918 scandal of the Sixtus affair. For Prince Sixtus's own version see Sixtus–Manteyer, *op. cit.*, pp. 275 *et seq.*; for an anti-Czernin Austrian version, Polzer, *op. cit.*, pp. 268 *et seq.* For a recent 'pro-Czernin' account see Ladislas Singer, *Staatsmann Einer Zeitenwende*. See also Demblin, *Czernin and the Sixtus Affair*; and, for a contemporary French and less partisan version than that of Manteyer, *La Paix des empires centraux* by F. Charles-Roux.

Though, as stated, Czernin says nothing of substance about either the Sixtus negotiations of 1917 or the 1918 scandal in his Memoirs, some curious notes of his were

Off to this ugly and perhaps significant start, the affair rapidly gathered momentum. Clemenceau was at the front on 4 April when M. Mandel, his secretary, called him from Paris with the text of Czernin's statement. He barked back down the telephone: 'Count Czernin is lying.' This, thought the secretary, was too good to spoil. He handed over the French Prime Minister's comment without elaboration to the official news agency Havas.

A war of communiqués was now unleashed between Paris and Vienna. For four days, they centred on the Armand–Revertera contacts which Czernin claimed (and Clemenceau denied) had been started up by the French only to be destroyed by the French over the Alsace-Lorraine issue. As he fired back each salvo, Czernin dug deeper and deeper into his archives for ammunition until most of this secret but relatively unimportant exchange was revealed. But, by the second round, the really big ammunition was on Clemenceau's desk. When he got back to Paris, he found in front of him not the Armand–Revertera file (which he knew all about and had himself closed) but the full account of Prince Sixtus's earlier mission, with copies of the Austrian Emperor's two Laxenburg letters.* The French Prime Minister was learning of this whole episode for the first time. The French President, M. Poincaré, had kept his personal vow of silence to Charles over the affair. And even the ineffective M. Ribot, who had told the Italians all about it, had not revealed the secret to his own successors in office in Paris. Now both the French Foreign Office and the French President (though the latter with great reluctance) decided that the time for disclosure had come.

Clemenceau knew a good thing when he saw one. His next note to Vienna of 6 April, though still on the Armand–Revertera exchanges, contained this ominous hint:

---

recently brought to light by the American historian Robert Kann's *Die Sixtus Affäre*. They are a rambling series of jottings written in the hieroglyphics of the old nineteenth-century Gabelsberg stenography. The notes are partly in first person, partly in third, partly indecipherable and partly ungrammatical. Their date of origin is unknown. If Czernin wrote or dictated them when in a rational frame of mind then they speak volumes for his instability and evasiveness. They cover for the most part entirely familiar ground. Almost the only new and concrete point is the allegation that the reference to French peace-feelers in his 2 April speech was specifically approved by the Emperor Charles 'to demonstrate the solidarity of the German alliance'; and Czernin implies that the whole speech was, in fact, 'cleared' with his sovereign. This must be recorded, for what it may be worth, against the categorically opposed evidence of the Empress, who even remembers the Emperor's exclamation of horror on reading the particular passage in question.

* A copy of Count Czernin's separate Note of 9 May which had accompanied the second letter was marked (appropriately 'No. 13') in this Paris dossier, but was missing. Why has never been explained.

Is there not somewhere in Count Czernin's memory a record of an earlier attempt of the same kind, addressed to Paris and London only two months before the Revertera enterprise began, and addressed by a personage of far higher rank? Of this too, an authentic and much more significant proof exists.

The description, coupled with the exact date, could only mean one of Charles's Laxenburg letters which Sixtus had carried with him to Paris the previous year. As we have seen, Czernin knew the gist of these letters since he had helped to draft them. He knew also that they were the highly personal concern of his Emperor. But in his determination to win this public debate, to which the whole of Europe was already listening with incredulous ears, he now committed the folly from which the final *débâcle* flowed. Czernin ignored Clemenceau's warning shot and sailed straight into the mouths of the enemy cannon.

Without consulting his Emperor, he sent back (and again published) a reply in which the Austrian Foreign Minister 'unhesitatingly affirmed' that he remembered those other exchanges, 'but will be bound to add, to complete the story, that this earlier attempt proved as unsuccessful as the later'. In other words, the Sixtus affair, like the other contacts, had failed solely because France had refused to abandon Alsace-Lorraine.

The French, who had thought that their warning of 6 April would silence the chatterbox in Vienna, could scarcely believe this new imprudence. There was now nothing for it but to 'put the dots on the i's'. For the first time, Charles's name was dragged into an official news-agency contest which had begun like a schoolboyish wrangle but was fast ending up as high politics. Why, retorted Clemenceau on 9 April, should Czernin insist that it was France's wrong-headed claim to Alsace-Lorraine which had always blocked negotiations? His own Emperor, after all, had 'said the last word' on this. 'For,' the French note went on, 'it was actually the Emperor Charles who, in an autograph letter of March 1917, gave his definite support to the just claims of France relative to Alsace-Lorraine. A later letter establishes the fact that the Emperor was in agreement with his minister. The only thing left for Count Czernin to do is to make a full admission of his error.'

The fat was now slipping properly into the fire, and the Emperor with it. For the first time there is now a record of the Foreign Minister consulting his sovereign on the quarrel. Czernin had been obliged to leave at this juncture for Bucharest, from where he could only safely communicate with Charles (who was at his Supreme Headquarters at Baden near Vienna) by means of the so-called Hughes apparatus. This was a primitive form of teleprinter and was about the most awkward instrument imaginable for the unravelling of such a highly complex tangle. According to the machine slips of this brief conversation, published two years later,* the Emperor began:

Good evening. I am very glad you rang me. I have just heard from the [Foreign] Ministry that Clem[enceau] wants to make some disclosures concerning me. Quite obviously everything that he produces is lies and deceit *apart from that which you anyway know about*. . . . [Author's italic.] If Clemenceau should say anything *which goes beyond the bounds of what you know already* [author's italic] I intend to send the Emperor William a telegram expressing my disgust of this enemy web of lies and again assuring him of our absolute loyalty to the alliance. . . .

Czernin in his reply expressed delight at the telegram proposal but warned his Emperor that Clemenceau was mentioning 'a later Imperial letter stating that the Emperor was of one mind with his minister'. Had His Majesty perhaps forgotten about something further he had written after the March letter? At any rate, Czernin wound up, he was now hurrying back to Vienna, where he would arrive the following evening, so would the Emperor wait with any more telegrams or communiqués until then?

It is plain even from this cautiously disguised exchange that what Czernin was already concerned about was his own position rather than his Emperor's. His main anxiety was to make sure that his own accompanying note to the second Laxenburg letter should not be produced against him. He was also clearly concerned that a gigantic confusion might arise if the Byzantine tale of the Sixtus affair now had to be translated a year later into public Austrian communiqués. On the first point, he need not have worried. Unbeknown to him, his unsigned note of 9 May 1917 was mysteriously missing from the French files. But on the second point his worries were to be more than justified. The muddle that now arose in Vienna as to precisely which secret letter to Paris had been written by the Emperor and when might well appear comic if it were not all so sombre in its consequences.

Before attempting to explain it, the battle of the communiqués must be followed to its noisy end. The next day, 10 April, without waiting to consult his Emperor as promised, Czernin fired off another public message to Paris† declaring, among other things, that 'M. Clemenceau's claims regarding the Emperor Charles's written statements are a lie from beginning to end'. In view of this, Charles had no option but to despatch

* See Demblin, *op. cit.*
† It is thought that he used the same Hughes apparatus for transmission while *en route*.

immediately his own prepared telegram to the Emperor William. This flatly denied Clemenceau's allegations that he 'had ever recognized any so-called just French claims to Alsace-Lorraine'. Then came an emotional assurance which looked somewhat odd over Charles's signature. 'At a time when Austro-Hungarian cannon are thundering alongside German guns on the Western front * proof is scarcely needed that I am fighting and will continue to fight for your provinces as though I were defending my own.'

Charles's telegram produced the desired and anticipated response from William that he had 'never doubted for one moment' his ally's loyalty. Czernin's final message to Clemenceau, on the other hand, produced an unexpected and unwanted bombshell. On the evening of 12 April the French news agency published the full text of Charles's Laxenburg letter of March 1917. This, it will be remembered, contained the Emperor's fateful promise that, in the interests of securing a general peace, he would 'support with all means, and by exercising all his personal influence with his Allies, the just French claims on Alsace-Lorraine'.

The best Czernin could do against this was to claim, quoting the authority of his Emperor, that the published letter was a forgery. Charles, the statement alleged, had merely written, in a purely personal letter to his brother-in-law, that he would have supported such French claims had they been legitimate, 'which in fact they were not'. It was almost his last act as Foreign Minister. Though, as we shall see, it had been taken at a heavy cost to his sovereign, it was not nearly good enough for Czernin's purpose. The French had the proof in their hands and rubbed this home in a sarcastic reply. Czernin was made to look, before the whole world, a liar as well as a fool. The Emperor now appeared before the same audience as a dissembler and a traitor.

Before coming to the final dramatic clash between the Emperor and his minister let us see how much of the mystery, muddle and contradiction in the story so far can be explained by the one central surviving eye-witness of the whole episode.

The Empress Zita relates the following:

'First, as to our surprise that the March 1917 letter should be published from Paris. This was because it had been agreed that the document should be shown to the French leaders by Prince Sixtus, but never left with them. Both President Poincaré and M. Briand accepted this. But it was in fact left long enough in their hands for a secretary of M. Briand's to get it copied.

* With great reluctance Charles had agreed to transfer some Austrian regiments to the West to take part in the great March offensive.

'Next, the Emperor's telegram of denial to the Emperor William. It had also been agreed with the French side the year before that, in case these secret negotiations should ever be exposed by any indiscretion, my husband should send a formal and public denial to the German Emperor. The point of this, so far as Paris was concerned, would be to convey to the French that they should not insist further in the matter as the whole position might become politically dangerous. This arrangement was made with Prince Sixtus and the French Government in 1917 and explains the Emperor's telegram of 10 April 1918.

'Then as to our own confusion after the first Sixtus letter was published in Paris. To explain it, one must recall the atmosphere in which those letters had been written. We lived under the constant fear of subversion and espionage, not only from hostile forces within the Empire but also from our German allies who had all their plans laid to march in and occupy Austria if need be – a fact that Czernin was to make full use of. It was essential that as few people as possible should know about, let alone see, this highly secret correspondence and it could obviously not be kept in any secretariat. And in fact, for greater security, the Emperor had all the Sixtus documents locked up in a desk in my bedroom.

'We opened the drawer when Clemenceau published his text and now the trouble began. Several drafts had been made of that first message and they were all preserved. But there was nothing now to show us which of these drafts had actually been given to Prince Sixtus in the end. No copy had been made of the final version and marked as such. As the events were now more than a year old and had anyway been written off we could not reconstruct them exactly from memory. Thus, though we knew there had been a reference to French claims on Alsace-Lorraine in the March 1917 letter, we had no means of proving or disproving that the exact words quoted by Clemenceau had been finally used by the Emperor. Forgeries, mistakes in transmission – anything could have been possible; the French had not yet released a photo-copy, only a text. Our failure to have a true copy made and not to destroy all the drafts was, of course, a costly mistake, though in the end it turned out that what Clemenceau published was the genuine March letter as it was sent off.

'The position regarding the second and less important letter of May 1917 – which referred mainly to the offer of peace which had just been passed to us by the Italian General Staff – was very different. A properly marked copy of this was made at Laxenburg – only one copy – but this sole copy Count Czernin took away with him and kept. He still had it in his keeping when the trouble broke out in April and this is what he was referring to in that Hughes conversation from Bucharest. He never produced it for the Emperor, who had quite forgotten it – so much had happened since.'

We must now move to the domestic scene for, with the publication on 12 April of the Emperor's secret peace moves, the matter developed into a political crisis in Austria as well as an international scandal. The parting of the ways had come at last for Charles and his brilliant but ungovernable and unpredictable Foreign Minister. The manner of their parting was that of high and occasionally grotesque melodrama. Neither the Emperor nor Czernin ever put anything on record and for fifty years various colourful versions based largely on rumour have been circulating. Here is the account * given by the only other eye-witness of those exhausting and eventful days. The Empress Zita relates:

'We were at Baden when, after lunch on 12 April, Czernin telephoned. Soon after he arrived himself and stayed with the Emperor until five o'clock when he returned to Vienna. The Emperor had other audiences to deal with then but once these were over, at 7.30, he called up Czernin and was talking on the telephone with him for two and three-quarter hours, until 10.15. By now the Emperor had put off his planned departure for Budapest.

'Czernin had brought out to Baden with him, already written out in his own hand, a so-called "Declaration of Honour" which he wanted my husband to sign. This contained various points such as a declaration by the Emperor that he had only written one letter to his brother-in-law,† that it was a purely private letter; that Belgium had not been mentioned in it and that, above all, it had not contained the version about Alsace-Lorraine quoted by Clemenceau.

'The Emperor told me some of the wild threats Czernin had been using to get the document signed, but the following morning I had the experience of hearing them all again myself. This is what happened.

'The Emperor awoke on the 13th feeling very unwell and his condition was not helped by a further telephone call from Czernin in Vienna. At 10 A.M. Czernin arrived again himself at Baden. The Emperor had in fact suffered a heart attack ‡ and asked me to receive Czernin on his behalf

---

* Based on brief entries in a diary as well as from memory. This was one of the few periods when the Empress felt compelled to risk keeping a personal record of events.

† It was the second letter (of which he had the only copy) that Czernin wanted above all to suppress because this one, of 9 May 1917, had been accompanied by a four-point note in the Foreign Minister's own hand.

‡ Some time before the Czernin crisis, Charles had ignored a warning from his personal physician, Dr Delug, that a complete rest of at least six weeks was imperative to safeguard the Emperor's heart and general health.

while he rested. This I did. We were over an hour alone together in the Emperor's study of our small Baden house while the Emperor rested in his bedroom nearby.

'Czernin behaved absolutely like a madman.

'He said to me: "Of course I know what really happened but still I need the Emperor's signature on this oath. I know it is a false oath but I must have it. I need it for myself and for the honour of my family."

'I replied: "But Count Czernin, do you realize what you are asking? You cannot expect the Emperor to sign and it would be more to the honour of you and your family if you do not want him to."

'At this he seemed to lose all control and shouted: "The Emperor can sign or not sign. But I will say this. If he does not, I will go immediately to Berlin and then it will be finished for Austria. I know – and Your Majesty knows – what plans the Germans have to invade us in an emergency. They will be carried out and I shall take over and I shall then be the Iron Chancellor."

'There was nothing I could do or say to bring him to his senses. At another point he burst out: "If the Emperor does not sign there will be nothing left but for all three of us to commit suicide – you, the Emperor and I." * And then he returned to his threats that if the Emperor did not sign Austria would "pay the price and be taken over by Germany".

'After a while the Emperor got up and joined us again from the next room. Czernin now repeated the same threats to both of us. (This was in fact more or less the language he had already used with the Emperor the day before.)

'In the end two things – apart from the desire to end this dreadful episode – persuaded the Emperor to sign a declaration that he knew to be false. There was first and foremost the fear that Czernin must be pacified in case in his frenzied state of mind he really did sound the alarm in Berlin, and we had good reason from our intelligence source to be anxious on this score.†

'The second was the hope – however faint – that, as Czernin kept on repeating, he only needed this declaration of the Emperor's for his own personal security and honour and that, once the Emperor had signed it, he

* If, as some versions have it, Czernin actually produced a pistol and threatened to shoot himself on the spot, it was not while the Empress was present.

† The General Staffs of most countries have theoretical plans for invading any of their neighbours but the German Plan 'O', designed to occupy Austria and force her to follow Berlin in total war should her resolution falter (as in fact it was doing), was more than abstract theory. In the last days of the collapse it became partly a reality when German troops marched uninvited into the Tyrol.

THE PRICE OF HONOUR

[Czernin] would lock it away in his desk and nobody else would ever see it. Though the Emperor never really believed his promise, he eventually, after a desperate inner struggle, put his signature to the false declaration.'

Charles was in truth so afraid of what Czernin might do that at one point on this tense 13 April, the Empress further relates, he telephoned the President of Police in Vienna and said: 'Look, Count Czernin is here and is behaving like a madman. If he is left to run around like that he could be a danger for the whole Empire. Can't we arrest him before he does something?' To which the Police President replied, with impeccable bureaucratic logic: 'No, Your Majesty, I am afraid not. We can only arrest him *after* he has done something.'

As to the second factor – Czernin's promise of no disclosure – the Emperor's suspicions were instantly confirmed by the way the Foreign Minister could not wait to start for Vienna the moment his sovereign had put his signature to the sheet of paper. Again according to the Empress, as soon as Czernin had left in his car, Charles telephoned orders to a sentry to take up position on the road at Laxenburg, which lay on the route to the capital, stop the vehicle and bring the Foreign Minister back to Baden. From the report that the wretched *gendarme* had to give his Emperor a little later, it was evident that Czernin too suspected something was afoot. When the sentry tried to hold the car up, it accelerated instead, and the man only saved his life by leaping back at the last second. On hearing this, Charles immediately rang the Foreign Office and left orders that the Foreign Minister should publish nothing without first consulting him.

Czernin now broke this direct order as well as his own solemn promise. He published his Emperor's 'word-of-honour' statement to the world that same night, well knowing, because he had himself drafted it, that it was a lie. This was almost the last Austrian document in that ignominious 'war of the communiqués' described above. It was also Czernin's personal swansong. After that breach of faith he could be kept no more. The crushing reply which came from Paris overnight, offering further proof of the authenticity of their disclosures, had anyway made Czernin's position untenable. At a stormy Cabinet meeting on the morning of 14 April, Czernin resigned.*

The Foreign Minister's resignation was not the only political drama of the day. Before leaving office, Czernin had tried to provoke an even greater crisis of a constitutional nature – the temporary 'resignation' of his

---

* Werkmann, *Deutschland als Verbundete*, pp. 260–1, suggests that it was Czernin's formal proposal to the Crown Council on 14 April that a Regent should be appointed which led to his resignation. Charles had, however, determined to dismiss him after his breach of faith over publishing his 'private' signed statement.

sovereign and the appointment of a Regent more to his taste. This was not the first time the thought had entered Czernin's head. Whatever the truth of the rumours that he had been intriguing for months past with other members of the Royal Family, as well as with senior civil servants, with a Regency in view, the Empress recalls that he had often asked her husband: 'What shall we do if you are ever cut off or even captured on your travels to the front? Who will take over in Vienna?' It is possible to argue, of course, that these questions reflected nothing more than the concern of a loyal minister for the continuity of government in wartime. It is also arguable, given Czernin's behaviour throughout the April crisis, that they reflected motives rather less pure.

Here is the Empress's account of this episode:

'Czernin made his Regency proposal during the confrontations of 12–13 April and not afterwards as has been assumed. It was a suggestion he made repeatedly during those endless heated arguments at Baden. His idea was that the Emperor should temporarily withdraw on the grounds that he was overstrained and tired and that a Regent should take over. The names of the popular Archduke Eugene, or the Archduke Frederick (with whose family Czernin was in the closest contact) were mentioned.

'It has been said that I vetoed the idea. The Emperor did not even discuss it with me. He always dismissed it out of hand himself. He told me afterwards he had retorted to Czernin: "It's out of the question. What shall we come to once we start declaring monarchs to be lunatics?"'

So far from abdicating, Charles, as soon as Czernin's resignation was settled, set out on his postponed visit to Budapest, where further strain and unpleasantness awaited him. Two days later, on 16 April, the Baron Burian who had been Foreign Minister at Charles's accession was brought back to replace Czernin. It was a case of the reliable old pack-horse taking over again from a fractious, and at times vicious, thoroughbred.

What were the motives behind Czernin's speech of 2 April that had touched off those two weeks of nightmare? It has been said that, in referring to secret French peace-feelers, he wished to discredit and perhaps even topple Clemenceau from office as well as cause disarray in the *Entente* camp. This idea may have figured somewhere in his unpredictable thoughts. It was the sort of diplomatic *coup de maître* after which he yearned. But it is more likely that what was uppermost in his mind was the determination to hitch the Austrian wagon once and for all to the Prussian star.

Ever since the German-led victories on the Isonzo of October 1917 Czernin seems to have abandoned all his earlier reservations about an Austrian policy of blind faith in Germany and total commitment to

Germany. That was the message of his 'Strasbourg–Trieste' speech of the previous December. That was the reason for his unpublicized capitulation to German pressure over the Ukraine treaty at Brest-Litovsk in February – since which 'triumph' he had been in a mood of nervous exultation. Those were precisely the sentiments which had echoed in that final message drafted for President Wilson only a week or two before. The April speech was in fact further evidence that, by now, Czernin had accepted Austria-Hungary's status as a German satellite. As a conservative Bohemian noble who hated the Slavs more than he loved the Austrians, his decision had a certain personal as well as political logic. Retiring in outward grace, he was given the Grand Cross with diamonds by his own sovereign, and the Iron Cross by the Emperor William. The latter, at least, he had earned.

If the motives behind Czernin's 'mad fortnight' can still be disputed, their results are clear. On the international plane, the Empire stood discredited as a fickle intriguer and its Emperor stood dishonoured as a liar. Since Charles had based the whole of his peace diplomacy on the integrity of his own person and the prestige of his dynasty, this was the heaviest blow of all. As for the German alliance, Berlin now demanded concrete reassurances of fidelity from Vienna and Charles had no option but to oblige. The Spa Treaty of May 1918, to which we now come, was a baleful revenge for Czernin's political ghost.

For the most fitting prelude to this next glum episode in the Empire's history we must go back to August 1914, and a long walk near Schönbrunn Palace which the young Archduke Charles was taking with his wife just before leaving to join his regiment at the front. The Empress recalls:

'There were of course many family and personal matters that had to be settled before his departure and we went through those first. Then my husband suddenly turned to the political situation and said:

'"I leave with a heavy heart because when this war is over, whatever happens in it, this Austria-Hungary that I know and love will no longer exist. Either there will be two purely German Empires in the heart of Europe with a big Slav group alongside them. Or, more likely, the Slav group will be pulled to Russia and we in turn will be swallowed up by Prussia.

'"It's like La Fontaine's fable of the *pot de fer* and the *pot de terre* who go walking out together. The Germans are the pot of iron and if we go too far and too fast walking hand in hand with them we will bang together as in the story and it will be our Austrian pot of clay that will be shattered."'

This prophecy was not in fact to be fully realized until Hitler's bloodless triumph of March 1938. But the long-term menace which German militarism represented to Vienna as well as to the rest of Europe was something that Charles kept constantly before his eyes as Emperor. It is indeed one of the greatest paradoxes of the First World War that the Central Powers camp, whose Austro-German basis* looked so homogeneous, was in fact a partnership of incompatibles. True, the Austrians and the Germans spoke the same language, shared the same culture, and bordered on common frontiers. True also, the political and military alliance between them had existed ever since 1879 in Bismarck's day and had become one of the constants of the European power equation. How much more natural and solid this looked than the opposing alliance of the *Entente* powers, whose basic members, England and France, had been at each other's throats until 1904; whose third partner, Tsarist Russia, was an autocracy remote in both geography and politics from the Western democracies; and whose fourth great member, America, lay across a great ocean and outside Europe altogether! Yet appearances deceived. As Bismarck had shrewdly perceived, even in his day, the aims and interests of Berlin and Vienna could never be smoothly harnessed together in the long run.†

Sure enough, many of these basic discrepancies had come to the surface in Charles's time. Some were merely questions of military prestige and grand strategy such as those disputes, already described, over U-boat warfare, over the organization of the Supreme Command or the priorities of the various battlefronts. Others were political confrontations which went deeper because they concerned the peacetime map of Europe. Into this category came, above all, the long wrangle between Berlin and Vienna over the future of the new Poland. On the political as on the military plane it was the Germans who nearly always won.

But there was one discrepancy more vital than any of these. This was the contradiction between the basic political philosophies of the Habsburg and Wilhelmian Empires which sprang from contrasts in the character and history of their peoples and centred on their opposing attitudes to nationalism. The German Empire was built upon and could only thrive upon an unvarnished and blatant nationalist ego. The multi-racial Dual Monarchy was built on ancient if shaky supranational foundations and simply could not survive if these were knocked away. When Bethmann-Hollweg, one of the more moderate of Germany's statesmen, spoke of the 1914 war as 'a fight to the finish between Germans and Slavs', meaning, of

---

* The other two members, who counted for relatively little, were Turkey and Bulgaria.

† The reason, of course, for his expulsion of Austria-Hungary from the German Confederation in 1866.

course, the Russians, he put his finger unwittingly on the fatal breach between the two allies. In many ways they lived in and for different worlds. Slavs accounted for some fifty per cent of the Empire's fifty million subjects. Vienna's real 'fight to the finish' was to keep them in the fold at all. This was the clash that Charles had seen and dreaded between the Prussian pot of iron and his own very breakable pot of clay. The two were now to come far too close together for his comfort.

Throughout April, pressure on the Emperor to take some dramatic step to 'clear the air' with Germany had increased. The very active and influential German Ambassador in Vienna, Count Wedel, pulled all the wires he could – and they were many – among Austria's indignant pan-German camp. He also attacked frontally. In a talk with the reinstated Burian on 23 April, he told the Austrian Foreign Minister bluntly that 'since Germany's confidence in its ally had recently come in for some severe buffeting, his country had to demand a clear and binding answer'.* On top of this pressure came the sobering telegrams from his opposite number in Berlin, the Austrian Ambassador Prince Gottfried Hohenlohe. This sorely-tried envoy had known nothing of the whole Sixtus affair and his task had not been exactly simplified by its sudden revelation now. Hohenlohe had hurried home for enlightenment and instructions when the Czernin crisis broke out and his first report to his new chief, Burian, on returning to his post, made grim reading.†

'I had never doubted,' it began, 'that the events of the past week would influence opinion against the Monarchy in the most unfavourable manner imaginable and unfortunately I have found these fears more than justified on my return.' Whenever, the envoy added, he tried to discuss with German officials anything affecting future relations between the two countries, he was met with 'evasive answers from which one could recognize only too clearly a total reserve and a boundless mistrust'.

In Vienna, the pan-German press‡ shouted for an act of atonement and the call was echoed in Budapest which, as ever, was steering on a Berlin tack. Among the Emperor's principal advisers, Burian pleaded for a gesture of solidarity with Germany in order to restore something of the alliance's shattered image abroad. Arz, the Chief of Staff, offered his own resignation if it would help the cause of military solidarity at home. When this was declined by Charles, the general pressed his sovereign, in the interests of the two Armies, to have an early meeting with the Emperor

* German AA, Oesterreich 95, 24 April 1918.

† Austrian State Archives: 174 PA III Preussen 1918. Telegram No. 4522 of 24 April 1918.

‡ It was rumoured that Czernin not only encouraged this newspaper campaign but actually helped to finance it. These allegations have never, however, been proven.

William, which could easily be arranged through staff channels. This was the solution adopted. On 11 May 1918, Charles arrived with his suite of advisers at the Belgian town of Spa, then the Headquarters of the German Army, where the Emperor William awaited him.

The Spa meeting has often been called Charles's 'journey to Canossa'. It may have been that in a political sense, but it was not in any personal sense. He seems to have been on the attack himself from the moment the German Emperor greeted him on the railway platform. The Sixtus 'disclosure', Charles told William, was exactly what he had spoken of at their Homburg talks in April 1917, when he had informed the German Emperor that secret peace-feelers had been put out from Vienna to the *Entente*, through the trusted intermediary he had refused to name. Furthermore, in ministerial contacts between the two allies at the time, Austria had specifically offered to sacrifice Galicia * if Germany were prepared to make the necessary concessions over Alsace-Lorraine in the cause of general peace. If the German side had not tried to veto such talks then, Charles pointed out, it had no right to climb on a high horse now.

Yet if Charles escaped from Spa with his personal dignity – and indeed his warm friendly relations with his fellow Emperor – more or less intact, a reckoning still had to be settled between the two Governments. The understanding between the two sovereigns and their chief ministers was couched in general terms: it recorded their agreement on basic principles to prolong and to broaden further the existing alliance. But the copy of this memorandum which has survived in the Austrian archives † shows that what Germany was really after was to convert the alliance into a disguised annexation. It set out the following three aims, to be realized 'with the greatest possible speed':

I. The construction of a close and long-term political treaty between the two Empires which would serve their mutual security and defence.

II. The conclusion of a military pact (*Waffenbund*).

III. The achievement of maximum possible economic co-ordination between Germany and Austria-Hungary *with the final aim of creating one unified economic territory*.

This was not far short of the *Zusammenschluss* or fusion policy which Adolf Hitler originally had in mind for Austria when German troops marched over the border twenty years later, only to be tempted into a

---

* See p. 75.

† PA Rot 505 Liasse XLVII 3/23–9 Krieg Geheim. I say 'survived' because so much on Austrian foreign policy and especially on relations with Germany was removed by the Nazis in 1938 or disappeared during the first months of the Russian occupation in 1945.

complete take-over by the ecstatic welcome given him by the Republic's misguided pan-Germans.*

At Spa, the Austrians did, it is true, manage to resist any immediate political commitment and to insert one important general reservation. It was agreed that: 'A final solution to the questions listed I–III above is conditional upon agreement on the Polish issue.' This gave endless opportunities for delay and bargaining in the ensuing political discussions over Point I. These began in Berlin the following month and meandered on from draft to draft † until the collapse of November 1918 blew both empires to pieces. It also helped the Austrian economic experts, who talked with their German colleagues throughout the summer at Salzburg on Point III, to conclude a tariff deal in the last weeks of the war that was not too unfavourable from Vienna's point of view.‡

But it was the military front, Point II, which was the only one that interested Hindenburg and Ludendorff for the moment. Here, the Germans carved out their pound of flesh straight away on the table. Before the Austrian delegation left Spa, General Arz put his signature alongside Hindenburg's on 12 May 1918, to some very detailed and far-reaching commitments concerning the new *Waffenbund*. The most important of these seven articles laid down that, in the interests of total mobilization, the rules guiding the organization and deployment of the two Armies would be synchronized; that all their weapons and ammunition would be standardized and their supply unified 'for future wars'; and that an exchange of officers, including commanding officers, should be introduced.§

A contemporary document dealing with these military provisions is in the Austrian Archives,¶ marked in pencil 'German proposal'. With one exception, the seven points it lists are identical with those actually signed at Spa. A single sentence of this German draft was omitted from the final version. It ran: 'Troop contingents from one army must be made capable of incorporation within the other.' Evidently Charles and his advisers had been able to convince even the eager Hindenburg that Croat or Slovene regiments from the Austro-Hungarian Empire could not very well be transferred bodily to German divisions who were supposed to be waging a 'fight to the finish against the Slavs'. However, the principle that German

---

* See *The Anschluss*, by the present author.

† For photostat of one draft extending the political treaty until 1 January 1940, see Appendix 4. (Austrian Archives. PA Rot 505 Liasse XLVII, as above.)

‡ Nearly all Austrian goods were to have free access to the German market whereas a wide range of Austrian products were given tariff protection. The agreement, of course, was almost immediately a dead letter.

§ See Arz, *op. cit.*, p. 251.

¶ Also in PA Rot 505, Liasse XLVII.

officers might command Austria's multi-racial formations had been conceded. Like much else in that *Waffenbund* General Arz had signed, it was something Charles had always managed to resist in the past.* Indeed, he had first fought successfully against this particular German proposal when still an Archduke commanding the 12th Army in Galicia in August 1916.

Yet, as Emperor, he now had to accept it all as necessary to relieve the ugly tensions of the day. The Empress, who did not accompany him to Spa, recalls the grim reluctance with which he set out, and also his attempts to talk some courage into his accompanying advisers – all of whom, except the experienced Burian, seemed quite cowed by the approaching encounter. In this respect, the Spa talks were to bring Charles one moment of light relief. The Empress recalls:

'Though my husband knew he had to go to Spa, if only to clear the air with the Emperor William and keep our own pan-Germans quiet at home, he was determined not to sign any actual political treaty there and he tried to imbue his ministers with this same firm line.

'At one moment when a new treaty of this sort was being advocated by the Germans in plenary session, the Emperor William suddenly cried out to the Austrian delegation:

' "What's wrong about it? Bavaria has already signed the same convention with us, and is quite happy with it."

'Bavaria, of course, was one of the units of the German Empire, ruled from Berlin, and to compare her in status with the Austro-Hungarian Empire was a dreadful *faux-pas*. There was an awkward silence, and Ludendorff was seen to go red in the face with embarrassment at his Emperor's blunder. My husband was able to look across at his ministers in silent delight, as much as to say: "What did I tell you, gentlemen, they *do* want to make a second Bavaria out of us." '

But what mattered, alas, was not what Charles and his ministers had thought and made of Germany's intentions at Spa, but how that meeting

---

* The whole Spa agreement represented, for the Germans, a victory for the policy of a closer alliance under tighter Berlin control which they had been urging ever since the outbreak of war. As early as 13 November 1915, the Austrians received a memorandum from their German allies suggesting a customs union and a military convention between the two countries, a proposal to which Vienna returned a cool reply. Hindenburg went further by openly advocating German interference in Austrian affairs exactly a year later, in November 1916, the month Charles came to the throne. On 22 October 1917, Czernin actually drew up with the German State Secretary Kuhlmann a strictly provisional set of six Articles for a new treaty of which the first sets the exact pattern for the Spa provisions of six months later. (PA Rot 524, Liasse XLVII 13.) These Articles do not appear to have been brought to Charles's notice at the time.

was viewed in the *Entente* camp. And to the Western allies it *did* look as though the Dual Monarchy was fast on the road to becoming a second Bavaria in the spring of 1918. This – not the actual concessions that the Austrians made – was the real tragedy of the Spa meeting for the Empire, and the real measure of the harm Czernin had inflicted on his country.

As soon as the scandal had broken out the month before, President Wilson expressed forebodings that it would 'rivet' the Dual Monarchy to Germany. All those weak doves of Austrian peace which had been fluttering towards him via Madrid were indeed scarcely worth receiving now. His Secretary of State Lansing was even more outspoken. In a memorandum written on 12 April, when the crisis in Vienna was at its height, he described Clemenceau's action in publishing the text of the secret Sixtus letter as 'a piece of the most astounding stupidity for which no sufficient excuse can be made'. The American Secretary went on:

If Clemenceau sought to prove that Count Czernin was a liar he possibly succeeded, but at what a cost! His disclosure has thrown Austria bodily into the arms of Germany.*

The summit meeting of the two allies at Spa seemed rapidly to have borne out these fears. A special appreciation, drawn up for the British Cabinet by the Foreign Office on 30 May 1918, stressed that the proposed new treaty between the two Central Powers had converted their existing military alliance into a 'permanent community of interests' for peacetime as well.† Furthermore, the Western allies soon had evidence that, even in short-term military questions, Vienna was now being strung more tightly to the Prussian bow. Between June and September 1918, six Austro-Hungarian divisions which had hitherto been fighting on the Italian front were identified in action in the West.

It was no wonder that the *Entente*'s very important psychological warfare campaign ‡ – which was by now getting under way in earnest under London's direction – should begin to harp, as one of its main themes, on Austria being 'yoked' to Germany. Nor was it surprising that Western statesmen should come to believe their propaganda. At the beginning of the year, as we have seen, the feeling still prevailed in Washington, London and Paris that the Habsburg Empire – if only it could put its own political house in order – was the natural counterbalancing influence in a continental Europe more overshadowed than ever by Germany following the Russian collapse.

* Robert Lansing, *War Memoirs*, p. 265.
† Public Record Office, CAB 24/53.
‡ See Chapter 12, pp. 163–4

Now, it seemed, this counterbalancing weight had transferred itself bodily to the Berlin scales. The whole purpose of Lloyd George's 'diplomacy of mobility', the whole message behind those eloquent pleas General Smuts had put to Austria in his name at Geneva – all this seemed written off. For most *Entente* statesmen, the Dual Monarchy had now become part of that menace of a German *Mitteleuropa* whose shadow loomed over Europe in peace and war.* So, to remove the menace, the Austrian Empire had to go as well. The irony that its Emperor dreaded Berlin's dreams of hegemony just as much as they did was left for the history books to record. The strong personal sympathy felt for Charles on the enemy side had anyway been sharply reduced by the baffling but disturbing implications of the Czernin scandal. From the summer of 1918 onwards, hardly an influential voice was raised any more in the *Entente* camp to preserve the young ruler or his archaic realm. The *émigrés*' cry of '*Austria delenda est*' was picked up instead, and soon swept all before it.

* For the most recent compendious treatment of this familiar theme, see Fischer, *Germany's Aims in the First World War.*

7 The Emperor Franz Josef on his death-bed, 21 November 1916. So ended at last the longest reign – sixty-eight years – in Europe's history. His relatively unknown great-nephew, the Archduke Charles, then only twenty-nine, now stepped into the place of this legendary figure, in the middle of a war that threatened the very existence of the multi-racial Austro-Hungarian Empire.

8 The legend is borne to the grave. On 30 November 1918, the new Emperor Charles, the new Empress Zita (completely veiled) with, between them, the new Crown Prince Otto, follow Franz Josef's coffin through the streets of Vienna at the head of the long procession of foreign princes and notabilities. The Emperor William of Germany, Austro-Hungary's principal ally in the war, was a notable absentee. He did not attend the full ceremonies 'for security reasons'.

9 Prince Sixtus of Bourbon-Parma, Charles's French brother-in-law, and his principal intermediary in the Emperor's famous secret peace overtures to Paris and London, in 1917, which have gone down in history as 'The Sixtus Affair'. The young prince had a keen political intellect and, despite his passionate French patriotism, was a fair go-between in this famous and ill-fated piece of old-style 'dynastic diplomacy'.

10 Charles's right-hand man at home during the first year of his reign, Arthur von Polzer-Hoditz. From his key confidential position as Head of the Emperor's Private Office, Polzer strove relentlessly and unsuccessfully to get a federal reform programme launched within the Empire during war-time. The conservatives throughout the Empire – and above all the powerful Hungarians, whom Polzer had sworn to 'cut down to size' – always managed to block his schemes.

A Contrast in Styles

11 The Villa Wartholz (right) was a Habsburg
family shooting lodge below the Rax Mountains
of Lower Austria which Charles loved more
than all his palaces put together. This
unpretentious and somewhat ugly building, set
in peaceful pine forests, was always, for him,
'home', and he escaped to it whenever he could.

12 Schönbrunn, the great Habsburg 'summer
palace' in Vienna (here seen from the park at the
rear) symbolized the pomp and protocol that
Charles tried to get away from. But it was in this
palace, built by the Empress Maria Theresa in
the 18th century that, in November 1918,
Charles and Zita watched their Empire dissolve
around them, and where they spent their last
days of rule.

13 The Empress Zita of Austro-Hungary (right) with the Empress Auguste Victoria of Germany, on a visit of the German royal couple to Laxenburg near Vienna in July 1917. Their parasols, like their husbands' policies, tilted different ways.

14 Allies and friends, but not soul-mates.

A wartime meeting in September 1917 between the two German-speaking monarchs, Charles (left) and the Emperor William. As was customary on such occasions, each is wearing the other's uniform. Charles said of his fellow-monarch: 'If Austria has a friend in Germany, it is the Emperor William.' But Charles feared and fought the Prussian militarists, symbolized by Ludendorff, who dominated the German ruler, and who pursued 'final victory' until it turned into total defeat.

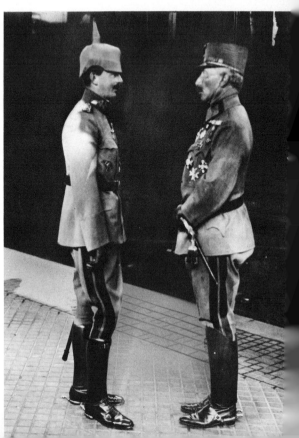

Chapter 12

AN EMPIRE CRUMBLES

Why and when does an avalanche actually start? Before it breaks loose, one can watch the snow piling up before a gale and sense that an unavoidable peril is there. Afterwards one can see where the trail of destruction has ended and what has been obliterated in its path. But how to mark that final thrust which sets even the inevitable into motion?

As regards the collapse of the 650-year-old Habsburg Empire in the autumn of 1918, two blows can perhaps be singled out from all the others to establish the beginning of the end. The first was political: the recognition by France, on 29 June 1918, of the Czechoslovaks' 'right to Independence' and of their *émigré* National Council in Paris as the 'basis of the future government'. The second came three months later and was military: the collapse on the battlefield on 25 September of Bulgaria, the smallest and weakest member of the Central Powers' alliance but the one who guarded the whole South-Eastern flank of the Austrian Empire. From this point onward the distinction between political and military disaster – always a complex inter-acting one in Vienna's case – becomes almost too blurred to separate any longer.

In a sense, of course, the first of these two events had been implicit in Wilson's Fourteen Points of January, with its pledge of 'autonomous development' for the peoples of the Dual Monarchy. But if this had been a disguised sentence of death on the Empire it had also been a suspended one. Austria-Hungary could still, in the *Entente*'s eyes, have saved herself by one or both of two desperate measures: wartime political reform at home and diplomatic defiance of Germany abroad. The refusal of Budapest to listen to the voices of reason and of the twentieth century continued to block all Charles's efforts in the first direction. The spring and early summer triumphs of the German Army in the West, and the heyday these brought to Austria's powerful pan-Germans, ruled out the other until it was too late.

With each month of 1918 that internal reform was further postponed, it became an even greater task to tackle. Radicalism, both in the domestic and in the *émigré* politics of the Empire's Slav peoples, was now rapidly gaining the upper hand. By the spring, for example, the extremist wing of the Slovenes, led in Ljubljana by Korosec, was already supplanting in influence Slovenia's traditional clerical leaders, who had always been loyal to the dynasty.* Even more startling was the parallel transformation at this time in the neighbouring South Slav territory of Croatia. For centuries, the Croats had been regarded as 'black-yellow'† almost to a man. A mixture of sentiment and political calculation (Vienna was their main hope of wriggling away from the Hungarians' grasp) had indeed made them a music-hall joke of dynastic devotion.

Now, this touching joke was ending. On 3 March 1918, the extremist wing of the so-called 'Party of Law', led by Starcevic, came out with a declaration calling for 'national independence and a democratic state for the Slovenes, Croats and Serbs'. Here was a solution at last to that famous South Slav problem, and one that had been looming up ever since the leaders of the three peoples, both in exile and at home, had met to compose their differences at Corfu eight months before. But it was a solution which excluded the Habsburg Empire and Crown, neither of which Starcevic had deigned to mention. Even Brutus was now drawing his dagger.

Throughout the winter months, this new mood of South Slav discontent had been fed by the example of the Bolshevik triumph in the great Slav brother country of Russia. It had been immensely stimulated also by those tens of thousands of the Empire's soldiers of all races and creeds who streamed back into the homeland from the now liquidated Eastern front, impressed (or 'infected' as the authorities would say) by what they had experienced there. Indeed, Trotsky, the Soviet negotiator at the later stages of the Brest-Litovsk conference, openly admitted afterwards that he had tried to draw out the parleys with the deliberate aim of spreading the Marxist creed into the enemy's camp by fraternization across the cease-fire lines. Royalist Russian officers warned Austrian officers of this danger at the time. The Austro-Hungarian prisoners of war who also now returned home from Russian camps presented an even graver problem of 'contamination'.

The Emperor, who had earlier opposed the smuggling of Lenin back to Russia even as a calculated move by Germany to weaken the enemy's resistance, now personally supervised emergency measures to contain the spread of the Bolshevik bacillus in his own lands. On 1 April 1918, a new 'counter-propaganda' department was set up at Austrian General

* For an excellent brief survey of these events, see Nowak, *op. cit.*, pp. 165–76.
† The Habsburg family colours.

Headquarters. Special reception camps were established where the return-ing prisoners could, it was hoped, be politically 'cured' before being released among the civilian population again. The hope was only partly fulfilled. Vienna – unlike Munich on the one side and Budapest on the other – was to be spared even short doses of the Bolshevik fever in power. But everywhere in the Empire the example of Marxism triumphant served to inspire and strengthen the radical cause. From the moment the first crown on the continent toppled, all the others began to slip.

Then, to round off this momentous spring, had come that Czernin scandal and its political pendant, the Spa Treaty, whose effect on the Slav peoples of the Empire was to stir up still more the restlessness and dis-content which had already seized them. However limited Charles's so-called 'capitulation' had been in fact, in appearances the Spa meeting was a long-term victory for the pan-German cause and therefore a long-term menace to Slavs anywhere under the Habsburg sceptre.

It was typical that it should have been the Czechs – the people of the Empire whose whole history and life in Bohemia had been one long struggle against Germanic domination * – who showed the most dis-cernible reaction. Already in January, as we have seen, the Czech and Moravian deputies of all parties had produced, in their co-called 'Epiphany Declaration' a clear-cut demand for 'a free national life and self-determina-tion'. The following month, in the mutiny at the Gulf of Kotor, Czech sailors had carried that defiance into the Imperial Navy. Now, on 13 April, eleven days after Czernin's disastrous speech to the Vienna city fathers, the Union of Czech Deputies produced a direct retort to the anti-Czech remarks the Foreign Minister had made. It took the form of a renewed oath to a Czechoslovak state over which no Habsburg double-headed eagles would fly. And on 22 May 1918, only ten days after the communiqué of the two Emperors' meeting at Spa, even the right-wing Czech Christian Democrats were moved to demand independence; though, in their case, this was still envisaged within a federal monarchy of sorts.

While events in Vienna were sharpening these Slav spears, new tips were being simultaneously produced for them in the *Entente* camp. Early in 1918, the English journalist Wickham Steed and the Scottish historian R. W. Seton-Watson had begun work in London as special advisers to Lord Northcliffe, the Director of Propaganda in enemy territories. Both men were convinced that the Habsburg Empire must be pulled up by its

---

* Even the great feudal landowners of Bohemia – most of whom owed their estates to the Habsburgs and all of whom owed the dynasty their allegiance – were split roughly half and half between Czechophil and pan-German sentiments. Czernin was in the latter camp. In fact he hardly spoke his 'native' Czech tongue.

roots and cast aside to allow all the thrusting nationalities on its soil room for separate statehood. Both men were personal friends and political sponsors of the Empire's Slav *émigré* leaders like Masaryk, Benes and Trumbic. Both now put their heads together to secure, first from the Foreign Office and then from the War Cabinet, permission to promise national independence in the leaflets that they were preparing to unload over the multi-racial Austro-Hungarian formations fighting deep on Italian soil.*

Agreement was finally wrung out of a hesitant British Government in mid-March. The Cabinet, while still refusing to work for the dismantling of the Austro-Hungarian Empire as a political aim, consented to do so as a propaganda device. The reason, of course, was pragmatic: the serious military outlook for the *Entente* on both the Southern and Western fronts at that time. Thus in the same week that the Czernin scandal broke out in Vienna, the Empire was first declared dismembered down on the Italian front. All this, and those legendary battle-feats of the Czech Legion in Russia which followed, immeasurably strengthened the hand of the Czech *émigré* leaders. Through them, the status of all the exiled anti-Habsburg politicians – whether Polish or Serb, Croat or Rumanian – was in turn increased.

The French Government's formal recognition of the Czech National Council at the end of June was therefore the logical and even the likely outcome of a long preliminary process. It was nonetheless historic. Speeches could be offset by other speeches. Secret promises could be dishonoured. Army leaflets could be disowned. But diplomatic recognition of a small group of wandering exiles as the heirs to a slice of the Dual Monarchy set an irreversible official process in motion. On 14 August, six weeks after the French move, Britain followed suit by declaring the Czechs to be an 'Allied nation' and by bestowing upon all their military units fighting in the East, West and South the status of 'allied belligerent forces' waging regular war with the *Entente* against the armies of the Central Powers. Finally on 3 September, the United States, which had started off the whole process by rhetoric, completed that process by action and recognized the Paris-based National Council as the '*de facto* belligerent government of Czechoslovakia'.

As we shall see, this was to invalidate all Charles's attempts to negotiate an eleventh-hour settlement with President Wilson in October before they had begun. By then, he was no longer regarded in Washington as an Emperor but as the importunate owner of a large mansion that was being split into apartments and handed over to new tenants. Due largely to the

---

* See on this whole subject, Wickham Steed, *Through Thirty Years*.

dictates of a military emergency, the *Entente* powers, in the summer of 1918, thus proceeded to dismantle the Austrian Empire on paper three months before it began to crumble to pieces on the ground. It was the *coup de grâce* of the many blows that the battlefield dealt the home front of the Dual Monarchy.

That critical summer of 1918 was also the last period in which Charles and Zita could snatch even the illusion of a normal family life within their kingdom. The pressure on the young Emperor had, if possible, increased as the climax of both the war and the Empire's own political crisis bore down on him together. His brief spells with his wife and children (there were by now five of them: Otto, Adelheid, Robert, Felix and Karl Ludwig)* had to be prised by his adjutants out of a working day that very often lasted eighteen hours. These personal aides were five in number and they normally worked on a rota of twelve days' continuous duty, followed, in theory, by twelve days off. As one of them † commented: 'By the time our own twelve-day spell on duty came to an end, we were always exhausted although what we did was really only secretariat work without any great responsibility. But the Emperor kept going on the same schedule day after day without any off-duty or rest periods, and having to carry all the time the colossal responsibility for his decisions.'

In a typical day at Laxenburg, Charles would get up at 6 A.M. After hearing Mass in the castle chapel, he then breakfasted on that extraordinary meal of warm meat and mineral water which the Empress has described. 'Office hours' began at 7.15 A.M., either with the first audiences in Laxenburg itself or with the short drive across to Army Headquarters at Baden where the Emperor would often pass the rest of the day. Lunch with the Empress was cut to forty-five minutes – sometimes less – and work began almost immediately afterwards, lasting without any break until seven or eight in the evening. Dinner was an equally brief meal and then the procession of audiences, reports and conferences was resumed until around midnight, the final hours normally being reserved for General Arz, the Chief of Staff, and his daily survey of the military position on all fronts.

---

* Otto had been born at Reichenau on 20 November 1912; the eldest daughter, Adelheid, was also a pre-war child, born on 3 January 1914, at the Vienna palace of Hetzendorff which the Emperor Franz Josef had allotted to the young couple. Robert (8 February 1915) and Felix (31 May 1916) were both born in wartime at Schönbrunn when Charles was already heir-apparent. Karl Ludwig, who was born at Baden on 10 May 1918, was their only child as ruling sovereigns.

Three more children were to come during the years of exile: Rudolf (5 May 1919) and Charlotte (1 March 1921) in Switzerland and finally Elisabeth, who was born in Spain on 31 May 1922 – eight weeks after her father's death.

† Schonta, *Erinnerungen*, Vienna 1928. The details which follow are taken mainly from this book and from the Memoirs of another secretary, Baron Stefan Kray.

Only once did Charles's slightly suspect heart and his strong nerves give way for an hour or two, and that was under the unique personal stress of the Czernin scandal. That they held up under the strain at all other times was due, apart from self-control and an innate capacity for hard work, to the way the young ruler managed to build some simple pleasures into this relentless official programme. An occasional evening stalk after deer in the woods that surrounded his beloved Reichenau was all that the hunter could now allow himself (throughout the war, he never seems to have laid hands on his shotguns). But he satisfied his love of nature, and that craving for being in the open which underlay all his sportsman's enthusiasm, by transferring as much of his desk work and Court life as possible away from offices and audience-chambers and out into the open air.

At Laxenburg he received even highly secret visitors like Prince Sixtus in a corner of the castle park which was always specially reserved as an 'outdoor study'. At Baden, where the small two-storeyed 'Emperor's house' did not even run to proper grounds of its own, another villa with a decent garden close to the park of the spa was hired so that Charles could walk and talk under trees even at his Supreme Headquarters. At Schönbrunn, maximum use was made of the so-called 'Emperor's Garden'. All this, of course, was anathema to the old guard of courtiers for whom the crown was synonymous with ceremonial and to whom an imperial audience was inseparable from successive relays of chandeliers and anterooms. Charles respected their views without heeding them. The simplification and modernization of Habsburg Court etiquette was something he had resolved upon even as a young Archduke in peacetime. The austere demands of war had now given him, as Emperor, an excuse to let fresh air into the palaces, as well as to keep it in his own nostrils.

Charles also eased the burden by keeping his family life as much within the framework of his official life as the running of an Empire allowed. General Arz describes how, especially in the small house at Baden to which he was a daily visitor, the two existences were too close on top of each other to be kept apart all the time. Sometimes when the General arrived in the one study of the house to make his regular late-night visit, he would find Charles and his wife sitting together and occasionally the Empress would remain in the room, sewing or reading, until the report was finished – though Arz never recalls her intervening in the conversation, however casual it became.

Then there were the occasions, all too rare, when an official ceremony could be conducted throughout in a domestic setting. Such a day, for example, was 17 August 1918, the Emperor's thirty-first birthday, and the last he was ever to celebrate in his homeland. He spent it at that unpretentious and rather plain Villa Wartholz at Reichenau which he preferred to all his palaces. On this occasion, a small flock of generals, admirals and ordinary soldiers in field-grey uniform mingled with his family and the normal members of his household. Charles, who first of all received himself the Field-Marshal's baton as a birthday salute from his Army, then took the opportunity to pin the Maria Theresa Order, the highest military decoration the Empire had to bestow for bravery in the field, on twelve of his officers and men. Normally, the parade-ground of a barracks or the courtyard of a castle would have been the stage for such a ceremony. One who was present * said that the scene was none the less moving for being held on the terrace of a rambling shooting-box built against the background of the mountains.

Finally there were the state visits, either inside the Empire or abroad, which could sometimes bring Charles and his wife relaxation as well as work. One such example was the journey to Sofia and Constantinople which they made from 17–21 May as a goodwill pilgrimage to their Bulgarian and Turkish allies. Though in two and a half years' time they were to sail past that same Turkish capital in vastly different circumstances – as prisoners in a British cruiser on their way to final exile – this spring visit was a happy and glittering affair, and a contrast to that sombre journey to the Germans at Spa that had gone before it.

Six weeks later, on 16 July 1918, the royal couple paid an equally unforgettable visit to Pressburg, the principal city of their own Slovak people. It was unforgettable because the welcome they were given at this tense and bitter period equalled anything a popular sovereign could expect from his contented subjects in peacetime. The Empress recalls:

'The journey to Pressburg, which was for the Harvest Festival, was a wonderful experience. We went down the Danube by steamer, taking Otto with us and – because she so insisted – our eldest daughter Adelheid as well. The enthusiasm from the crowds was everywhere enormous and so obviously spontaneous. It was as if there was no war, and no separatist movements at home.

'The reception was such that we asked ourselves: "Is it all a dream?" In a sense of course it was. In the midst of all this joy there was for us sadness because we both knew that the cheering was genuine but deceptive. It had no substance, and the Emperor warned me against forming any illusions. He knew that, however much the ordinary people waved and cheered, the Empire simply could not go on much longer without peace abroad and reason at home.'

Two months later, all Charles's presentiments came true. King Ferdinand

* Schonta, *op. cit.*, pp. 116–17.

of Bulgaria, who had fêted him as a loyal ally that same spring, suddenly opted out of the war, and the Empire's swift slide into oblivion began.

The news from Sofia on 25 September came as no surprise to Charles. He had felt for some months, the Empress recalls, that the German-born Bulgarian monarch was 'looking for a way out'. Indeed, on more than one occasion he had expressed these fears to the Emperor William and had urged a precautionary strengthening of the south-eastern forces. The reply had always been that his apprehensions were groundless as 'Ferdinand knows it's to his own interest to stay with us'. But now, after the over-running of Bulgarian troops in Macedonia by the Allied 'Army of the Orient' under the French General Franchet d'Esperey, Ferdinand decided that his best interests were to drop his crown and run. At first he wanted to run to Austria and settle as a private citizen in the Marchfeld near Vienna, where he had an estate. But Charles would have none of that, for personal as well as political reasons. As the special train carrying this dubious ally away from his adopted kingdom rolled across the frontier, the Emperor sent out one of his court officials, Count Berchtold,* to intercept it. After a heated conversation in the middle of the night at the little Lower Austrian station of Marchegg, Ferdinand was persuaded to continue with his train back to his native Coburg.

But though Charles had lost no time getting rid of the Bulgarian King himself, the consequences of Ferdinand's flight could not be so easily dismissed. The collapse of Bulgaria was all the more menacing because it came at a desperate period in the fortunes of the Central Powers as a whole.

The previous month had seen not merely the end of the great German advance on the Western front but, on 8 August (Ludendorff's famous 'black day'), the beginnings† of that even greater *Entente* counter-offensive which was soon to bring the entire war to a finish. The implications of the German failure were discussed between the two Emperors at another conference at Spa on 14 August. (Though neither could have imagined it, this was to be the last time the two allied sovereigns would ever meet.)

The occasion and the mood were very different from that previous encounter of theirs in May. Even the buoyant, over-inflated confidence of Hindenburg and Ludendorff had now been punctured at last. This time, they made no objection when the Austrians repeated their old arguments

---

* The same man who, as Austro-Hungarian Foreign Minister, had helped to draft and had signed the ultimatum to Serbia in July 1914. Ever since Charles's accession he had been relegated to minor Court duties, which he fulfilled conscientiously and apparently contentedly.

† The first counter-blow was made by British troops who on that day launched a highly successful flank attack on the German positions between Ance and Avre.

that it was simply not possible to achieve an adequate peace through a military victory. There was not even a protest when General Arz, echoing the warnings of 1917, declared categorically that 'Austria-Hungary could only continue the war until December'.* Finally, there was now acceptance in principle on the German side that a new peace initiative would have to be made to the enemy camp.

But only in principle. The plan that was already forming in the Austrians' minds of a meeting on neutral soil between joint emissaries of the two sides† was not yet acceptable to the German Emperor and his advisers. Clinging to the hopes of at least partial military success in stemming the *Entente* advance, they wished to avoid anything that smacked of a premature 'act of desperation' and argued instead for more discreet mediation through a neutral third party such as the Queen of the Netherlands. This stultifying debate was to continue for weeks between Berlin and Vienna, wasting more precious time with every fruitless exchange of views that passed.‡

Such was the general atmosphere of gloom and frustration in which, at 7.30 in the evening of 25 September, King Ferdinand's telegram of surrender arrived at the Austrian Headquarters at Baden and was taken over to Charles in the little 'Emperor's House'. Though the event was not comparable in world significance with the German defeat in the West, its impact on the fortunes of the Dual Monarchy was instant and decisive. The Empire was suddenly cut off altogether from its fourth ally, Turkey, and the whole of its weakly-held Balkan front was now open to the advance of Franchet d'Esperey's Allied forces. As Burian succinctly put it: 'In jumping clear from us, Bulgaria has knocked the bottom out of the barrel.'

That remark was passed at a meeting of the Crown Council, presided over by Charles, which was held two days later, on 27 September 1918, to consider the lessons of the new situation. The Protocol, which shows that these lessons had been grasped in all directions, makes fascinating reading.§ Burian, who spoke first, said that the 'Bulgarian catastrophe' had severely worsened the Empire's position in every respect. In a prophetic comment which, if anything, undershot the mark, he added: 'It will have direct repercussions and also longer-term effects which we shall only begin to feel as time goes on.'

* See Arz, *op. cit.*, p. 284.

† It had first been submitted to the Emperor by Burian on 23 July 1918, and instantly taken up by the sovereign. (See Burian, *Austria in Dissolution*.)

‡ See, for example, Hohenlohe's reports from Berlin of 20 and 26 August 1918, Austrian Archives (PA Rot 505 Liasse XLVII 3/23–9).

§ Austrian Archives, XXXX 315 PA Interna 1918.

Burian then turned to the political moral to be drawn from the military collapse on the Empire's Balkan front:

The South Slav danger in its broadest form now stares us right in the face and positively demands a solution. The subversive trend whose most radical aspect can be found in the Korosec movement * has recently gathered the swiftest momentum. Today there is no time left for further deliberation. We must act, act as quickly as possible as long as we can still avoid the impression of our hand being forced. There is not a day to lose. . . . The longer a solution is postponed, the more unfavourable will be the impact of the South Slav movement on our other political problems. . . . Once a South Slav state has been created of its own accord, then the Bohemian question will arise to square the circle.

After much more in this domestic vein, the veteran diplomatist ended by stressing the parallel importance of 'continuing to spin our threads of peace' abroad and he foreshadowed the possible need for a 'concrete peace offer' to be made even within the next fortnight, 'formulating our conditions in fairly precise terms'.

It must have been an impressive speech to come from this normally reserved and cautious minister. Though the Hungarian Prime Minister spoke after him (still Wekerle, and still preaching the 'territorial integrity' of Dualism) and though General Arz added a detailed military appreciation of his own, it is above all Burian's plea for urgent political action which is reflected in Charles's summing-up. According again to the Protocol, the Emperor ordered 'the speediest start on the internal reconstruction of Austria' combined with 'a request to the Hungarian Government to state its views on the South Slav question'. Finally, picking up Burian's diplomatic argument, he called for 'energetic pressure on Germany in the peace question'.

On the peace issue, there seemed little hope of concrete progress. That wrangle with Berlin which had lasted throughout August as to whether a single mediator or a general conference was to be preferred had ended in deadlock. As a result, only a fortnight before this Crown Council meeting, Burian had been encouraged by his Emperor to act independently of Berlin. His 'Peace Note' of 14 September 1918 had called for an end to the speech-making on both sides and had proposed that the Governments of all states taking part in the war should meet on neutral soil for the 'confidential and non-committal discussion' of a peace settlement. The note had been virtually ignored by the statesmen of the entire *Entente* camp. In Berlin, it had only caused further irritation and blunt telegrams had been exchanged between the two Emperors. Appearances were soon to prove

* See p. 109.

deceptive, but it seemed in September that without a sudden change of heart in Germany nothing much could now be achieved on the diplomatic front.

On the closely-related home front, however, the decisions of that Crown Council of 27 September produced immediate and momentous results. The South Slav question, which four years before had touched off the Empire's last and greatest war, now sparked its last and greatest act of reconstruction. And what the old Emperor Franz Josef had always felt in his conservative bones was to come true. In reforming itself, the Empire destroyed itself.

The so-called 'Peoples' Manifesto' of 16 October 1918 – in which Charles proclaimed his Empire from that day forward to be a federation of independent nation-states – was the most far-reaching act both in his own life and in the life of the Dual Monarchy he had inherited. Like those other two initiatives with which he will always be associated, the July amnesty and the Sixtus diplomacy of 1917, it was essentially another move to end the fighting. That it ended the Empire as well showed how well-nigh impossible the task of wartime reform had always been, as well as how high the price of peace had now risen. But the link between the two, home and abroad, is still there, as always in Charles's reign. The October Manifesto is usually regarded as one of the last milestones in the Empire's domestic history. This, of course, it was. But it can only be fully understood when it is also seen as one of the Emperor's last stepping-stones to peace.

Though the final version was published in a rush, the origins of the Manifesto go far back. Even before he became heir to the throne, Charles, as we have seen, had fervently proclaimed himself a federalist to the one person he was least likely to deceive, his own fiancée. And when, early in his reign, Polzer's attempts to launch a federal reform in the thick of war had failed, at least there had been, by way of consolation, the setting-up of that special study group to work on the problem full-time.* This obscure body of men, already powerfully reinforced, began to come into their own on 27 July 1918, when Seidler, who had served as Austria's 'caretaker' Prime Minister for more than a year, was finally worn down by inter-racial parliamentary intrigue and resigned.

As usual, there was no statesman of the first order anywhere on the Vienna horizon to replace him. Nor was another second-grade politician easy to find with enough resolution to compensate for his lack of talent. The man Charles finally picked was Baron von Hussarek, a Professor of

* See p. 106.

Canon Law and a former Minister of Education. And the reason for this, the Empress recalls, was first that all the other candidates suggested proved unacceptable either to the Austro-Germans, the Czechs, the Poles, or the Magyars; and second that Charles thought he had found in this compromise choice the Prime Minister he could most easily bend to his will over the constitutional issue. The appointment of Hussarek was a sign that the Emperor had determined, if humanly possible, to give President Wilson an early and concrete answer to the 'self-determination' demand.

The new Prime Minister thus took office as the declared instrument and apostle of internal reform. Contrary to popular belief, however, he was not, and he never became, the apostle of all-out federalism. Hussarek saw the federal device primarily as a means of giving autonomy to the South Slavs *as a group of nations* and he originally envisaged an Empire consisting of four such independent groups under the Habsburg crown. These were to be: Austria in the centre with the German-speaking Sudeten areas added; Croatia and the neighbouring lands in the South; Hungary in the East, now stripped of those same Slav lands; and Galicia in the North with the Ukrainian territories tacked on. Like all of the dozens of theoretical ways of cutting up and re-stitching the Habsburg patchwork quilt, this one too left many rough edges sticking out. How was Budapest ever to be persuaded to abandon part of King Stephen's sacred heritage? Would the Czechs, rid at last of their German Sudeten fringe, ever be content with anything less than a pure Bohemian Republic or Kingdom?

But what concerns us here are not the practical flaws in Hussarek's reform ideas (there were flaws in everyone's) so much as their restricted scope. This particular approach was Quadralism, a curious variant of Franz Ferdinand's old ideas. It was not the true federalism of the Manifesto, giving equal independence to each of the Monarchy's races, that Hussarek finally signed. The real author of that was the prime federalist of the Empire, the Emperor himself.* It was also Charles, more than anyone else, who realized the futility of trying to chop the whole Empire up into four new units simply because the rearrangement looked more logical. He, as the crowned King of Hungary, knew that the Magyars would fight the loss of their Slav territories with something more than logic. And he, who had taken the oath in Budapest to safeguard those territories, and who had swung the ceremonial sword to all points of the compass to symbolize that oath, was the last man who could enforce that sacrifice against the will of his Hungarian Government. Throughout the summer, further attempts had been made to get the sacrifice accepted willingly by Buda-

* For an interesting new study of the October Manifesto, which makes use for the first time of Hussarek's family papers, see Rumpler, *Das Völkermanifest Kaiser Karls.*

pest: all in vain. The lesson was clear. Weeks before he issued his Manifesto, Charles was resigned to it being at best a two-stage operation. The idea of national autonomy for all the races of a new federal Empire could, of course, still be proclaimed by the Emperor as a principle. In practice, he knew it could only be immediately implemented in the Austrian half of the Dual Monarchy, where no Coronation oaths tied Charles's hands. His only hope was that the pressure of Vienna's example and of world opinion would drive the other half of the Empire into following suit.

If the Bulgarian collapse gave the first decisive impetus to the Manifesto, it was an unexpected development on the diplomatic front which provided the final thrust. In the last days of September, the miracle finally happened. This was not so much the defeat of the mighty German Army as the fact that the German generals admitted it. On 29 September Ludendorff and Hindenburg confessed to their Emperor that they could no longer offer even those 'partial successes' promised in August when the Austrian peace drive had been blocked at Spa. On 2 October the German High Command itself drew the conclusions from this confession by demanding from its own government and its allies an immediate armistice with the enemy to enable negotiations to start. Berlin now became as precipitate in its rush towards the conference table as, for four years past, it had been reluctant to move one inch from the battle-field. Only with difficulty did Burian in Vienna secure a forty-eight-hour delay. This was needed to enable the armistice move to be made jointly by the three surviving Central Powers and also to give Germany's new 'Peace Chancellor', the liberal Prince Max of Baden, time to take over office from Herling, the now discredited tool of the generals.

On 4 October Austria-Hungary, together with Germany and Turkey, duly addressed their parallel notes to President Wilson asking for an armistice, to be followed without delay by peace talks on the basis of the Fourteen Points. The Austrian message added its own gloss. The Dual Monarchy reminded Washington of all its previous attempts to secure peace and justice and claimed that it had only fought in self-defence. Peace-reform; reform-peace. Again came the direct interaction of the diplomatic with the domestic.

Already on 1 October Hussarek had read out to the Vienna Parliament the constitutional declaration foreshadowed in that Crown Council of 27 September. As can be imagined from what has been said of his personal views on reform, this eagerly-awaited bugle call had a few wobbly notes. True, it proclaimed national autonomy as the 'fruitful principle' on which the 'internal reconstruction of the Austrian lands' should be based. But though the four racial groupings of his Quadralist solution were no longer mentioned, it was still left vague as to how the autonomy promise would apply. Was it *territorial* self-determination leading to separate nation-states he was talking about, or simply a variant on that old Habsburg device of giving the nations greater cultural, linguistic and administrative freedom within the existing order? This latter was the game which Vienna had played for generations with the Czechs in a German-dominated Bohemia. It would not do to satisfy the naked and uncompromising *political* demands of the day. Nor did it satisfy Charles who knew, now more than ever, that those demands could only be met by a truly federal adventure.

There was something else that bothered Charles. Wekerle, still trying to gain both time and freedom of action for Hungary, was now pressing Hussarek to leave the Emperor out of the reform programme altogether. Why not, he urged, simply issue parallel declarations of intent by the *Governments* in Budapest and Vienna, of which Hussarek's speech to his Parliament could be regarded as the Austrian contribution? Such talk, the Emperor strongly suspected, was but another piece of Magyar procrastination, and his fears were confirmed by Wekerle's behaviour at another Crown Council meeting held on 2 October. This was the very day Vienna had learned of the German decision to sue for peace. Now, if ever, was the time for the domestic scene to be brought into step with the military-diplomatic one. Yet the Hungarian Prime Minister tried to get inserted in the note to President Wilson, which was under discussion, a passage declaring that the Dual Monarchy 'would look after the settlement of its internal problems by itself'. This would of course have made nonsense of that central principle of self-determination which the Empire was agreeing with Washington to adopt.

It was becoming increasingly plain to Charles that he would have to move ahead of both his Prime Ministers and, if some constitutional formula could be found, act alone. He can only have been strengthened in his convictions by the fact that, a fortnight before, his own Chief of Staff, General Arz, had made a rare incursion into politics by urging his master to solve the constitutional problems of the whole Monarchy by an Imperial manifesto, and had even submitted a draft.[*]

In the Crown Council of 2 October, the twin threads of peace and reform had actually crossed and re-crossed in the discussions. Yet in a sense the link between them was symbolized not so much by what happened at that meeting as by what failed to happen after it. Two days later, as we have seen, the notes to President Wilson had been sent off. And now

* Text in Rumpler, *op. cit.*, pp. 74–6. In his own Memoirs, curiously enough, General Arz gives no details.

everything hung fire in Imperial Vienna, including the great constitutional debate, until the bourgeois oracle of the White House gave utterance.

For five days nothing happened at all. Then, on 9 October, there was a partial answer. President Wilson acknowledged receipt of the German note, and demanded the immediate evacuation of France and Belgium as a pre-condition for the negotiations requested by Berlin. On the 11th, Germany accepted, after consulting her Austrian and Turkish allies. But there was still no American reply to Vienna. Hopes were not high. Lansing's comment to the Swedish Ambassador in Washington when this intermediary had handed over the Austrian message had been a taciturn: 'The response won't be very encouraging.' Yet somehow the delay, and the official news that the reply to Austria was still being prepared, gave some ground for optimism. Surely, the tone to Vienna would be milder than that adopted to Berlin? The suspense was in any case unbearable. It was to break it and, if possible, to influence Wilson in the right direction in drafting his response that Charles now decided to take matters into his own hands. His federal Manifesto was the result. In its purpose, it was as much a diplomatic document as a domestic blueprint, though in its effects, the balance was to be very different.

As though to emphasize the fact that, in the last analysis, the Emperor would indeed have to march ahead alone, both the Hungarian and the Austrian Governments resigned on that same 11 October. Both had been rent by arguments over Germany's acceptance of the Wilsonian conditions. Now that the American terms had been met, the two Prime Ministers felt obliged to throw in their hands at once. The sorely-tried Emperor decided to keep both of them in office in a *de facto* capacity until the great act of reform which they had all begun together had been launched. Hussarek's status was comparatively irrelevant. But the Hungarian crisis destroyed the last hope that Budapest might soon follow Vienna's example over reform, for it had reopened all the flood-gates of Magyar chauvinism.

Only the day before, 10 October, Wekerle had hurried to Vienna with three other Hungarian political leaders – Andrassy, Apponyi and the former Prime Minister, Tisza – to ask the Emperor in person whether it was true that he intended to proclaim a federal state. When assured by Charles that it was, they returned to Budapest to fill the air with cries of Hungary's 'thousand-year rights' and attacks on the whole Dualist system. Any faint prospect that may have existed of a compromise formula for eventual South Slav independence was swept away by this wave of national Hungarian fervour.

But by now the Emperor was past heeding the voice of Budapest. The fighting was clearly in its last weeks, so the massive argument for post-poning radical reform so long as the war continued was no longer valid. It had to be federalism or nothing to satisfy Wilson, especially as regards the Czechs, whose nationhood he had recently recognized, and Charles himself had always been a federalist at heart. Above all, something radical had to happen now.* After five days of feverish consultation with all manner of advisers over the drafting – during which time it was the Emperor, not his resigned Prime Minister, who stood at the centre of the discussions – the final text was agreed at a Crown Council meeting of 15 October.† On the early evening of the 16th, after further 'last-minute' revisions (which in fact went on throughout the day), Charles gave the signal from Schönbrunn Palace for it to be proclaimed.

The vital passage of the 'Peoples' Manifesto' ran as follows:

Following the will of its peoples, Austria shall become a federal state (*Bundes-staat*), in which each racial component shall form its own state organization in its territory of settlement. . . . This reconstruction, *which shall in no way affect the integrity of the lands of the sacred Hungarian Crown,*‡ shall guarantee to each national individual state its independence. . . . Until this reorganization is completed through legal processes, the existing institutions shall remain in force unchanged to safeguard the general interest. . . .

To those peoples on whose rights of self-determination the new Empire will be built, *my call goes out to help implement the great work through National Councils* ‡ which – made up of the parliamentary deputies of each nation – shall represent the interests of the peoples with each other and in contact with my government.

The origins of these critical passages were as remarkable as their content. That definition of the proposed new units, for example (races within the 'territory of settlement'), was, to anyone familiar with the Empire's political jargon, the pure language of the old Czechs-versus-Germans struggle in Bohemia: which of those two races had settled first and where and with what rights, in the twelfth century and before? § Indeed, the phrase does seem to have been taken over by the Emperor from a draft reform plan originally composed by Vienna's Austro-German deputies and submitted to him by the Minister of Agriculture, Count Silva-Tarouca, on 10 October.¶ To its authors, this formula was, of course,

---

* Messages just received from Skrzynski in Berne, and quoting American confidential sources, had confirmed the need for immediate action.

† Unfortunately, the minutes of this historic meeting have not survived. There is a gap in the Austrian Archive records for that day marked, 'Never entered in the files'.

‡ Author's italic.

§ See p. 34.

¶ See Eichhoff, *Die Wahrheit über das Oktobermanifest, Neues Wiener Journal,* 31 March 1945.

designed to stabilize the position of what later became known as the 'Sudeten Germans' in the face of growing Czech nationalist pressure all around them. To the Emperor, the wording seemed convenient both as a means of pacifying Wilson over this same Czech issue, to which the American President was particularly committed, and as a general description for the new basic units into which the Austrian half of the Empire was to be split. Thus the great reform project which had started off three weeks before primarily as a means of solving the South Slav problem in the wake of the Bulgarian military collapse was ending as an instrument to settle the North Slav problem in the face of American diplomatic pressure.

That passage which specifically exempted Hungary from the provisions of the Manifesto was also the product of outside interests. As we have seen, Charles had reconciled himself – certainly for weeks past and perhaps for months – to the fact that Budapest would not join with Vienna in any immediate reconstruction of the Dual Monarchy. The only hope was for *subsequent* parallel action by his Hungarian Government. The limitation of the Manifesto to 'My loyal *Austrian* peoples' was not therefore, as is usually suggested, the result of any last-ditch fight made by Wekerle on 15 October. What the Hungarian Prime Minister did fight for on that crucial day * was something else: his own wording of the exemption clause, which was more categoric than either the Emperor or his Austrian advisers would have preferred. It seems strange, however, that Wekerle would need to threaten to cut off all Hungarian food supplies (as Hussarek once claimed) just to achieve this amendment. Charles's loyalty to his Budapest coronation oath, which the Emperor had himself stressed at the opening of the 15 October Council,† ought to have sufficed.

As for the Austrian Prime Minister, he had found himself putting his signature under that of his Emperor to a drastic reform plan which was very different from his original intentions and into which he had finally been hustled by his sovereign. Gone was all thought of dividing the whole Empire into three or four racial groupings, each of one or more nations. There was no longer even talk of splitting just the Austrian half into such regional components.‡ There was, in fact, no longer the hope nor the intention of maintaining a centralized control from Vienna in any form except through allegiance to the dynasty. The Manifesto's call to each

* He did not arrive in Vienna until after the decisive Crown Council meeting of 15 October was ended, but spent most of the afternoon with the Emperor, Hussarek and other Austrian politicians.

† Though, as stated, no official minutes have survived, accounts of the proceedings have been given by participants like Hussarek and Spitzmüller.

‡ One such plan for Austria only envisaged four separate states: a German-Austrian, a Czech, a South Slav and a Ukrainian.

nation-state to help itself to independence with noth hands by creating its own responsible National Councils had sounded the death-knell of this. It also marked the end of that centuries-old confrontation between the individual races of the Empire and the 'historic' provinces of the crown which had always enveloped them. The races – now declared by their common sovereign to be nation-states – had won, and a new sort of history had begun to be written.

In its vital diplomatic aim – that of persuading President Wilson to negotiate with an Empire now publicly dedicated to federal reform – Charles's Manifesto was a bitter disappointment. The White House waited four more days to digest the contents and the implications of the Emperor's latest move and then, on 20 October, sent Vienna the eagerly-awaited reply. Its message in effect consisted of two words: 'Too late.'

The President stated that he was 'unable at present to entertain proposals from the Austro-Hungarian Government because certain events of the greatest importance, which have occurred since his statement of 8 January, have necessarily changed the attitude and the duty of the United States of America'. Quoting the Tenth of the Fourteen Points, dealing with self-determination, that he had announced on that day, Wilson's note continued:

Since that sentence was written . . . the government of the United States has recognized that a state of belligerence exists between the Czecho-Slovaks and the German and Austro-Hungarian Empires and that the Czecho-Slovak National Council is a *de facto* belligerent government clothed with proper authority to direct the military and political affairs of the Czecho-Slovaks. It has also recognized in the fullest manner the justice of the nationalistic aspirations of the Yugo-Slavs for freedom.

The President is, therefore, no longer at liberty to accept the mere 'autonomy' of these peoples as a basis for peace but is obliged to insist that they, and not he, shall be the judges of what action on the part of the Austro-Hungarian government will satisfy their aspirations. . . .

In logic, this reply was as full of holes as a fish-net. Charles had granted more than 'autonomy'. He had introduced into his Empire Wilson's own principle of 'self-determination' in the terms in which it had been proclaimed nine months before. Indeed, it was the American President, befuddled by the *émigré* leaders, who now called this principle into question by announcing support for two new composite 'nations', the Czecho-Slovaks and the Yugo-Slavs, which had never existed in history and did not exist then. But such debating points were irrelevant. The United States had decided by October that Europe could now do without its Central Empires, whereas it had still been a continent of the old order to which

Washington had addressed itself in January. It was no longer reform that the White House wanted from Charles. It was his crown.

But if the Manifesto disappointed its author by having too little effect abroad, it now startled him and everyone else by having too much effect at home. The ultimate of all the Habsburg ironies was that this one instrument which was capable of knitting the Empire's peoples together was now used by them instead to slash the whole dynastic fabric apart. Over his own signature, the Emperor had called on his peoples to claim their independence – assuming, though not actually insisting, that they would remain as free nations under his rule. One by one, they staked their claims for separatism. One by one, they ducked under the sceptre.

The Czechs, those pacemakers in radicalism for whom, in the end, the Manifesto had been largely designed, led the way yet again. A week after the Manifesto, their principal leaders had gathered in Vienna on their way to Geneva to confer with their triumphant colleague in exile, Eduard Benes. (The Austrian Government, now anxious not to appear obstructive even to its declared enemies, had issued them with the necessary travel documents in what was to be one of its last acts of authority over Prague.) Only two of the five-man delegation, Kramar and Stanek, were still rated as monarchists, and they never appear to have got to the Emperor while in Vienna. Their colleague who did, the Socialist Klofac, left Charles under little doubt, after an audience on 22 October, that the Czech lands were slipping away from the crown altogether. This too was the general mood at their critical Geneva talks with Benes a week later, at which the Prague leaders, by implication, accepted the leadership of the anti-Habsburg *émigrés*.* By the last week of October, therefore, the Czech politicians, already constituted as the new National Council on the authority of the Manifesto, were poised to take over power from the Imperial authorities in Prague. But, once again, it was Charles's search to end the war which helped to end his Empire as well. On 27 October the Emperor replaced Hussarek – *in statu demissionis* for more than a fortnight – with the well-known Professor of International Law, Heinrich Lammasch. At the same time, Burian was succeeded as Foreign Minister by Julius Andrassy, son of the great Hungarian statesman who had signed the Empire's treaty of alliance with Germany nearly forty years before.

The son was being called upon to dismantle his father's work in an attempt to save his sovereign's inheritance. For just as Hussarek had been appointed to carry out reform at home, this shadowy 'Government' of Lammasch had been put there in its place to make one final appeal for

---

* At least they agreed to take no further action in Prague without the consent of the exiles' committee in Paris. (See Zeman, *op. cit.*, p. 225.)

peace abroad. The time pressure was such that the appeal obviously had to go direct to President Wilson and be drafted without previous consultation in Berlin. Charles decided to go one step further and formally exclude his German ally from the Austrian move. In a warning telegram sent to the Emperor William on 27 October he informed his 'dear friend' of his resolve in terms of dynastic duty that he hoped the Hohenzollern ruler might accept:

Even the closest fraternal and friendly feelings of brotherly alliance must yield before the consideration that I must save the existence of those states whose fate has been entrusted to me by divine providence. For this reason I must inform you of my unalterable resolve to sue within the next twenty-four hours for a separate peace and an immediate armistice. I cannot do otherwise; my conscience as a sovereign commands me to act in this way.

Immediately the German Emperor telegraphed back to Vienna expressing his pained surprise at the message and appealing to Charles to approach the United States only jointly and 'in the fullest agreement' with his own Government.* But Charles could no longer afford to listen. On the same day that the Emperor William's appeal reached Schönbrunn, 27 October, the Austrian note was sent on its way to Washington via Stockholm. In this, the Austro-Hungarian Government declared itself ready to conclude an armistice and commence peace talks 'without waiting for the results of any other negotiations'. The famous 'separate peace' had been launched at last, in the hour of desperation. An official commentary issued simultaneously in Vienna pointed out that the federal reforms just started in the Empire went even further than President Wilson's original 'autonomy' demands and stressed that there was anyway no longer any dispute over the 'completely free decision' to be made by the South Slavs and the *Czechoslovaks*. The 'nation' that Masaryk and Benes had created from exile was now, for the first time, included in the Empire's own political vocabulary.

The immediate and only effect of Charles's note, which failed completely to influence Wilson, was to bring that new state into being on the ground. Vienna had publicly severed that bond with Berlin which the Czech leaders feared so much. Henceforth they need look only to the American President, and they knew where they stood with him.

The very next day, 28 October 1918, the National Council in Prague stretched out for power. To their surprise, they took it from the limp fingers of the Emperor's custodians without a single shot being fired. Two of their members began the day by walking into the Corn Distribution Office in the capital and taking it over in the Council's name. This gave

* For photostat of text see Appendix 5.

them command of the country's food supplies. They then entered the office of the Imperial Governor and simply informed the staff that henceforth they had decided to run the administration of the country themselves 'in the public interest'. In the evening, the Council met in full to proclaim, in its first law, what was by now an accomplished fact: 'The independent Czechoslovak state is herewith founded.' Later that same night, the last danger to this swift and bloodless transfer of power was removed when the commander of the imperial garrison in Prague pledged his co-operation.

There was no question of treason in all this. Like the rest of the Emperor's servants that day in Prague, the bewildered general no longer knew for certain where logic or legitimacy or the true path of duty lay. The path of prudence, on the other hand, looked broad and inviting enough. Events seemed to be moving of their own accord in a limbo between past and present. Yet the momentum still came from the past. For even if the Habsburg double-headed eagle was already being torn down from some public buildings, the National Council men who now sat inside those buildings had got there on the Emperor's sanction. He had called them into being and nothing short of that twelve-day-old Manifesto could have enabled this almost trance-like end to four centuries of Habsburg rule in Prague to take place. The greatest tribute to Imperial authority had been the swift and bloodless way in which it wound itself up.

There was soon no doubt that even its title had ended as well and that the new nationalist leaders intended to take the Czech and Slovak peoples right out of the monarchy. Their representative in Vienna, Vlatismil Tusar, who had hitherto been merely the delegate of an undefined Government in embryo, was now given full powers by the Prague Council to liquidate all ties with the Habsburg crown. The Austrian Government accepted the inevitable with grace. On 30 October came Tusar's well-known interview with Professor Lammasch.

'Your Excellency,' the Emperor's new Prime Minister announced, 'I take pleasure in welcoming you as the Ambassador of the new Czechoslovak state.'

'Sir,' the even newer ambassador replied, 'the pleasure is all mine.'

The Empire's other Slav capitals rapidly followed Prague's lead. For all practical purposes, the Croats had themselves been independent of their Hungarian overlords since the beginning of the month. Charles had

* To placate the Croats further (and also to forestall an imminent meeting) Charles, on 30 October, ordered the transfer of the entire Austro-Hungarian Adriatic fleet to the newly independent Croatian state. South Slav joy at this was unconfined but brief. Within the week, Italian, American and French squadrons sailed into the Adriatic harbours of Pola, Sebenico and Cattaro, hauled down the new flags, and proceeded to divide the former Imperial navy up among themselves.

certainly not discouraged them in this, hoping to keep the loyalty of at least this one traditionally pro-Habsburg people.* But when, on 29 October, the Croatian 'Sabor' or Diet met in Agram to pronounce on the nation's future, it was to sever all ties with Vienna as well as with Budapest. The territories of Croatia, Slavonia, Dalmatia and Fiume were declared independent of both Austria and Hungary, and proclaimed part of the 'Common Sovereign National State of the Slovenians, Croatians and Serbs'. Though there was still total confusion as to what precisely this new state was and how it should be formed, the National Assembly of the Slovenes in Laibach promptly copied the Croat example and, on 31 October, proclaimed their independence.

By this time the Polish National Committee in the north, though not so well established politically and diplomatically as the other Slav bodies, had taken over the day-to-day administration of all the territories under Austro-Hungarian occupation. Next door to them, their bitter rivals, the Ukrainians, had proclaimed a West Ukrainian Republic at Przemysl. By 31 October, when the Rumanians in the East of the Empire declared their independence, all the outer ramparts of the Dual Monarchy had crumbled away.

What, in the meantime, of that central bastion of the 'lands across the Leitha', the twin capital of Budapest itself? Charles had left Vienna with his wife for his Hungarian kingdom on the evening of 22 October and he was there during the five critical days in the Empire's life that followed. His first destination was Debrecen, the great Calvinist centre of Eastern Hungary, and the town from where, on 14 April 1849, Louis Kossuth had declared the House of Habsburg to have forfeited St Stephen's crown for ever. A second and far deadlier revolution was just about to erupt in Hungary. Yet the reception that Debrecen now gave its royal couple, who had gone there to open the university, seemed to mock both the memories of Kossuth's threats sixty years before and the realities of Count Karolyi's radical challenge in the present. It was that Harvest Festival visit to Pressburg all over again: scenes of wild popular enthusiasm, real yet unreal, a salute that was almost hysterical, perhaps because the crowds sensed that it was final.

That strange day in Debrecen was indeed to be the last that Charles and his wife were ever to spend away from all the shadows of war and politics and in the sunlight of old-fashioned dynastic devotion. As the Court train turned westwards again they seemed to run straight back into the thunder-clouds. The train was soon halted by urgent signals trying to contact its Hughes telegraphic apparatus. The messages which now came through on the printer all spelled disaster. Revolt had broken out in Fiume, with Croat military units on the side of the demonstrators. Ahead of them in Budapest, riots and plundering had taken place and the Government of Wekerle had now fallen for good. It was a sombre Emperor who, late that night, reached his lovely baroque palace of Gödöllö close to the capital.

The alarm bells continued to ring throughout the next day, 24 October. A major enemy offensive was reported from the Italian front, with powerful new contingents of French and British troops in action. From Berlin came the first serious hints that the Hohenzollern crown was none too secure on the Emperor William's head – a prospect that posed some hitherto unaskable questions about Charles's own future. Vienna pressed for the Emperor to return. Austria, like Hungary, was without a Government. A new Foreign Minister had to be appointed and the final appeal to President Wilson drafted and despatched. But the Hungarian crisis, which was just as grave, had to be solved as well. As he was at its centre, Charles stayed on at Gödöllö (where his children had by now arrived) for three more days in a vain attempt to unravel it.

The Hungarian political kaleidoscope was shifting from hour to hour. At its centre there still stood the old phalanx of the conservative Magyar aristocracy, with the former Prime Minister Tisza as its dominant figure. But their power was fast flowing out to the three 'reform' parties of the Left: the Social Democrats, the Radicals, and the Independents. This last group was headed by Count Michael Karolyi – an ill-starred idealist whose fate it was to be both the renegade of the old order and the victim of the new. Though it lacked the broad-based support of the Socialists, his was the only faction with parliamentary representation. And though Karolyi himself, with his torn loyalties and his speech impediment, was far from being a natural leader of the masses, his was the magic name of the hour. On 24 October, as the news of the Croat mutiny in Fiume spread through Budapest, the streets echoed with calls for Karolyi to be made Prime Minister. As if to prepare for the event, the three reform groups merged into a Hungarian National Committee under his control.

Still Charles hesitated to put power in the hands of this strange man who seemed to have destroyed his own identity and that of Hungary by trying to live in two worlds at once. After two more days of fruitless audiences with all and sundry at Gödöllö, the Emperor left again for Vienna with no Government appointed but taking an expectant Karolyi with him on the Court train. However, when the new Hungarian Prime Minister was announced on 29 October, it was another Count, Johann Hadik, whose name came out of the Imperial hat. Charles had selected him from a meagre choice of reluctant candidates in a last attempt to broaden the Hungarian government without handing it over lock, stock and barrel to the Radicals. Furthermore, as Charles could not be in Vienna and Budapest simultaneously, and as the situation was now so desperate that a continuous Imperial 'presence' seemed necessary in both of the twin capitals, he appointed the Archduke Josef, who had strong Magyar roots and sympathies, as his *homo regius* in Hungary.

But neither Emperors nor Archdukes could hold the situation in Budapest much longer. Political union with Vienna (as opposed to personal union through the crown) had already been declared dead a fortnight before, in the wake of the October Manifesto. Almost the only act of Hadik's may-fly ministry had been to separate the two armies of the Dual Monarchy. When the news reached Budapest that the Croat lands of St Stephen had broken away (allegedly with the Emperor's encouragement) all emotional links with Vienna seemed to snap. A report – in fact untrue – that the Budapest garrison commander, General Lucacics, had been told personally by the Emperor over the telephone from Vienna not to use force removed the last restraints of caution. The mob that the radicals had prodded into action on their behalf now took over completely. The Magyars have never been ones to do things by halves. The Empire's traditional capital of feudalism became overnight its capital of anarchy.

On 31 October Hadik resigned after forty-eight hours of shadowy 'office' and Archduke Josef, yielding to popular clamour, appointed Karolyi in his place. The confusion was total. The Austrian double-headed eagles were torn down; but so, as well, were the insignia of St Stephen's crown. Protection was demanded from the *Entente* armies looming up from the South; yet the inaugural statement of Karolyi's brand-new Minister of Defence, the raw young Socialist artillery colonel Bela Linder, was the immortal: 'I never want to see another soldier again.' Karolyi himself and his ministers at first took the old oath of loyalty to their Emperor and King, only to wriggle out of it under threats of abolishing the Monarchy altogether a day later. As for the *homo regius*, he turned his name fashionably into Josef Alcuth, and, having sworn in Karolyi's Government of the Left, begged the Emperor's permission on the telephone to be allowed to melt away from the scene altogether and retire to his country estates. However, when Charles from Vienna sternly commanded him to stay where he was and do the job for which he had been appointed, the magyarized Archduke meekly obeyed his powerless sovereign. Nobody for the moment seemed to know quite what they wanted or indeed quite who they were.

One exception was a group of three soldiers who, as dusk came, burst into the Budapest Varosliget villa of Count Tisza. They had come to murder the statesman whom they regarded, correctly, as the symbol of arch-conservatism and, quite wrongly, as the principal instigator of the war. Their victim also knew who he was. He refused to escape by the window when the soldiers pounded on the front door, and even threw away his revolver to save his family from counter-fire. He met his assailants in the hall with the words: 'As I have lived, so shall I die.' He had spoken his own epitaph on all the splendid but foolish stubbornness of his life. A minute later, riddled with the bullets of his self-appointed executioners, he lay dead in the arms of his wife.

The news reached Karolyi up in the royal palace at Buda five minutes before he was to take the oath of office before the Archduke. Only a short while before, while the argument over his new Government was still raging, Karolyi had shouted across at Tisza: 'Your time is over, and our time has come.' The first part of that prophecy had been swiftly and gruesomely fulfilled.* The fulfilment of the second part was to prove deceptive. On 16 November 1918, Karolyi was duly elected first President of Hungary's first so-called 'Peoples' Republic'. On that same day, the Hungarian Bolshevik agitator Bela Kun arrived in Budapest from Moscow. Barely three months later, Kun took over power from Karolyi's nerveless fingers. Whatever the motives behind this aristocratic Radical's actions (and eloquent cases have been made for him as saint and Satan), the results, both for himself and for his country, had been disastrous.†

November and Vienna, the last days in the Imperial capital itself, belong to a separate chapter. But before going on there, it might be appropriate at this point to look at all these earlier autumn events once again through the eyes of the Empress, who had sat at the centre of them, a helpless spectator at her husband's side. These are some of her recollections of the whole chain of disasters set loose by the triumph of the Czech exiles in June and the surrender of the Bulgarian Army in September.

'The collapse was just as sudden as it was expected. But the real fight in those last months, as the Emperor once said, was less against the Governments outside the Empire than against the peoples within. No peace could

* There are no grounds for supposing – whatever the rumours and accusations that flew around – that Karolyi had any hand in the murder of his political opponent. In his own Memoirs (p. 374) Karolyi says he was warned, on the afternoon of 31 October, of the imminent danger to Tisza's life and that he 'gave the necessary instructions'. What these were is not stated. No guard seems to have been placed on Tisza's villa to protect him, and according to one version a guard there was actually withdrawn shortly before the murder took place. Perhaps it is kindest to blame the prevailing chaos for this sordid episode.

† See *Faith without Illusion*, Memoirs of Michael Karolyi. Also Burian; Kray, pp. 175 *et seq.*; Glaise-Horstenau, pp. 279 *et seq.*; Zeman, pp. 241 *et seq.*, etc.

be concluded with the *Entente* powers without an internal reconstruction of the Monarchy, yet at home everything was in a nationalistic tumult that simply beggars description. Nobody would give way. Everyone wanted everything for themselves – the Poles, the Ukrainians, the various Slav groups in the North and South, and, of course, the Hungarians.

'After France's recognition of the Czech exiles, the Emperor knew full well that all his attempts to bring Bohemia round, or even to hold her to the idea of Empire, might well prove fruitless. Indeed, he felt that Clemenceau, in being the first to make this gesture towards the Czechs, was only trying to encourage the Monarchy's disintegration. We had a lot of Czech troops at the front and they, like the rest of the troops, were of course already war-weary and hungry. This success of the exiles made the Emperor realize the importance of reform now more than ever. But his ministers lagged behind him. Most of them, still believing in "final victory", simply didn't grasp the significance of the Paris move. Too often one heard the scornful attitude: "The *Entente* can *talk* about recognition, but what can they *do*? It is we who are sitting here on top of Bohemia, not they."

'It was not until a month after the French step that the Emperor managed to find a new Prime Minister to replace Seidler and get on with the urgent work of reconstruction. A change couldn't be made earlier because candidate after candidate was rejected by this or that national group, who, like the political parties, were all torn with bitter strife. Hussarek was appointed after interminable negotiations because he was the only man who seemed to be at least tolerated by all sides. The Emperor, who was always steering towards federalism, thought Hussarek's ideas about reform were at any rate less rigid than anyone else's. As he was also a pliable man by nature, the Emperor hoped that he, if anyone, could help us reach a solution to this indescribable confusion of the rival races and nations.

'Hussarek at first wanted to apply reform only to the South Slavs, which, because of the oath to the Hungarian constitution, was not possible. Indeed, because of this the Emperor could only in the end proclaim a reconstruction in the Austrian half of the Empire. This was an enormously hard and a virtually hopeless decision for him to take. But he did it to show to his own peoples and the powers abroad that – at least in the Austrian lands where his action would be fully constitutional – he was determined to give to the nations their independence within the common fatherland.

'His hope was that the Hungarians might be shamed into following suit. There was no chance of their acting simultaneously. This was finally made clear on 10 October when their leaders (including Wekerle and Tisza) came to Vienna. After his audience that day with both his Hungarian and his Austrian ministers he was in no doubt that no one was ready to go all the way with him. So he went on alone.

'The main thing was somehow or other to get peace before the whole Dual Monarchy went under. Of course he knew there would be problems in implementing his own federal solution announced in the Manifesto. There had always been problems with any solution. But he hoped to meet them by adopting the least rigid approach. His idea was really for a *confederation* rather than a federation of his people. Time and again he repeated in these last weeks what he had first said to me before we were married: that some of the nation-states of the new Empire could be Republics if they chose, like the Hanseatic towns in the German Empire.

'But it was not to be. Each day from then on brought a new hammer blow and another crisis to succeed the last. On 22 October – before leaving for Debrecen in the evening – the Emperor saw some of the Czech leaders who were on their way from Prague to the meeting in Geneva. There was little comfort from this, though, by a coincidence, two of them had direct personal links with the Emperor. Klofac still remembered with pride the telegram my husband had sent him in 1916 when his son, who was a gallant soldier, had been killed on the Italian front. Another one in Vienna at the time, Kramar, owed his life to Charles who, as Archduke in 1915, had successfully interceded with the Emperor Franz Josef to have his death sentence commuted.

'Another visitor to Vienna in this period was Mihalovic, the last "Banus" of Croatia. He could get no instructions out of Budapest, which still in law and in theory governed Croatia, and didn't know whether or not he should hand over power to the new Council which had now been formed, after the Manifesto, out of the old Croatian Parliament. So he made the difficult journey to Vienna – partly on foot – to ask his Emperor.

'My husband told him that, due to his own Hungarian Coronation oath, he could not simply authorize such a step himself. But he added: "*Ultra posse nemo tenetur*". The Emperor was very moved by this loyalty shown by the Croats right up to the end. But he could only tell Mihalovic what he had been trying to din into the Croat leaders for months. This was that they had to take the first steps themselves and demand their own freedom in the proper place, which was the Hungarian capital. Only then and there could he constitutionally back them – in Budapest as King of Hungary, not in Vienna as Emperor of Austria.

'As for those last days in Hungary itself, they began with the Debrecen visit which was terribly moving but also somewhat ghostly. I remember feeling a tremor of hope that perhaps after all something might be salvaged out of our poor homeland. But the Emperor said, "No, cheering cannot stop things now".

'Then on to Gödöllö and the endless stream of audiences there with the Hungarian leaders to try and form a Government to succeed Wekerle. They all came one after the other and some of them many times – Apponyi, Toth, Serenyi, Ugron, Szabo, Batthyany, Huszar, Jaszi, Garami, Hadik as well as Michael Karolyi himself. Not one of them would take it on, except Karolyi, whom the Emperor regarded as too unbalanced for office, as well as too fanatical. He was not bitter about the reluctance of all the others. He once commented: "It's always difficult to find a crew for a sinking ship." But he had to go on trying, though now – as throughout these last weeks – he was existing on two or three hours' sleep a night, despite his doctor's repeated warnings.

'Finally came the decision to postpone a decision and meanwhile take Karolyi back on the train with us. This may in fact have saved our lives. We learned later that some extremist elements had made plans to blow up the Court train during its journey back to Vienna on the night of 26–7 October and that this plan was only abandoned when they learned that Karolyi was aboard. The unexpected appointment next morning of Hadik as Hungarian Prime Minister owed much to the attitude of the Emperor's newly appointed "peace" Foreign Minister, Count Andrassy. Though Michael Karolyi was in fact his own son-in-law, Andrassy disliked and distrusted him politically to such a degree that at first he refused to remain Imperial Foreign Minister in Vienna if Karolyi became Hungarian Prime Minister in Budapest. This was just another of those endless frictions and complications which had somehow to be sorted out.

'Our children we had left behind us at Gödöllö. It was a dreadful decision to have to take but we did it deliberately. It was the only way to show to the Hungarian people that their King and Queen did not intend to flee Hungary for good. It would have been the last straw had that idea spread about! But our children were not left there as hostages against our will. Nobody asked that they should stay. It was our own decision and it was helped by two things. First, at that particular moment, the situation in Vienna looked if anything even more dangerous than in Budapest. We were not moving from trouble into peace but from one storm into another. Second, our children were by now so used to their parents being continually on the move that they were in no way anxious or frightened at being left alone. But the Emperor and I knew that there was now danger everywhere and though we made our leave-taking appear quite normal, it was with a very heavy heart that we said good-bye to them at Gödöllö. *

'Our feelings in this respect can be imagined when the Revolution broke out in Budapest. It was I who actually heard the news first. The Emperor had not got to bed in Schönbrunn until long after midnight on 30 October. In the small hours, just as he had fallen asleep, an urgent telephone call came through for him from Budapest. I answered. It was General Lucacics, the commander of the garrison there, who told me, beside himself with agitation, that revolution had broken out in the city and that he simply had to speak to the Emperor.

'There was nothing for it but to wake my husband. As I was naturally very worried about the safety of my children I listened for once to the whole of the conversation which followed. In it there was no question, as is alleged and as was believed at the time in Budapest, of the Emperor giving his general orders not to use force. Lucacics did indeed begin by asking point-blank whether he was to fire at the demonstrators or not – which was an improper way of trying to shield his actions, considering that the immediate military responsibility for preserving law and order was his and his alone.

'The Emperor told Lucacics that if it was within his power to hold down the gathering revolution, *he must on all accounts do so*. He was only to refrain, and so avoid even greater bloodshed, if the forces ranged against him were so great as to allow *no prospect whatever* of containing them or of saving his own soldiers' lives. Lucacics pressed the Emperor to authorize an immediate surrender, which he absolutely refused to do. Then it came out. The general complained that he had only (apart from a few Bosnian troops) the so-called "Budapest House-Regiment" available and that these battalions could not be relied upon.

'Now when, earlier that year, the Emperor had appointed Lucacics (who held the highest military decorations and was known as the "Iron General") Commander of Budapest, he did so in order to have the right man on the spot to deal with the trouble he knew was brewing. And the Emperor at that time issued Lucacics with specific orders to re-shuffle the "House-Regiment" – which was made up mostly of Budapest men – as quickly and quietly as possible, and to replace these locally recruited soldiers with others drawn from outlying areas of Hungary. My husband realized that, in plain humanity, it was too much to ask troops to use force against crowds that might well include their own friends and relations. He explained all this to the general, who said he fully understood and

---

* After the Revolution in Budapest broke out four days later, the children had to be smuggled back to Vienna, where they all arrived safely a day or two later after an adventurous car journey via Pressburg.

undertook to carry out the exchange of units with all possible speed. Now, in the early hours of 31 October, with the mob already on the move (though still not yet across the Danube bridges to Buda and the seat of government), the Emperor had to learn that his instructions had never been carried out.

'Despite this, the Emperor still urged Lucacics on the telephone to do everything he could to put down a revolt that threatened the well-being of the people and the security of the Government. In the event, the general not only opened all the flood-gates of rebellion in Budapest but also falsely maintained that his sovereign had told him to do so.

'In 1923 or '24, Lucacics once visited me in exile at Lequeitio in Spain on a mission from Admiral Horthy. When I revealed that it was I who had first answered the telephone in Schönbrunn on that October night five years before and had then heard the whole conversation that followed, he had to admit that he had in fact acted contrary to his ruler's orders. He promised me to put the record straight in a book or an article, but this was never done. When he went on to talk of his earlier war career and of the exploits that had won him the Maria Theresa Order, the phrase slipped out: "In the days when I was a hero. . . ."'

Maria Theresa would not have been very proud of the general's behaviour in October 1918. Budapest was the one capital of the Empire where the Monarchy was at the heart of both the national legend and the national pride. Indeed, it was to stay a monarchy in theory until the Second World War. Yet not a shot had been fired to keep it a Monarchy in fact at the end of the First World War.

Chapter 13

SCHÖNBRUNN: NOVEMBER 1918

It was fitting that the last act should be played out at Schönbrunn. The great summer palace of Vienna had already seen so much of the Habsburgs' triumphs and tragedies since the Empress Maria Theresa first moved into its yellow baroque walls more than a century and a half before. Here in the 1750s the great Austrian Chancellor Kaunitz had engineered the famous defensive treaty with France – a reversal of Europe's alliances that Charles had striven to repeat in his own brief reign. Here in 1809 Napoleon had slept as a conqueror. Here, but five years later, the monarchs and statesmen of the whole continent had gathered to re-dispose of his conquests at the Congress of Vienna, and the most glittering age of Austrian diplomacy, under her even greater Chancellor, Prince Metternich, had begun.

In the autumn of 1918, it was here that the last of the Habsburg Emperors now returned to preside over the dissolution of his Empire. The threat that faced him was ten times as desperate as any that the armies of Frederick the Great or Napoleon had posed to his ancestors. To help him meet it he had no Kaunitz and no Metternich in Vienna, but only a handful of political mediocrities. Some of these were already too frightened to stay loyal at any cost. However, none of them proved desperate enough or bold enough to play the traitor outright. The Empire thus subsided on a typically Viennese ground of half-truths and half-measures.

It was Sunday, 27 October, when Charles got back from those five exhausting days in a smouldering Hungary where his children had been left behind.* Among the first to report to him when he arrived at Schönbrunn with the Empress was the Chief of Staff, General Arz. His news was graver even than the political chaos in Prague and Budapest or the hopeless diplomatic duel with President Wilson. The Italian front, always *the* battle-front for Austria-Hungary, had just collapsed. The last, the worst, and the most muddled military crisis of the Empire's long life had begun.

---

* They finally got back to Vienna on 31 October.

191

The only amazing thing about the collapse itself was that it had been so long in coming. Months before the *Entente* powers launched their crucial October offensive, the Austro-Hungarian army facing them had been reduced by food and equipment shortages to a polyglot skeleton. Already in the summer, the basic rations of the Empire's soldiers on the Piave had been reduced to a diet of thin black coffee with nothing solid whatever for the morning and evening 'meals', and only an unpredictable mixture of dried fruit, cheese and cabbage at midday. A complete set of under-clothing was a rare treasure – even if the only thing that matched in the two halves were the holes. The supply of uniforms was no better. During this final campaign, one Austrian General Staff officer reported coming across a detachment of infantry shivering in a cave high up on the Asolone plateau, clad only in their ragged undergarments. Their commander explained that they were still 'on duty and standing by', but that he only had enough uniforms and greatcoats left to clothe his other platoon which was actually fighting up in the forward trenches. As one of the Emperor's soldiers said to the inhabitants of a Venetian village where he was quar-tered: 'We are not heroes any more but beggars.'* Indeed, deserters lived better off berries in the woods than did their comrades who continued to queue up at the near-empty and meatless regimental field-kitchens.

On paper, this army still numbered 57½ divisions (out of the Empire's total strength of 78 fighting formations – proof enough of the importance of the Italian front). But of those 57½ divisions, nineteen were between quarter- and half-strength in the autumn of 1918; nine were riddled with malaria; and a further seven were still being re-formed after transfer from the East. On 24 October 1918, the combined *Entente* forces of Italian, French, English and American troops struck at these tattered and hungry opponents in the mountains between Brenta and the Piave.

For three days the motley legions of the Dual Monarchy held firm. Austrians, Czechs, Poles, Magyars, Croats, Rumanians, Slovaks and Ukrainians stood together and fought together for every ridge and ravine as though weakened neither by privations nor by political propaganda; as though indeed a common fatherland still existed just as solidly behind them. The achievement impressed – and probably surprised – even the German liaison officers attached to the two Imperial Army Groups of Field-Marshals Kovess and Boreovic. Yet this last feat of defiance of the 300-year-old joint army was as unnatural as it was splendid. It was the deceptively true note that a violin string goes on giving out although frayed to within a hair's breadth of extinction.

* See, for the whole campaign, Arz, *op. cit.*, pp. 333 *et seq.* Also Werkmann, *Deutsch-land als Verbündete*, pp. 312 *et seq.*

On 26 October the string snapped. A mixed Magyar and Slovak unit, the 25th Infantry Regiment, defied an order to march to the front in view of the appeals that Count Karolyi was making from Budapest to all Hungarian troops to cease fire. Almost immediately, two entire Hungarian formations already in the line, the 27th and 28th 'Honved' divisions, refused to fight on and demanded transport back to Hungary to defend 'St Stephen's Lands' from those other *Entente* armies which were now striding up the Balkans. The High Command's call to Budapest to issue reassurances and come out with a rallying cry instead fell on deaf official ears – indeed, on non-existent ears, for Hungary was then without a Government. Within two days, mutiny or passive resistance had spread to twenty-six of the fifty-seven divisions on the Italian front. That proud and true greeting sent by an earlier Habsburg Emperor to his troops: 'In your camp stands Austria', had overnight become a mockery. The Army of the Dual Monarchy had split apart at last, right along its racial seams.

Such was the grim military situation that Charles had returned to on 27 October. Arz pressed him for an immediate armistice with the Italians. The Emperor could only in principle agree, though he added wearily that some of the political problems awaiting him in his capital would have to be tackled first.* When this tide of domestic worries had been pushed back for a few hours and the Chief of Staff renewed his plea in Schönbrunn the following day, Charles gave his formal consent. As a result, at 6 A.M. the next morning, 29 October, an Austrian General Staff officer named Captain Ruggera clambered nervously out on to a railway embankment north of Serravalle. Accompanied by a white-flag-bearer and two trumpeters, who shattered the dawn air with the sounds of the 'General March', he walked into the Italian lines carrying his Emperor's request for a cease-fire. The ill-starred negotiations for an Italian armistice had begun. Before the week was out, they were to produce on the battlefield the most ludicrous 'victory' of the entire war. On the home front, they were to complete Charles's isolation in his own capital.

The political picture here was bizarre in the extreme. The Emperor's German-speaking Austrian subjects had duly fallen in step with his other peoples by accepting the invitation in his October Manifesto to set themselves up as a separate and independent unit of the proposed new federal Empire. But these Austrians, and particularly the cosmopolitan Viennese, were a race apart – if indeed they were a race at all. They had never been a

---

* This was the same critical day on which Professor Lammasch had been appointed 'Peace Prime Minister' in Vienna and the Austrian plea for separate peace talks with President Wilson had been despatched to Washington despite the protests of the German Emperor.

proud and compact nation like the Magyars, for whom even the Habsburgs were essentially only a historical convenience to embody their statehood. For six centuries, the only solid political identity of the Austrians had been as the privileged servants of the dynasty. They were the stewards of a multi-national Empire that had grown up as one vast feudal estate around them, rather than a nation with any vitality of their own. And, now that this double-headed eagle they had ridden upon or nestled under for so long looked like being knocked off its ancient perch, the Austrians, unlike any other people of the Empire, had to get up, look in the breaking mirror, and ask themselves the disturbing question: Who *are* we? Did they, as German speakers, really belong to that great Germanic mass to the north of the Empire, whose culture they shared? Should they, as the Emperor's subjects, join up with other German speakers within the Empire, like the Sudetens of Bohemia, whose history they shared? Or was there conceivably such a thing as a *homo austriacus*, an Austrian with both a culture and a history of his own, who could live and feel as such even when the dynasty which alone had given him his profile had gone? A clear answer was to be more than a generation in coming.* It was little wonder that this riddle – hitherto unposed, let alone unsolved – did so much to compound the confusion in the last weeks of Imperial Vienna. This confusion covered not only the constitutional form and the legal authority of the incipient Austrian state, but even its name. Significantly, one of several titles suggested was 'South-East Germany'.

The process by which the Austrians began to extract themselves from the thicket of the Empire began on 21 October 1918, when the German-speaking deputies of the last elected Parliament (1911) assembled in Vienna to declare themselves 'The Provisional National Assembly of the independent German-Austrian State'. This was the Austrian equivalent of those National Councils which the Emperor's Manifesto had just summoned into being throughout the Dual Monarchy. Unlike its fellows, however, the 'Provisional National Assembly' of the Austrians made no direct bid to seize power. For one thing, that unique dynastic background was too strong. The Emperor was still in residence in Vienna, the 'Imperial city'; his own Government still stood, however witless and bewildered, at his side; and all that ponderous machinery of Empire still tried to grind on in the same capital, dispensing ordinances, titles and decorations into the very jaws of oblivion.

* One may date the beginnings of a solid and almost universally accepted Austrian patriotism from the Second World War. The Austrians, taken over with mixed feelings but without resistance by Hitler in 1938, found their own fatherland at last, as soon as they had lost it.

This was altogether too frightening a thing to touch. Moreover, as it was dying anyway, there seemed little point in provoking it into any last convulsions. The Austrian National Assembly, having elected an all-party executive committee of twenty members (soon re-named the State Council), therefore simply settled down as close as it could to the weakening centre of power, and waited for it to expire. Yet even though that power was fast ebbing away from Charles by the end of October, his would-be successors insisted that he should shoulder full responsibilities right to the end. They wanted to ride the eagle until its wings dropped off. The most dramatic example of this was the conclusion of the Italian armistice, which was the last major and independent step of Charles's reign.

Captain Ruggera's walk down the railway embankment at dawn on 29 October had led, not without complications, to the opening of fully-fledged talks with the Italians two days later. The parley was held in the Villa Giusti near Padua, with General Badoglio (later of Abyssinian fame) as the Italian representative and General Weber as the Emperor's spokesman. The latter's instructions were to accept 'all terms which did not impair the honour of the Army and which did not amount to capitulation'.*

The Italian conditions reached Schönbrunn on the evening of the following day, 1 November. They came, in fact, as close to an Austrian capitulation as made no difference. The principal demands were for the complete demobilization of the Austro-Hungarian Army and its subsequent reduction in peacetime to a strength of twenty divisions; the withdrawal of all Austro-Hungarian forces right back to the Brenner Pass, thus handing over to Italy not only the Trentino province but most of the other Habsburg territories promised to Rome in the secret treaties of 1915; and finally, the right of *Entente* troops 'to move freely inside Austria-Hungary and occupy strategic points'. This last condition (which Charles was determined if possible to resist, since it opened up his territory for an attack against his own German ally) was the immediate concern of the Emperor and his General Staff. But the first two demands vitally affected the future of the new Austrian state, whatever form this was to take. Charles therefore decided to invite the representatives of that new Austria to come and discuss the Italian armistice with him and his advisers. In doing so, he formally acknowledged the fact that they were already a parallel government which was slowly displacing the last Imperial Cabinet of Professor Lammasch he had appointed only the week before. Towards four o'clock on the afternoon of 2 November, the five leaders of the State Council (the Parliamentary Presidents of the three main parties

* Arz, *op. cit.*, p. 345.

represented and two specially appointed 'State Secretaries') duly arrived at Schönbrunn.*

The encounter got off to an unfortunate start. As the five parliamentarians were being escorted up to the state apartments, one of them, the veteran Socialist Viktor Adler, who was in fact already mortally sick,† had a heart attack right on the grand staircase. The commotion of his comrades and his own loud gasps for breath brought the Empress from her rooms. She immediately ordered a glass of cognac to be brought to the suffering man. But Adler, who had been forbidden all alcohol by his doctors, waved the drink aside with a horrified 'Do you want to kill me?' Eventually he recovered and the party moved on into the so-called Blue Chinese Saloon behind the Great Gallery of the palace. Here the Emperor, with two aides, joined them as they grouped themselves on the gilt and satin armchairs around his sofa. The fading dynasty and its inheritors were face to face for the first time.

The Empress relates: 'The Emperor began by showing them the message from General Weber with the Italian terms. He also passed round his own exchange of telegrams with the Emperor William in which he had assured his ally that he would personally lead the fight if need be to stop the *Entente* armies from attacking Germany across his territory. Then he outlined the position. On the one hand, the Italian demand for troop transit was unacceptable. But, on the other hand, our army was simply not fighting any more. Our troops were flooding back uncontrolled from the front, rioting and blowing up their own ammunition dumps as they went. So in practice the *Entente* forces could not be stopped if they did decide to march through. The military choice therefore lay between letting them in without any attempt at resistance or blocking their advance on Germany by blowing up all the main bridges and railway lines in the Tyrol. This, however, would aggravate the already desperate food distribution problem of our own people. What should we do?

'The State Council leaders promptly replied that all further bloodshed must be stopped but without damaging Germany's interests. However, they had no ideas and no proposals as to how this might be done. Instead they began a discussion on responsibility for the war. They, Viktor Adler said, had not begun it and they did not want to take any responsibility for ending it. The decisions on the armistice must continue, therefore, to be made by the Emperor.

'My husband replied: "I no more began this war than you did. But I have always tried to stop it and you, gentlemen, have never supported me

---

* See Werkmann, pp. 340 *et seq.*, and Arz, pp. 363 *et seq.*

† He died ten days later.

in my peace efforts." There was no answer to this. The Emperor then asked them to withdraw to another room to think things over while he attended to other urgent business. At about six o'clock they reappeared to say that, though they accepted the necessity for an armistice, they were still not prepared to share any of the responsibility for it. They then left the palace.'

The heirs to the Habsburgs in Vienna thus approached their legacy with what was an act of shrewd pragmatism or of plain moral cowardice – depending on the viewpoint. Its immediate effect was to complicate an already tangled situation. Charles had still not abandoned hope of getting some sort of State Council backing for the inevitable Italian armistice. But for that he needed time, and time was the one thing the crumbling Southern front would not give him.

As soon as the five delegates of the 'German Austrian National Assembly' had departed – with a promise to report to their plenum at 10 A.M. the next morning – Charles summoned a meeting of his own Austrian Cabinet, to be followed, at 9.15 P.M., by a session of the Imperial Crown Council. This body, which had always been the supreme political forum of the Empire, a conference of the joint Austro-Hungarian ministers under the chairmanship of the Emperor, was now a pale shadow of its former august self. There was indeed no common finance policy with Hungary any more and no common foreign policy. That same night also destroyed the last vestiges of a common Army. Colonel Lindner, the young Social-Democrat War Minister of Count Karolyi's newly-formed Radical Government in Budapest, rang up Schönbrunn in the middle of these armistice deliberations and declared that if the Emperor from Vienna did not order all Hungarian troops to cease fire, then he would issue the order himself, from Budapest. Here, at least, was someone prepared to take responsibility, even if it was unwanted. The Emperor had little choice but to comply, to avoid even greater bedlam at the front. At 9 P.M., just before his last Crown Council meeting began, Charles authorized his Hungarian soldiers to stop fighting – a few hours ahead of the general cease-fire. 'Inseparabilitur ac indivisibiliter', 'Inseparable and indivisible', the motto on the double eagle, was thus wiped out a few days before the rest of the Imperial crest.

The Emperor had hoped by this step to keep the threads, however tangled, still in his own hands. But the confusion now began in earnest. Messages from the Army Group Commanders poured in while the Crown Council was sitting. They became steadily more frantic. Charles's generals were commanding only chaos. The bitter decision had to be taken to accept the Italian terms virtually as they stood. In the confusion of this hectic evening, the Austrian generals, both at Supreme Headquarters in Baden and at the Emperor's elbow in Schönbrunn, went on the false assumption that detailed cease-fire arrangements had already been concluded with the Italians and would automatically come into effect with acceptance of the severe armistice conditions. By midnight the necessary telegram of authorization to General Weber in Padua had been drafted and it was despatched, after further amendments, an hour later. It contained little more than a pious wish that the *Entente* forces should not be allowed to attack Germany across Austro-Hungarian territory. Of Charles's ringing promise to the Emperor William only a few days before to lead the fight against any such attack in person there was no longer any mention. It was now becoming clear to the last Habsburg ruler that he might soon be fighting instead for his crown and even for his own life.

His immediate concern, however, now that the Italian terms had been accepted, was to pin down those evasive gentlemen of the State Council. To inform them officially of the news, General Arz and the Prime Minister, Lammasch, were despatched after midnight to the Parliament building on the Ringstrasse. They found that the State Council was not merely evasive but was missing altogether. On this of all nights in their country's history, they had decided, possibly deliberately, to dispense with an emergency session. Two of their members still on the premises declared themselves unauthorized even to comment on the Emperor's step; nothing whatsoever, they declared, could be done until their Council met again in nine hours' time. When Arz returned to Schönbrunn with this information, the Emperor made one last attempt to hold up the battlefield to suit the State Council's schedule. In the early hours of the morning, he ordered a temporary suspension both of the acceptance telegram to Padua and of the cease-fire order. The first message was duly held up but it was too late to stop the second: it had already gone out from the Army Groups to the troops. There was nothing for it but to countermand the cease-fire suspension and let things take their original course. Charles's generals down on the Italian front must have been as weary as he was by the time that sleepless night of 2 November was over; as weary, and a great deal more perplexed.

But the really disastrous confusion was to come with the new day that dawned. Once or twice during the Padua talks, the Italians had in fact been hedging over a precise date and time for the cease-fire to take effect, saying that this should come twenty-four hours after *their* acceptance of the armistice terms. The motive behind this calculated vagueness soon emerged. At five minutes past ten on the morning of 3 November (after another vain attempt to contact the State Council first), the Emperor's delayed telegram to General Weber authorizing him to conclude the proposed armistice was finally sent off. By now, following the Emperor's earlier cease-fire orders, the Austro-Hungarian forces in Italy had virtually stopped fighting. The Italians, however, were only just beginning to fight their own sort of battle.

For a few hours there was silence from Padua while Italian troops continued to attack all along the front. Then came a blatant piece of procrastination from General Badoglio. Would the Austrians please provide a written copy of the Emperor's message, as the telegraphic text was insufficient? This was done. All the time, the Italian attacks continued against an army that, by now, was barely raising its hand before its face. Arz could do no more than order his front commanders to protest, while Vienna still waited. Not until late that night did the official news arrive from Padua. It was precise and deadly. General Weber reported that at 3 P.M. that afternoon the Italians had at last signed the armistice instruments but had stipulated that all *Entente* troops would only cease hostilities twenty-four hours later, at 3 P.M. on 4 November. The perils of a one-sided cease-fire preceding a general armistice agreement were now brought home.

In those twenty-four hours, the Italians thrust specially organized flying columns of cavalry and motorized infantry clean through the soggy, unresisting, disorganized mass of the Austrian armies. Many Austrian units, believing it was all over, were just sitting, with rifles stacked, on their kitbags. The Italians thus rode unopposed into all that Austrian territory which, in twelve previous campaigns since 1915, they had failed to conquer by force. When they duly stopped, at 3 P.M. on 4 November, they had reached a general line running from Male and Val Sugano across to Pontebba and the Adriatic town of Grado in the East. The Italians were sitting on their long-coveted '*fino al Brennero*' at last.

The bewildered Austrian divisions to the South of them – in so far as these could still be classed as formations – were now mostly cut off from their last retreat routes up the Etsch valley. They were all promptly declared prisoner, as indeed many were. Some got away, but 350,000 Austro-Hungarian troops and enormous quantities of war material dropped, almost without a shot being fired, into the Italians' laps. This was the famous 'victory' of Vittorio Veneto, to which great monuments were raised in Italy. It was, of course, no feat of arms. It had been won by a mixture of Italian cunning and Austrian muddle. These were the traditional qualities of the two peoples respectively and they had now lethally combined.

Charles's own reaction, when this mournful state of affairs became plain, was typical of the man and symptomatic of his plight. There was no bitterness, nor word of reproach for a team of military advisers who had not exactly distinguished themselves – complex though the task had been – over the negotiations. Just a weary sigh of relief. 'At least no more soldiers will fall on *that* front,' the Empress heard him murmur. Yet the unexpected Italian disaster was nonetheless a heavy blow at his personal position. Hard on the heels of the political defections in Prague, Budapest, Zagreb and other centres had come the dissolution of the Army, and in far more humiliating circumstances. For the first time, the prestige of the crown began to sink along with its dwindling power. This was expressed in a number of ways.

To begin with, Charles himself now relinquished the Supreme Command over his armed forces. At first he chose General Arz, who was handed a six-word letter of appointment by the Emperor at 3 A.M. on 3 November in Schönbrunn; the next day, at Arz's request, he nominated instead Field-Marshal Kovess, who had managed to extricate himself in time from the *débâcle* on the Italian front. It was not responsibility that Charles was avoiding (for him there was never an escape from that) so much as the stain of treachery. He did not wish to sign in person any armistice which might endanger his German ally. Yet, whatever its specific motive, this handing over of command was also a public admission that defeat was now inevitable and that only the technicalities of surrender remained.

But there was more to this new military disaster than that. Significantly, the turmoil of that same terrible night of Saturday to Sunday, 2–3 November, brought with it the first threats to the safety of the Imperial family itself in its own capital. Though it seems scarcely credible that one night could contain so much stress and drama, a domestic crisis had also flared up that evening and had gone on parallel with the military crisis until the early hours. In the Empress's words:

'It was a night of indescribable confusion. In the middle of the endless armistice discussions, the Police President of Vienna, Dr Schober, rang us up to announce that the security threat to the palace was getting absolutely out of hand. This was the first time anything like this had been reported, but Dr Schober was emphatic. The Emperor must leave the palace with his family that same night and go elsewhere for safety.

'But where? From all sides suggestions rained down on us – all different, all emphatic. We should move to Reichenau; to Brandeis on the Elbe; to the abbey of Kremsmünster; to Innsbruck; to Pressburg; to Prince Starhemberg's castle in Upper Austria. There were as many pressing suggestions as advisers. The ministers present repeated the Police President's warning to us to get away from Vienna that same night. There were even stories that thousands of workers were already marching on Schönbrunn. But the military urged us to stay where we were.

'In between all this and the armistice talks came repeated telephone calls from Budapest. One was from the Emperor's *homo regius* there, the Archduke Josef. The Emperor took the call. The Archduke was complaining loudly about the threat to himself and his own family. He called on the Emperor to abdicate as King of Hungary. This appeal was refused point-blank. The Archduke tried to insist, saying that unless he did so he, the king, would be murdered. The Emperor retorted that he was quite indifferent to threats of this sort and repeated that he would not abdicate. With that, the *homo regius* had to be silent if not content.

'As to the threat to us, at 4.30 A.M. a decision was finally taken. Dr Schober rang up from police headquarters again to say that the danger to the palace had "somewhat receded" and that we might as well remain. So stay we did. Soon afterwards, at nearly 6 A.M., we all went to early Sunday Mass in the palace chapel. Then, the sleepless night nearly over, we tried to get a little rest.'

The Archduke Josef was not the only one to mention abdication that night. The dreaded word had also been dropped for the first time in Schönbrunn itself by a group of courtiers who had gathered in the Blue Chinese Saloon while the Crown Council was meeting in the Emperor's study. One of those present, Baron Werkmann, has described the scene:*

The Archduke Max, Count Hunyady, Count Alexander Esterhazy, and I were discussing the situation. We could only agree that the Emperor had no joint government any more. As for the Austrian government, of Dr Lammasch, this could no longer decide anything, administer anything or be responsible for anything. The newly-formed national governments, even the one in Vienna, were seeking no contact with the throne. The Emperor also had no *de facto* control over the army any longer. . . . In the heavy atmosphere of the capital, in the frenzy that had seized both the troops and the civilian population, nothing could be organized. And the question was: what would be the position tomorrow, when news of the shaming armistice got around?

Then Archduke Max produced a sheet of paper. His father-in-law, Prince Conrad Hohenlohe, had told him after an audience with the Emperor at 10.45 that morning that there was only one possibility: the Emperor should hand over power to those who were clamouring for it and then withdraw from the capital to some more peaceful place, there to await the hour when a truly imperial power could be restored. The Archduke then read out to us the draft of an appropriate Manifesto drawn up by Hohenlohe which he had in his hand.

Werkmann goes on to describe how, in a brief midnight pause between

* Werkmann, *op. cit.*, pp. 343 et seq.

all the other calamities and emergencies of the hour, the Emperor received three of this group, including himself, to hear the proposal. Without altering his stand on abdication, Charles listened to the arguments for and against each 'more peaceful place' suggested. Then, in Werkmann's words: 'General exhaustion brought our deliberations to a stop.' *

The Sunday did not bring those angry reactions and mass marches on Schönbrunn that the police and the Court had feared. Indeed, it began on a note of ghostly loyalty. 4 November happened to be the Emperor's name-day and the usual High Mass was celebrated in St Stephen's Cathedral that morning in his honour. Vienna's great church, which in its time had shared so much of the Habsburgs' rise to glory,† was crowded for the occasion and almost the full complement of ministers and other notabilities were in their places on the front benches. But they had deliberately come out of uniform and had slipped in through the side doors. The *Te Deum* during the Mass and the Imperial anthem *Gott erhalte* which closed it were in fact a memorial service for the dynasty. Appropriately, all eyes were wet at the end. A few strong arms would have served the Emperor better.

The last week in the Empire's life had now, indeed, dawned. After further overtures by Lammasch to the State Council had failed to produce any programme for joint action, only one hope remained for saving the crown in some form in Vienna. This was to rally the pro-Monarchist forces in the 'Provisional National Assembly' itself for the imminent confrontation over 'German-Austria's' future. In theory, the prospects here were far from bleak. When that Assembly had first met a fortnight before on 21 October, two of the three political parties represented in it had declared their continuing support for the dynasty.

The largest of the old Austrian right-wing parties, the Christian Socialists, had declared that their delegates to the new Assembly 'would use their influence towards a democratization of German-Austria while preserving the principle of a Monarchical form of Government'.‡ Though the word 'Empire' was not actually mentioned, their Tyrolean spokesman Josef Schrafl (who was deputizing for the party's sick leader, Prelate

---

* According to Spitzmüller, *op. cit.*, p. 295 and p. 299, Charles also briefly discussed the Hohenlohe Manifesto during that night with his principal Austrian and Hungarian ministers summoned to Schönbrunn for the Crown Council. All of them at this point still supported him in rejecting the idea.

† The famous 'double wedding' in the sixteenth century, for example, which had gained the crowns of both Bohemia and Hungary.

‡ One of their inner group at this time, the noted journalist Dr Funder, has stated that in October 1918 'only a small minority' of the Christian-Socialist deputies leaned towards the idea of a Republic. (Funder, *Von Gestern ins Heute*, p. 581.)

Hauser) went on to support the Emperor's concept of a 'union of the new nation-states into one federation', should this be the general wish. Even the German-Nationalist delegates, despite their programme of a closer union of all the Germans, had declared themselves to be 'convinced supporters of a constitutional monarchy'. Only the Social Democrats thought and spoke otherwise. The dying Viktor Adler called on the German-Austrians to 'form their own democratic people's state', and while he too advocated a union with their neighbours, he spoke significantly of 'a federation of free peoples' and not a federation of Governments under one political roof. The Social Democrats now wanted no part of the old Habsburg house – roof, walls or foundations. They were determined from the outset of this final crisis to construct a new republican building of their own.

Still there was no call on the Emperor to step down – neither at the Assembly's initial meeting of 21 October nor at its second session on 30 October. November began with the constitutional form of 'German-Austria' as yet undecided and with a majority of its newly-appointed delegates still formally pledged to the crown. The Provisional Assembly was, however, only a weather-vane which would turn with any prevailing wind. A fierce and growing storm had already started to blow up against the dynasty. It came from the streets and not from the corridors of Parliament.

Many blasts of anger or frustration fed it. Some were artificially produced or fanned. Rumour-mongering, for example, reached an unprecedented peak in these last days even by Vienna's standards – the stories ranging from old favourites such as the Emperor lolling hopelessly drunk in Schönbrunn to new refinements such as the 'Italian' Empress having helped her 'countrymen' to victory by selling them the Austrian defence plans. Their points of origin seemed to stretch everywhere from the radical wing of the Republicans to the German Embassy in the Metternichgasse, which had by now become virtually a hostile mission.

But the main force of the tempest, whether misdirected or not, was spontaneous. Pan-German feeling throughout Austria (which at that time ran just as high among the left wing as the right) had been incensed by the Emperor's decision of 27 October to sue for a separate peace over Berlin's head. Anti-Italian feeling (which was an almost universal sentiment among the Austrians) had been inflamed by the Piave *débâcle* of 3–4 November and all the humiliation of an unnecessary defeat. The Emperor, who had taken the responsibility for both, now felt the backlash from both across his face.

Above all, it was the entire social and political landscape of a once-great power that was crumbling away around the dynasty, and with it were falling all those natural windbreaks of custom and authority that normally sheltered the crown. To the growing despair of hunger and war-weariness which had gripped Vienna for three winters past was now added the sudden pandemonium of military defeat.

The armed forces, formally demobilized by the Emperor on 6 November in compliance with the Padua armistice, had spilled out over the homeland in the wake of the earlier deserters like a horde of angry scavengers. Discipline was trampled underfoot in the scramble for plunder. Whole units, sometimes forcing their own officers along with them as hostages, turned themselves into free-booting gangs, raiding farms, looting shops and factories, emptying army depots, selling their equipment, slaughtering their horses. The civilians, including some erstwhile pillars of bourgeois society, were not far behind these erstwhile soldiers in the universal orgy of theft.* And underlying everything was that new note of class strife which the Russian Revolution had first injected into the Austrian scene. So the bands of authority and convention which had held the old order of things together began to snap fast. The Emperor, who was the symbol of that order, could not hope to survive alone. The Irish poet, W. B. Yeats, though writing of neither this Viennese time nor scene, found some words which perfectly describe it:

> *Things fall apart; the centre cannot hold;*
> *Mere anarchy is loosed upon the world.*

Yet the symbol itself had not been touched. There was still no sign of any 'storming of the Louvre'. Austria's would-be revolution had loud lungs, but little heart and no head. Indeed, until the last forty-eight hours of the Empire's life, the situation in the capital was so volatile and disorganized that one division of loyal and disciplined troops might have swung it, temporarily at least, in the Emperor's favour. Instead, the entire Army seemed to shrink away from Schönbrunn and its Emperor. How could this happen?

The Empress, in describing life in the palace just before the final crisis, has given some interesting clues:

'At midday on 2 November, the main element of the palace guard,† the Hungarian battalion, simply marched out. They told us they were leaving because the Emperor was no longer in Schönbrunn. When the Emperor

---

* See among others, Redlich, *op. cit.*, Arz, etc., Funder, pp. 597–8.

† At the beginning of October this had consisted of a company of life guards, some 200 so-called 'palace gendarmes' and the infantry battalion, which was drawn from the Hungarian Infantry Regiment No. 69. Both the life guards and gendarmes had been dwindling in numbers as the month ended.

proved to them that he still was by showing himself in the little private garden, they left just the same. The immediate reason of course was the order issued that morning from Budapest by the new Revolutionary Miniser of War, Lindner, that all Hungarian regiments everywhere should lay down their arms. That same afternoon, Lindner rang the palace and tried to get the Emperor as King of Hungary to sanction his action retrospectively. Lindner had realized that one result of his order would be that the Rumanians would simply march into Hungary (as they did) and he wanted to place the blame for this on the King. My husband, of course, refused to give his sanction. At this, Lindner asked if he could speak to me on the telephone. I declined.

'Our own life guard troops were also disappearing, but it was the departure of the Hungarian battalion which first created a really dangerous situation. The whole palace was now open. There were not even sentries at the main gates. The only people permanently in Schönbrunn from now on – apart from the Emperor and myself and our children – were about half-a-dozen ladies-in-waiting and aides, a few remaining servants and retainers and the life guards officers who had stayed behind after their men had left.

'Then, without being asked or prompted, the military cadets suddenly appeared to guard us. The first to arrive were from the Wiener Neustadt Academy, led by Walter von Schuschnigg (a cousin of Kurt, who later became Chancellor of the Republic); and they were soon joined by other cadets from the Traiskirchen Academy. The Emperor was deeply moved by their loyalty. But though he never told them, in order not to wound their pride, he never had the slightest intention of exposing them in a fight if the palace ever should be stormed. They were little more than boys.

'Why, despite all the confusion, no proper troops could be found instead to replace the Hungarian battalion I do not know. Perhaps due to an error, no regular reinforcements seem to have been available from the Vienna garrison, which would have been the natural place as it controlled, among other forces, the life guards. One attempt was, I remember, made by the War Office to replace the Hungarians. An order was sent to the Regiments 14 (Linz) and 49 (Salzburg) who were stationed quite near at Wiener Neustadt to make up a special battalion to guard the Emperor. But on the twenty-five-mile journey to Schünbrunn most of the unit evaporated. All that arrived at the palace were the officers of the battalion and fourteen men.

'But I do know that several messages were sent to Vienna at this time from commanding officers in the field offering to march to the capital with such troops as they could still muster and fight for the Emperor. *And I also know that not one of these offers was ever passed on to Schönbrunn or reached the Emperor personally*. They were turned down outside the palace in the Emperor's name, but not by him.

'Sometimes – as we learned later – units had tried despite this to get through to Vienna just to be on hand if needed, but had never managed it. The commander of one regiment which was returning home to Salzburg in the first days of November, for example, was determined to march on the capital and find out what was going on although his offer to help had been refused there. But the regiment simply melted away on the platforms of Salzburg railway station. On the journey back from the front the troops had seen from the train all the plundering and looting going on in the countryside. Once they got out at their home town, their only thought naturally was to rejoin and protect their own families.

'But in other cases these negative replies from Vienna may have prevented aid actually reaching us. We only learned later, for example, that the Commander of one of the Isonzo Army Groups, Field-Marshal Boreovic himself, who had brought a large part of his forces in good order and discipline back to Klagenfurt, twice cabled the Emperor personally from there offering to move on to Vienna. Twice the offer was declined in the Emperor's name. In fact, we never even got to hear of it at all at the time.*

'Thus all stories that the Emperor turned these offers down – whether from Boreovic or from anyone else – are quite false. He was a soldier himself and would have jumped at such aid. He had fought throughout the whole war for his country and his crown and, after such sacrifice, would certainly have been ready to fight on when everything was at stake – provided there was a real chance and that blood would not be spilt uselessly.†

'The Emperor was not surprised and therefore not bitter that military

---

* The Field-Marshal died on 4 April 1920. In recognition of his loyalty, Charles had sent him from exile some money to ease the hard times he had fallen upon. For his own account of his offer, by which he planned to occupy Vienna in the Emperor's name, see Funder, *op. cit.*, pp. 549–50.

† The explanation why no regular troops ever managed to march on Vienna and come to the Emperor's aid is partly to be sought in the confusion and muddle of the time and partly in the fact that several commanders in key places were, to put it mildly, 'dragging their feet'. One such officer was the Commander of the Vienna Garrison itself (where many of the messages offering help from the field were received) General Dankl. He later excused himself for not accepting these offers by saying that, if he had done so, 'it would have made it look as though the Emperor was afraid'. In the last critical phase, the General never once came out himself to Schönbrunn, let alone sent reinforcements there.

support never reached him. He had confidently hoped for it, of course. Even if he knew only too well in those last weeks that the end in some form was coming – with occupation by the *Entente* armies or revolution or both – the presence of a few loyal regiments would have enabled him to keep some semblance of order and legality in order to deal with events as they came. But he realized that the country was utterly exhausted and that the point of breakdown had now come. Once again it all came back to that old fear of his, that prophecy now coming true that he had so often expressed to the Emperor William and to his own ministers: "If we don't make peace, then the peoples will do it for us over our heads."'

By the second week of November, it was too late for all the loyal troops left in the Army to have saved the crown. Again, though the crumbling went on all the time inexorably inside the Empire, the decisive blows came from outside. Three were struck within forty-eight hours and together they set the seal on the dynasty's fate.

The first two were diplomatic. Since 2 November, Prince Windisch-graetz (now a senior Foreign Office official under the new minister Count Andrassy) had been in Berne talking to the British, French and American representatives there. The aim of this last-minute salvage operation – in which nobody but the irrepressible Prince seems to have shown much optimism – was a modest one: to offer the Allies the services of the Emperor in the 'orderly liquidation of the past', without even stipulating that the Empire itself should continue. The pessimists were, of course, right. These unrealistic contacts ended on 7 November with identical replies from the three missions stating that 'as the peoples of the erstwhile Austro-Hungarian monarchy had decided on the dissolution of the Danube state, the *Entente* powers were precluded from negotiating further with the government of his royal and imperial majesty'.

The next day, 8 November, President Wilson underlined the point in an unmistakable and irreparable fashion. He sent a greetings telegram to the Chairman of the State Council in Vienna, Dr Seitz, expressing his pleasure that 'the constituent peoples had now thrown off the yoke of the Austro-Hungarian Empire'. Parallel messages were despatched to Budapest and Prague. Ten days before, the State Council had reported their formation, not to the monarch in Schönbrunn, four miles down the Mariahilferstrasse, but to the President in the White House, four thousand miles across the Atlantic Ocean. Now the American President had replied in the same way. The Dual Monarchy had been privately written off for months in Washington. This made the news both public and official. Thus, in effect, it was Wilson who first proclaimed the November Republic in Austria just as he had prepared its earlier path with his slogans of self-determination in January.

That same day, Lammasch and the other members of his now paralysed 'Imperial Government' went out again to Schönbrunn. They had already been discussing among themselves the question of the Emperor's abdication or withdrawal without agreeing on any formula which would reconcile such a glorious past with such a wretched present. They had also tried, in the wake of the Italian armistice catastrophe, to lay down their own offices, only to be pressed by Charles into staying on at his side. This process was now repeated again. Nothing was decided; nothing was settled; nothing was done. The Empire was running down like an engine out of gear, only waiting for someone to switch the motor off.

This feeling of trance-like helplessness in a setting of such resplendent power is well conveyed by Professor Redlich, who, as Finance Minister in the Emperor's last Government, was with Lammasch that day in Schönbrunn:

That splendid view across the park from the aide-de-camp's room brought me no pleasure. It was as though I was on the stage of a historic tragedy, but not a noble one.... Across the parquet floor strides the charming Countess Bellegarde, herself like a rococo marquise come to life, and around her the elegant officers of the guard, and hovering over everything, this breath of dissolution mixed with the fragrance of a culture still exquisite though faded. Will those others who will soon be spreading their legs here understand that culture and be able to develop it? ...

Then, three-quarters of an hour with the Emperor in his study. He begins by saying we must stay as ministers for if we go he must go too. He gave the impression of being quite in control of himself and clear as to what was coming. He said to me: 'Always, I only wanted peace, and *how* I have striven for it!' ...

I found him talkative, calm and looking better than he did ten days ago, also speaking again quite shrewdly. But again I got this feeling that all these happenings no longer touched his innermost being, a feeling of a strange emptiness, of the unreality of it all. ...*

The next day, 9 November, came the event which put an end to this painful trance. The Emperor William fled his capital, abdicated, and a Republic was then proclaimed in Berlin. Charles's position had been hopeless before this event, but it was the flight of his 'dear brother' that set the inevitable in motion for him as well. The fall of the Hohenzollerns finally dislodged the Habsburgs. So, in the end, the German 'pot of iron' had indeed shattered the Austrian 'pot of clay', though not quite in the way that Charles had predicted to his wife when war broke out.

* Josef Redlich, *op. cit.*, p. 315.

That same night, the Committee of the Austrian Social-Democrat party spoke out publicly for a 'democratic socialist republic of German-Austria'. This was little more than the proclamation of the inescapable. In the constant feelers he had maintained from Schönbrunn with the right-wing politicians of the capital (particularly with the rising Catholic priest, Dr Seipel), Charles had sensed over the last fortnight a steady draining away of monarchism as a political force. He made one more despairing effort to rally it after the dreadful news from Berlin arrived.

At midnight he called two of his close advisers, Count Hunyady and Baron Werkmann, to his study and told them calmly:

Austria will collapse on the example of the German revolution. A republic will be called for and the monarchy will no longer be defended. . . . I will not abdicate and I will not flee the country. To step down from the throne will deprive me of no rights as long as I do not renounce these myself. But I want to know whether the [political] parties which only a few days ago declared themselves for the monarchy still have the courage of their convictions.*

Werkmann was sent into the town to find out. He returned in the small hours to give his sovereign a mixed report. The German-National deputies in the Assembly were now wavering. They would swim with the strongest current. The Socialists, predictably, were determined on a Republic. Everything depended on the main right-wing group of the Christian Socialists – traditionally the party of Empire, dynasty, property and the Church. Above all, in this final emergency, the Church. Their leader, Hauser, was a Catholic prelate. The brightest of their younger stars, Seipel, was also an ordained priest. Could the party as a whole perhaps still be held to the black and yellow flag by an appeal to this strongly clerical leadership through the head of the Catholic Church in Vienna, Cardinal Piffl himself (who four days before had celebrated that mass in St Stephen's for the Emperor's name-day)?

Charles, who, on this night as well, had barely managed to snatch two hours of rest, was awakened by Werkmann and Hunyady again at 6 A.M. with the proposal. They found him so tired that, despite the excessive heat from the great porcelain stoves, he was shivering with cold and exhaustion. But he was calm and clear-headed as usual. Within minutes, he had penned an urgent appeal to the Cardinal. Within the hour, Werkmann had driven through the still darkened streets and was handing it over to the Prince-Archbishop of Vienna in his palace alongside the cathedral. The great man received it with a delphic: 'I shall do my duty.' Almost immediately he set out to find Prelate Hauser in the Parliament building, where the

---

* Werkmann, *Der Tote auf Madeira, op. cit.*, pp. 13 *et seq.*

unexpected arrival of Vienna's Cardinal early on a Sunday morning caused no little stir.

But the republican current was simply too strong by now for anyone to fish the heavy crown out to safety. Throughout that day Lammasch and his ministers were discussing the Emperor's position, both among themselves and with Seitz and Renner as representatives of the State Council.* All were agreed that the revolution in Berlin had already settled the main issue in Vienna. There was no question in any of their minds of the Emperor staying on his throne. All that remained to be decided was the exact form in which he should step down and – as regards the Christian Socialists – how they could extricate themselves with some show of dignity from their recent pledge to keep him there. Renner made it clear that they only had until the next day to sort both problems out, for on Monday, 11 November, the State Council intended to pronounce and put to the vote the basic laws of the new German-Austrian state.

A message passed to the Emperor by the Cardinal immediately after his visit to Parliament showed how the solution was shaping. His Majesty, the Cardinal Piffl suggested, would make it simpler for the Christian-Social deputies to support his case when it came to the vote if he first agreed to 'put aside his rights and place the constitutional decision in the hands of the people'.† This verbal advance warning was given to the sovereign already by 11 A.M. on 10 November. But despite his repeated enquiries and urgings, the official formula in writing was not put in his hands until 11.10 the following morning – less than four hours before Parliament was anyway due to pronounce his Empire in Austria extinct. Before coming to those events, these are some of the Empress's memories of that last week-end in Schönbrunn, which was also to be their last as ruling sovereigns.

'It was an almost unbroken series of conferences, audiences and reports – day and night. The situation changed almost from hour to hour and our plans and contacts changed accordingly. The whole palace was echoing with suggestions as to what we should do next.

'But there was one suggestion that the Emperor never at any time entertained for one moment: that he should abdicate outright. It was not a question here – as has sometimes been suggested – of him saying perhaps and me saying no. He always felt, and he repeated it again now at the end: "This crown is a responsibility given to me by God and I cannot renounce it." He never wavered on this point and could not have been influenced by anyone. To abdicate, he said, would be like deserting from the front.

* See Redlich, *op. cit.* p. 317.   † Werkmann, *op. cit.*, p. 15.

'Apart from the ministers and other advisers, who were constantly coming and going, there was a stream of all sorts of visitors during these last days. Three stand out in my mind – each very different from the others.

'The first was a familiar figure clad in dark green shooting-clothes who suddenly appeared late at night in Schönbrunn, produced a military rifle from under his cloak, and asked if he could be of any help. He was Count Franz Karl Waldendorff, a friend and officer-comrade of my husband's when he was an Archduke serving in the 7th Dragoons. Waldendorff had been convalescing from war injuries at his home in Alt Bunzlau in Bohemia when the November crisis gathered, but had got up and somehow managed to make his way to Vienna through the streams of soldiers and refugees in order, as he told his wife, to protect his Emperor. Lots of people came to us with advice. He was one of the few who came bringing a weapon and offering to fight.

'Then there was Admiral Horthy, who had come up from the Adriatic to discuss the handing-over of our fleet to Croatia.* He couldn't contain his grief now that the decision had to be taken and he burst out in tears in front of the Emperor. Charles was so moved that he sent a message to me in my rooms asking me to come over and say a few soothing words to Horthy to try and console him. This, of course, I did.

'Then suddenly – I can still see it now – Horthy, the tears still in his eyes, braces himself, stands upright, raises his right hand and swears, quite unasked: "I will never rest until I have restored Your Majesty to his thrones in Vienna and Budapest." An interesting episode, when one thinks of what we were to experience three years later, when Horthy, as the Emperor's Regent, fought his sovereign in the suburbs of Budapest and even had him arrested and deported to keep Hungary in his own hands.

'Equally unforgettable was an energetic bright old lady of nearly ninety who turned up at Schönbrunn on our very last day there. Who should it be but Princess Melanie,† the last daughter of the famous Chancellor Metternich who, of course, had played such a role in this same palace in the Napoleonic era more than a hundred years before, only to be driven from office by the revolt of 1848. In those last hours there was no protocol any more and no appointments book. So she had just arrived, asking to see me with a message to give to the Emperor. I received her in my sitting-room on the first floor of the East Wing.‡ This was the message she brought: "Tell the Emperor he shouldn't worry too much. Revolutions

* See footnote to p. 181.
† Then eighty-six years old; born 27 February 1832.
‡ Occupied in the autumn of 1945 by the author when the Palace was the head-quarters of the British High Commission.

are like floods. They pass over the land and cover it. But they do not last
for ever. And when the flood-tide falls, the land comes up again.'' '

It was eleven o'clock the next morning that the 1918 flood of revolution
reached Schönbrunn. It was not borne by a mob but carried decorously in
a motor-car by two members of the last Imperial Cabinet – Lammasch, the
Prime Minister, and Gayer, the Minister of Interior. They brought with
them, for Charles to sign, the text of the Manifesto which the politicians of
the old and the new Austria had finally agreed upon and which salvaged
the consciences of the former while meeting the demands of the latter.
Lammasch himself, his Finance Minister Redlich, the Social-Democrat
leader Renner and several others had taken a hand in drafting this document, which had to say so much while still leaving some things unsaid.
But the passages that were crucial to the whole compromise are generally
attributed to the astute Christian-Socialist priest Ignaz Seipel. These
stipulated that the Emperor, recognizing in advance any new constitution that German-Austria might decide upon, should relinquish 'all
participation in the affairs of state'. Thus, whatever the practice turned
out to be, in law the Habsburg dynasty was to renounce its power but
not its crown.

Though, as stated, these republican tidings were not actually brought
out to Schönbrunn by the mob, this was probably not very far behind.
Certainly such was the impression given by the two ministerial messengers, though how far they were influenced by nervous strain and how
far by a desire to put maximum pressure on the sovereign is impossible to
estimate. Both were in a parlous state. Gayer, in great agitation, urged
Charles to sign because 'that same afternoon would see the workers'
masses before Schönbrunn ... and then the few who refuse to abandon
Your Majesty would fall in the fight and with them Your Majesty himself
and the All-Highest family'.* Lammasch was even more excited and
distraught, listening half to one speaker and half to another, beginning
sentences without finishing them. They both pressed the Emperor to sign
immediately as the Manifesto was due to be published all over Vienna at
3 P.M. and had still to be printed in the State Printing Office. One by one,
the Emperor's other advisers joined in the chorus.

The Empress recalls: 'The Ministers pursued the Emperor in a panic
from room to room demanding his signature. They had been promising to
let him see this famous compromise formula for two days. Now they
arrived at 11.10 A.M. and wanted it proclaimed in fifty minutes' time, at
noon. At one point, the Emperor literally had to shake them off with the

---

* Werkmann, *op. cit.*, pp. 18–22; Redlich, *op. cit.*, pp. 317–18.

exclamation: "If you won't even let me *read* it, how do you expect me to *sign* it?" '

At this Charles was left at peace for a few moments to study 'his' Manifesto. Then, quite calmly, he put some final questions to his advisers. Werkmann was asked to repeat the story of his mission to the Cardinal. Gayer was asked again to confirm that any attempt at armed resistance from the palace could only do more harm than good. A revolution, he tearfully declared, could not be held back by force. The Empress was called in to read the fateful document. At a first quick reading she mistook it for an outright abdication and burst out in protest:

'A sovereign can never abdicate. He can be deposed and his sovereign rights be declared forfeit. All right. That is force. But abdicate – never, never, never! I would rather fall here at your side. Then there would be Otto. And even if all of us here were killed, there would still be other Habsburgs!'*

All this while there were knocks and shouts at the door of the study. First the aides, then Minister Gayer himself appeared on the threshold, begging for an instant decision as though the hordes of Genghis Khan were already galloping across the palace flower-beds. The Emperor withdrew with the Empress and Werkmann into the next salon, the so-called 'Porcelain Room'. Here, for a few more minutes, he went through the arguments again. The Empress now realized that this was no formal abdication but a voluntary withdrawal from power. Finally Werkmann, asked for his opinion, also urged the Emperor to sign, arguing that the document still left all constitutional roads open for the dynasty in the future, in the other crown lands as well as Austria. and, as for the present: 'Madness reigns today and a madhouse is no place for a sovereign.'

Charles took up a metallic pencil† and put his bold clear signature at the foot of the document. Then he told Werkmann to inform the Prime Minister that the Manifesto could be published in the form in which it had been submitted. Minutes later the two ministers were in their motor-car, heading back to the city centre with the news.

This was the Emperor's message to his people, as it was rushed off the presses that same day:‡

* These are the Empress's words as recounted by Werkmann, *op. cit.*, p. 19. The Empress does not remember exactly what she said at this hectic point but thinks Werkmann's account may well be the gist of it.

† The Empress states that the fact that the Emperor signed in pencil had no significance. He nearly always carried a pencil with him, often talking with it in his hands, and signed most documents this way.

‡ For photostat, see Appendix 6. This is a photostat of a true copy. The original was destroyed when the Palace of Justice in Vienna was burned down by rioters in 1927.

Ever since my accession I have tried ceaselessly to lead my peoples out of the horrors of a war for whose inception I bear no trace of blame.

I have not hesitated to restore constitutional life and I have opened up for the peoples the path of their development as independent states.

Filled, now as ever, with unwavering devotion to all my peoples, I do not wish to oppose their free growth with my own person.

I recognize in advance whatever decision that German-Austria may make about its future political form.

The people, through its representatives, has taken over the government. I renounce all participation in the affairs of state.

At the same time, I relieve my Austrian Government from office.

May the people of German-Austria, in unity and tolerance, create and strengthen the new order! The happiness of my peoples has, from the beginning, been the object of my most ardent wishes.

Only an inner peace can heal the wounds of this war.

And, at the bottom, that one word in pencil which had put an end to six and a half centuries of Habsburg rule.

The time was soon after noon on 11 November 1918. A hush now fell over Schönbrunn, a strange quietness, which, in Werkmann's words, 'almost hurt'. It was as though life itself was draining out of the great palace now that the power had gone.

On the morrow the Republic would be formally proclaimed. But that same night the Emperor determined to leave the palace with his family. It was not only anxiety for their safety, in case those dire prophecies of 'red hordes' should prove true. Schönbrunn itself – deserted, unguarded – had become, with a few strokes of the pencil, a magnificent irrelevance, and its atmosphere was unbearable.

One ghostly procedure had to be gone through first: the formal removal from office of the last Imperial Government. Soon after two o'clock, Lammasch was back in the palace again with all his ministers to enact the macabre ceremony. Redlich described the scene as 'almost a physical pain'. Charles's bearing throughout the whole exhausting crisis had impressed even his opponents. Now too, he seemed to be the only calm person present. All of his ministers were choking with emotion. Some had just given up the fight, like Professor Lammasch himself, who had tears streaming down his white beard as he struggled through a brief speech of farewell.

But even in all the drama and sorrow, certain eternal Austrian priorities were not forgotten. Two ministers, on their formal retirement, were each awarded pensions of 20,000 crowns a year. Lammasch was given the Great

Cross of the Order of St Stephen to dry his tears on and lesser awards of this and the Order of St Leopold were distributed among the other ministers. Two of them who had particularly hoped for the title of 'Geheimrat' or 'Secret Councillor' were frustrated by their colleagues. It was a very Viennese as well as a very dynastic finish.

When that was over and done with and the ministers had departed for the last time, the Emperor had to decide on his own destination. After a final talk on the security position with Gayer, Charles plumped for Eckartsau on the Marchfeld north-east of Vienna where he had a shooting-lodge. The Empress has stated that there were several reasons for this choice. Eckartsau was removed from the capital but not too remote. It was in the middle of a Lower Austrian countryside which was by tradition loyal. It had a small game preserve which, in those desperate days, would come in useful as a source of food. Above all, it was indisputably the private property of the Emperor's and not a state dwelling like any of the palaces, which were about to be declared the property of the Republic.

This is how the Empress remembers the leave-taking:

'The whole day was a nightmare. There had been many visitors in the afternoon coming to say good-bye and to wish us well. Also – though we hadn't heard about it immediately – the Swiss Minister, Burckhart, and his Dutch colleague, van der Weede, had approached the palace on behalf of all the neutral missions in Vienna, offering their personal protection to escort us abroad. When the Emperor was told about the approach he sent back a message thanking the diplomats warmly but declining because he wanted to stay in his country.

'Our preparations for departure had to be made in the middle of all this with the greatest secrecy. Raiding parties were already out in the streets of Vienna and there was a danger that the whole family would be taken prisoner by the Red Guard. From five o'clock onwards we waited for our cars, which however couldn't get through on time to Schönbrunn. Then at half-past six, they began to arrive.

'The Emperor and I went with our children into the palace chapel, where we said a short prayer that we might one day return here. After that, we went up to the so-called Hall of Ceremonies where all those who had still remained behind with us were gathered. We said good-bye to them and thanked them one by one.

'Then down the stairway to the small inner court below where the cars were waiting. Along the sides of the arcades, drawn up in two ranks, were our cadets from the military academies, sixteen- and seventeen-year-olds, with tears in their eyes, but still perfectly turned out and guarding us to the end. They had really lived up to the motto the Empress Maria Theresa had given them: "*Allzeit Getreu*" ("Loyal for Ever").

'It was dark by now, and a misty autumn night. We got into the vehicles. The Emperor and I and all the children except Karl Ludwig squeezed into the back of one car with Count Hunyady at the front. In the next came the infant Karl Ludwig with Countess Kerssenbrock and the children's nurses. The order of the other cars I forget.

'We did not risk driving out of the main gate in front of the palace. Instead we continued parallel with the main building along the broad gravel path that leads to the eastern side gate. We slipped out of this and left the capital by a special route. Late that night – without any trouble or incidents – we arrived at Eckartsau.'

Before following them there, one last little episode at the palace they had just left is worth recording.* It speaks volumes for the chaos in Vienna that night and for the gap it created between the old order and the new.

In order to conceal their departure as long as possible, the Empress had taken only one of her two personal maids with her. The other was left behind in Schönbrunn not even knowing that the family had left. In the early hours of the morning this maid was awakened by the call-bell from the Empress's bedroom. It shrilled on and on like no ordinary call and the maid dressed hurriedly and ran down to the first floor, wondering what had happened. As she got to the state apartments, she noticed for the first time that there were no guards to be seen. She also noticed something even stranger. Though nobody was answering, other call-bells were sounding from all directions.

A shock awaited her as she burst into her mistress's bedroom. There was no sign of the Empress. Instead there were three or four intruders of doubtful appearance who, having found the Imperial palace open and unguarded in the middle of the night, had just walked in to see what they could steal. As the maid surprised them, they were working away with a set of tools to try and prise open the wall-safe where the Empress normally kept her jewels. And one of the burglars, to be more comfortable while he worked, had sat himself down on the edge of the bed without moving the covers.

Underneath these, and right underneath him, was the Empress's *sonnette* board with its rows of call buttons still linked to all parts of the palace. He would have been alarming everyone – had there been anyone to hear or care.

* This was told to the Empress a few days later at Eckartsau by the maid concerned.

Chapter 14

ECKARTSAU: EXILE AT HOME

The night drive to Eckartsau was no journey into oblivion, like the German Emperor's flight to Holland. Charles now had less than three and a half years of his short life ahead of him. Yet almost every day of them was to be filled with politics, and exile itself was to bring him even greater dramas and tragedies than the throne. Indeed, all Europe was to be more startled by this powerless wanderer than it ever had been by the reigning monarch.

In those first months of exile inside what had been his own Empire he was in the position of a spectator who – without willing it or even raising a hand – overshadowed the action he was watching. Events in what had been his Dual Monarchy moved on without him, but always with a sideways look at the young Habsburg in Eckartsau who was still technically undeposed as Austrian Emperor and still quite unchallenged as Hungarian King. In both of the old twin capitals, however, the new leaders lost no time in staking out their claims.

On 12 November, Charles's first day in his new 'Court', the Republic of German-Austria was formally proclaimed in Vienna, amid gestures of protest from both political extremes. The challenge of the left-wing radicals was an ugly one. A group of Communist-led soldiers and demonstrators tried to storm the main entrance to the Parliament building, only to have it slammed in their faces just in time. Foiled in their bid to invade the chamber, they then made their contribution to the inaugural debate on the steps outside. Seizing the red-white-red flag of the new state, they ripped out the white middle strip – a symbolic call for a Communist 'Peoples' Republic' of the type that was actually to spring into life in four months' time in both Bavaria and Hungary.

Compared with this, the protest gesture from the right wing was a tame affair indeed. The Christian-Socialists had dropped their last despairing campaign for a 'democratic monarchy' and as a party decided to go republican with the rest. Only three of their number, including the later

President, Wilhelm Miklas, voted against the one word 'Republic' in the basic law. Of that emphatic Christian-Socialist support for the crown announced three weeks before * there now remained, apart from this minuscule protest vote, only the technical objection that the new constitutional form should have been decided by plebiscite rather than by the politicians.

After this ritual declaration by the erstwhile monarchists, Germany-Austria was proclaimed a 'democratic Republic' (Article I of the state law). It was also hopefully declared to be 'a part of the German Republic' (Article II). Apart from some nationalistic aberrations in the 1930s, Article I was to be duly carried out. But to achieve Article II, the Austrians had to await the sobering experience of Hitler's *Anschluss* twenty years later, which cured their pan-Germanism for good by the simple process of fulfilling it at last. As regards this infant Austrian Republic, it was the victorious *Entente* powers who now forced Vienna to try and stand on its own unsteady feet. The France of Clemenceau, above all, was determined to prevent anything which might give strength to the prostrated German colossus. Her will was to be reflected in the Peace Treaties of 1919 which not only declared the German and Austrian Republics to be two separate and independent states but went on specifically to forbid any union between them. Thus in 1919, as before in 1806 and 1866 and as afterwards in 1938 and 1955,† the Austrians had their new identity decided for them. And in this particular move, the *Entente* powers were acting after Charles's own heart. For him, as for France, the Berlin of the generals spelled a greater menace than all the restive Slavs of Christendom.

Thus on 12 November all the Austrian politicians (though not all the Austrian people) forsook their Emperor. The next day, their Hungarian colleagues arrived from Budapest in an attempt to shake off their King. The delegation which arrived at Eckartsau on the morning of 13 November was headed by no one less than the Prince-Primate of Hungary, Cardinal Csernoch,‡ assisted by the President of the Hungarian House of Peers, Baron Wlassics and two pillars of the old feudal order, Prince Nicholas Esterhazy and Count Dessewffy. Their mission was commensurate with their splendour. As the Empress recalls the day:

'Count Karolyi, who by now of course was Prime Minister of the radical government in Budapest, wanted the Emperor to abdicate outright, and had sent this delegation to achieve it. The four men all seemed

---

* And repeated, the Empress states, by Hauser and the other Christian-Socialist leaders as late as the morning of 11 November in Schönbrunn, in return for the Emperor's agreement to sign the 'renouncal of power'.

† When the Four-Power occupation was ended on the condition that Austria proclaimed her 'perpetual neutrality'.

‡ Who had assisted at the coronation of Charles in Budapest two years before.

to be in a boundless panic. One or two of their number – including Tisza, of course – had already been killed in Budapest and they wanted an abdication to save themselves as well as the situation. But the Emperor refused point-blank and a hard battle of wills and wits began which went on the whole day. I noted in my diary that they first had an hour before lunch with my husband from 12.30 to 1.30 and then two long sessions afterwards – from 14.30 to 15.45 and from 16.45 to 18.00. In the end they had to settle for the same sort of compromise the Austrians had got two days before. I was not present and not involved in any of this. The Emperor did not need me to know what to do about his Hungarian crown.'

The compromise was a brief statement of only three sentences.* The operative words read:

I do not wish to stand in the way of the evolution of the Hungarian nation, for whom I still feel the same unchanged love. Consequently I resign my part in the business of state and accept this decision as regards the new form of Government in Hungary.

When he signed this modest-looking document it was as though Charles had taken the thousand-year-old crown of St Stephen off his head and laid it for a while in his lap. But he never took his hands off it and neither did the nation whose history it symbolized. Hungary remained a Monarchy in abeyance right down to the Second World War, ruled in the name of the dynasty by defectors from the dynasty. It is this that makes Charles's two descents on Hungary to reclaim his kingdom something far removed from wild adventures, even if they did end in failure and fiasco.

Before being launched on all this, however, there were immediate problems enough for the royal family to face at Eckartsau. As there had been no formal deposition, the Court had simply moved from the great palace of Schönbrunn to this quiet shooting-lodge, close to the Czech and Hungarian borders in the so-called 'Three Countries Corner'. Here, tucked away in the damp wooded meadows of the Danube within half an hour's stroll of the river itself, it continued to function, or at least revolve in a painful and ghostly fashion for all those who still openly or secretly acknowledged it. The facts, of course, scarcely matched the theory. It was an Imperial Court in title only. In appearance and resources it was more like the swollen household of a country squire who ate less well than the peasants on his surrounding fields. Austerity was nothing new to Charles and Zita; nor was it anything particularly distasteful to either of them. Yet now for the first time they met privation and hardship as well – two of the

* For photostat of original, see p. 343.

many baleful companions they were to travel with in the years ahead. This is the Empress's description of daily life at Eckartsau in the six weeks up to their bleak Christmas there:

'The numbers at Eckartsau varied but there were never less than fifty of us. Often there were many more because in addition to ourselves and the children and the handful of people who had fled with us from Schönbrunn there was a small detachment of Vienna police who were supposed to guard us; the servants and keepers who lived permanently at Eckartsau; and finally a constant flow of visitors and what one could only call refugees – former retainers and so on driven out of the capital by fright and hunger or both and who came out to us for food and protection.

'Not that we could give them much of either. Food was quite literally insufficient and had it not been for the game we could shoot in the woods we should have been in a desperate way. The Emperor did his share of this until he fell ill on 15 December. Food supplies were supposed to be sent out to us from Vienna but the lorries arrived irregularly and, more than once, they were attacked and picked clean on the way.

'Everything else was in short supply – soap, for example, so that the children were obliged to wear dark clothes to reduce the need for washing. The electricity was more off than on and some everyday essentials like matches were missing altogether.

'As for the security position, the local population was utterly reliable and so was the tiny force of so-called "castle gendarmes" (later recalled) which the loyal Vienna Police President Dr Schober had at first provided. But the danger – and it was a big and unpredictable one – was from the plundering bands of deserted or demobilized soldiers in the countryside around us, and, even more, from units of the newly-formed radical "Red Guard" which was largely Communist-led. They posted up on the park gates their threats to hang us all and carried out their raids right up to the boundaries of the estate. Indeed, it got so bad that when our keepers went out to shoot game quite near the house they had to take an armed police-man with them. At least one of them was shot at while on patrol.

'Christmas 1918 was therefore a rather sombre festival – especially as the Emperor, who was anyway suffering from repeated heart attacks and general overstrain, went down with a severe attack of Spanish influenza ten days before and was now really ill. All the children caught it as well; some only mildly it is true, but some severely – Karl Ludwig, for example, who was then barely eighteen months old, very nearly died.

'However we did our best to make it a cheerful occasion. We had a Christmas tree of course on the evening of the 24th and at the foot of it we spread our pile of little gifts. We had found at Eckartsau a trunk nearly full of minor presents which we had once used on our official journeys and this came in most useful. To the staff I remember we gave mainly the things they wanted most – bits of chocolate and other scraps of food we had saved and wrapped up for the occasion.

'The Emperor got up for Christmas Eve but was so weak that he had to remain seated in an armchair while the presents were being exchanged. He was quite exhausted afterwards and his temperature went up again. That same night, we heard, there were toasts to the Emperor drunk all over the capital. This rather bore out that well-known remark of the new Socialist Chancellor Renner: "Austria is a Republic without republicans!"

'And in fact we could have drunk toasts ourselves had we been in the mood. There was wine enough for us at Eckartsau due to an interesting episode. After the Emperor, who rarely touched alcohol of any sort, went down with 'flu, the doctor had ordered him to drink wine for his health. At that our Count Hunyady went up to Vienna and made straight for the Imperial cellars. Here he found in charge one of our former servants (not a very good one, as a matter of fact) who was now an ardent Socialist, in name at least. When Hunyady demanded some wine for the sick Emperor the man replied: "Of course. Take all you want, and I hope it will do His Majesty some good."'

So the new year opened, the first of the powerless years. Before it was a week old, the pressure to force the Emperor either to leave his kingdom or renounce its crown for good began in earnest. Before Christmas, on 22 December, Renner had already raised the matter in the State Council of this infant Republic that still had the ancient dynasty in its midst. He had wanted then to intervene personally with Charles but had been dissuaded by one of the Emperor's spokesmen in Vienna, Baron Werkmann.* To tackle the problem afresh seems to have been one of Renner's New Year resolutions. In the first week of January, the Chancellor of the Provisional Government of German-Austria suddenly appeared himself at Eckartsau – unannounced and unexpected – and asked to see the Emperor. He was to learn that the shooting-lodge was still, despite everything, a Court to its inhabitants. While Charles and Zita remained on the first floor, Renner was served the best lunch that Eckartsau could provide downstairs, but with only Zeno von Schonta, one of the Emperor's aides, to keep him company.

The Chancellor's message was much as expected. The monarch was urged to leave Austria with his family as soon as possible, firstly to get away from the unhealthy damp atmosphere of the Danube meadows and

* *Der Tote auf Madeira, op. cit.,* p. 33.

secondly to avoid 'unpredictable actions by impetuous elements'.*
Schonta, knowing his master's wishes, replied with more conviction than
he felt that there was nothing wrong with the local air, while security –
which was anyway the visitor's responsibility – presented no problem.
The meal ended and Renner left without even clapping eyes on Charles.

From his own point of view as leader of the Austrian Socialists and head
of a republican regime that was still only provisional, Renner's concern to
get the monarch out of the country was perfectly understandable. Elections to return the Republic's first proper Government were due to be held
in a few weeks' time and the mere presence of the Emperor on Austrian
soil might well have served as a rallying point for right-wing sentiment, as
well as a flash-point for Communist agitation. When those elections were in
fact held † on 16 February 1919, the representatives of the *bourgeoisie* (and
to some extent of the old order as well) easily outnumbered the left wing.
But the Social Democrats with seventy-two seats just outnumbered the
Christian Socialists with sixty-nine seats as the largest single party. (The
various German-national groups collected twenty-nine seats among
them.) Charles could draw some consolation from the fact that in the local
elections at Orth, which was just beside Eckartsau, a German-national
deputy was returned who had openly fought his campaign as a monarchist.
Yet this was little more than a flash of light relief on a darkening horizon.
With a Republic now formally constituted in Vienna under Socialist
leadership (and, in the eyes of its leaders, recognized in advance by the
Emperor's declaration of 11 November) Charles's own position in the
country became overnight more tenuous.

Then, the very day of the elections, coming right out of the blue and
from the hostile *Entente* camp a thousand miles away, a hand suddenly
stretched across the continent to Eckartsau in greeting and protection. It
was indeed no ordinary hand. It was that of the British sovereign, King
George v himself. Hearing of his fellow-monarch's plight and danger, the
ruler of another Empire that still had a generation to live had ordered a
British officer to be made personally responsible to him for Charles's welfare and safety. This was the beginning of a strange link, which for-
tuitously renewed itself in the years ahead. From now until the end of their
adventures, the British Army and the Royal Navy were to be inextricably
bound up with the fortunes of Charles and his family, first as saviours and

---

* Schonta, *Erinnerungen, op. cit.*, pp. 59–60.

† They were held according to the direct and universal suffrage already introduced
under the monarchy. But it was something of an irony that the Socialists opposed
making voting compulsory, fearing that their working-class supporters would somehow resent it.

then as sympathetic captors. What lay behind King George's extraordinary gesture of chivalry to a young Emperor who, less than three months before, had been his enemy in war?

The dynastic gesture had a dynastic background. The prime movers behind this help which the victorious House of Windsor extended to the defeated and overthrown House of Habsburg were the Empress's two brothers, the French Princes Sixtus and Xavier of Bourbon-Parma. And their most eloquent argument had been the fate of yet another European dynasty, the Romanovs. There is no record in the Windsor Castle archives of when Sixtus, the elder of the two Princes, had his private audience with the British monarch and Queen Mary. Nor is there even any mention of the meeting – let alone an account of what transpired – in King George's own personal diary.* But other evidence suggests that the audience took place in the first days of February 1919. As to what happened, here is the Empress's general account, based on information supplied by the princes afterwards:

'My two brothers acted entirely on their own responsibility in approaching King George on our behalf. Cut off at Eckartsau, we had no means of communicating with the outside world and had not been in direct touch with them since their activities – alas unsuccessful – as intermediaries in the Emperor's secret peace-feelers to London and Paris in 1917. But of course they had all the news from Vienna and, as our position worsened in the New Year, they decided to act.

'As a first step, Prince Sixtus immediately went to see the French President, M. Poincaré, in Paris, to ask for French intervention and protection. Poincaré replied that he indeed thought something ought to be done, especially in view of the contacts he had had with the Austrian Emperor through my brother during the secret peace negotiations of 1917. But he could only hold out the hope of a diplomatic step through the Ministry of Foreign Affairs and he stressed that, as President of the Republic, he could not intervene directly. Prince Sixtus replied that, though one would be grateful even for that, such a slow process would have no effect on a revolutionary government and that only a direct and immediate step by the President could prevent a repetition of the Russian Royal Family's tragedy. Poincaré answered that a decision of this sort could not come from him but that he would try to get some action out of the Prime Mnister (Clemenceau) as soon as possible.

'At that, my brother – seeing that Poincaré intended to rest on his legal position as a President without power – said: "M. le Président, we cannot

* I am indebted to the Queen's librarian, Mr Mackworth-Young, and his staff for their help on this and many other features of the episode.

afford to lose a minute. I shall leave straight away for London." And Poincaré replied: "You are doing the right thing, for the King of England has more freedom of action than I have; but I shall do whatever I can on my side." At that, Prince Sixtus telegraphed to London and crossed the Channel that same evening with his brother Xavier.

'The next day – the day of his arrival in England – after a call on the Foreign Office, he was received by King George v at Buckingham Palace in the presence of Queen Mary. He described to them what was happening in Austria and the dangerous situation which the Emperor and his family were in. He then alluded to the assassination by the Bolsheviks of the Russian Imperial family at Ekaterinburg the previous July and said that the same tragedy might well now be repeated. This warning had a profound effect. It was known that the King always reproached himself for the fate which had been allowed to overtake his cousin, the Tsar Nicholas, after the plan had been dropped to send a British cruiser to Murmansk to bring him and his family to safety in Britain.

'Queen Mary, very moved, turned to the King and said: "What Sixtus has told us is very serious." And King George, who was equally disturbed, replied: "We will immediately do what is necessary."

'At that, Prince Sixtus took his leave, stressing at the end of the audience how urgent the need was for *military* protection, and adding that he was assured that France would give at least her diplomatic support.

'As a result, we were suddenly informed at Eckartsau a week or so later that a British officer was being attached to us for our protection. The Emperor was just as astonished as everyone else when the news arrived at the house: astonished and overwhelmed with gratitude and relief and also deeply touched by this gesture of solidarity from one monarch to another across all the barriers of war. As we now had direct contact with the British authorities in Vienna, my husband immediately wrote a personal letter of thanks to King George for them to transmit to London.'

No copy of that message was kept – or at least none has survived in the Habsburg family documents. But the original letter has been preserved among King George's personal papers at Windsor. Charles wrote it in French, then the accepted language for all personal communications between European sovereigns or Heads of State.

Majesté,

Je suis heureux de pouvoir venir remercier Votre Majesté de la si délicate attention de m'avoir envoyé le colonel Summerhayes. Je suis fort touché de cet acte si courtois et en même temps j'en suis très reconnaissant. Le colonel est un homme charmant qui remplit sa mission avec beaucoup de tact et d'amabilité. La situation dans le monde entier est très difficile surtout pour nous souverains. Que Dieu ait pitié de l'humanité souffrante et lui rende bientôt le repos dont elle a si besoin!

De Votre Majesté le bon frère et cousin,

Charles

*Eckartsau, ce 21 février 1919.**

King George had sent his personal help not only to a man who was a fellow-sovereign in an hour of need. Charles was still remembered in London as the most insistent and the most persistent of all the voices from the enemy camp who had spoken up for peace, and the one who had almost wrecked his own alliance in his attempts to achieve an end to the war by personal diplomacy. Indeed the last time that same brother-in-law of his, Prince Sixtus, had stood before the British monarchs was on 23 May 1917 when, in the presence of Lloyd George, he had pleaded the case for peace negotiations with Vienna on the Emperor's behalf.† Finally, quite apart from the shadow of the Romanov massacre, King George may also have felt another purely personal association flash through his mind as the French Prince talked to him again. It was this same prisoner on the Danube flats at Eckartsau who, as the Archduke Charles, had come to London in June 1911 to represent the old Emperor Franz Josef at his own Coronation in Westminster Abbey. A memory both of a happier Europe than that of 1919, and of another order of life that Sarajevo had blown to pieces for good.

King George's response was understandable therefore; almost predictable. For some reason which has never been cleared up, the King's decision was nearly a fortnight in taking effect. For what happened next, we can best turn to a little-known account given by Colonel Sir Thomas Cunninghame ‡ who, at Christmas 1918, had been posted to Vienna as British Military Representative on the joint *Entente* Mission there (a job he arduously had to double with that of British Military Attaché in Prague and unofficial observer of all that was happening in Hungary). He writes:

In mid-February of 1919, when in Prague, I received from the War Office in London a telegram to the effect that an intention to murder the Emperor and Empress of Austria had been indicated by a reliable report. The same source had also suggested that lack of medical attendance was causing great hardship to the Empress. I was directed to send a reliable officer of the Military Mission to

* For photostat, see Appendix 7. Published by Gracious Permission of her Majesty the Queen. Royal Archives reference CV M1466/4.

† See p. 89 above. Prince Xavier was not present at either audience.

‡ Found in the *Hungarian Quarterly* (Budapest–London–New York), Volume 5, No. 4 (Winter 1939–40), pp. 633–46. I am indebted to helpers in present-day Hungary for pointing the article out.

Eckartsau who should endeavour by every means in his power to ameliorate the conditions of life of the Emperor and Empress and give them the moral support of the British Government.

Dated 4 February and not received by me until 15 February, the origin of this telegram still [i.e. in 1939] remains a mystery. It was never explained who it was who wished to murder the Royal Couple, nor was it ever said whether the supposed plot was local or otherwise. The Chief of the Austrian Police – Dr Johann Schober, afterwards State Chancellor – was a devoted and faithful servant of the Habsburgs. His best detectives kept unremitting watch over the Château of Eckartsau. . . . From the working men of Vienna – as a body – no danger was to be apprehended at all. They had much personal sympathy with their late ruler and thought him a man of progressive ideas and a good fellow. Besides, at the time, food and clothing were so short that I doubt whether men or boots would have lasted the sixty kilometres from Vienna to Eckartsau. The *Volkswehr*, a force raised by the Socialists to keep unemployed off the streets, were in the main composed of decent men. There were groups of them however who were out of hand, and the evil of exaggerated political opinion rendered trust in them, as instruments of public security, an uncertain factor . . .*

Cutting short my visit to Prague, I hastened back to Vienna on 16 February 1919, having in mind for the post of *Ehrenkavalier* [*sic*] at Eckartsau a certain Colonel Summerhayes of the Royal Army Medical Corps who had been employed evacuating prisoners-of-war in Germany and Austria. He accepted the post with alacrity and proved himself a good choice, for he was of cheerful disposition and was able to do much to dispel the gloom which had settled upon the unhappy family; for the latter was suffering not only from cramped quarters but also from actual shortage of food.

Colonel Cunninghame then relates how, on a date later in February which he unfortunately does not name, he drove out to Eckartsau himself to introduce Summerhayes to the Emperor, whom neither of them had ever met. In a talk with the Emperor which he describes as 'long and very interesting', Cunninghame told Charles outright that he personally considered that 'the famous plot against his life was mythical' as far as the Austrians were concerned. But the sceptical Colonel then went on to suggest another danger from a totally different quarter which even the Emperor himself does not seem to have envisaged.

The *Entente*, Cunninghame pointed out, had bestowed Slovakia – which was a province of the old Hungary – on the new-born composite state of Czechoslovakia. Moreover, the Czechs had been given sanction to occupy it in advance of the peace treaty which was still to be concluded with the

---

* This elaborately phrased passage refers to precisely those elements from whom Charles had most to fear – the Communist groups in the 'Red Guard' who were threatening to murder the Royal Family. Colonel Cunninghame, however, never really believed in the danger.

Hungarian Government. This process of occupation had already begun and the Italian section of the Czech Legion, under General Piccione, was on the march. Its Headquarters were now at the old Slovak capital of Poszony,* which was only a few miles to the East of where they were all sitting at Eckartsau, across the River March. The Hungarians – nationalistic Magyars whatever the flag they flew – were becoming increasingly restive and resentful about this. Colonel Cunninghame added that, when he had been in Budapest a few days before, Count Karolyi himself had warned him that unless Hungary got special consideration from the *Entente* in this matter the position might get out of hand, with the radical left-wing leading the field. The Colonel, to return to his account, went on:

As there was not the slightest prospect of the *Entente* listening either to Karolyi or the Socialists, danger from the Red element in Hungary was to be expected and it was no use blinking the fact. In Vienna, owing to the conditions of distress, there was much inflammable material and it was vital to keep the two regions from igniting simultaneously. . . . I then added that I thought there would be advantage in his removal from a spot so near the March river. It was not proximity to Vienna that was in my mind but proximity to Poszony. The Hungarian troops were at that time cantoned in the eastern provinces but there were already reports that they had been ordered to move westwards. Poszony was a vital point and a military clash in its vicinity was far from being an impossibility. I suggested that he should move to Gmunden † where the Duke of Cumberland had an estate or to the frontiers of Salzburg province where the Bavarian Wittelsbachs were taking refuge. I was careful to say that I did not suggest departure from Austria.

I then asked laughingly what the Emperor would feel if a troop of Red Hussars suddenly came over the frontier, surrounded Eckartsau, and seized his person. His reply surprised me. He said simply that he wished it could happen but was afraid it couldn't!

Thinking over this answer since [the Colonel commented twenty years later], I find much sense and foresight in it because the Hungarian protest to the *Entente* was always in essence much more National than Red. That this would be so could not, of course, have been foretold by any of us so early. But that the Emperor anticipated it is clear.

Back in February 1919, however, Colonel Cunninghame was not to be burdened for long with the problem of the Imperial family's safety. Indeed, he had barely returned from Eckartsau to Vienna when totally different instructions came from London. A personal letter arrived from his own chief there, General Sir William Thwaites, telling him that the

* Its Hungarian name. Pressburg to the Austrians and Bratislava to its new masters, the Czechoslovaks.

† On Lake Traun in Western Austria.

British C.-in-C. in Salonika, General Sir Tom Bridges, had been asked to find and send a suitable officer to relieve Colonel Summerhayes. That this was more than just a change of personnel was made clear by the order which followed: 'It is an instruction that you have nothing further to do with this matter and that above all you refrain from giving advice to the new officer, or to the Emperor, or to anyone else.'

Colonel Cunninghame knew his Whitehall and he guessed accurately what had happened. As he records his own reactions at the time:

> This was sufficiently comprehensive. The British War Office did not wish to be mixed up with a business which was in essence political. The new officer was obviously to be the representative of the Foreign Office and the go-between authorized in all that concerned the fate and movements of the Emperor. I was therefore precluded from helping in any way and could only await the arrival of the new man in the hope that he would prove capable of giving sage advice to the Emperor in a situation which was becoming more and more difficult.

So, at this point, a third Colonel of the British Army enters the lives of Charles and his family. He is an infinitely more colourful and engaging personality than the other two, who seem to have been respectively the very prototypes of the competent but unemotional staff officer and the amiable doctor in uniform. Furthermore, unlike Cunninghame or Summerhayes, whose contact with Charles had been both brief and conventional, this newcomer was to develop for the Austrian Emperor and his family an almost passionate devotion which was to endure down to his own death nearly thirty years later. It is an extraordinary personal saga that now begins: that of a British officer who came to serve the Habsburg double eagle and the black and yellow colours of an ex-enemy dynasty with a fervour second only to his loyalty to his own King. Indeed, there were to be indignant voices raised later on in London suggesting that the fervour had grown so intense as to nibble away at the loyalty. The reproach seems both untrue and undeserved. But certainly this third British Colonel never shirked from putting his own career in jeopardy to help a foreign sovereign in his troubles.

The officer General Bridges had selected in Salonika was Lieutenant-Colonel Edward Lisle Strutt, D.S.O., of the Royal Scots, who was then doing liaison duties with the combined *Entente* armies operating in the Balkans under the overall command of the French General Franchet d'Esperey. Even a glance at Strutt's paper qualifications fifty years later makes it easy to see why the choice had fallen on him. As a grandson of the first Lord Belper, his social credentials were appropriate. He was a Catholic, like the Emperor to whom he would be assigned. He was a linguist whose languages included German – indeed he had done a spell as a student at an Austrian University (Innsbruck) between his education at Beaumont College and Oxford. Yet these academic achievements had not softened his calibre as a fighting soldier. If there was to be trouble ahead on this assignment, Colonel Strutt's list of decorations on active service to date suggested he would be well capable of handling it: South African War 1900–2 (despatches, Queen's medal and four clasps, King's medal and two clasps); European War 1914–19 (wounded, C.B.E., D.S.O., despatches four times, *Croix de Guerre* with four palms, Chevalier and Officer of the Legion of Honour, Chevalier of Order of St Leopold, Belgian *Croix de Guerre* and palm and Order of the Star of Rumania).

The choice, on paper and in practice, was indeed the perfect one. Strutt, it proved, even had the ideal temperament and outlook for his task. He was a plain uncompromising soul who saw everything political in terms of black and white, or rather black and red. All radicals, whether of Socialist or Communist stamp, seemed automatically suspect as the instruments of evil. By instinct and by emotion he was a partisan of the old European order to whose fringes he himself belonged. What more could a Habsburg Emperor in distress desire?

General Bridges can scarcely be blamed for not foreseeing two quite unpredictable complications. The first was that Colonel Strutt was to hate Colonel Cunninghame virtually on sight – a feeling that was returned with interest. The second was that he was to form this unusual devotion for his imperial charges – also virtually on sight and also a sentiment that was to be reciprocated.

We are lucky that Colonel Strutt was, beside everything else, a diarist. The story of the Eckartsau 'rescue' can now therefore be taken forward mainly in his own words.* The flavour of the man is conveyed very early on:

21 February 1919. Hotel Danieli, Venice.

I was just pushing off from here when the Hotel Porter brought me a w.t. message stating that I was to await urgent orders arriving from Padua. I returned to the Hotel and slept there.

22 February.

At 2 p.m. I was handed the following message from Tom Bridges, Constantinople: 'You will proceed at once to Eckartsau and give Emperor and Empress moral support of British Government. They are stated to be in danger

* Though extracts from Colonel Strutt's writings appeared shortly after the First World War, this is the first time the full diary has become available. I am indebted to his widow and his legal executors for permission to reproduce it. The main burden of his narrative has been confirmed by the Empress. A copy was deposited at Windsor Castle.

of their lives, to be suffering great hardships and to lack medical attendance. Endeavour by every possible means to ameliorate their condition. (Signed) *General Bridges*.' We all concluded that the Emperor must mean the Emperor of Austria but disagreed as to interpretation of 'moral support'. None of us had any idea where Eckartsau was.

23 February

On board H.M.S. *Hydra*, destroyer. Arrived in torrents of rain at Fiume at 15.10. . . . A train was stated to be leaving for Zagreb at 22.00 hours. A first-class carriage, old style, was reserved for us. It contained no cushions, no lights, no glass in the windows, and through the opening in the roof, where the lights had once stood, poured a continual stream of water.

24 February

R.T.O. had assured us that no train took less than twenty-four hours to Zagreb (Agram); however, at 07.10 we steamed into that station in a snow-storm. Found a train left for Steinbruck on the Vienna–Trieste route at 13.10.

Haughtily ordered compartment to be reserved and stowed away our kit and seven days' rations in it. The officials were all Austrians and were as polite as before the war. Guard asks us for our tickets, but quails at my retort and retires backwards murmuring the inevitable '*Küss die Hand, Excellenz*. . . .' At Graz a prolonged halt is made and everyone has to descend and be searched. We naturally refuse to dismount and the officials retire bowing. The same thing goes on all night at every big station, but the train runs well in the intervals and our *coupé* is free from vermin. . . .

25 February

Arrived at the Süd Bahnhof, Vienna, at 12.10; a most successful journey, under sixty hours from Venice. Crowds gazed curiously at me, without sign of hostility. My luggage was passed through at once and loaded on to a cab, miserably horsed, while the rest of the wretched tired passengers were once more searched. Knowing nothing, I determined to proceed to the Hotel Bristol, where I used to stay in former times. Went for a short walk in the Ring where the first person I bumped into was Kary Czernin (the ex-Foreign Minister). We stared at one another and then burst out laughing and shook hands warmly. He asked me to lunch, adding that they had nothing to eat. Accordingly I secured a loaf and some tins of bully beef and jam and we proceeded to Kary's enormous apartment in the Schwartzenberg Platz [*sic*]. Found Maritschy (Countess Czernin, *née* Princess Kinsky) looking charming as ever but thin and worn. I forgot myself and embraced her before Kary. They informed me that Lieutenant-Colonel Sir Thomas Cunninghame was at the British Embassy as head of the British Military Mission to Czechoslovakia. I hurried off at once, leaving the rations and promising to return later. Found Cunninghame, a shifty-eyed odd-looking fellow, beautifully dressed – shining brass-hat and all – rather deaf, who gave the highly misleading first impression of being a fool. He knew all about my mission and told me he had sent a British doctor, belonging to the Food Commission, out to Eckartsau pending my arrival. We walked over to the Bristol for lunch, the German officials glaring insolently at us from their Embassy as we left our own. Found little to eat, but Cunninghame produced some excellent French burgundy.* Ashmead Bartlett, *Daily Telegraph* correspondent, sat down at our table and was as objectionable as ever.

That night, at about nine o'clock as I was writing in my room, a very pretty girl came in and asked me for some food, saying she was starving. I gave her some and she asked to be allowed to eat it in my room as it might be taken from her on the stairs. Her gratitude was pathetic.

26 February

Received a message from Summerhayes to say he could not leave Eckartsau till tomorrow and consequently I could not be fetched till then. Walked about the city most of the day. The sight of the starving children was ghastly. Italian officers were swaggering about the streets and the crushed-looking passers-by edged off the pavement to avoid them. A large and truculent Italian Mission was occupying the whole of the Hotel Imperial. None of them ever dreamed of saluting a British officer. Saw Cunninghame in the evening. He is off to Prague. He has not been of the slightest help to me.

27 February

Packed up my few belongings (I really am ashamed of my kit), and found a large six-seater open 60 h.p. Austro-Daimler awaiting me. The imperial arms on the panels had been painted over. . . . We started at 11 A.M. After Aspern the road became very bad. It rained and snowed alternately and the scenery was depressing in the extreme. As we approached Eckartsau and the vast, ugly woods surrounding it the road became a morass through which the car threshed and skidded its way on second speed till we came to a neglected drive where a Civil Policeman and a fierce-looking dog [Gussl, the Emperor's favourite] were on duty. At 12.25 P.M. we drove into the courtyard of an imposing building. The distance from Vienna was sixty kilometres. A naval officer, a dependable and cheerful individual, Commander Schonta, met me at the door; with him was Summerhayes, who impressed me less favourably but had contrived, as I discovered, to make himself popular with everyone. He always addressed me by any name except my own which, he declared, he was unable to pronounce. . . .

I was taken through a large hall to a kind of dining- and sitting-room where

* That Colonel Cunninghame also found little joy at this first encounter is shown by his own account. He records that, at this first meal together in the Hotel Bristol, Strutt declared 'that every Socialist was a knave and that the only thing for England to do was to occupy Austria and Hungary in force and to rule both through the person of the Emperor'. This, not unreasonably, Cunninghame dismissed as 'baby-talk'. It strengthened his impression that though Strutt 'seemed outwardly to have all the necessary qualifications, closer acquaintance revealed an undesirable wish to support the Emperor's claims at an inopportune moment'. (*Hungarian Quarterly, op. cit.*)

I was introduced to the two ladies-in-waiting, Countess Agnes Schönborn and Countess Gabrielle Bellegarde. With them was an old acquaintance of mine, Count Joseph Hunyady, head of the great Hungarian family of that name. It would be difficult to speak too highly of these ladies. Countess Schönborn was a cousin of the Empress: both were clever and accomplished and devoid of any fear. I was conducted to the bedroom now vacated by Summerhayes, a fine apartment with bathroom attached. The first thing I noticed was a deplorable screen covered with photographs of the late Archduke Franz Ferdinand and William II of Germany surrounded by hecatombs of dead stags. [Eckartsau had been Franz Ferdinand's shooting-box and the scene of gigantic slaughterings of game.] Among these photographs I actually perceived one of myself taken with Franz Ferdinand and Rumerskirch, his A.D.C., many years ago at St Moritz! Schonta informed me that the Emperor would receive me in ten minutes and I asked Summerhayes for a few tips on the general situation. All he could say was that I should address His Majesty as 'Sir', adding that he always did so himself!

Schonta conducted me up a great staircase and ushered me into the Emperor's sitting-room. The Emperor is of medium height, very slightly built, with quite a good-looking, well-bred, but weak face. His age is thirty-one. He was wearing full Field-Marshal's uniform, with a handsome sword and a mass of medals, decorations and 'plaques'. Amongst these I recognized the Order of the Golden Fleece, the Iron Cross and our G.C.V.O.! He was most affable and expressed his gratitude to the Allies. I stayed about twenty minutes with him and nothing could have exceeded his cordiality. I may say here that I almost always spoke French to the Emperor, and he replied in German. His English, he told me, was very indifferent, but his French was excellent as regards pronunciation, if rather deficient in vocabulary. The Emperor's appearance describes his character. It was impossible to avoid liking him; an eminently lovable if weak man, by no means a fool, and ready to face his end as bravely as his ancestress, Marie Antoinette. I lunched with the Court. As far as food was concerned, it was a complete failure. We all went for a walk afterwards and I saw several stags feeding in sodden and depressing-looking clearings. There were then, owing to the depredations of poachers, *Volkswehr* and *Soldatenräthe*, only some 200 of these remaining out of a pre-war 2,000. We strolled at the usual continental crawl to the Danube, which is about 500 yards wide here and very swift.

On our return I was summoned to the Empress Zita and had tea with her in her sitting-room, she laughingly apologizing for its vile quality. She was very simply dressed in black wearing her wonderful pearls (I came to know those pearls well later), and looked pale and ill. About medium height and with a slim figure she looked younger than her age, twenty-six. The first impression I had was one of extraordinary strength of character softened by her own remarkable charm. Determination was written in the lines of her square little chin, intelligence in the vivacious brown eyes, intellect in the broad forehead half hidden by masses of dark hair. Without extraordinary claims to beauty, the Empress would always attract attention in a crowd. As I entered the room I realized that she must always share with the Queens of the Belgians and Rumania the honour of being one of the three great royal women of the war. What might have happened, I could not help wondering, had she sat alone on the dual throne during those last two years? Nor did I ever hear one word of complaint from her, who certainly felt her position more deeply than her husband. No more affectionate and devoted couple than these two could possibly be found. So much for the foul lies * of the gutter press in Austria and Germany.

On being dismissed I had a long talk with Schonta and discussed with him the most vital requirements of the household such as bread, milk, petrol, etc. The electric light engine was almost out of fuel and the house was in almost complete darkness. Nor were there any candles. I found that there were over 100 persons living in the house. Dined at eight with the Emperor, Empress and Archduchess; Countess Schönborn also there, and the Bishop in attendance – Seidl, a good fellow. The menu was as follows: vegetable soup, fried vegetable cutlets and dry biscuits. (The Austrian press was continually publishing articles on the fifteen-course dinners and gorgeous wines daily consumed by the Imperial family at Eckartsau. The Northcliffe press naturally followed suit.) There was some thin Tokay and good coffee – not *ersatz* at least, this last item. No ceremony once we had sat down. Afterwards we played bridge. I won, thanks to my partners, and was compelled to smoke a pipe! Just as I was going to bed the Empress sent for me and asked me to allow Summerhayes (who had left for Vienna) to accompany the fourth infant, the Archduke Felix, to Switzerland where he was to go for his health. (All the Imperial children were suffering from want of nourishing food.) Of course I gladly consented and a message was arranged to be sent by telephone to Vienna.

28 February

Arranged about sending out a British lorry next day with rations for the entire household, also cypher telephone messages to Vienna (our telephone was continually being tapped) in case it came to a flight.

1 March

Took the Court out for a walk and we all got lost in the woods. Eventually found our way back by following the Danube. Nearly everyone was dead to the world. Rations and petrol arrived by British lorry. Great excitement over the white bread. (This appeared to have been baked at Fiume or Padua and was at least a fortnight old, but still quite good. It was the first white bread any of the Court had seen since the beginning of 1916.) The children were reported to have consumed one tin of bully beef, one loaf, one tin of jam and one tin of milk apiece – probably exaggerated. Had a long talk on the situation with the Emperor; he appears to rely on King George alone.

Suggested that as we could only supply tinned meat – the Italians held up all refrigerator cars – our *Jaegers* (of whom two or three were still left) should shoot a stag every now and then for food. This was hailed as a brilliant idea and

* i.e. newspaper gossip that the marriage was an unhappy one.

worthy of Great Britain's representative. This was duly done and the meat was quite good.

Discussed our means of defence with Schonta. We have ten reliable police armed with carbines and revolvers but very little ammunition. There are about twenty servants who might be of some use, and Schonta, Ledochoffski [*sic*], Ashmore, my batman, and myself. The house could be rushed by twenty men in a few minutes. The ground-floor windows are barred but the hall opposite the courtyard has only shuttered french windows. (Some 300 Red Guards with armoured cars were continually reported to be cruising around Orth. As a matter of fact there were not more than twenty to thirty with three cars armed with a machine-gun apiece, and the roads were fortunately too heavy for these cars to come into the grounds, but I often used to meet them and always was afraid of their coming upon the Imperial Family suddenly and opening fire.) I always slept with a revolver under the pillow but on testing the cartridges – which I had in France in 1914 – three months later in Constantinople, found they were nearly all 'duds'!

3 March

Drove out with the Emperor in a small victoria over swampy paths for three hours. We talked of every subject under the sun, but everything led back to Bolshevism. We spoke of German atrocities and of the sinking of hospital ships. 'That I cannot believe,' he said. 'If you tell me that they pillaged, murdered, outraged – *that* I can more than believe, for they did all that in my country; but hospital ships, no. Even they would not dare.' Eventually I think he did believe me. My personal knowledge of instances at Salonika did much to convince him.

Again and again he repeated that he had not abdicated. 'I went into retirement on 4 November 1918, pending the restoration of order. I am still Emperor.' He asked me to write home to the King and Lloyd George to send British troops to Austria-Hungary – '10,000 or even 5,000 would do. My officers are still loyal; they will organize what is left of my old armies behind yours. If you cannot send British, send Americans, but no French or Italians.'

I wrote this and much more, and sent it by the Prague bag, addressed to Leo Amery and Bradford, who had just been made a Lord in Waiting. To Bradford also I sent Albert Mensdorff's private notes for King George. The letter, but not the enclosures, **reached** Bradford; he subsequently recovered the enclosures from Curzon of Kedleston's pocket. These letters were all opened by the censor in spite of the destination of their contents. The censorship apologized to Bradford but stated in excuse that Colonel Strutt had written a most indiscreet letter to Lady Evelyn Cotterall, hence their action. This letter, incidentally, contained no mention of political events as I subsequently verified. Several political telegrams were also sent by me to the War Office all asking for acknowledgement of their receipt. No reply or acknowledgement was ever vouchsafed. When I met Mr Balfour in Paris some weeks later I asked him why no reply had been sent. 'We did not know how to reply,' he said. 'But could not a simple acknowledgement have been sent?' I asked. 'Oh no, that would have been tantamount to confessing that we did not know how to reply,' laughed the philosopher.

The Emperor spoke about his reign. 'I first tried to rule autocratically, and then democratically; both were errors, but of the two the latter was the greater.' We drove down to the Danube. A few fishermen were hauling in a seine net and we watched them. The men took off their caps politely – the Emperor was as usual in undress *feldgrau* uniform. H.M. asked them to go on: they drew in three small coarse fish. H.M. thereupon borrowed 200 Kr. from me (the money was returned as soon as we got home) and gave it to them, and after a few minutes' conversation we left them bowing. I never saw or heard of any peasant being anything but polite to the Imperial Family; moreover they always showed real pleasure at any chance meeting in the wood....

16 March

To Vienna with Ledochoffski and Countess Bellegarde. We overtook a train full of demobilized soldiers near Aspern. A light railway ran alongside the road for several miles there. I was sitting next the chauffeur and the other two were behind, both wearing goggles. The soldiers evidently mistook my companions for the Imperial couple and yells of derision and insult went up as we passed them. About 200 yards farther on one of our back tyres burst just as we came opposite a small wayside platform and we had to stop, the train also pulling up about five yards off. I got down and addressed the men who were still booing furiously. They stopped, and there was a dead silence. I can't remember a word of what I said but they all saluted and there were several cries of '*Um Verzeihung, Excellenz*', as the train moved off. The whole thing lasted for perhaps three minutes. Ledochoffski was nervous; Countess Bellegarde laughed. Went to the Embassy; still no means of deciphering my telegrams.

17 March

Went for a long walk with His Majesty. He told me that the papers were commenting very rudely on his having given the Golden Fleece to two or three distinguished people (I made no note of their names), and said he had done it on purpose to prove that he was still Emperor. He informed me that the escutcheons of distinguished British people who had received high Austrian decorations or honours were still hung up in the Stefans-Kirche and presumed that King George had taken no action as regards those Austrians whose banners hung in St George's Chapel, Windsor. I replied as tactfully as I could that the insignia of all Germans had been removed, but that I was quite ignorant as to what had happened to those of other enemy nationalities.

As these diary entries would suggest, the fortnight since Strutt's arrival at Eckartsau had been something of an idyll for Charles and his family, at any rate when compared with much of what had gone before and most of what was to come afterwards. Adequate supplies of food, including the near-miracle of white bread, had descended as though from heaven on the beleaguered household. The other necessities of everyday life had also been restored and proper medical attention was now provided for the Emperor and Empress and their ailing children. Above all, the presence of this resolute British Colonel, sent at the personal initiative of King George v, spelled both security and an equally precious link with the outside world. (Dr Schober, the loyal Police President in Vienna, had described this link to Colonel Cunninghame as: 'A pleasant plot and one of which I much approve – a plot to interest Buckingham Palace in the shooting-lodge of Eckartsau.') *

But this happy interlude, during which the Emperor strolled in the wintry park with his new champion, discussing everything from Bol- shevism to German bombing and from stag-shooting to the banners in St George's Chapel, Windsor – almost daring to hope that somehow, some- where, England herself might actually come to the rescue of the House of Habsburg – such an idyll could not last.

Charles did his level best to turn the dream into reality. During these last weeks at Eckartsau, for example, he managed to despatch another appeal for help to King Alfonso, the royal intermediary in those abortive secret peace exchanges of his with President Wilson twelve months before. In March 1918, as reigning Emperor, he had pleaded with the Western Powers to save the Dual Monarchy from destruction. In March 1919, as a dispossessed ruler sitting amidst the remains of his former kingdom, he could only beg his ex-enemies to come and pick up the pieces for him again.

In this letter sent by special courier to Madrid, Charles asked Alfonso to pass on to the *Entente* Governments a warning that Bolshevism might soon devour all the countries of the old Empire one by one † unless they acted swiftly to prevent it. The measures he suggested were:

1. The despatch of *Entente* troops into the Danube area specifically to keep radicalism under control;

2. The delivery of as much food as possible to prevent unrest due to famine; and

3. *Entente* support for a confederation to be formed again of the old nations of the Empire under the leadership of the Habsburg dynasty.

It was indeed a tall order. But King Alfonso, who appears to have received the letter just after the Communist *coup* in Budapest had taken

---

* Cunninghame in *Hungarian Quarterly, op. cit.*, p. 638.

† Within a week of Charles penning his warning from Eckartsau on 17 March 1919, Bela Kun seized power in Budapest.

place, acted as a loyal and solicitous postman. On 29 March 1919, he sent Charles's warning to (among others) King George v with the following covering note in English:

Dear George!

I enclose you a copy of a letter of the Emperor Charles of Austria. You will see the danger for us all of what he says.

If you can do something, do it directly, as minutes must be gained [*sic*] to arrive in time. I am quite at your disposal if I can be of any use, and let me know what I can answer. . . .

(signed) Alfonso R.H.*

To send a single British officer as *Ehrenkavalier* to Eckartsau was one thing. To despatch an entire British army to turn the Danube blue again was quite another. All King George could tell King Alfonso was that a translation of Charles's letter had been sent to the British Prime Minister in Paris 'with a view of his referring its contents to the Peace Conference'.*

Charles's appeals to King George for military help (like his earlier messages to London passed via Colonel Strutt) were not, in fact, quite the hopeless arrows fired into the blue that they may appear today. The *Entente* powers were themselves gravely concerned at this time about the dangers of a Bolshevik take-over in all the lands that had formerly been under the Habsburg and Hohenzollern sceptres. Indeed, some of their officials operating in the ruins of the Dual Monarchy in the spring of 1919 were actually echoing Charles's plan for the despatch of Allied troops to keep the Communist menace at bay. One was the young American diplomat Allen W. Dulles, who was responsible for preparing intelligence reports about the former Habsburg territories for the Paris Peace Conference. Several members of the American Coolidge Mission to Vienna and Budapest echoed this view, especially in the harsh light of the Bela Kun *coup*.†

Yet, despite their anxiety, no leading *Entente* statesman felt able to risk another war in order to restore to power those who had been their enemies in the one that had just ended. Nor, with the important exception of a group of French politicians, was there any sympathy for Charles's concept of a revived Habsburg confederation. For most Western leaders, the efforts of Charles and his tiny Court were but a charade of Imperial actors who were now miming the great roles they had once played in earnest. With every day that passed, the Austrians were, after all, getting a

* Windsor Castle Archives. Published by Gracious Permission of Her Majesty the Queen. Reference GV M1466/10.

† For an excellent survey of this, see a very recent work: A. J. Mayer, *Politics and Diplomacy of Peace-making*, especially pp. 575–7 and 720–1.

little more used to the single-headed eagle of their new Republic, just as the outside world was accommodating itself to having this suddenly shabby and bourgeois Vienna in its midst. Time may not conquer all, but it blurs all.

On 4 March 1919, the Republic's first Parliament, as elected in the February poll, had duly assembled. Ten days later, on 15 March, what seemed to be a reasonably stable Government had then been formed. It was a left-right coalition between the two traditionally largest parties of the Social Democrats and Christian Socialists, with the German nationalists excluded. Renner, as the leader of the senior partner in the Coalition, became Chancellor. The other portfolios were divided among the nominees of the two parties with a system of mathematical precision that was to persist in Austrian politics down to the 1960s. This was the Republican Government to which foreign missions now had to be accredited and which was now fully entitled to speak for Austria in the peace talks with the *Entente*. The problem of the illustrious squire at Eckartsau simply had to be tackled.

Cunninghame had never ceased, in his reports to London, to stress the risks that the Emperor's mere presence seemed to him to constitute, both to the security of the Czech–Hungarian–Austrian border triangle and to the stability of the new Austrian Republic itself. He received plenty of encouragement in this from Renner who, during the early part of March, came to warn him of the danger that control in Vienna 'was fast slipping out of the hands of the Socialists and into those of the Communists'. In a troubled political arena like this, the *Entente* powers now decided that the black and yellow banner could only act as a red rag to the Marxist bull.

Since early March, the instructions sent to Vienna for Colonel Strutt had been taking on a steadily more concerned and urgent tone. On 15 March, Cunninghame received from London a definite order with the words: 'Most desirable to get the Emperor out of Austria without delay. All possible steps to be taken to expedite departure.' * Perhaps significantly, this was the day that Renner's Government was formally constituted.

The news reached Strutt at Eckartsau just after lunch on 17 March. A personal telegram from the War Office told him that it was 'highly advisable to get the Emperor out of Austria and into Switzerland at once' and then added the remarkable warning that 'the British Government can in no way guarantee your journey'.† Strutt kept his mouth shut and left for Vienna at once to find out what was going on.

There he discovered that the newly-formed Government had decided to force the issue of the Emperor's presence in their midst. Both partners in

---

* Cunninghame in *Hungarian Quarterly*, *op. cit.*, p. 642.

† Strutt, *op. cit.*, *Diary of a Special Mission*.

the Coalition (including, that is, the conservative and formerly monarchist Christian-Socialists) had decided to confront Charles with three alternatives:

(*a*) If the Emperor and Empress would abdicate all rights they could live in Austria as private citizens.

(*b*) If he refused to abdicate he must be exiled.

(*c*) If he refused both to abdicate and to leave, he would be interned.

This was uncompromising enough and, taken together with the flat instructions from London, left the Emperor's British 'bodyguard' no choice. He did not waste time on useless argument. Within five minutes he had arranged for a special train to be assembled at Vienna's Westbahnhof on receipt of the single code-word 'Act' passed by him to the British Embassy. He then called on the Swiss Legation and asked, in his capacity as British escort officer, for the royal family to be received in Switzerland. (The War Office appears to have nominated that country as a destination without even enquiring in Berne whether the Swiss themselves were agreeable.)

The worst part of Colonel Strutt's task was before him – to break the bad news to the Emperor and persuade him to agree with the action planned. As he describes the struggle:

I returned at once to Eckartsau, arriving about 9 P.M., had a talk with Schonta and then asked to see the Emperor. He was in bed, feeling seedy, but saw me at once. I told him I intended to take him to Switzerland the following night; that he must shave off his moustache, wear my spare uniform and Glengarry bonnet and take a bag and one servant only. I would leave him in Switzerland and come back and fetch the Empress and the children. At this point the Empress came in. 'Just let me speak to Zita alone,' he said. I knew then that the plan was dished, as she would never allow him to go.

At 10.30 he sent for me again. He was alone; he said he would not go. 'I will take your Majesty by force then,' I said, and for a moment I thought he had yielded. But he only smiled, saying: 'I cannot leave Zita and the children.' It was out of the question to take the whole family secretly across Vienna to the West-bahnhof; they must have been recognized at the station even if the cars passed unnoticed. I knew he was right. He then wrote out the following telegram for the British Government (I have the original still): '*Der Kaiser will das Land nicht verlassen, weil er nicht der Überzeugung ist, dass die Situation dies erfordert. Eine Abreise ohne seine Familie ist ausgeschlossen.*' (The Emperor will not leave the country as he is not convinced that the situation calls for such a step. In any case, he could never leave without his family.)

He then dismissed me in the most friendly way possible.

18 March

Went to Vienna at 8 A.M. with the Countess Bellegarde. Translated and sent off the Emperor's telegram and went to the Swiss Legation. Burckhart appeared, beaming: the Swiss Government would receive the whole family 'if the worst came to the worst in Colonel Strutt's opinion'. Countess Bellegarde was all for staying – like the splendid girl she is. She and I returned to Eckartsau at 9.30.

19 March

All the male portion of the Court very depressed: the ladies confident as ever. I could not stand the gloom of it and suggested to Schonta that the Emperor, he and I should try to shoot some woodcock at Stopfenrieth. He jumped at the idea and we three, with Ledochoffski, went out. Just as it became almost pitch dark two woodcock came over my head and I killed them both – the first right and left I ever got at woodcock. No one else got a shot.

On returning home I was given some ominous news. On its return this afternoon one of the carts which had been sent to Schönbrunn to fetch coffee and sugar had been attacked by some soldiers at Engersdorf under an Oberleutenant, pillaged and smashed to pieces. The driver, who had been roughly handled, had returned on foot with the horses, carrying a letter addressed to *Herr Karl Hapsburg*. This letter contained a receipt for the articles stolen and an obscene note signed by the Oberleutenant.

This determined me to have it out with the Empress as the real head of the family. I told her of my fears for their safety, that I entirely agreed with her that in spite of every danger they should stay if the country wanted them to do so; but, I pointed out, I heard on all sides that the country was against them, that Budapest was in a state of revolution, and that the situation in Linz and Salzburg was little better. I promised somehow to get them out without the Emperor having to abdicate so that they could come back when the inevitable reaction set in. She listened but still showed no sign of assent. Finally I concluded by saying: 'A dead Habsburg is no good to anyone, whereas a live one, with a family, may yet be.' She smiled, shook me warmly by the hand, and said simply: 'I will do all I can to help. We will leave under your orders and arrangements and trust you to avoid Karl's having to abdicate.'

The Colonel's troubles were far from over, however. Having talked his Imperial charges into leaving Eckartsau, he now ran into unexpected trouble from Renner. The Chancellor, a master of opportunism, had seen that the tide was flowing his way and had decided to make one last-minute attempt to drown the Habsburg dynasty in it for good and all.

Strutt had his first brush with Renner (whom he describes, in very rough language, as 'a hairy, cunning-looking rascal with intelligent eyes') on 20 March. He had called to get an official denial of Socialist propaganda statements that the Emperor had himself applied to the Swiss for asylum and also to sound the Chancellor out on the possibility of the Emperor being allowed to live in the Tyrol. He succeeded on the first count but failed on the second.

The Tyrol had been Charles's last hope of prolonging his exile from power on Austrian soil. Strutt broke the bad news to him late that night back at Eckartsau and told him there was now no alternative but to leave the country. Charles looked at him hard in the face and replied simply:

'Only promise me that I shall leave as Emperor and not as a thief in the night.'

'Sir,' said the British officer, 'I promise.'

He was to keep that promise with interest. But first there were some further and far more dangerous confrontations with Renner to be surmounted. Strutt had no mandate to act for the Emperor in these clashes. What was more, in view of that ominous phrase in the London telegram refusing to 'guarantee the journey', he now had only a very shaky mandate from his own Government. Yet he was still a Colonel of the Royal Scots on the territory of a defeated ex-enemy power, so he decided to let a British Army uniform speak for itself. Already in that initial encounter of the 20th he had somewhat shaken the Chancellor at the outset by bawling in what he describes as his 'best boche style': 'Please stand up in future when I enter your room!' Renner had instantly jumped to his feet as though stung by a hornet – though the 'nervous twitching' that Strutt records was probably more anger than fear.

Whatever it was, the reaction to the Colonel's 'brain-wave' had shown him the diplomatic possibilities of the military approach in a capital that had always been susceptible to uniforms. He employed the same tactics when he returned to Vienna the next day. First, mindful of his promise to Charles, he ordered the Austrian railway authorities to re-assemble once more the Imperial train in all its splendour with three saloon carriages, one kitchen- and one dining-car, two luggage-vans and one open truck to carry motor vehicles. This was told to manoeuvre itself somehow by that Sunday, 23 March, up the light track to Kopfstetten, a tiny station only two miles from Eckartsau. With his own colleagues, Strutt next arranged for a British Military Police guard of one sergeant and six men to accompany the train.*

He then called again on Renner, who this time was 'already standing up' when he entered the room. The Austrian Chancellor showed relief at the news that the Imperial family were about to leave for Switzerland at last and that Colonel Strutt had decided himself to escort them on their

---

* Cunninghame (*Hungarian Quarterly, op. cit.*) states that when he had once asked the Vienna Police President about the risks involved in the Emperor travelling through Austria, Dr Schober had replied: 'It is as safe, dear Sir Thomas, as a drive to the Derby.' But Strutt was taking no chances against the radical bands of *soldateska* he had already encountered near Eckartsau.

journey. But he promptly embarked on what by any standards, and particularly those of a former Imperial official, must be regarded as a niggling campaign of harassment. He began by demanding that the Emperor and his family would have to be searched – their persons as well as their luggage – before leaving. Strutt flatly rejected this, 'in the name of the British Government', and gave his own word of honour that the Emperor would take nothing with him that was not his own personal property.

Renner had to accept this but countered with another demand that his Government should send a 'High Commissioner' to the train to see that 'no disagreeable incidents occurred'. This seems to have angered Strutt. He now suspected that the Chancellor's only purpose was somehow to stage-manage for the Republic a visible show of authority over the dynasty it had been too afraid to touch itself and whose fate had finally been arranged on its behalf by a British officer. He retorted that the Chancellor could send his representative if he wanted but that, at the very first 'incident', the Commissioner would be shot and that he, Strutt, would do the shooting! Nothing more was ever heard, let alone seen, of the Republic's 'High Commissioner'.

But the crucial clash of wills between these two oddly-contrasting men, the British officer of the old world and the Central European politician of the new, came on the following day, 22 March, which was the eve of the journey itself. Strutt was in Vienna again, arranging details of the train's time-table, when a telephone message came from the Chancellery asking him to call on Dr Renner at once. What the colonel did next showed that he was endowed with brain as well as brawn. Guessing what was afoot, he drafted a telegram to London, put it in his pocket and then went to see his adversary.

His suspicions were confirmed when Renner at once demanded that the Emperor would have to abdicate before he left the country.* Unless Charles complied, the Chancellor continued, he would be interned. Strutt said nothing but simply pulled the prepared telegram out of his pocket and laid it on the table. It read:

En Clair

To Director Military Intelligence London

Austrian Government refuses permission for departure of Emperor unless he abdicates. Consequently give orders to re-establish blockade and stop all food trains entering Austria.

(signed) Strutt

---

* This incidentally disposes of arguments that Charles's declaration of 11 November was an abdication. Renner, himself a jurist, knew better.

It was the wildest and most improbable of bluffs. As far as the British Government was concerned, there could be no possible link between the first sentence and the second. And a mere Director of Military Intelligence was hardly the man to order such a grave step on behalf of the Cabinet – indeed of the whole *Entente*.

Yet it worked. Renner looked at the 'telegram', threw up his hands in despair and exclaimed *'Grosser Gott!'* Then after a short pause he added: 'All right, he can go.' 'Without any conditions?' the colonel asked. 'Yes,' came the reply. Strutt picked up the piece of paper and walked out, leaving the Chancellor gazing gloomily out of the window. The colonel had kept his word. The Emperor was to go as Emperor.

The story of the twenty-four hours that followed, when the last of the Habsburg rulers was taken safely out of his realm under the protection of the British flag, is best told by returning to Strutt's own diary:

23 March (Sunday)

From nine o'clock in the morning people began to arrive by car. My worst forebodings were fulfilled. Was there going to be another Varennes? At 10 there was Mass in the Chapel which was crammed to suffocation. The Imperial family was in the Gallery. The Bishop said the Mass and the seven-year-old Otto acted as server. At the end the Austrian National Anthem was sung by all – perhaps for the last time before an Austrian Emperor. Everyone was sobbing.

At 2 P.M. Parker from the British Mission turned up in his car convoying two British lorries containing four men apiece. Parker and I went to Kopfstetten and met the train which arrived punctually at 3.45. It looked immense in the open plain and must have been a great strain on that very light railway. The British Army was in full evidence (the escort – one N.C.O., and six Military Policemen was exactly half the armed British strength in Vienna!). A large Union Jack was flying between the two cars in the truck (the Daimler and the Emperor's fine Mercedes limousine). The last van-load of luggage left at 4.45. Everyone had worked like niggers, including the women. At five o'clock Parker started back for Vienna with his two lorries and their perspiring crews, Schonta plying them with bottles of wine and other titbits as they went off. As soon as the lorries had gone I hurried off, with an axe and a saw, to the previously located intersection of the Vienna–Pressburg–Marchegg telegraph wires. I hacked down the posts for some fifty yards and cut all the lines, a filthy job in the dark. . . . There remained only one line, a single line from Orth, which I did not cut as it would have inconvenienced Schonta.

There had now collected in the hall a large group of peasants, *Jaegers* and the Mayors of two or three villages round about, some thirty or forty persons in all. Their Majesties sent for me and informed me that they were taking a large trunk full of jewels and a heavy box full of Habsburg documents, both labelled with my name. I was handed the Empress's pearls (six rows), the Maria Theresa diamond stomacher, and the keys of the boxes. All these I crammed into one of my pockets. The Emperor then handed me a pocket book containing a large sum of money which I stuffed into another pocket. In addition I carried in my haversack some other jewels belonging to the Archduchesses Maria Theresien [sic] and Franziska. . . .

At 6.35 the Emperor and Empress walked down the great staircase arm-in-arm. The crowd in the hall, now reinforced by the numerous servants we were leaving behind, all fell on their knees. The dignity of the Imperial couple at so heart-rending a moment was superlative. As an anti-climax the Emperor's widowed mother, Maria-Josefa, hung about like a Christmas tree with jewels and trinkets and with her two horrible old collie dogs on a lead held by her maid, came struggling down the stairs behind. Up to that moment I swear I had forgotten her very existence. Four cars were waiting outside. Their Majesties, after touching farewells, got into the first; the children, delighted at the prospect of travelling with British soldiers, into the second; Maria-Josefa, her maid and dogs into the third; Schonta and I into the last. We bumped over the pot-holed road to Kopfstetten, which we reached at 6.55.

It was pitch dark and raining. The blinds of one saloon carriage on the train, the last, were up and the lights were on inside. What with that and the car headlights, the faces of the nearest of a crowd of some 2,000 people were visible, all absolutely silent and many, as I could see, weeping. In front of the last saloon stood the British Police rigidly at attention and in front of them four or five wounded Austrian soldiers. The Emperor, who was in Field-Marshal's uniform, saluted the Police and he and the Empress then shook hands with the wounded men. They then entered the train and stood at the open windows of the saloon. Schonta and I scrambled up into another saloon carriage from the far side and I told the train officials to start. The Emperor leaned forward and said simply: '*Meine Freunde, Auf Wiedersehen,*' and the Empress bowed. Schonta then said good-bye. The train started at five minutes past seven, and as we steamed off a sort of low moan went up from the crowd. I joined their Majesties and led them into the middle saloon. 'After 700 years,' the Emperor said to me sadly.

In the train, exclusive of the guards and escort, we were twenty-five people; seven of the Imperial family, the two ladies-in-waiting, Ledochoffski, the Bishop and I. The rest were servants, including the two admirable chauffeurs. The train was very well equipped and decorated. We had some supper in the dining-car, the Empress joining us. I sat next to her, and in the course of general conversation, she said: 'My family * has been exiled from France, Italy and Portugal. When I married I became an Austrian subject, and now am an exile from Austria. Colonel Strutt, tell me, to what country do I now belong?' I could find no answer. By 10.30 everyone had gone to bed. I sat all night in the ante-room at the back end of the Imperial coach on a camp stool with a revolver on my knee.

* Bourbon–Parma–Braganza.

24 March

At about 7 A.M. I met the Empress, looking her best. She said, laughingly: *'Qu'avez-vous donc fait de votre mitrailleuse?'* (My revolver was rather a heavy one.) At 7.30 the Bishop celebrated Mass on the train. We passed through Zell-am-see, the lake still frozen over; climbed the steep grade to Kitzbuhel and down again to Wörgl on the main Munich line. We had all the blinds up now and people gazed curiously at the splendid train. At Schwaz, which we ran through at full speed, we could see the familiar uniforms of French *poilus* who were slouching about the platform. At Innsbruck the station was full of scruffy-looking Italians. The Duke of Aosta, G.O.C. 3rd Army, courteously sent his A.D.C. to enquire after our needs, a pleasant-looking fellow who saluted everyone all round on retiring. There was some delay there, and Italian soldiers smoking cigarettes and with their uniforms unbuttoned began to crowd outside the train, some even climbing up on the shoulders of their comrades to gape into the windows. The police at a nod from me cleared them off, helped by Gussl, the Emperor's hound. I also spoke to some Italian officers near by and requested them to control their men. We left at 10.15 twenty minutes late.

At Imst we stopped to put on a mountain engine. The platform was completely cleared and two pickets of British troops held the Fern Pass road about 200 yards east and west of the station. On the platform stood a fine British guard of twenty-five men,* and as the train moved out this guard presented arms to their Majesties, who were standing at the window of their saloon – the only official honour paid to them on leaving their country, and that at the hands of their 'enemies'. I was in another saloon with the rest of the party, who were immensely touched, poor old Ledochoffski bursting into tears. These troops were, as I ascertained later, from the H.A.C., and were as smart as Guardsmen. I heard later from the Empress that it was on this occasion that the Emperor broke down, for the first and last time. On the Emperor's instructions I sent a warm telegram of thanks to the Officer Commanding at Imst when we got to Switzerland. . . .

At Braz I joined the Emperor and sat with him till we reached Feldkirch where, according to Ledochoffski, there would be trouble over passports. (We had no passports, of course.) But a gentleman in top hat and frock coat, M. Weber-Deteindre, met me on the platform and, courteously introducing himself, informed me that the Swiss authorities were waiting to receive us at Buchs. The train started at once and I left his Majesty, who went to change into civilian clothes. Presently we crossed the Rhine and were in Switzerland, and ran into Buchs station dead on time at 3.45 P.M. Swiss troops lined both sides of the railway. On the platform were Monsieur F. J. Borsinger de Baden, of the Swiss Foreign Office, representing the Government; Colonel Bridler, commanding the 6th Infantry Division, and several of his staff. A large and respectful crowd

---

* They were from the Honourable Artillery Company – an odd coincidence since their Colonel at the time, Lord Denbigh, was from the Fielding family which claims relationship with the Habsburgs.

were kept well back by the troops. M. de Baden and the officers greeted me with the utmost courtesy and cordiality, and, after a few moments' conversation, I took them into the train and presented them to the Emperor.

The Emperor then got out of the train, said a few words to my British military policemen and shook hands with them. Ledochoffski presented each man, on behalf of His Majesty, with a watch bearing the Imperial monogram and a cigarette case embossed with the Austro-Hungarian and Habsburg arms. They were to stay at Buchs until our train returned from Staad and were then to return in it to Vienna. The rest of us, with M. de Baden, Colonel Bridler and his staff, then got back into the train which took us half an hour farther on to the tiny station of Staad where arrangements similar to those at Buchs had been made to receive us. The Swiss military and railway authorities, by admirable organization, had all the luggage piled under guard within thirty minutes of our arrival, and the train started back at once for Buchs. Bridler most kindly conveyed me in his car to the Hotel Anker at Rorschach and overwhelmed me with hospitable attentions. He assured me I could go anywhere and do anything I liked, the only stipulation being that I should not wear my sword – an article which I had last seen in July 1914!

It was all over, the pain anaesthetized for the moment by the politeness, the punctilio, and the efficiency of the Swiss, so practised at giving asylum. It must have also helped Charles and Zita that the first stage of their exile was spent with relatives. By previous arrangement, the Imperial family and party were now driven to the small château of Wartegg which belonged to the Bourbon-Parmas, and which lay conveniently near by in wooded grounds on the shores of Lake Constance. It was here that Colonel Strutt drove from his hotel the next morning to hand back the Empress her jewellery. The date was now 25 March 1919. A fortnight later, a telegram arrived for him at the British Legation in Berne ordering him to 'proceed forthwith' to Constantinople. His 'special mission' was completed.

Two other extracts from his diary are worth recording. The first describes his parting from the Royal Family after a farewell lunch at a hotel on the road to Zurich.

10 April

We talked till about two o'clock and then, as it was getting cold and windy, I suggested that their Majesties should return to Wartegg. I walked with their Majesties (and Gussl) along the road towards Aarau. People stared curiously but very respectfully at them and many saluted (a very unusual thing for the Swiss to do). Outside the town we said good-bye. I can remember little of what was said; it was all like a dream. Her Majesty's last words were: 'Only an Englishman could have accomplished what you have done for us.' I knelt and kissed her hand. People began to collect as the Emperor's car drove up. I last saw them waving their hands to me as the car turned into the town.

And the last is an entry on his arrival in Constantinople on 27 April:

A month ago I had been almost a Dictator. Today I am a humble unknown British soldier.

Colonel Strutt's days as dictator were certainly over. Yet, had he known it, his part in the adventures of the exiled Austrian Emperor was only beginning.

Chapter 15

A KING RETURNS:
THE 'EASTER BID'

In following Charles over the Austrian border into Switzerland through the bluff military eyes of Colonel Strutt, we have lost sight for a moment of politics. Not that the Emperor himself ever did, or indeed ever could.

To mark his exile from Austrian soil, Charles now signed the so-called Feldkirch Manifesto. This document, which had been under preparation for some time, was designed to demonstrate to the Austrian people and to the world that the Emperor had only undertaken an act of voluntary self-banishment which was without prejudice to any of his ultimate sovereign rights in his homeland. It went further: the authority of the Republican government which now ruled in Vienna in his place, though not in his name, was denounced outright.

The German-Austrian Government [it read], has put aside my proclamation of 11 November 1918, which I issued in a dark hour, in that on the same day it decided to lay before the Provisional National Assembly a resolution proclaiming the transformation of German-Austria into a Republic, thus pre-empting the decision which, according to my proclamation, should only have been taken by the whole German-Austrian people. . . .*

What the German-Austrian Government and the provisional constituent National Assembly has decided and done in this regard since 11 November 1919, and what it resolved to do in the future, is therefore null and void for Me and My House. . . .

And so I leave German-Austria. . . . It was in war that I was called to the throne of my ancestors. It was to peace that I sought to lead my peoples and it is in peacetime that I have desired and still intend to be their just and faithful father.

Feldkirch 24 March 1919 †

* The same legal point that the formerly monarchist Christian-Social deputies had made in much feebler terms when agreeing to proclaim the Republic.

† This date of issue, though deliberately chosen to mark the frontier crossing, is almost certainly incorrect. The document was in fact issued a few days later.

Proud yet pathetic, logical yet unrealistic, the Feldkirch Manifesto was also a historical curiosity in that it was proclaimed, so to say, in dead silence. A few days before, in Budapest, the Government of Count Karolyi had suffered the fate of all amateur left-wing radicals who play with real fire and had been duly smoked out of office by the Communist regime of the Moscow-trained Bela Kun. A reign of terror had begun in Hungary, with the conservative leaders shot, jailed or fleeing for their lives – as they were to do thirty years later when another Moscow-trained Communist, Mathyas Rakosi, took over power after another world war. It was partly to avoid further dangerous provocation to the extremists that the Emperor's Manifesto, with its ringing assertion of undiminished Habsburg rights, was not published.

But only partly. The Empress recalls that another and even more important reason for the suppression of the declaration had been the attitude of Austria's Christian-Democrat leaders, Hauser and Seipel, backed by Cardinal Piffl himself. The Manifesto question had been discussed, via intermediaries, with these priestly gentlemen while Charles was still at Eckartsau. All of them, the Empress remembers, had begged Charles 'not to throw a blazing torch into the Austrian powder-keg while he moved away to safety'. The Emperor's predictable reaction to this appeal was to keep silent rather than endanger those who still professed their loyalty. Thus, in order not to provoke the extreme left-wing in Budapest and not to imperil the extreme right-wing in Vienna, the Manifesto was never publicly declared. Instead, with a covering message, copies were privately distributed 'for the record' to the Pope and the heads of various friendly states.

No copy, needless to say, was sent to Vienna, though the next act of Dr Renner's Government reads almost like a retort to Charles's defiance. On 3 April 1919, the so-called Habsburg Law was adopted without opposition by the new Parliament and incorporated in the Republic's constitution. This not only banished the House of Habsburg for good from its own homeland (with the exception of certain selected members who swore allegiance to the Republic); it also declared even the private property of the family to be forfeit. The Austrians of the Second Republic were still struggling to amend the injustices of this measure fifty years later.* It was the most uncompromising act of political revenge to be enacted against any of the dethroned dynasties under the so-called rule of law. But, of course, it was not law that ruled in Vienna in that dreadful spring of 1919, but hunger, panic, hate and fear.

*It was only in 1967, after years of byzantine negotiations with the Second Austrian Republic, that arrangements were finally worked out permitting the late Emperor's eldest son Otto to return to his homeland for the first time since 1919.

There is no record in the Royal Archives at Windsor that King George V was among the recipients of the Feldkirch Manifesto – though for Charles he was certainly a friendly head of state if not the head of a friendly state. But, once settled on Swiss soil, the Emperor lost little time in thanking the British monarch once again for that remarkable helping hand which had brought him safely into exile. This second message, more personal and more emotional than the first, has been preserved at Windsor. It reads, in the original French:

Monsieur mon frère,

Arrivé sur le sol hospitalier de la Suisse avec l'escorte militaire que le gouvernement de Votre Majesté a bien voulu mettre à ma disposition, je désire vous exprimer directement et sans délai les sentiments de gratitude que me fait éprouver l'appui sûr et généreux de l'empire britannique dans ces circonstances cruelles que je veux croire momentanées.

Votre Majesté le savait mieux que personne: j'ai tout fait dès les débuts de mon règne, pour arrêter cette guerre funeste dont le prolongement insensé plonge maintenant l'Europe dans une crise sociale qui, de proche en proche, menace de tout englouter.

Je n'ai rien à me reprocher et cette certitude que Votre Majesté avait de mes actes est, sans doute, ce qui a fixé les dispositions courtoises du gouvernement britannique, dont j'ai à vous remercier.

Elles viennent ainsi de se manifester noblement à l'égard de mes chers enfants, de l'Impératrice, ma femme bien aimée, de ma mère et de moi-même. Vous n'avez pas voulu que l'exemple injuste et sauvage donné par la Russie égarée, se renouvelle contre moi et les miens. Je vous serai, quoi qu'il arrive désormais de nous, toujours très profondément reconnaissant de cet appui fraternel et effectif. Je n'ai eu qu'à me louer, en particulier, des dispositions prises par le Colonel Strutt, qui m'a accompagné jusqu'ici et dont le caractère plein de droiture a été hautement apprécié par moi.

Dieu veuille Vous épargner de voir jamais, dans l'avenir, ce que j'ai dû voir auprès de moi. Je suis, de Votre Majesté, le très obligé et le bon frère.

Charles

*Wartegg, le 11 avril 1919.**

The château of Wartegg on Lake Constance had been acquired in the 1860s by the Empress's father, the Duke Robert of Bourbon-Parma, who had added it to those other properties which together made his 'retirement' after the *Risorgimento* such a placid and comfortable one. But it was too small for the demands now made upon it. Apart from Charles and Zita and their five children (the Empress was then expecting her sixth child) relatives from both the marriages of Duke Robert had streamed to Wartegg to welcome the exiles. The château was filled to the very attics with Habsburgs, Bourbons and Braganzas so that even the Emperor's own servants and tiny suite had to be put up in near-by houses and hotels.

* Published by Gracious Permission of Her Majesty the Queen. From the Royal Archives, Windsor Castle, Reference Number GV AA43/224.

Moreover, one of the very mild conditions* that the Swiss Government had made on receiving Charles was that he should take up residence in a canton either in the interior or in Western Switzerland – at any rate away from the Austrian border whose mountains he could gaze upon every fine day from the windows of Wartegg.

After a few weeks' search, a pleasant alternative was found. This was the Villa Prangins on Lake Geneva, a roomy house with outbuildings set in a secluded park near the water's edge. The family moved there in May. Despite the never-ending pain of exile, which made even happiness a bitter-sweet sensation, there now followed some of the calmest months of Charles's life. He was still up before seven every morning, and each day was largely taken up with reports from his own small but busy staff and with audiences given to a stream of visitors who came from all parts of the dismembered Dual Monarchy to this miniature Court in exile on Lake Geneva. But, for the first time since the outbreak of war, there was now leisure and rest as well as work and strain. Charles was able, for example, to indulge in the stolid Swiss passion for reading fat newspapers from end to end. Above all, he could now devote more of each day to his family, taking part in the games of the smallest ones and helping in the education of the two eldest, Otto and Adelheid.

It was at Prangins on 5 May 1919 that the royal couple's first child in exile was born. Another son, he was named Rudolf, after the founder of the Habsburg dynasty six and a half centuries before. The infant's parents had not yet accepted that the wheel of history was indeed closing around their heads. Charles, on the contrary, was serenely confident that the natural geographical unity of the Danube Basin would eventually smother all the wrangling of the new succession-states and that he or his successors would still have a role to play there when the tumult had subsided.

It was above all Hungary that riveted his attention – the land of the thousand-year-old St Stephen's Crown, and the only one that had actually been placed on his own brow. This Hungary, which had been his heaviest burden as Emperor, was to bring him disaster as an exile. To begin with, however, it seemed to bring only hope. Throughout the summer of 1919, as the tension in Budapest mounted so also, gradually, did the prospects of the banished monarch. Already in April, an opposition 'government' of sorts to the Communist regime of Bela Kun had been formed under French protection at Szegedin in the extreme South, which was still occupied by those French forces that had marched all the way from Salonika the year before. Here, over the weeks, the rudiments of two

* The only quasi-political one was that he should refrain from any activity which might embarrass the Swiss authorities – a formula which left nearly all options open.

loyalist battalions were formed, largely out of officers fleeing from the Communist terror. One of them, the Ostenburg Battalion, was to play a vital role in Charles's coming fight to regain his Hungarian crown. This monarchist nucleus in Szegedin did not amount to much and what there was of it lay at the mercy of the local French military command. Yet it was a start and it soon gained its vital opening to the West – and ultimately to Charles on Lake Geneva – when it established regular contact via Serbia with the so-called 'Action Committee' in Vienna.

The Committee was an assemblage of Hungarian politicians of all colours except red who had taken refuge from Bela Kun in the Austrian capital under the leadership of Count Stephen Bethlen. They were a mixed bunch and they contained some pretty irresponsible elements. On one occasion, for example, it was left to the redoubtable Frau Sacher of Sacher's Hotel – that imperishable legend of legends among Central Europe's vanished hoteliers – to stop them making fools both of themselves and of the Emperor, to whom she, too, was devoted. She overheard a group of about twenty of them deciding, in the flush of an alcoholic evening at the hotel, to hire half-a-dozen taxis then and there and simply drive to the border 'to liberate Hungary'. A call to the police by the prudent old lady stopped the escapade just in time.

On another occasion, however, the *panache* of the 'Action Committee' proved rewarding, in the literal sense of the word. They managed to break into the Hungarian Government building in Vienna – appropriately situated in the Bankgasse – and seize all the mission's funds. Thus, for months, Bela Kun's money was used to finance the campaign against him. Part of these 'sequestrated' funds were used to raise another Hungarian loyalist force ready to strike when the moment was ripe. This was the so-called 'Lehar Division', led by a brother of the composer, and recruited and trained in Eastern Styria throughout the summer. Colonel Lehar, whose devotion to Charles was to become a monarchist by-word, eventually led these troops back across the border in early August and formed a Carlist stronghold in Western Hungary that was not to be shattered for fifteen months.

But Lehar was not the only newcomer to the Hungarian political scene. It is now that Admiral Horthy – humble aide-de-camp at Charles's wedding in pre-war days and his brilliant naval commander in wartime – begins to enter the picture again, a picture he was soon to dominate. The Admiral, though high on Bela Kun's 'liquidation list', had escaped the Communist execution squads by fleeing from Budapest to the country estate of his parents-in-law near Arad. On hearing that he was alive, Charles had him appointed, through the Bethlen Committee, as Minister of War in the Szegedin 'counter-government' – a post which Horthy subsequently exchanged for that of Commander-in-Chief of the incipient anti-Communist army.* The Emperor had unwittingly placed the asp in his own breast.

From now on things moved swiftly. At the end of July, the Rumanian occupation troops holding Eastern Hungary marched on Budapest. Bela Kun and his comrades promptly downed their gory tools and, in the first week of August, fled to Vienna. They were succeeded by Peidl's may-fly Socialist Administration; then by Friedrich's Nationalist Government under the aegis of the Archduke Josef (Charles's *homo regius* of the previous autumn); and finally, in November 1919, by Huszar's Coalition. This was, in effect, appointed by the *Entente* powers under strong pressure from the Czechs in order to have an all-party Hungarian Government ready to negotiate the Peace Treaty.†

While the politicians changed seats in the capital, Horthy bided his time and slowly built up his forces in the South. His moment came on 16 November 1919, when the Rumanians finally withdrew from Budapest. Two days later, the admiral turned soldier-of-fortune entered the city in triumph at the head of 'his' monarchist army. He had marched this far as the Emperor's man and it was on the shoulders of the dynasty that he now climbed much higher.

A wrangle had broken out as to whether Charles was still the undisputed King of Hungary or whether his Eckartsau Declaration of 13 November 1918 was tantamount to an abdication which entitled the nation to fill the throne with any candidate of its choice.‡ Though the majority of the people held to the orthodox legitimist view, there was among the politicians a very sizeable and very active group of so-called 'free electors' – sustained by a variety of diplomatic machinations outside the country as well as a variety of intrigues within. The new right-wing Coalition Government returned by the elections of January 1920 tried to settle the dispute by shelving it. This compromise acknowledged that though Hungary was still a monarchy, no Hungarian King could, for the time being, exercise his due powers. A Regent would therefore be appointed in his name, elected by the Parliament and answerable to the Parliament to

* See Boroviczeny, *Der König und Sein Reichsverweser*, pp. 21–2.

† The Treaty of Trianon, finally signed on 14 June 1920. It lopped off vast areas of Hungary to give to Czechoslovakia, Rumania and Yugoslavia and even fragments to Austria, Poland and Italy. Of the 325,411 square kilometres of 'St Stephen's lands' only 92,963 remained, and the population of what had once represented half of the Dual Monarchy dropped by more than thirteen millions.

‡ The act of coronation in Hungary was always a mutually binding contract between king and nation in which each party assumed certain historic obligations.

discharge provisionally the functions of Head of State. On 1 March 1920, Admiral Horthy, who was the secret hope of the 'free electors' while remaining the public symbol of the legitimists, was appointed to this curious post. His was the classic case of the absolute corruption of absolute power. He soon became answerable neither to Parliament nor to his King. As for the 'provisional' discharge of functions, this was to be stretched out by him over the next twenty-five years, and only broken in the end by war.

Horthy began modestly. To do him maximum justice, he was perhaps even unconscious of all the temptations ahead and, at this early stage, irresolute about pursuing them. He was rather slow, it is true, in reporting his appointment officially to his exiled sovereign. But when his message did reach Prangins, it still sounded like the passionately loyal voice of the dashing courtier and admiral of former days. The Regent assured the monarch of his unshakeable loyalty; of his conviction that Charles's restoration would come; and of his intention in the meantime to report fully on events in the homeland. He even begged special permission to be allowed to move into a side-tract of the Royal Palace as this was, after all, his master's house.

But once the Regent settled down in the gilt and brocade chairs on the Buda hill, his ambitions quickened. Despite all his attempts at camouflage, this changing mood could be sensed even on faraway Lake Geneva. Proclamations sent to Budapest by secret courier for the Regent to give out in the King's name were received but never published. Specific orders to Horthy to prepare the path for the King's return and to indicate the most suitable time* were either evasively acknowledged or not answered at all. Most disturbing of all, the Regent compelled all the officers of Hungary's armed forces to swear a personal oath of allegiance to him – with no mention either of King or dynasty. This oath was, for Charles, the turning-point. From this day on, though he still hoped for Horthy's loyalty, he no longer counted on it. And once when the Empress, whose own faith in the Regent persisted a little longer, debated the point with him, he put an end to the discussion with the firm remark: 'There can be no two ways about it. An officer's oath is a crucial matter and it is a military matter. I understand these things and you, my dear, do not.'

So, by the late summer of 1919 (when the Treaty of Trianon had been signed and settled),† Charles had decided to return soon to Hungary at all

---

* One such message from Charles was delivered to Horthy in Budapest on 4 June 1920. (See Boroviczeny, *op. cit.*, p. 80.)

† Any restoration attempt before then could have resulted in even fiercer peace terms. On this point Horthy and Charles had agreed.

costs – with or without the invitation of his enigmatic Regent. Two things had to be established well in advance. The first was what backing, if any, he could count on from the major European powers to contain the certain hostility of the small 'succession-states' which now ringed Hungary, each holding fat portions of Hungarian land. The second problem was even more basic: how to get from Lake Geneva to Budapest. The Emperor, who had never held a passport in his life, was without travel documents of any sort now. Moreover, the Swiss authorities,* however correct and polite, watched his every move, shadowed all his messengers and controlled his mail. The difficulties would begin from the moment he set a foot outside the gates of his private park at Prangins.

From this position of isolation, so remote and closely guarded, Charles had decided it would be almost hopeless to try and organize any pre-arranged mass movement of support to coincide with his return. In any case, at this stage, both he and the vast majority of his advisers hoped it would probably turn out to be unnecessary. Once Charles IV of Hungary arrived in person to reclaim the thousand-year-old throne of King Arpad which was his anointed right, the people would surely cheer and even the ambitious Admiral would presumably step aside. In the meantime, the best tactics seemed to be to lull him by friendliness until he could be displaced by surprise. Thus when Horthy coolly bestowed upon himself the title of Duke, Charles swallowed the impertinence and even brought himself indirectly to sanction it by addressing this self-ennobled Regent as 'Your Grace' in his next message to Budapest. Yet these developments – the oath, the title, the evasions, the silences – all pointed in the same ominous direction and they all called for drastic action. By September 1920 Charles had become more precise. In a walk around the villa grounds during that month he suddenly turned to his press secretary Werkmann and said: 'I cannot afford to delay my return beyond next spring.' †

By the time he spoke those words, Charles had already found the powerful sponsor he needed. Of the *Entente* powers Italy, he knew, would be at best indifferent towards his return. The Italian Government had ambitions of its own in the Danube Basin now that Vienna's supremacy there was broken. Indeed, there was even talk at one point in January 1921 of a 'political marriage' between Princess Jolanda, daughter of the Italian King, and the young son of Archduke Josef, the magyarized Habsburg in Budapest who, though formerly Charles's representative there, had become one of the darlings of the 'free electors' for the vacant throne.

---

* The espionage services of the Czechs, Rumanians and Jugoslavs, soon linked together as the 'Little *Entente*', were also formidable pursuers to be shaken off.

† Werkmann, *op. cit.*, p. 149.

England, though not actively hostile at this juncture to a restoration bid, was at best neutral and was expected to 'wait and see'. Her main concern, which came out more strongly as time went on, was the stability of Central Europe as a whole and a fear that the Hohenzollern dynasty might be awakened out of its slumber in Holland by any spectacular success of its former comrades-at-arms, the Habsburgs. For the rest, weighed down as she was with the post-war problems of Empire, the perennial question of Ireland and with a deepening economic crisis, all that England asked of the Danube Basin was that it should stay calm, and she did not much mind how.

But France was a very different story. There were politicians of many shades in Paris who wished to counter both the Italian thrust up the Balkans and at the same time restore some friendly Catholic bloc along the Danube as a permanent counterweight to Protestant Prussia. Among the most ardent supporters of this line was Aristide Briand, who had already played a leading role before his overthrow in 1917 in encouraging Charles's initiatives for separate peace talks. In January 1921, Briand returned to power again as Prime Minister and Foreign Minister combined. One of Charles's warmest personal supporters, and one of the best advocates the Habsburg dynasty as such had in Paris, was now at the helm.

Well before this, however, the Villa Prangins had managed to spin its contacts to Briand and his circle and had received the most encouraging messages in return. There has been much controversy as to how categoric this private French backing was for Charles's Hungarian adventures since, not unnaturally, Briand himself later denied everything in public. Here is the Empress's full account:

'The secret exchanges with Paris over a restoration bid began in the summer of 1920. They went on continuously until shortly before the Emperor's first return in March 1921 and, despite the failure of that attempt, they were immediately resumed in preparation for the second bid in October 1921. A variety of deputies and ministers expressed sympathy and support. They included some Socialists who remembered the Emperor's peace efforts of 1917; some Nationalists who were appalled at the dominant influence the new Czech leaders Benes and Masaryk exerted over the Quai d'Orsay; and a section of the Radicals who hated Horthy's military dictatorship and would have preferred to see a liberal monarchy in its place. The French General Staff and most of the Army leaders also favoured our cause.

'But our principal contact, our most outspoken supporter and, after January 1921, our most powerful one, was Briand himself. He always made it perfectly clear, however, that, before he could come out in the open with French Government backing, the restoration bid would first

The two evil geniuses of Charles' life

15 Count Ottokar Czernin. Charles'
brilliant but erratic and disloyal Foreign
Minister. He was a gifted dilettante, a man
of Bismarckian ambitions but hardly any
Bismarckian talent. His foolhardy public
disclosures about Austria's secret peace
moves to the Entente precipitated a major
Austrian crisis as well as a European
scandal in the spring of 1918.

16 Nicholas von Horthy. A humble naval
Aide-de-camp to the Emperor Franz
Josef at Charles' wedding in 1911, he
was promoted Admiral of the Austro-
Hungarian navy by Charles himself
during the war. In 1920, in a confused
political situation in Budapest following
the collapse both of the Empire, and then
of a short-lived Communist regime,
Horthy was appointed Regent of
Hungary. He swore to Charles that he was
only keeping the throne ready for him.
But in 1921, when Charles left his Swiss
exile to launch his two restoration bids,
Horthy ejected his master, the first time
by cunning, the second by force. Horthy
himself was deposed and driven into exile
by Hitler in 1944 and died in Portugal in
1957.

17 The 'People's Emperor'. Charles listens patiently to the pleas of poor peasant women during a 1917 tour of Karst province, while all his aides look studiously the other way.

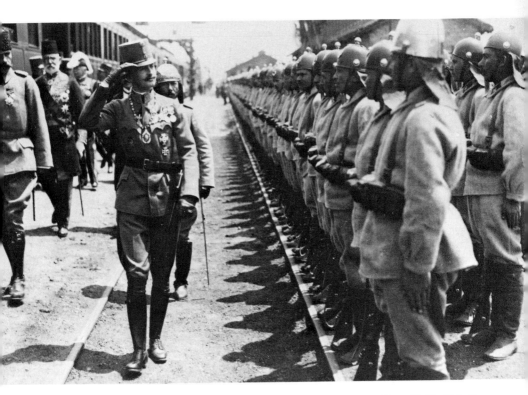

18 The Emperor inspects a picturesque Guard of Honour during a state visit to his Turkish ally in the summer of 1918. The visit provided a last illusion of the Central Powers' solidarity as well as a last untroubled journey abroad for Charles and Zita. Three months later, the Bulgarian-Turkish front started to collapse.

19 A happy moment during a wartime visit to Innsbruck in 1917. Charles and Zita acknowledge the cheers of their Tyrolean subjects.

Exile in Switzerland: family happiness amid political cares

20 The Emperor stands by as Crown Prince Otto (sitting) and two other of his children fish in untroubled neutral water at Prangins, their first Swiss residence in 1920. One of the few joys of exile was the extra time he now had for his family.

21 Charles and Zita photographed with their seven children at Hertenstein, their second Swiss residence, on 3 October 1921. Less than three weeks after this picture was taken, Charles set out for Hungary on his second restoration attempt – this time by secretly chartered private plane and accompanied by the Empress.

have to succeed. His attitude throughout – which my husband accepted and understood – was: "If the attempt goes well and the Emperor looks secure in Budapest, then we shall support him officially and keep Hungary's neighbours quiet. If the attempt fails, we can of course do nothing."

'The contacts with Briand – in order to protect his own position – were all verbal. The French go-betweens were at all levels. They included my brothers, the Princes Sixtus and Xavier; a number of former French diplomats and politicians; the secretary to the then French President, M. Deschanel; and a number of plain messengers. The Emperor and Briand organized a system whereby these "official" verbal messages were always repeated again in conversation to some trusted person about to travel between Prangins and Paris in order to make sure that the original had got through and had been understood.

'In this way, over the months, it was possible to "negotiate" a very detailed arrangement. It is quite untrue that M. Briand's support was only of a vague and general nature. These were his seven specific promises given to my husband before the first restoration attempt was launched:

1. Immediate recognition of the Emperor as soon as he had taken over as King of Hungary.

2. Immediate setting-up of economic links.

3. Immediate granting of French state credits.

4. French military aid, should the Emperor need it in Hungary against foreign attacks.

5. A pledge, on the other hand, that no French troops would be forced on the Emperor if he did not require them.

6. An undertaking to "look again" at the large territories of Hungary allotted to her neighbours and to "readjust the position to some extent".

7. A promise, as regards those same neighbouring states, to keep them in check and to cut off all the French credits on which they so heavily depended should they give any trouble.

'This seven-point verbal pact was only finalized after repeated exchanges. In Point 1, for example, Briand originally proposed "early" recognition. My husband insisted it must be "immediate" in view of the strategic vulnerability of a Hungary now greatly reduced in size. This was also the Emperor's argument in having Point 4 (military aid) added and, as an extra weapon, Point 7 (economic sanctions). Even if French armed intervention was threatened, the Emperor pointed out, the succession-states might shrug their shoulders and repeat the old saying: "The heavens are high and the Tsar is a long way off." But the cutting-off of French credits would apply direct and immediate pressure on them. All these arguments were accepted by Briand.

'As to the urgency of the operation, it was not so much the Emperor who was pressing the French during the final weeks as Briand – and the circle around M. Deschanel – who were pressing the Emperor to act with the greatest possible speed. As Briand once exclaimed to my brothers and to a Hungarian diplomat in Paris, M. Halmos, during this last preparatory stage: *"Qu'il rentre su plus tôt et nous le reconnaîtrons immédiatement."*'

The restoration bids of 1921 were thus no wild adventures launched out of the blue. At least on the diplomatic side, they were operations 'cleared' in advance, meticulously if only verbally, with several French leaders, including the Prime Minister of France himself.*

But though the French authorities were also even prepared – by various 'unofficial' means – to provide Charles with the necessary false travel documents to get back to Hungary, there was one problem they could not very well tackle, and that was spiriting him out of Switzerland in the first place. And here who should reappear upon the scene but Colonel Strutt, the Emperor's British champion in the dark winter of 1919.

The colonel had maintained regular contact by letter and by messenger with the Imperial family, first from Constantinople, whence he had gone after his 'special mission' at Eckartsau, and later from Danzig, where he had later been posted as Assistant High Commissioner. In February of 1921 he was holidaying in Switzerland, probably by arrangement with Prangins, when the affairs of the House of Habsburg caught up with him once more. The account which follows is not from any diary of his. It is taken from the confidential report on his activities which he submitted himself to the perturbed authorities in London on 31 March 1921, when Charles was already back in Hungary wrestling with Horthy, and Europe was resounding with alarms and rumours. He wrote it to Alexander Cadogan in the Foreign Office, in a handwriting which was so bad that he apologized for it himself and suggested the recipient ought to get some copies typed.†

On February 19th last whilst staying at St Moritz I received a telephone message to expect 'someone' by the afternoon train on the following day. I accordingly proceeded to the station at 1500 hours on February 20th, and met Commander Schonta, A.D.C. to the Emperor Karl. He brought me a verbal message from the Emperor begging me to come to Prangins at once. Schonta had no idea what I was wanted for and asked me not to speak of his (Schonta's) presence at St Moritz to the Archduke Max, the Emperor's brother,

---

* M. Briand had to continue his public disavowals even after the Emperor's death. Thus in January 1924 he privately begged the Empress to try and prevent the publication of a book (it was that of Boroviczeny) which would reveal the existence of the 1921 links with Paris. He warned the Empress that he would again be compelled to deny this account as and when it appeared.

† Strutt's original manuscript, available in the Public Records Office: C 6930/180/21.

who had also been spending the winter there and with whom I happened to be dining that night. Schonta and I started the next morning, February 21st, by the same train but in different compartments. We arrived at Lausanne at 20.15 and while Schonta proceeded direct by car to Prangins I slept the night at Lausanne as Prangins was quite full of doctors and near relatives owing to the approaching confinement of the Empress Zita.

I went to Gland the next morning, February 22nd, and was met by car and driven to Prangins. The Emperor met me just inside the park and we walked to a clearing in the park – so as not to be overheard – and conversed for over two hours.

The Emperor said that he had sent for me to ask for my advice and assistance in an absolutely secret matter which I was not even to mention to the Empress.

He stated that on February 19th he had heard from Prince Sixtus in Paris that Monsieur Briand had been to see him (Sixtus) and had stated that 'if the Emperor went back to Hungary and proclaimed himself King, thus showing a *fait accompli*, neither France nor Great Britain would make the slightest opposition'. Briand had added that the move should take place at once and not later than March 15th–30th; the Emperor must throw off his lethargy.

The Emperor asked for my advice as to whether he should start or not, but he gave the impression that he intended to move whatever I might say.... He requested me to proceed to Paris, interview Prince Sixtus and confirm the Briand statement. I agreed and asked him to allow me to go to London and if possible interview the Prime Minister as well. He refused.

I lunched with the Emperor and Empress *en famille*. I went for a walk of 1½ hours with the Empress afterwards. She was in great spirits but mentioned nothing about the family's future. I then proceeded by car to Lausanne, picked up my bag and left by the night train to Paris.

The next day, February 23rd, I called on Prince Sixtus at 47 Rue de Varenne in Paris and he confirmed the whole Briand story, adding that his (Sixtus's) great friend Maréchel Lyautey was present at the interview, and was most anxious that the *coup d'état* should be brought off as soon as possible. Briand had stated to Prince Sixtus on February 14th that the Italian Government was trying to marry the half-witted son of the Archduke Josef to Princess Jolanda of Italy and then proclaim a joint Italian–Habsburg dynasty over Hungary – all this *pour embêter les Serves*. If the Emperor Karl, added Briand, returns *now* and seizes the throne, we shall have a faithful ally to France and Great Britain as King as well as a French Princess as Queen of Hungary. Doubtless, Austria will soon follow. 'Now is the time for the Emperor to show all the energy he may possess.'

Sixtus was enthusiastic about the whole scheme and laughed at difficulties; he said Prince Xavier would accompany the Emperor. The only difficulties would be a passport to leave Switzerland, but that could be procured. Sixtus asked me to try and cross the Austrian–Swiss frontier at Martinsbruck, Lower Engadine, without showing my passport. As this suited a long-standing engagement of mine to meet Count Czernin at Landeck, I consented. I had already obtained a

Swiss–Austrian visa. I saw Sixtus again in the evening and received from him (I believe) a passport for the Emperor. I returned to St Moritz that night arriving there on the evening of February 24th. . . .

I left St Moritz on February 26th, by train to Tarasp, and then arrived by sleigh at Remus. With a 'letter from a friend' in my pocket betting me 5000 frs. that I could not cross the frontier without showing my passport, I left the inn at 21.00 hours on foot, and crossed the frontier by the steep rocks above the left bank of the river Inn. I duly returned by the same route approximately at 05.30. I met no one but of course used no path. The journey was most unpleasant in the dark and suited only for a practised mountaineer.* At 09.00 on the same morning, February 27th, I started on a sleigh, crossed the frontier with no trouble as regards the officials and arrived at Landeck at 16.30. . . .

I returned to Switzerland via Buchs on March 2nd. . . .

On March 4th, I went to Geneva, breaking the journey at Prangins, handed over Prince Sixtus's letter to the Emperor and pointed out to him the difficulties of my journey to Austria. He appeared quite determined to start. . . . I then asked him 'what the hurry was now' and did my utmost to prevent him starting for another year at least. Briand's remarks about 'apathy' etc. appeared to rankle; he was adamant.

He begged me to take a letter home to the King George v to assure H.M. that his, Karl's, friendship for the *Entente* was profound and the move was only to save his own country and the throne which he had never abdicated. This letter was to be handed to the King after the arrival in Hungary. I requested the Emperor not to give me this letter but to hand it to Mr Hohler, the British representative, at Budapest. He then said that he entrusted the Empress and his family to my care and begged me to do all I could for them. I accepted gladly. He preferred not to tell me the date of his departure or the route, but thought it would be either via Simplon–Venice–Tarvis–Neunkirchen–Hungary, or via Bavaria–Passau–Linz–Vienna. . . .

I saw the Emperor again on March 6th when he bade me a most affectionate farewell. I was of course unable to see the Empress.

On my return to London I saw Colonel Twiss of the War Office and Mr Cadogan of the Foreign Office. I gave them as much information as I could. I also saw Mr Lindley and as a result of my interview with him, wrote in the strongest way direct to the Emperor Karl imploring him not to start. I have received today a letter dated the 25th March, acknowledging receipt of my letter, containing affectionate messages and 'hopes to see me very often shortly'.

31 March 1921   Lieutenant-Colonel E. L. Strutt
                                  117 St James's Court,
                                  Buckingham Gate, S.W.

* Colonel Strutt was. After his abrupt retirement from the Army he went out to the Himalayas the following year as second-in-command of the 1922 British Everest expedition.

In this hitherto unpublished memorandum the French Prime Minister is shown again, and from a different quarter, not merely as backing Charles's restoration bid up to the hilt but as urging the exiled monarch on to strike immediately, and even naming a definite fortnight for the operation (a recommendation which Charles, in fact, acted upon). It is also, of course, remarkable for the frank admission of the part played by Colonel Strutt himself – still a serving British officer and at that time actually attached to the Foreign Office – in preparing the Emperor's journey, this time without the vaguest of mandates from the British Government.

This bit of private enterprise was to get the Colonel into the hottest water in Whitehall. Lord Curzon, the Foreign Secretary, declared when all the excitement was over, that he

could not help being doubtful of the propriety of a British subject, who is understood to be on the Special Reserve of officers, continuing to associate in the manner explained with an ex-enemy sovereign and discussing with him political plans which must gravely affect the interests of this country and the policy of the British and Allied Governments. . . .

One of the noble Marquess's senior officials at the Foreign Office thought the Colonel's 'ambiguous meddling . . . worthy of the strongest censure', and the Foreign Secretary in due course approached the Chief of the Imperial General Staff for 'such disciplinary action as may be possible'. Indeed, Strutt only escaped trouble thanks to the petty and almost schoolboyish hostility between the two government departments now involved. The War Office, incensed that civilians should try to censure an Army officer, replied that Colonel Strutt had 'not been guilty of any technical military offence' and was anyway at the moment attached to the Foreign Office for service in Danzig. An even more infuriated Foreign Office commented that this must be a lesson to them in future 'not to trust too implicitly' in War Office recommendations for secondment. The upshot of it was that Lord Curzon wrote a reprimand which the Army Council transmitted to Strutt but without suggesting that they agreed with it to any marked degree.*

This all happened, of course, after the dust had settled in Budapest. Meanwhile, we must follow Charles there. It had been decided at Prangins that the hazardous route reconnoitred by Strutt would be too risky to take. A suitable alternative was eventually found and, on 24 March 1921, Charles slipped safely across the Swiss frontier on foot into France and was on his way home. It was two years to the very day from the start of that journey into exile from Eckartsau.

* For this whole Strutt episode see Public Records Office: C 6930/180/21; C 7033/180/21; C 8699/180/121; and C 12075/180/21.

The elaborate travel arrangements worked out in advance and put into operation from this point forward were in the best tradition of Central European adventure. A car met Charles at the border and drove him direct to Strasbourg. Here, in the early morning of 25 March (it was Easter Friday) he boarded the Vienna-bound express as it came in from Paris and was taken straight to the sleeping-car, number 1717. Waiting to greet him was one Count Lasuen y de Reischach, a Spanish nobleman living in Bordeaux who had reserved both the berths in one compartment (numbers 11 and 12) for the whole journey from Paris onwards. This Spanish–French blend was reproduced in the travel document which the Emperor now handed to the sleeping-car conductor. It was a Spanish diplomatic passport made out in the name of Sanchez which had been issued by the Spanish Consulate in Paris, stamped by the Head of the Third Division of the Paris Prefecture of Police, and furnished with Czech and German visas from the Paris passport office of these two countries as well as a third visa from the German-Austrian Legation in France.

So at Salzburg the 'Spaniard' – who feigned illness and kept to his compartment throughout, wearing a pair of large dark spectacles – crossed back into his former Empire. A host of Austrian notabilities were on the same train, all blissfully unaware that the Emperor was travelling in their midst. They included two of Charles's former Ministers, Dr Spitzmüller and Prince Ludwig Windischgraetz and, as an added coincidence, Dr Coumount, the lawyer who represented the Habsburg dynasty's financial interests in Vienna.

The train arrived at Westbahnhof at 10.50 P.M. that night and Charles got off the platform unnoticed in the throng of Easter passengers. To preserve anonymity, an ordinary Vienna taxi* was hired and, to dispel any suspicions, perfunctory enquiries for hotel rooms were made. They were all in any case full over the Easter week-end, and Charles and his companion now drove to their real destination – Landkrongasse No. 5 in the Inner City where Count Thomas Erdödy, his faithful messenger of the 1917 Sixtus negotiations, had an apartment. The Count was fortunately at home. He came to the door to find his Emperor standing on the threshold.† This was to be the one and only night of his whole exile that Charles was to spend in Vienna. It was in marked contrast to the last one passed in his Palace at Schönbrunn on 10 November 1918. Attempts to

---

* Generously but unwisely Charles gave the driver, one Petrak, a Swiss 50-franc note – a small fortune in the inflationary Vienna of those days and a fat enough tip to make any taxi-driver talk. This one duly did – to the police.

† Count Erdödy, the Empress relates, had in fact been warned some days before that the Emperor would pass through Vienna. But it had not been possible to tell him exactly when or how, or that he might be called on to put Charles up for the night.

contact a few trustworthy friends by telephone and warn them of his presence failed. All were away from the capital; Easter again. This scarcely mattered, however. Budapest was the target, not Vienna, and for tomorrow's journey into Hungary itself further elaborate preparations had already been made.

On the Easter Saturday, a relay of two taxis, each driven by chauffeurs who had formerly worked for the royal family, took the Emperor and his companions on their way. The first car did the stretch from Vienna to Seebenstein in the Burgenland, and the second took them on from there via Aspang and Mönnichkirchen to the border post at Sinnersdorf. Here Count Erdödy barely needed to show his papers to either the Austrian or the Hungarian officials. He regularly travelled to and from his estate on the Hungarian side and was a well-known figure. But when the 'Spaniard' – the collar of his brown coat pulled up to his ears and his head and face masked in a motoring hat with thick goggles – produced his papers, he was a Spaniard no longer. Charles was now travelling as William Codo, an official of the English Red Cross! Where that passport came from remained forever a mystery despite all the determined efforts of the British Foreign Office later on to clear it up.*

These are Charles's sensations as he set foot again on Hungarian soil. They are taken from a personal account of the 'Easter bid' which he dictated to the Empress as soon as the whole adventure was over: †

A strange feeling to be back, unrecognized, in the homeland ...

The man at the Hungarian border was an old gendarmerie sergeant from Debrecen, a real brown son of the *puszta* who hardly knew which end of a passport to look at first. Next to him a soldier in summer drill trousers. ...

Then on to Pinkafö, where we eat at the *Gasthaus* Jenner. The first warm food for two days – *schnitzel* with sour cucumbers! The landlord later preserved the cutlery and the remains of my cucumbers as souvenirs. It was interesting to

* The fullest account of the Emperor's travel arrangements was later pieced together by the Austrian police after thorough interrogation of the various sleeping-car attendants, taxi-drivers and frontier officials concerned. See Austrian State Archives, Fasz. 891, Liasse 2/11, Documents No. 1279, 1292, and 1490.

For the startled reaction of the British Foreign Office – who enquired at the British Red Cross and at all their own relevant passport offices abroad about 'Mr William Codo' – see Public Records Office C 6930/181/21.

† Published in 1925 in an edition intended for limited private circulation by Werkmann under the title *Aus Kaiser Karls Nachlass*. This, the Empress states, was the authentic account of what happened. The earlier version published by another courtier, Boroviczeny, in his *Der König und Sein Reichsverweser*, was based on material which had been deliberately shortened and diluted in order to avoid provoking an irreparable breach with Horthy. When the Regent challenged even this version, the whole truth was let out.

watch how the people jumped at foreign money. The meal we paid in French francs and the car in Swiss francs.

From Pinkafö we drove to Oberwart, where the Easter procession was just winding through the streets as we arrived. We got out and knelt down as it passed. The town's garrison was out, and dressed in our good old uniforms, the artillery with their *kartusche*. It was an uplifting moment, especially seeing the first of my old uniforms again. . . .

Next we drove to St Mihaly. . . . I asked some people there what their king looked like. I thought they might produce photographs, but no one recognized me.* Finally we all drank the king's health and they grumbled at me because I didn't drain my glass, as they did, at one go. I couldn't – the wine was too heavy. As the car had broken down, we now continued by horse and cart to our first destination, Szombathely.

We arrived at about ten o'clock at night in front of the Bishop's Palace there. The Bishop [Count Mikes] was still dining and happened to have one of the Hungarian Ministers, Dr Vass (who was himself a priest) at table with him. When Thomas [Erdödy] sent a servant up to request accommodation for the night for himself and another gentleman, the Bishop was rather put out. But – good host as he was – he came down to the great hall of his palace to greet us. He gave us both his hand and then there was a pause. Thomas asked the Bishop if he didn't recognize who his companion was. The Bishop regretted he didn't know the gentleman.

Then Thomas, in a ceremonial tone, declared that it was none other than his Apostolic Majesty the King. The Bishop started back and took me into a side room where he asked:

'Are you really he?'

I told him I was. And so the ice was broken.

The Bishop, whom Charles described as 'terribly excited and shaking all over', immediately informed his ministerial guest of this apocalyptic event which had shattered the calm of their country supper. Dr Vass, equally astounded but more under control, immediately presented himself to the King. He acknowledged his loyalty in that he declared himself a minister no longer since 'the Cabinet of the Regent ceased to exist the moment the crowned King set foot again on Hungarian soil'.

But Dr Vass was not the only member of that Government to be in or near Szombathely that evening. By a strange coincidence, the Prime Minister himself, Count Teleki, was spending the week-end shooting snipe on Count Sigray's estate of Ivancz only twenty miles away. The devoted Colonel Lehar, now Hungarian Army Commander in the Western region, had meanwhile reported to his King and had instantly offered the services of himself and his troops. It was one of Lehar's officers who was

---

* He was wrong. The girl who served him had.

now sent in the early hours to Sigray's estate to get the Hungarian Prime Minister out of bed and bring him at all costs to Szombathely.*

Count Teleki arrived at the Bishop's Palace at 4.30 A.M., not knowing in the slightest what to expect there but fearing he was about to learn of some *putsch* in Budapest, and perhaps even of the Regent's murder. When told that the great event was the arrival of King Charles, who was awaiting him upstairs, he is said to have scratched his left ear with his right hand passed behind the head – a characteristic gesture of his when troubled – and to have murmured, 'Too soon, too soon'. The Prime Minister did not, like Vass, place his office unreservedly at Charles's disposal. Indeed, with his first breath he spoke of retreat as well as attack. But however ambivalent, the advice he gave was also accurate. The King, he declared, must either go on to Budapest or go back to Switzerland. There was no other way. Hungary could only be taken from the capital.

This Charles knew well enough. The very fact that he had made first for Szombathely showed not his disregard of the capital's importance but his doubts about the Regent's attitude. Here, in western Hungary, were the only battleworthy army units upon whose loyalty, under Lehar's command, the King could absolutely count. The question now was: should he order them eastward and risk starting a civil war, or could the operation be completed without a show of military force? In the debate which followed it was Teleki's opinion which was perhaps decisive. The Prime Minister of Hungary said he was convinced that the Regent would step aside and place himself at the King's disposal the moment Charles reached his capital. Even Lehar, who had already tasted something of Horthy's ambitions and intrigues, could not envisage serious resistance on his part.

So the fateful decision was taken to proceed without even a single platoon of armed soldiers as escort, which was a blunder whatever advice Charles had been given. At first light on Easter Sunday, around 6.30 A.M., Teleki and Vass left for Budapest by car an hour ahead of the Emperor. Their task was to clear the air there by informing Horthy of Charles's imminent arrival. Charles himself, accompanied only by Count Sigray and two officers of Lehar's command, followed in a second car. Up to now, the 'Easter Bid' had gone well, too well perhaps. From this point on nothing went right. It becomes a sorry tale of muddle, treachery and disaster.

The first complication – strange as well as serious – was that Teleki never reached Budapest before his King. According to one version, his car 'took the wrong turning' and headed south instead of east. According to

* The American High Commissioner in Budapest, Mr Grant Smith, who was another week-end shooting guest at Ivancz, was allowed to sleep on, doubtless deliberately.

another account, the vehicle broke down. For Teleki's sake, the second variant is to be preferred. Not even a carload of foreign tourists could easily stray off the main road to Budapest in broad daylight, let alone a party of Hungarians. At all events, when the King's car drew up in front of his Budapest Palace at two o'clock that afternoon, nobody presented arms, nobody waved flags and nobody in fact seemed to realize that he was even in the country. A puzzled Charles sent Count Sigray ahead with one of Lehar's officers to announce his arrival to Horthy. Then the King went in alone, changed into a military uniform he had brought with him from Szombathely, and prepared himself for the interview at which he intended to take back formal power from his Regent's hands. Sigray's words on returning to fetch Charles were not exactly encouraging: 'Your Majesty will have to be very forceful.'

The King-Emperor and his Admiral now came face to face for the first time since that emotional parting in Schönbrunn in November 1918 when Horthy, the tears running down his face, had sworn never to rest until he had restored his monarch to his throne. Now, three years later, he proceeded to push Charles from the very steps of that throne. He was helped in this by all the shadowy confusion of an old order that, in Budapest, had neither survived nor collapsed but which simply hung like a mist over the city. This same confusion of divided loyalties – assuming it was genuinely present in Horthy's mind – offers the only moral explanation that can be advanced for the Regent's treatment of his sovereign. Just as neighbouring Austria was, in Renner's words, a 'Republic without Republicans', so Hungary had become a kingdom without a king. Charles had the rights and the title but Horthy had the power, even if this was exercised only in his visitor's name. It was a case where possession was nine parts of the law. The Regent's motives for making it all ten parts must be judged from the way he now behaved.

As the two men met head-on in what had been Charles's study, Horthy burst out: 'This is a disaster. Your Majesty must leave at once and must return immediately to Switzerland.' Charles replied calmly that this was out of the question as he had already burnt his bridges behind him. At that the battle of wits and wills began with a country at stake. It lasted well over two hours.*

After thanking his Regent for all he had done, Charles then formally

---

* The account which follows is Charles's own, as given in *Aus Kaiser Karls Nachlass*. It has been confirmed by the Empress, to whom the Emperor dictated it and who has also supplied a few extra details. Horthy always denied strenuously in public this account of what happened, but in private he is said to have admitted that only one particular in it was incorrect. This was the suggestion that he had failed to offer his sovereign any proper refreshment during their debate.

called on him to hand over the reins of government. Horthy's reply was so astonishing that Charles had to ask him to repeat it. But it was the same the second time: 'What does Your Majesty offer me in return?' Controlling his feelings with an effort, Charles began to bargain. In the next hour he offered Horthy successively the confirmation of his self-bestowed ducal rank; the post of Commander-in-Chief of the Army under the King; of Admiral-in-Chief of the Navy, which, apart from a few Danube vessels, no longer existed; and finally, forgetting for the moment that Horthy was a Protestant, the Order of the Golden Fleece.* After each successive bribe demanded by the Regent had been given, Charles repeated his call for the transfer of power. Every time Horthy hedged or refused outright. He advanced a variety of reasons: the certain hostility of Hungary's neighbours and of foreign invasion; the 'unreliability' of the Army; even the 'impossibility' of finding a Prime Minister to serve under the King.

When all the rewards he could think of had been claimed and all the political and diplomatic excuses exhausted, Horthy fell back on moral compunctions. Up to now, he admitted, he had 'only been thinking of himself'. But there was also his oath to Parliament on taking office as Regent. A long and bitter exchange followed over this:

Charles: 'But before that you swore an oath to me.'

Horthy: 'That is no longer valid. It's been superseded.'

Charles: 'Nothing of the kind. I have released no officer from his oath to me. And you, Horthy, are also bound to me by a second and highly personal oath – that of a court official.'

Horthy: 'All that no longer counts. . . . The only oath that is valid now is the last one I swore to Parliament.'

Charles: 'And that oath can contain nothing against the King, for Parliament has no power to change the old constitution and it has not in fact done so. . . . With my arrival here your responsibilities towards the nation are completely dissolved. It is I alone who bear the responsibility before God and the fatherland for it is I swore the coronation oath and not you!'

The King had won the point, but not the debate. Again, Charles ordered Horthy to hand over power, this time not as King talking to Regent, but as the former Supreme Commander addressing his former wartime Admiral. Again Horthy refused. The time was not ripe, he pleaded. There would be bloodshed. There was not 'one half of one per cent probability' that the King's cause would prevail.

It was a tragic but also a somewhat farcical situation. Charles was dead tired. He had not slept a wink the previous night and had had hardly any rest for two nights before that on the tense journey from Lake Geneva.

* This could only be bestowed on members of old Catholic families.

Moreover, here, in the very heart of his old kingdom, he stood alone. The ante-rooms outside were full of the Regent's men and Captain Gömbös, the most ruthless of all Horthy's supporters, had by now arrived in the castle to stiffen their hostility. Charles had no idea where Teleki and Vass had got to nor of what had happened to the two officers who had been his only escort from Szombathely. How bitterly he must have regretted now that, despite all the Prime Minister's assurances over Horthy, he had not brought along even one lorryload of Lehar's troops as reinsurance. A score of armed men at his side could have turned the tables. As it was, he could not even threaten the recalcitrant Regent himself. As Charles later ruefully confessed to the Empress, he had left his own revolver behind. There was nothing for it but to argue on, in the hope of finding some chink of fear or shame in the Admiral's armour of self-righteous ambition.

He nearly found it a few minutes later when, pressed by the Regent on the question of outside support, he named in strict confidence the French Prime Minister, M. Briand, as his secret champion. Horthy began to flounder at this, and now promised to hand over in a few weeks, as soon as he had got the situation 'right under control'. But characteristically he immediately increased the stakes in another direction. His new condition was that Charles should use Lehar's reliable troops in western Hungary to march on Republican Vienna and then they would all have their 'beloved old Austria-Hungary back again'.

This was a cunning move indeed. The plan to 'recapture Vienna' was a favourite one of Horthy's and he reasoned that, if the French Government really stood behind Charles's journey to Budapest, it would presumably support his return to Vienna as well. In any case, if the King led the armed descent on Austria, what would the Regent risk? On the other hand, if the story of French backing proved untrue, or simply conditional, he would by this proposal have got the King safely out of the capital, and preparing to march in the opposite direction.

After further fruitless argument and threatening, Charles reluctantly accepted the plan – less in earnest than simply to get out of this nightmarish situation and back to the safety of western Hungary. He tried to rescue what royal dignity he could at the finish. Pulling out his calendar, he declared: 'Today is 27 March and three weeks takes us to 17 April. Remember Horthy, if on that day you do not join me in Szombathely, I shall be here again in Budapest.'

So the King-Emperor and his Admiral parted. They were to fight once more, but never again face to face. Their parting was now courteous and Horthy even managed to wheedle one more decoration out of this sovereign of his whose very authority he had just denied. The Chapter of the

Knights of Maria Theresa in Vienna, he said, had promised him the Order of the Grand Cross. Could the Emperor perhaps confirm it? Charles obliged, his stomach turning over, and hurried out through a side door away from his Regent and his Palace to the waiting car outside. The return journey to Szombathely, plagued by breakdowns, took all that afternoon and evening and most of the night. Charles finally got back, frozen to the marrow, at half-past five on the Monday morning, after a fourth consecutive sleepless night.

From the moment he left the palace with power still not in his hands the King's 'Easter Bid' was in fact doomed. Firstly because, as Teleki had said, Hungary was Budapest or it was nothing. The former twin-capital of the Dual Monarchy completely dominated the truncated country of the Trianon Treaty. Whoever held the city held the land. Szombathely was at best a spring-board; it could not serve as a refuge. The attempt was also now doomed because, as Briand himself had warned, success had to be complete and rapid in the eyes of the world, or not at all. Horthy lost no time in exploiting both of his adversary's weaknesses.

As soon as he was alone again, the Regent called the French High Commissioner in Budapest, M. Fouchet, to the Palace and gave him a suitably amended version of what had just happened. The King, he claimed, was already on his way out of the country having failed to secure the transfer of power. Then, despite his promise to Charles not to reveal to anyone the name of the secret protector, Horthy proceeded to ask Fouchet whether it was true, as the King had claimed, that the French Prime Minister was supporting his return. The puzzled diplomat, who had not the slightest inkling of what his master in Paris might have been up to, could only offer to cable home for enlightenment and instructions.

The result was the inevitable disavowal in public, whatever attempts Briand may have made in private to hold the ring a few days longer for Charles.* Fouchet was told to disclaim all French responsibility in Budapest and, at a meeting of the Allied Conference of Ambassadors held in Paris on 1 April, the French Government formally followed suit with its *Entente* partners. All reports, the French chairman M. Jules Cambon declared, that France had encouraged the former Emperor to return were false. Indeed, the French Government 'were in entire accord with the

---

* Charles was told later that soon after his arrival on Hungarian soil, a French Cabinet meeting, with President Millerand in the chair, had been held at Rambouillet to discuss the matter. One group under the Minister of Interior, Loucheur, who knew nothing of Briand's secret role in the affair, attacked the restoration bid as a 'move inspired by Germany'. But the majority present – including Millerand, Barthou and, of course, Briand himself – favoured a policy of benevolent non-intervention in the hope that Charles would speedily establish himself.

policy of the Allies in opposing the restoration of the Habsburgs'.* The Conference of Ambassadors thereupon instructed all the *Entente* High Commissioners in Budapest to present a note to the Hungarian Government in their name repeating the terms of their previous declaration of February 1920. (In this, Hungary had been warned against the consequences to the peace of Europe of restoring a member of the Habsburg family to the throne, a question which, it was stressed, did not concern Hungary alone.)

This cut the diplomatic ground from under Charles's feet. His only hope of sustaining his secret support in Paris was somehow to achieve from the Bishop's Palace in Szombathely what he had failed to achieve in his own Palace in Budapest. Though he wrestled with the task for another week, it was a well-nigh hopeless one. Colonel Lehar's loyal military forces in the West would have been sufficient for the lightning blow which had not been, dealt. But, at an effective strength of only some 1,500 men, they were not enough for the sustained battle against Horthy's men they would now have to fight. Nor was this the only battle Charles had to take into his calculations. The leaders of the 'succession-states' (Yugoslavia, Rumania, Czechoslovakia), whose countries had grown fat at Hungary's expense, were all shouting their heads off and threatening the direst military reprisals unless Charles left his kingdom. The loudest of them in voice, Benes in Prague, was probably the least dangerous on the ground. Even the Serbs in the South seemed at first to be waving their rifles rather than loading them. Yet, if Hungary's neighbours did decide to pass from threats to action, the Hungarian Army of the King's troops and Horthy's combined would probably have been inadequate to hold them.† If this Army were split, defeat would be inevitable. These unpalatable facts were to be explained in detail to Charles soon after his return to Szombathely by an objective emissary of the General Staff, Colonel Say.‡ The Colonel's report only confirmed what he had already assumed.

There was nothing for it but to conduct the final battle with Horthy by telegram. At first there seemed to be hope left. The Prime Minister, Count Teleki, had also got straight back to Szombathely – this time, it appears, without breakdowns. On the afternoon of that same Easter Monday, he received a message from Horthy in Budapest to the effect that the Regent was prepared to hand over power 'under certain conditions', and was only keeping the machinery of government in his hands until then. Opti-

---

* See telegram from Lord Hardinge, Paris, to Lord Curzon 1 April 1921 (Public Records Office C 6803/180/21).

† Let alone to 'invade' Austria at the same time, as Horthy was proposing.

‡ See Boroviczeny, *op. cit.*, p. 128.

mistically, the King fell to discussing with Teleki arrangements for his instant return to the capital and even had a Manifesto drafted for his arrival there.

But by evening it was clear that Horthy had been only playing for time until he could safeguard his domestic front with the Army and secure his diplomatic rear with the *Entente*. An Order of Day he now issued to his troops contained the ominous passage: 'Any violent and abrupt change of government would threaten the very existence of the State. That is why I have persevered in my resolution despite the events of these past few days. . . .' More ominous still, he then thanked his army for its 'unanimous fidelity to the oath of loyalty sworn to me'.* The King of Hungary was not even mentioned, let alone acknowledged.

From now on, as notes and ultimatums from the Big and Little *Ententes* rained down on Szombathely and adviser after adviser – including the impeccably loyal Lehar as well as the more doubtful Teleki – urged the King to call the attempt off, it was really no longer a question of whether he would leave but only of when and how. Things were delayed by a severe attack of influenza and bronchitis, brought on by that icy twelve-hour journey in an open car back from Budapest, which forced Charles to take to his bed on 1 April. A final flicker of encouragement came as he lay ill in messages which arrived both from Paris and from the anxious Empress herself in Prangins. (The unsigned Paris telegram, which told Charles to 'stand firm' as Hungary's neighbours would be 'calmed down', was in fact brought to him by hand of one Fitz-Williams, a British doctor from the mission in Vienna, who had been officially summoned to Szombathely just to attend the King's illness.)

But as the days passed, the neighbours showed no signs of 'calming down'; indeed, the first serious indications of hostile mobilization against Hungary's frontiers were now reported from Serbia. As for 'standing firm', the Emperor had no ground left to stand on, unless he was prepared to conjure up both civil war and foreign invasion by lingering. In any case, by 4 April, Horthy had sealed off the entire monarchist enclave of Szombathely from the rest of Hungary, with nine control posts set up on the road to Budapest.† It was time to go. As in Eckartsau two years before, however, Charles was determined to go as a King. The outward appearances of this departure from Hungary were, if anything, even more important than those of the journey out of Austria, since Charles had

---

* Copy of text in Public Records Office C 6855/180/121.

† Horthy had also despatched two 'liaison men' to safeguard his interests in Szombathely itself. One was General Hegedüs (of whom we shall hear much more later) for the military side and the other Kanya (later a Foreign Minister) for the diplomatic side.

already decided to return for another battle *à l'outrance* with his renegade Admiral.

Charles accordingly demanded from 'his' government (which in fact meant Horthy) three conditions for his departure: the publication of a manifesto to the Hungarian nation which the defeated King had already drafted; dignified and secure transit arrangements to Switzerland and the right to resume his asylum there on the same basis as before; and finally, immunity from arrest or persecution of all those in Hungary who had supported him. All three conditions were formally accepted in a telegram from Budapest which was handed to Charles just as he was starting for the frontier. At first, the unfortunate monarch thought that this eleventh-hour message being rushed to his train was to recall him to his Palace after all. The telegram turned out to be a double disappointment. None of the conditions which it 'guaranteed' was to be met in practice.

As regards the first part of his journey into exile, however, the Hungarian people themselves gave Charles a worthy send-off. Indeed, when he appeared on the balcony of Bishop Mikes's palace to say good-bye to the crowd, he was met with a burst of frantic cheering more appropriate to a returning conqueror than to the departing vanquished. There were roars of '*Eljen!*' and '*Viszontlatasra!*' ('Long may he live!' and 'Until the next time!'); flags and handkerchiefs were waved from all corners of the square and all windows around; and all joined voice in the Hungarian anthem – Charles, in uniform at the salute, singing as well. It was the same story on the drive to Szombathely station, where a special 'court train' had been assembled, and on the journey from there to the frontier. At almost every station on the way the train was stopped to allow declarations of loyalty to be handed over and further enthusiastic supporters (including the American-born Countess Sigray) to climb aboard. However gratifying it felt and looked there was of course a good helping of purely emotional Magyar froth in this display. For when Charles, temporarily carried away, suggested that he might remain in Hungary after all and that one of his companions should travel into Switzerland in his guise (a somewhat improbable idea, admittedly), there were no volunteers.

Finally, at the little border station of Gyanafalva, the ordinary people of the *pusta* paid a tribute in the language they spoke best of all. As Charles was inspecting the local *gendarmerie* school, all the gypsy musicians of the village came out and played to the King and to the crowd.

At Fehring, on the Austrian side, the officers of the three *Entente* powers who were guaranteeing the Emperor's transit into Switzerland were waiting to take over in a special train: the French Colonel Hinaux, the Italian Colonel Count Stoppo, and the British artillery Colonel C. W.

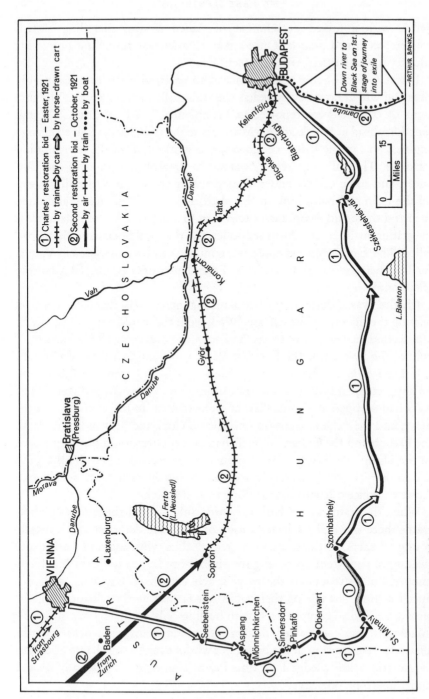

The two restoration bids

Selby, with a mixed detachment of Allied troops, including British soldiers, as armed guards. Once again, Charles was travelling out of his country under British Army protection.

It was Colonel Selby and his men who dealt with the one really ugly situation which now developed as the train rolled across Styria. The first signs of trouble were reported at Frohnleiten, north of Graz. The rail junction ahead at Bruck-an-der-Mur, where the train had to halt to change engines, was in the hands of 2,000–3,000 workers from the surrounding factories. They all, apparently, wanted to present a petition to the Emperor, and some of the wilder elements were threatening to pull Charles off the train and hang him on the platform unless he formally abdicated then and there and swore never to return to Austria. All attempts to clear the station made by the Austrian police and the local Socialist officials had failed. The *Entente* officers could not contact their own missions in Vienna for help because the tiny station at Frohnleiten only possessed a railway telephone.

Charles was delighted at this alarming news. His first comment on hearing the threats to himself was 'Well, well: this could get really lively.' * His second reaction was to try and turn the situation to his benefit. If neither the police nor the Socialist Party could control these firebrands, and if the *Entente* officers were unable to get fresh instructions, why not, he suggested, simply turn the train round and return to Hungary? The train had stopped at Frohnleiten at eight o'clock in the evening and the delay, and the debate, went on until two o'clock the next morning. Both the French and the Italian colonels had agreed after midnight to go back to the Hungarian border. But Colonel Selby was adamant. With a gruff 'I'll knock 'em out', he finally went on ahead himself with one or two Austrian police officials, to sort things out at Bruck.

When the train, with Charles aboard, duly arrived there shortly afterwards there was still a selected group of some 250 demonstrators, mostly young workers, in the station. A great deal of whistling and jeering and shaking of fists went on during the short stop. But as the British soldiers jumped out, surrounded the royal coach with fixed bayonets, and produced a loud rattling of their rifles' magazines as they loaded up, the crowd decided to content itself with hurling only epithets. One of these – 'Mass-murderer' – showed the primitive and demagogic nature of the affair. As a description of the passenger whom even the moderate Socialists of Austria acknowledged as 'the Peace Emperor', it was almost too ludicrous to be offensive.

After twelve tense minutes, the train moved on. The rest of the journey

* Boroviczeny, *op. cit.*, p. 138.

was uneventful. At 4.20 that afternoon they reached Feldkirch, the western border station of Austria. Colonel Selby and his two colleagues saluted and departed, and, half an hour later, after the brief run through Liechtenstein, Charles was on Swiss soil again.*

The first restoration bid was over. But plans for the second had already been laid. As Charles subsequently told the Empress, who was waiting to greet him at the frontier, he had left his uniform behind in Colonel Lehar's keeping. The collar with its rank badges had been removed. When Lehar received from Switzerland the code message, 'Stitch the collar on', it would mean that the King was coming again.

* For the official Austrian police report on the journey, see Austrian Archives, Fasz. 891, Liasse 2/11, No. 1630 dated 18 April 1921.

Chapter 16

HUNGARY: THE LAST THROW

⟲⟆⟲

'Nothing succeeds like success.' The reverse is also true, as Charles soon learnt on re-entering Switzerland after the resounding failure of his first restoration bid. The Swiss authorities, though as courteous as ever, were now a good deal more formal, and the severe conditions they demanded for accepting him a second time bore no resemblance to that easy-going tolerance shown when he had first arrived from Austria the year before. If they still had to have the ex-Imperial eagle in their midst, the Swiss were determined henceforth both to clip his wings and to bind him securely to a perch of their own choosing.

The struggle over these terms of residence, which was to last for several weeks, began before the Emperor's special train reached the border station at Buchs; and it began, for Charles, under the worst possible circumstances. He now discovered that Horthy had betrayed him not only in Budapest, but in Berne as well. One of the conditions Charles had laid down for agreeing to leave Hungary was that he would be re-admitted to Switzerland and treated there 'in the same way as before'. Just before his departure, Charles had been passed assurances from Budapest that this had all been arranged 'with the exception of certain difficulties about His Majesty's continued residence in the Canton Vaud, which would, however, be disposed of before his arrival'.*

While the train was still *en route*, however, the Swiss Press printed a list of conditions for a new asylum which, it was claimed, the Emperor had already accepted. Three of the five points restricted his movements in the country: not only the Canton Vaud but all frontier areas and also the towns of Zurich, Basel and Berne were now to be closed to him. A fourth condition stipulated in categoric fashion that both he and his suite must in future 'refrain from all political activity'. This was a considerable stiffening of the vague formula adopted in 1919, when the Swiss authorities had only expressed 'desires'. But it was the fifth demand which was the most

* Account given by the Empress.

serious. This laid down that Charles was to inform the Swiss Parliament forty-eight hours in advance of any intention to leave Switzerland. * There was no question of any sharp practice by the Swiss Government in all this. Whatever trickery had gone on had been Hungarian. All five points had been telegraphed to Budapest to be transmitted to the King before his departure and the mere fact that he had set out for Switzerland seemed to the authorities in Berne to signify his acceptance. They were not to know that Charles had never heard of the conditions, let alone accepted them, before starting his return journey. It was, in fact, the Empress who first broke the bad news as she greeted him at Buchs, which she had reached just in time after an all-night car drive from Prangins.†

There was nothing for it, as he was already on Swiss soil, but to accept these conditions for the time being, especially as Lieutenant-Colonel Kissling, the representative of the Swiss Government, was emphatic that this second asylum was strictly limited in duration and that the Emperor would anyway have to cast around for a new country of domicile. As though to rub this in, there were difficulties as to where that same night, let alone the following weeks, should be spent. The Swiss now forbade even a transit stop at the near-by Bourbon-Parma castle of Wartegg, which had sheltered the Imperial refugees the year before. Charles and Zita finally ended up, just before midnight and almost too tired to care, at the Hôtel National in Lucerne. This was too public as a long-term solution – too public and too costly, for money was already becoming a problem. So, once the Canton agreed to accept them, they moved in early May to the small château of Hertenstein near-by. It was a roomy building with a large private park, not unlike Prangins but at roughly half the rent. Another vigil on another Swiss lake had begun.

The first few weeks there were taken up with the battle over asylum. Barely had Charles concluded a one year's lease at Hertenstein (on the rumour that he would be allowed to stay that long after all) than another Swiss spokesman, Colonel Pfyffer, turned up with the demand that he must leave the country in six, eight or, at the most, ten weeks. The reason given was that his prolonged presence would only exacerbate the religious conflict between the Swiss Catholics and Protestants. True or not, it was a telling argument to a man of Charles's stamp, and he promised to leave Switzerland of his own accord within three months.

* See Austrian Archives. Liasse Ungarn 2/11 Telegram No. 1420 of 7 April 1921.

† The Empress had simply not been able to believe the Swiss newspaper reports of that afternoon stating the Emperor was already on his way back from Hungary and giving the allegedly agreed new conditions of asylum. But when, at one in the morning, Werkmann rang up from Paris to confirm the story, she got up immediately and drove right across the country to meet her husband.

Then, on 5 May, in response to an official enquiry, the Emperor wrote out in his own hand in French and signed at Hertenstein a declaration absolving anything or anyone Swiss from having played any part whatsoever in the Easter adventure. 'In the matter of my departure,' he declared, 'no Swiss citizen was involved; no Swiss citizen ever knew of it; no Swiss official was bribed and none committed any incorrect or illegal action on my behalf; and no Swiss passport was used.'* This categoric assurance that the political virginity of their own people had not been tampered with seems to have calmed down feelings in Berne considerably. A fortnight later, on 18 May 1921, yet another Swiss envoy, Minister Dinichert, arrived at Hertenstein to inform Charles of 'the desires' of the Federal Government in the matter of his continued residence. There was no longer any talk of a short time-limit and the conditions put forward were no worse – if no better – than those which the Emperor had first learned of at the frontier the month before.

Nothing was ever signed or even put on paper at these, the final talks. Indeed, there had been a marked reluctance throughout on the Swiss side to commit themselves to any formal agreement. A purely verbal device that Charles now resorted to in order to safeguard his future liberty of action becomes of crucial importance therefore in judging later allegations that he had 'broken faith'. Before Dinichert entered the room, Charles hid Boroviczeny in a large cupboard in the study and posted Baron Werkmann at the door outside in order to be witnesses when he said: 'I interpret the Swiss Government's wish in the sense that I am to inform Parliament forty-eight hours before I leave for another place of exile.' And, at the end of the conversation, the Emperor carefully repeated the phrase 'place of exile' again because, in German, the words for 'exile' and 'asylum' could easily be confused. Either the Swiss envoy did not grasp the meaning of this nuance, or he chose to ignore it. The words were as clear as they were deliberate. Hungary, of which Charles was still King, was not another 'place of exile' but his own forbidden homeland. He had been as blunt with the Swiss as any major political refugee could afford to be, and more than most had ever dared to be.

Though a pleasant roof was over his head for the time being, Charles none the less started to cast around for another European asylum, just in case the Swiss grew impatient again. But the heavy Habsburg crown, even without its sceptre, proved a very difficult object to deposit in the spring of 1921. As the Empress recalls:

'Norway and Denmark could not be considered, as the general feeling in both countries at the time was too hostile. For little Luxemburg we

* Habsburg Family Papers.

would have been too big a weight. Italy was impossible and Portugal too remote from the Emperor's lands to be practicable. Actually the Emperor would have preferred to stay in a Republic where he would have felt less constricted than in a country where he stood as monarch to monarch, with all the personal obligations that implied.

'But as the summer came and went, neither Republics nor Monarchies presented themselves as alternatives. From England* and Sweden we received firm refusals; from Holland an evasive reply and from Spain only a long silence. Finally we got an extension of our time in Switzerland, not at our own request, but at that of the Spanish and Hungarian Governments.'

As at Eckartsau and Prangins, so now from Hertenstein, Charles did what he could both to help the sufferings of the peoples he had once ruled and to demonstrate that he was still entitled to speak on their behalf. On 28 July 1921, for example, he sent personal letters both to King George of England and to President Millerand of France, pleading with them to use their influence in the matter of financial aid to a near-bankrupt Austrian Republic. The letter to King George v ended:

C'est le moment où, me souvenant des inoubliables preuves de magnanimité que Votre Majesté m'a données jadis, je viens joindre ma voix à celle de mon peuple si éprouvé, en priant Votre Majesté de bien vouloir intervenir, de Son Auguste Personne, dans la question des crédits susmentionnés.

Sachant comme quoi la vaillante et noble nation anglaise et son sage gouvernement ont, de tout temps et en toute chose, obéi aux sentiments d'humanité vrai et sincère, je me flatte que ce n'est pas en vain que je viens faire appel au cœur généreux de Votre Majesté, persuadé qu'elle pourra sans peine se rendre compte de la consolation que j'éprouverais, au milieu de mes peines, à voir l'Autriche secourue d'une manière prompte et efficace.

Et je n'ai guère besoin de mentionner à Votre Majesté la sincère et immuable gratitude que s'assureraient dans mon cœur, les bienfaiteurs de mon peuple infortuné.

Charles.†

Like those byzantine negotiations with the Swiss authorities, these activities, however necessary, were but shadow-boxing. The one vital task for Charles was to get back again to Hungary to carry out the implied promise in those parting words '*Viszontlatasra*' ('Until the next time'). As we have seen, this was at the back of his mind even when he was negotiating with Swiss spokesmen over his renewed asylum. By midsummer, with that problem temporarily resolved, he could apply himself in earnest to a second restoration bid. This time, he knew, it would be all or nothing.

* For Britain's refusal see Public Records Office C 12569/180/21, 17 June 1921.
† From Habsburg Family Papers. The original of this particular letter has not been traced in the Windsor Castle archives.

Two preliminary questions had to be tackled first. They were the same ones he had faced at Easter but they both confronted him now in a sharpened form. The first was whether his secret French sponsors, above all Briand, would still stand by him on the same strictly unofficial terms. The omens here looked good. Not unnaturally, the French leader wanted some clarification as to how the delicate secret of his own support for the enterprise had got out in Budapest, thus forcing him into the public denial. But he expressed entire satisfaction with the reply Charles sent back to Paris at the end of April, explaining that it was Horthy who had broken the confidence. By May, the Emperor's clandestine links with his French sponsors were as firmly tied as ever.

In some ways they became even stronger, for attempts were now made from the French side to formalize them as far as the highly unorthodox situation permitted. On 20 May a messenger from the former French President M. Deschanel arrived in Hertenstein to say that the French Government were thinking of recalling their High Commissioner in Budapest, M. Fouchet, because of his passive attitude towards Charles. What would the Emperor think of M. Doulcet, then French Minister at the Vatican, as his replacement?* The messenger brought another request that sounded even more promising. Would the Emperor nominate a personal representative of his, if possible with political or diplomatic experience, to be permanently available in Paris as his main channel of communication with the Briand group? This was exhilarating talk indeed for the exiled monarch and Charles set about finding the right man for this secret mission with more excitement than he had ever felt when selecting any of his formal ambassadors to the great powers in the past. Half a dozen names were canvassed. At least two of the candidates approached made polite excuses. Another was turned down by the French. Finally the choice fell on the Hungarian diplomat von Charmant, who was both willing and acceptable all round. Barely had this 'appointment' been made than another encouraging piece of news arrived from Paris. M. Berthelot, the very influential Political Director of the French Foreign Office, and an implacable enemy of the Habsburgs, had been removed from his post. The political path to Budapest seemed to be getting smoother every day.

But how was it to be travelled physically? This was the second major problem to be solved, and everything hinged on finding the right answer. Another journey by rail or road would be courting disaster, whatever disguises were used and false documents procured. The Austrian authorities, as well as Horthy's police, were watching every border crossing like hawks and any overland approach to avoid Austrian territory entirely

* For these conversations see Boroviczeny, *op. cit.*, pp. 203–7.

would have been too circuitous and uncertain. For a while, the Emperor's tiny court at Hertenstein eyed the Danube itself as a possibility. It was in some ways a tempting thought, to sail back downstream into the Dual Monarchy, borne on the fast current of the river that had always linked its twin capitals. Yet though the risk of detection would have been much smaller than by land, there remained some serious snags. The Emperor would have had to board the Danube upstream from Linz on Bavarian soil and then, assuming Vienna could be passed safely by night, his craft would still have to run the gauntlet of the Czechs, who now guarded a long stretch of the river's northern bank.

There was nothing for it, in fact, but to fly into Hungary by private aeroplane – a decision which was by no means as commonplace in 1921 as it is today. This method too had its own drawbacks, above all the danger of a forced landing. But the triple advantage it offered of maximum speed, maximum security and maximum surprise was overwhelming. It was Boroviczeny who put the suggestion forward and Charles instantly agreed, though he had never yet sat in an aeroplane in his life, let alone for a flight on which his kingdom depended. On his next visit to Hungary early in August, Boroviczeny* told Colonel Lehar of the plan and arranged for two completely loyal Hungarian pilots to stand by and await his signal to come to Switzerland for the operation. The second man chosen was Captain Fekete, an airman who possessed a brilliant flying record in the war and considerable technical knowledge as well. The crew were to need all their talents.

Back in Switzerland at the end of the month, the energetic young Boroviczeny – who was far better suited for these tasks than for his would-be role as the Emperor's political mentor – soon found the right aeroplane for his Hungarian pilots to fly. It was an almost new and completely enclosed Junkers *Monoplan* with a single 180 horse-power engine and room behind for six people. And it was conveniently sitting in a hangar at Dübendorf airfield near Zurich waiting to be bought or hired from its owners. The 'Ad Astra' Company now found their customer, though they had no inkling of his true identity.

There now remained only the time and the exact place of landing to be fixed. As to the time, the Empress states that they would all have preferred, if possible, to have waited for the spring of 1922. Another winter of

---

* Though he was well-known to the Regent as a 'King's man' and a member of the court in exile, Boroviczeny, who was still technically a Hungarian official, was allowed to enter Hungary and move around the country more or less as he chose – another example of that political no-man's-land of which Budapest was now the capital.

certain hardship – which Charles, even as King back in his own capital, could have done little to alleviate – would then have passed, and there would have been new hope as well as new warmth in the air of Budapest. But it became steadily clearer, while all the technical preparations were still being made, that they simply dared not wait that long. The blow had to be struck before Horthy had paralysed or neutralized the entire Legitimist camp inside Hungary itself and, with every week that passed, the Regent was drawing his net around them tighter.

True, he still preserved an outwardly correct front towards the sovereign he had driven into a second exile. Throughout August, Charles's principal political spokesmen in Budapest – men like Dr Gratz, the Foreign Minister, Dr Rakovsky, the President of the National Assembly, and Count Julius Andrassy – had been pressing the Regent both to stop his persecution of the Legitimist cause in Hungary and to reaffirm his own loyalty to the King outside Hungary. Count Bethlen, who had succeeded Teleki as Prime Minister after the Easter bid,* backed their demands. The result was a letter from Horthy which was delivered to Charles at Hertenstein on 4 September 1921. In this† the Regent maintained that the foreign policy situation had worsened for Hungary since what he euphemistically described as 'Your Majesty's Easter visit' and that, if only on these grounds, a restoration 'seemed at the moment impossible'. Horthy continued: 'Yet I want to take this opportunity of assuring Your Majesty that nothing is further from my thoughts than clinging on to the post which I now hold; indeed I yearn impatiently for the moment when I can step down from this seat of tribulation.' Even this sugary speech lacked the firm assurance that the throne was Charles's and his alone and that Horthy would, when called upon, step down and hand it over to him.‡

But what mattered far more than the words the Regent did not put on paper were those things he continued to do in practice. The systematic purge of suspected Legitimist officers went on unchecked throughout the Hungarian Army, for example, on the pretext of the overall reductions called for in the Trianon Peace Treaty. A similar process was applied, without even a pretext, to the civilian ministries. At the same time, while

* Teleki had not been able to stomach Horthy's Order of the Day to the Army of 30 March 1919, which the Regent had promised his Prime Minister he would not make public.

† For full text, see Werkmann, *op. cit.*, pp. 250–53.

‡ Horthy even had the aplomb to couple this letter (which was delivered personally by Dr Gratz) with a 'reminder' to his Emperor of that promise during the 'Easter visit' to bestow on his Regent the Grand Cross of the Maria Theresa Order, instead of the mere Knight's Cross which the Chapter in Vienna were proposing. Would His Majesty now take the necessary steps? Gratz simply could not bring himself to present the request and handed the task to Boroviczeny.

suppressing all pro-Charles manifestations in Hungary, Horthy went on giving full rein to the anti-Habsburg propaganda campaign which was conducted by the Government Press Chief Eckhard in person.

As for the 'seat of tribulation', the Regent was clearly finding this progressively more comfortable. He had taken up residence that summer in the Imperial palace of Gödöllö outside the capital and had resumed those famous shoots for which the Emperor, whenever he had resided there himself, had found neither the time nor the inclination. This combination of unctuous if evasive politeness towards the exile at Hertenstein and ruthless suppression of his cause at home told its own story. Like many a political adventurer before and after him, Horthy had by now so identified ambition with patriotism, egoism with idealism and even luxury with sacrifice that he probably no longer knew them apart.

Horthy's general attitude, therefore, combined with the growing influence of extremists like Captain Gömbös in his entourage, seemed to call for the King's earliest possible return. But it was a specific military action of the Regent's that now fixed the exact date. During the summer, Colonel Lehar's small but determined loyalist 'army' in western Hungary had been strengthened by the transfer to that area of a *gendarmerie* battalion commanded by another of Charles's supporters, Major Ostenburg. The battalion has been sent there for urgent foreign-policy reasons, to increase Hungary's military 'presence' on the western border while the tussle with the Austrian Republic over the Sopron enclave was being fought out by the diplomats. In September a settlement over the border dispute had been reached and was duly signed between the Austrian and Hungarian Governments in the so-called Venice Protocol of 13 October 1921.

Horthy promptly acted to reduce not only the military show of strength against Vienna but also the political threat to himself in Budapest. He ordered the Ostenburg battalion to be brought back to the capital, disbanded, and its personnel distributed among units of the National Army. The date provisionally fixed for the transfer to Budapest was 23 October 1921. The Empress recalls that, on learning this, Charles decided he could wait no longer, especially as the news was accompanied by an urgent appeal for action from the loyalist officers inside Hungary. So he made Horthy's date his own.

The two Hungarian pilots, to whom a Bavarian colleague had been added, were now brought to Zurich to try out the Junkers plane. It performed to their complete satisfaction on a test flight around the airfield on 18 October. At that, the private charter deal was concluded. It was to fly a 'Mr and Mrs Kowno' to Geneva on 20 October. Apart from the charter fee, an extra 50,000 Swiss francs was deposited in Berlin for the benefit of the 'Ad Astra' Company. This, it was reckoned, would compensate them for the trouble they would have to face when it became known that their machine had in reality been used to fly the Emperor and Empress of Austro-Hungary back to their homeland.

The final 'invasion' plan was quickly superimposed on an outline already formed in months of secret contacts – some very roundabout, others more direct – between Hertenstein and Charles's followers in Szombathely and Budapest. It envisaged the King landing before nightfall in western Hungary in a specially marked field on the estate of Count Sigray at Denesfa. He would then proceed to Sopron and board, in secret, the Government train already assembled there to take the Ostenburg battalion back to Budapest. Other loyalist forces of Colonel Lehar's would be on board as well. On arrival at the capital, the King would reveal his identity to his soldiers, draw his sword and lead the 'disbanded' troops straight into action to seize the Royal Palace. Charles's supporters in Budapest itself would have meanwhile prepared his path by arresting Horthy's key men there overnight and by securing the support of the local garrison commanders. It was a neat-looking plan; yet its success depended on two formidable pre-conditions. The first was perfect co-ordination of timing. The second was that everyone would stand by the promises he had made.* There were to be woeful shortcomings on both counts.

But first the flight, which now became more and more of an adventure in itself. The Empress had resolved to accompany her husband despite the fact that, like Charles, she had never sat in an aeroplane before, and was at that time expecting another child. When Boroviczeny attempted to dissuade her, he was met with the calm and emphatic reply: 'Do not try to change my mind. I am quite determined to fly as well. Nothing will happen to our children here in Switzerland, they are in safe hands. But the Emperor faces danger and thus my duty as a wife becomes greater than my duty as a mother. . . . So do not even attempt to describe those dangers – that would only strengthen me in my decision. . . . I am the Queen of Hungary and if the King goes back there, my place is at his side.' †

As it happened, the fact that the Empress was also making the journey helped the elaborate camouflage which was now arranged to cloak their

---

* Denials by some leading 'Carlists' after the failure of the attempt that they had encouraged the restoration bid (or denials on their behalf) were largely made to protect the ringleaders from persecution. The Empress states that all the principal Legitimist leaders had invited and encouraged the October bid, with the exception of Andrassy, who could not be consulted in time.

† Boroviczeny, *op. cit.*, p. 260: a version confirmed in general by the Empress, though she does not recall her actual words.

departure. It was spread abroad that the royal couple intended to celebrate their wedding anniversary, 21 October, in seclusion with their relatives; and at 9.30 on the morning of 20 October they were duly seen leaving Hertenstein in their usual car and taking the road to the Parma castle at Wartegg. But punctually at eleven o'clock they were met at a cross-roads *en route* by Boroviczeny. He was driving a new Daimler automobile, which nobody would connect with the Emperor, and which had been bought specially for the occasion. The royal passengers rapidly changed cars and, just before midday, they arrived as 'Mr and Mrs Kowno' at Dübendorf airfield. The mist of early morning had lifted and it was now a sunny and almost windstill autumn day, perfect for the occasion. Charles and Zita climbed into the waiting monoplane with only one tiny suitcase between them. (All the luggage had been sent ahead by car to Hungary both to save weight on the aircraft and to avoid suspicion.) A few minutes later, just before 12.15 P.M., they were airborne for the first time in their lives.

The Empress retained vivid memories of that flight: 'We had with us no passport or identification papers of any sort – real or assumed. The plane itself also carried no documents so that any landing *en route* in Switzerland, Germany or Austria would have been disastrous. And in fact there was one very anxious moment when the single engine suddenly cut out while we were over Bavarian soil and the machine lost a great deal of height. But the pilots managed to start it up again, and that was the only time our hired machine was to worry us.

'The Emperor and I were seated right at the back of the plane, behind the wings, and both of us felt somewhat giddy. But neither that, nor the seriousness of the occasion, could take away the novelty of a first flight in such beautiful weather. After clearing the Bavarian Alps, we flew over the Austrian border north of Salzburg and saw the spires of the town and its great fortress clearly. Then, following the Danube eastwards, we could pick out Persenbeug Castle – where of course the Emperor was born – and the Oetscher mountain, which he had so often climbed. We even caught a glimpse of Baden, the wartime Supreme Headquarters, though our castle at Laxenburg was out of sight and so was Schönbrunn and Vienna itself. I remember the Emperor saying thankfully once we left the Swiss mountain scenery behind us and were safely coming down over the plains of our homeland: "I would never have thought that a great flat stretch of stubble fields could be so beautiful."'

It was on one of these stubble fields that they had landed soon after 4 P.M. The pilots knew that, by now, they were on Hungarian soil and must be close to their destination, yet in the fading autumn light they had been unable to pinpoint the castle of Denesfa from the air. Peasants promptly emerged out of nowhere – as they always have a habit of doing in the apparently most deserted parts of the *puszta* – to gape at this astonishing visitation from the heavens. There had been nothing much wrong with the pilot's navigation. Denesfa, the peasants said, was two hours away 'by walking horse'. By flying bird it was considerably quicker. The Junkers took off again (just escaping, as it turned out, a band of pro-Horthy irregular troops who happened to be roaming the adjoining woods). Five minutes later, at nearly half past four, it came down with its royal passengers on the dairy farm of the Csiraky estate. Dusk was already gathering. They had completed the journey from Zurich just in time.

There was one jarring note amid all the relief and joy of safe arrival. The four recognition flares that should have been burning, one at each corner of the big field, were nowhere to be seen. Charles had an uneasy premonition of muddle there and then, as a peasant lad was despatched from the farm on horseback to fetch Count Csiraky from the castle. It was soon to be confirmed. Something had gone sadly wrong with the timing of the enterprise. At least one of their principal political supporters had no idea at all they were arriving. Even Colonel Lehar, whose little army was vital to the whole operation, seemed to be expecting them for the following day.

The Legitimist politician who had been left in the dark was Count Julius Andrassy, Charles's Foreign Minister in the last days of the Empire. But just as peasants had a habit of popping out of the emptiest woods in the *puszta* so, in the Hungary of those days, Counts had a habit of collecting at the remotest castles. It so happened that Andrassy was himself spending that week-end at Denesfa, to attend the baptism of the youngest child of the house, who was in fact his grandson. In her diary of these events, his wife records that Count Andrassy 'turned pale . . . and looked as though he were about to fall' when Boroviczeny arrived at the castle to say that the King of Hungary had literally descended from the heavens in the midst of these family celebrations. Countess Andrassy continues:

> He argued that he did not wish to be made responsible for an act which he had not advised and of which he had known nothing. This he felt he must tell the King as soon as possible. As a matter of course he would at the same time assure the King that, now this all-important step had been taken, he would place himself entirely at his disposal.*

There was indeed one very awkward political complication. Only three days before, Andrassy had at last reached an agreement with the Prime Minister Count Bethlen to form a single government party in Parliament

* Countess Andrassy's Diary, *From Sopron to Tihany* (Habsburg Family Papers).

for the forthcoming spring elections which would be Legitimist in character. And the very next day Bethlen was due to make the party's inaugural
speech at Pecs in which he would plead for time to settle the dynastic
question and would reject meanwhile both extremes of monarchist *coups
d'état* and calls for dethronement.* Now, on the eve of the speech, the
King was suddenly in their midst and he, Andrassy, as a well-known
Carlist leader, would look like a fool or a double-dealer. Even worse,
Bethlen, who was a more doubtful supporter, might be totally estranged.

For greater security, Charles had avoided the crowded castle and had
gone to meet Andrassy at a cross-roads near a keeper's cottage deep in the
woods of the estate. There was concern at Andrassy's story and at the fact
that he had somehow been excluded from the secret. But the King was far
more worried by the report he got from his other loyal supporter who had
been hiding in the cottage all day. This was Colonel Lehar, who knew
everything about the operation except the exact date of the King's arrival
and, in his uncertainty, had allowed the 'official' troop transport arrangements for Budapest to be called off for that night. This was a blow indeed,
for those soldiers were the core of the whole enterprise. How had this
ominous confusion arisen? It seems to have been again that blend of one
part confusion and two parts disastrous coincidence which dogged all
Charles's secret operations, in war or peace.

As the Empress explains it:

'The first mistake arose in the flurry of communications which passed
between Hertenstein and our principal supporters in Hungary in the last
days before our flight. All of these exchanges were purely verbal, which
made for greater security but also, of course, increased the possibility of
the misunderstanding which actually arose. The key message about the
timing as it was actually sent out of Hungary in mid-October said: "Not
before the 21st". But in the version which we got in Switzerland it ran:
"Not later than the 20th".

'In some of the messages we sent back, a margin of two or three days
may have been mentioned in case, for example, bad weather prevented our
flight at the last moment. But I remember there was one which the
Emperor sent just before leaving and which did give the exact date. It used
the code agreed in Hungary at Easter when the Emperor had left his
uniform behind with Lehar, the collar and its rank badges detached. The
telegram, which was sent to one of Lehar's officers, also by previous

* The operative passage from Bethlen's speech read: 'We wish to solve the dynastic
question with patience and honourable goodwill. Any other method can only lead to
civil war. In the ranks of our unified Government party therefore we will accept
neither those who think they can restore the King by force nor those who are only
concerned with taking his crown from him.'

arrangement, read: "Collar will be stitched on on 20 October". This was the clearest possible warning, sent by a method agreed long in advance. But it was never delivered. The officer told us the reason later. The authorities in western Hungary were having enormous problems with smuggling and black-market deals across the frontier at that time and many of these operations were signalled by coded messages. They couldn't stamp out the activity altogether, as some officers of the *Entente* commission were involved, but, in order to disrupt it, the regional Post Offices had orders every now and then simply to destroy all private telegrams coming from abroad. One of the days they picked was the day our coded message arrived.'

The practical effect of all this uncertainty was that most of the open railway trucks which had been carefully collected at Sopron railway station for the journey to Budapest were stolen during the night by the local peasants who were anxious to get their sugar-beet harvest loaded. (The very questionable decision had been taken, once it was thought the train would not be needed that day, to leave it unguarded 'in order not to arouse suspicion'.) The whole operation now had to be delayed for twenty-four hours while Colonel Lehar's men scoured the surrounding countryside for the missing trucks, emptied out the sugar-beet, and brought them back to Sopron to be filled with their intended cargo of Ostenburg soldiers. Though everything was done to keep Budapest guessing, and though a telegram and telegraphic censorship was imposed by Lehar's men over Sopron itself, it was clear that the advantage of total and sudden surprise was lost beyond recall.

For a long time after this initial set-back, however, it looked as though the battle itself was won. This second descent of the Emperor's on Budapest was far from the pre-doomed escapade it has so often been called. Like Waterloo, it was a 'close-run thing'; though, unlike Napoleon, Charles was to be beaten by trickery rather than by cannon-fire.

After a short rest on an estate near Denesfa, the royal couple were taken by car at three in the morning to Sopron and driven straight to the barracks of the Ostenburg Battalion, which became their headquarters for the day. Rakovsky and Dr Gratz (who, unlike Andrassy, were expecting the King's arrival in Hungary) were soon there to greet him and the former was promptly designated Prime Minister of the King's new 'Cabinet'. The barracks made a very rough-and-ready 'palace'. As Countess Andrassy relates, after her arrival there: 'The Queen was occupying a soldier's room. The furniture consisted of a soldier's bed and two wooden chairs. In a corner of the room lay some shovels, brooms and several pairs of military boots. From pegs on the wall hung some soldiers' trousers turned inside out. . . . Gyula [her husband Julius Andrassy] with Rakovsky and Gratz was in the room next to that occupied by their Majesties, and it was here that we passed the greater part of the afternoon. As there were no chairs, we sat on boxes which, however, were continually being taken from us by the soldiers who were busy packing up their kit.

'During the afternoon some thirty girls, dressed in white Hungarian costumes, came to offer the Queen flowers. . . . The swearing-in of the Ostenburg troops was a striking and touching ceremony . . . about 1,500 men – infantry, artillery and cavalry – marched past looking their smartest and saluted their Majesties. . . . Then the Queen, standing amid the white-clad Hungarian girls, listened with rapt attention to the oath of the troops as it was thundered out by thousands of voices: "Through water and fire, on sea, on the land and in the air for God, King and Country". . . .'*

Throughout the 21st, as Charles received deputations, reviewed troops, and discussed the military plan, the assembling of the railway 'armada' continued. It grew into a formidable array of rolling stock. First came a train full of officers; next the King's train, with a company of Lehar's men as guard; and behind that, two more separate trains, each crammed with soldiers. By eleven in the evening, all was pronounced ready. Charles and Zita drove out from the barracks through lines of cheering people to the station, where another massed crowd awaited them. It might have been a ceremonial drive in deepest peacetime. All that Colonel Lehar had been able to find for the royal couple was a Red Cross carriage with two cramped sleeping compartments made up with soldiers' blankets. The 'dining-car' had only a plain wooden table with stools and railway cushions for seats. To Charles and his wife it must have seemed more welcoming than their comfortable Court train in its prime. For this one was taking them home. The 21 October 1921 was, in fact, the tenth anniversary of their wedding.

The journey to Budapest was one long triumph. The King, it seemed, was simply scooping up his kingdom again from the lines of the railway track. At Györ, which they reached at lunchtime, a guard of honour from the local garrison was waiting, drawn up on the platform, and the royal train halted to the sight and sound of dipped standards, trumpet salutes, cheers and the old heart-warming cries of '*Eljen a Kiraly!*' The only bombardment the train received was of autumn flowers. True, the commander of the garrison, General Lorinczy, had played the situation both ways. Before turning out to greet the King with his troops, he had reported the fact of Charles's arrival to Budapest. This was the first news from Hungarian sources Horthy got that the second restoration bid was

* Countess Andrassy's Diary, *op. cit.*, pp. 10–11.

under way.* By a hair's breadth, it was to give the Regent just enough time to save the situation.

From Győr, with the secret out, the race was on. It still seemed to be going Charles's way. The Regent despatched instructions all along the route to hold up the train and tear up the tracks. Mostly, the orders were ignored and, where the line was torn up, it was quickly re-laid by pioneer units travelling with Lehar's forces. To every garrison commander between Győr and Budapest Horthy sent orders to fire on this railway cavalcade. In fact, hardly a shot was fired. At Komarom, the local battalion went out to block the line but promptly joined the King's men as soon as it was clear that these were in earnest. The entire garrison then turned out for the King's entry into the city at 8 P.M., and, as at Győr, formally swore its oath of loyalty. The same scene was repeated at Tata and again by the garrisons at Totis and Bicske.

Charles, the Empress remembers, was still very worried by the fact that his biggest weapon against Horthy – surprise – had nonetheless been lost. Nor was there any sign that that particular leopard had changed his spots. On hearing from the Győr garrison commander of the King's arrival there, the Regent had promptly resumed his Easter game of prevarication. He despatched one of his ministers, Dr Vass, to Komarom with an escort officer to conduct negotiations in the station there. Charles agreed to the negotiations but insisted they should be on the moving train. The envoys were hauled reluctantly aboard, with their car following along the parallel main road. Vass, who at Easter had declared unreservedly for the King, this time brought no message of personal loyalty. It was soon clear that his task was merely to gain time for Horthy, and information. Bethlen's Government, he said, were in permanent session in Budapest to decide what to do. They were 'naturally' loyal to the King and would 'probably' hand over power, were it not for their fear that the King's arrival in the capital would give the signal for a general invasion by Hungary's neighbours. Vass then tried, in vain, to discover what 'guarantees from any foreign powers' His Majesty had brought with him on this occasion.†

None of this was reassuring. Yet when Charles awoke at six the next morning it seemed to him and his Queen that the situation was resolving itself above the Regent's head. They had just stopped at the tiny station of Bia-Torbagy. The station master declared the next stretch of line to Kelenföld to be free. Kelenföld was the suburban station of Budapest

---

* Charles learned later that the first report of his arrival had actually reached Budapest the previous evening, via the *Entente* liaison officers in western Hungary. (See p. 292.)

† Boroviczeny, *op. cit.*, p. 293.

itself, on the eastern or Buda side of the city. From there, without having to cross the Danube, Charles's troops could march straight up to the Palace hill, whose outlines were now visible. They had arrived. It was 23 October, a Sunday.

The skirmish – it can hardly even be called a battle – which was fought that day in the suburbs of Budapest decided Charles's political fate for ever, and that of Hungary for the next generation. For such a crucial event it has, even today, a strange air of unreality and mystery about it. Not all the accounts put out afterwards by Horthy's men on the one hand and the King's men on the other, and not even the reconstruction made fifty years later by the Queen herself – who was an eye-witness of everything short of the front-line fighting – can quite explain why the King's cause, which seemed poised for certain victory, crumbled so swiftly into total fiasco. Treachery, as has been mentioned, played a major role. But so did the fact that, though Charles's camp did not lack bravery, it was lacking in that ruthlessness and improvisation so essential to any enterprise of this nature.

What also defeated him was something that was not tangible on the battlefield but was almost palpable in the air above and around it: the mood of Hungary herself. The country, three years after the collapse of 1918, rent by all the arguments about the dynasty and within the dynasty, and dazed by the nightmare of Marxist revolution and counter-revolution which had followed, this land was in a limbo – psychologically as well as politically. There were a few, like Captain Gömbös on the Regent's side and Colonel Lehar on the King's side, whose ambitions or loyalties were always crystal-clear. But the majority never saw their path so clearly because they were trying to look both ways at once. The 'Kingdom without a King' had become a realm of double-talk and schizophrenia. As in those last weeks of power in Vienna, it was this 'half-and-halfness' which really defeated Charles again. And this enemy was invincible, because it was invisible.

However confusing the episode, certain definite turning-points stand out. The first was in Budapest in the night of 22–3 October, the same Saturday night that the King's train was rolling triumphantly if slowly towards the capital. Despite all the confident versions put about after the event, there seems little doubt that Horthy was in a panic during these hours and, more significantly, was at a loss to find enough regular troops who might be relied upon to fire at the King. Indeed, the immediate situation was only saved by the formidable Gömbös, who spent the evening and night raising an emergency force of Budapest University students with the story that an army of the hated Czechs were besieging the Hungarian capital. By means of this monstrous fairy-tale he had managed by the morning to recruit and arm some three hundred students. These were rushed out, under the command of a few pro-Horthy officers, to 'reinforce' the single infantry regiment of the Budapest garrison which had been sent to hold the station at Kelenföld. This was the type of bold, if cynical, stroke by which gambles are won or lost. Had Gömbös been the King's man, instead of Horthy's, the whole outcome might well have been different.

How desperate the Regent's situation was on the Sunday morning is shown by the fact that it was this improvised force of students – imagining they were fighting the Czechs – who offered the only sharp resistance when Lehar's troops, leaving the royal train behind for the moment, tried to advance via Buda-Örs on Kelenföld. The infantry battalion there had declared it would not oppose the King but would simply await his arrival and then march with him into Budapest. Two of Horthy's artillery batteries had been overrun with little trouble and two others had come over of their own accord. But when Ostenburg's men, having cleared Buda-Ors, tried to push on and link up with the waiting regiment they were attacked from the flank by Gömbös's band of students who held the high ground above the railway. The King's soldiers retired with a few dead and several wounded and a council of war was held back at Bia-Torbagy.

Now the second decisive event of the day took place. Lehar, discomfited by this reverse, pressed Charles into relieving him of the top command and urged the King to appoint General Hegedüs in his place. Hegedüs had been serving as Horthy's regional commander in Szombathely when Charles had arrived. He had already played an equivocal role during the Easter events, when he had been sent to western Hungary as Horthy's 'watchdog', and he had continued with the same game now. Though ecstatically welcoming Charles and twice swearing the oath of allegiance, he had taken care to inform the three *Entente* liaison officers stationed in Sopron of the King's return, 'as it would make a better impression not to deceive them'. Hegedüs, in fact, was one of those gifted creatures who *could* see clearly when looking both ways, because it was the path of advantage, and not that of duty, he was seeking. How was it that Charles could hand over to him? Here is the Empress's account of this fateful decision:

'Lehar, though loyal to the core, was a very modest man. Despite the fact that he had been highly decorated in the war (he was a Knight of the Maria Theresa Order, for example), he seemed to have no great opinion of himself. Though the Emperor had promoted him General the day before, he still considered himself to be really under Hegedüs, who had commanded the whole western region. Now, after this one check, he was determined to hand over command. The Emperor had the gravest suspicions about Hegedüs but was in a dilemma when Lehar insisted that he, having actually worked with the General closely for months, knew him to be reliable and would vouch for him. It was difficult for the Emperor, who had spent those same months at Hertenstein, to argue. But it was only with the greatest reluctance that he gave way. Indeed, he ordered one of Lehar's most trusted officers to "shadow" the General from the moment he took over; but Hegedüs managed to shake him off.'

The King-Emperor's new commander (with Lehar now functioning as 'Chief of Staff') soon lived up to Charles's worst misgivings. Artillery units, summoned up by Lehar from the West, clattered through Bia-Torbagy by train, shouting confidently as they passed that 'a few shots' against Buda would disperse the King's enemies. But those few shots were never fired, evidently on Hegedüs's orders, as Lehar, before handing over command, had sent the guns into action. In the meantime, Horthy had replaced the Commanding Officer and several company officers of his disobedient Budapest regiment with men who would obey his orders, so that Charles now lost the co-operation of this vital unit. By ten o'clock an atmosphere of confused deadlock reigned over the battlefield, a deadlock which only a decisive blow or a parley could clear. Hegedüs suggested that he should himself go to the 'front line' at Kelenföld and try to persuade the Horthy Regiment there to march over bodily to the King's side. Charles, who at that time had no idea that the regiment's officers had been changed since early morning, agreed. Hegedüs disappeared, and walked straight through the battle zone into Budapest, where he sat down with Horthy and Gömbös to plan the King's defeat.

How this defection transformed the situation can be sensed in some of the despatches which the British High Commissioner in Budapest, Mr Hohler, sent back to London during the critical twenty-four-hour period of 22–3 October.* When Hohler, with his French and Italian colleagues, first visited the Regent on 22 October, as the King's train was rolling almost unopposed towards Budapest, they found Horthy 'by no means certain of himself and of the outlook as he had been last Easter'. Indeed, he exclaimed to them more than once that 'the difficulties of his position had become almost too great to deal with'. And when the *Entente* representatives, following the official policy laid down by the Ambassadors'

* Public Records Office C 20175/180/21: C 20178/180/21: C 20326/180/21: C 20324/180/21.

Conference in Paris, called on the Regent to prevent the restoration bid,* Horthy could only reply that he was 'taking all possible steps'.

It was quite a different story on mid-morning of the following day. When Hohler called at 10.45 A.M. on the 23rd to discuss the situation with Count Bethlen, the Prime Minister, he found Hegedüs already sitting there, fresh from the front line. The General, whose capacity for double-talk seems to have been boundless even by contemporary Budapest standards, assured his listeners that 'he had not taken the oath to the King and had refused to accept command of the Carlist forces'. Mr Hohler, who was personally strongly anti-Habsburg and anti-Charles, and who was anyway less inhibited in the matter than his wary French colleague, then said his set piece. England, he declared, 'would never recognize Charles and would never permit the return of a Habsburg in view of the very eventuality with which we are now faced, namely war'. Though nobody in Budapest was certain what role Briand might be playing behind the scenes in Paris, this forthright statement was not without its effect – most of all on Charles's own renegade 'Commander-in-Chief'.

When the British diplomat called on Horthy an hour and a half later (Hegedüs had preceded him at the Palace), he found that the Regent had 'got over his mental crisis' and seemed to be 'fully confident and determined'. The morale of his officers was now good, he said, and steps had been taken to eliminate the 'Carlist' ones. Those now in control had decided 'that their duty to their country came before their oath to the King'. He, Horthy, considered himself 'finally and definitely absolved' from that oath. By that same evening, he added, it was hoped to compel the King's forces to lay down their arms. The thoughts of his Government were already turning to which remote place of exile the King might be sent, and here the assistance of the Great Powers would be necessary. With Charles's own commander now on his side, Horthy could well afford such confidence.

---

* The formal note which the three *Entente* High Commissioners handed over reminded the Hungarian Government of the Paris Conference decision of the preceding 3 April (after the abortive Easter bid) which had set out their determination 'to oppose the accession to the Hungarian throne of a prince of the House of Habsburg'. The three powers accordingly 'required the Hungarian Government to take forthwith all necessary measures to secure once more the expulsion of the ex-King from his former dominions'.

A telegram sent to Budapest from the Ambassadors' Conference two days later went even further. It called on the Hungarian Government 'to proclaim without delay the dethronization of the ex-King Charles'. The pressure of the Little *Entente* – and above all the need to placate Benes in Prague – lay behind this demand.

(Public Records Office C 20162/180/21, telegrams of 22 October 1921; and C 21686/180/21, telegrams of 24 October and following days.)

Meanwhile Hegedüs himself, having arranged for armistice talks to happen – and for much else besides – returned to the King's camp at Bia-Torbagy, where he arrived soon after 2 P.M. Charles now learned for the first time that his own commander had been dealing not with the regiment at Kelenföld but with the Regent in Budapest. He was obliged to listen to the gloomiest possible report: the Horthy troops ahead were now determined to fight; Budapest was ready for any siege, with machine-guns bristling from the Palace; Horthy, Bethlen and the British High Commissioner were all spitting defiance. The only solution, Hegedüs urged, was an armistice which Horthy had offered. The General added, in another burst of double-talk, that such a truce would enable him to bring up fresh loyalist reinforcements overnight from the West and so resume the King's offensive the following day.

At this stage, the Empress recalls, Charles decided to throw all caution to the wind as regards the risk of capture (which would have automatically ended the whole operation) and to go up to the front line himself. True to her pledge at Hertenstein to be at his side in all danger, the Empress insisted on going with him. The only safe route forward was along the railway line and the only 'vehicle' available was an old locomotive. So a white 'flag' (according to Countess Andrassy, it was a towel fetched from the sleeping-cars) was tied to its funnel. A few officers perched as guards on its coal tender, and on to the narrow engine platform climbed Charles and Zita with Hegedüs and their chief political advisers all piling in behind. It must have been the first and last time in history that a royal couple drove into battle on a railway engine.

They were halted by their own soldiers at the signal hut of Török-Balint. Horthy's troops, they reported, had now officially asked for a cease-fire, and their envoys would arrive at any minute. This was the third critical moment of the day for Charles: to fight on or to parley? The Empress relates:

'The Emperor now had a talk with those officers of his, like Ostenburg, whom he knew to be still completely loyal. He suggested to them that our troops, which were anyway spaced too far apart, should be withdrawn from the front line altogether, regrouped and that we should then launch a night attack on Budapest with the Emperor leading them in person. For this reason, he proposed to reject the coming armistice offer. No one would agree to the plan. The officers pointed out that their men, who had already been two nights without sleep, were in no physical condition for such an operation and that the attack ought to be postponed until the Monday morning, giving them a chance to rest. The political advisers present – who included the irreproachable Rakovsky and Count Andrassy

– also voiced opposition, but for quite different reasons. They argued that if the King now rejected out of hand a cease-fire appeal that Horthy had offered, it would look as though only Charles was bent on further bloodshed.'

So the attack plan was dropped. Soon afterwards Horthy's emissary, Colonel Svoy, arrived on the scene, and an armistice was agreed. It was to last until 8 A.M. the following morning, at which time formal political talks between the two sides would begin at a farmhouse just inside the Carlist positions. The locomotive with its royal passengers puffed back to Torbagy, leaving General Hegedüs behind to fix the troop demarcation lines for the night with Colonel Svoy. This proved the costliest mistake of all in a day so full of treachery, half-measures and hesitations. The General allotted all surrounding heights not to Charles's troops, but to Horthy's, and agreed with the 'enemy' that, from these commanding positions, they would break the truce by three hours and move into position while it was still dark for a surprise attack on Charles's forces.

His work done, Hegedüs now returned to Torbagy and himself asked Charles to be relieved of his command. The reason he gave was that whilst in Budapest that morning, he had discovered that both his sons were fighting on Horthy's side. 'You could have brought them both over,' was Charles's bitter comment, as he duly dismissed Hegedüs. Why the General had not been replaced and locked up as well as soon as he had admitted an hour before to dealing with Horthy behind the King's back must remain a woeful mystery.

Just how woeful Charles was to learn by dawn. He had gone to sleep after giving orders for the last loyalist reserve battalion to be brought up from Komarom for the daylight attack and for the whole cease-fire line to be carefully patrolled in the meantime. At any sign of suspicious movement, he was to be awakened. But though the night passed without firing, it did not pass without enemy activity. At half-past seven in the morning a message was brought to Charles from Horthy's new Commanding General, Baron Than, which coolly declared the cease-fire to have been invalid for the past two and a half hours. As Dr Gratz and Lehar left dejectedly for the agreed 8 A.M. parley, lines of Horthy's soldiers had already moved down from the heights on either side of Torbagy. In the ensuing scramble, some of Ostenburg's troops had got away in time. Other units, their sentry posts overrun, were taken prisoner as they dozed over their rifles. In one or two cases, the Empress remembers, the sentries did not even bother to resist. They mistook the peacefully advancing Horthy men for their own reinforcements summoned from Komarom: the uniform, like so much on both sides of the line, was the same.

Two hours later, Gratz and Lehar were back with Horthy's 'peace terms'. These could now afford to be stiff, and they were. The Regent called for the King's soldiers to lay down all their arms and hand over all their war material and for Charles himself to abdicate his throne in writing. In return, a meaningless amnesty was promised for all of his supporters 'except agitators and ring-leaders'. As for the King's future, this would be decided by the Hungarian Government 'in conjunction with the representatives of the Great Powers', but his personal safety was guaranteed so long as he remained on Hungarian soil.

The second restoration bid was already doomed three hours, perhaps eighteen hours, before, when the decision had been taken to sit it out for the night in a position that had already been betrayed. Now it crumbled to pieces within five minutes. As Charles stood reading the protocol with Horthy's terms in the tiny station building, shots rang out – bullets or shells, it is not clear which. One hit the royal train. For a few moments, there was total confusion. Boroviczeny, in a panic lest the King might be hit, bundled him aboard the train and ordered it to back away. As soon as they felt it moving, Lehar and Ostenburg, who had been conferring aboard, leapt down and ran along the platform shouting for a 'last stand' and a 'fight to the last drop of blood'. This was the mood the King had sought for in vain among his exhausted officers the previous afternoon. Now, with only the demoralized remnant of an army left, surrounded on all sides and cut off from its ammunition supplies, it was too late for such heroics. Charles halted the train and called out from his carriage window:

'Lehar! Ostenburg! Stop and come back here! I forbid any more fighting. It's all quite senseless now. . . .' And from his compartment he dictated a surrender order to be taken down the line to what remained of his forces. Then the train pulled slowly out for Bicske – backwards. It was all over.

As has been said, that skirmish around Buda-Örs set Hungary's course for a generation. It was a dark and desperate course. By rejecting instead of encouraging the secret support of democratic France, Hungary was obliged to look elsewhere for the big power support she needed to re-establish her weakened hold on the Danube Basin. The dictators moved in to occupy the ground from which the Habsburgs had been driven. It was Gömbös himself, appointed Prime Minister by Horthy in 1932, who led his country into the arms, first of Mussolini and then, via the Duce, into the grip of Hitler.

The Regent, who had refused to come to terms with his Apostolic King, soon paid the price for his pact with the devil. When he tried to betray his Nazi ally as he had betrayed his sovereign, Hitler, in the closing months of the Second World War, struck back savagely. On 15 October 1944, German troops occupied Budapest, 'deposed' Horthy, and installed the Hungarian Fascist regime of Szalasi in his place. Three months later, the advancing Red Army formed its first 'Provisional Government of Democratic Hungary' at Debrecen. Hungary's second red terror had begun. Horthy, who had taken over from Communism in 1920, now fled for his life from it twenty-five years later. He died in exile in Portugal in 1957, taking a troubled conscience with him to the grave.*

As for Charles, his political life had ended when that train pulled out backwards from Bia-Torbagy station. For one more night, Charles and Zita were to be treated as sovereigns on their own soil. Count Esterhazy, who had joined the King's train on its journey to Budapest, now offered the royal couple the hospitality of his castle at Totis, near the Czech border. Given the King's plight and the Regent's power, it was a bold gesture. It was also one typical of a family whose loyalty to the Habsburg dynasty had been one of the old Empire's legends. (It was to this same castle, for example, that the Emperor Francis had once fled from Napoleon's armies in Vienna more than a century before.)

Totis and the Esterhazys gave all they could again now. The ten finest carriages from its stables – the horses all decked in ceremonial harness and the coachmen all in their gold-braided livery – were waiting when the train that had been Charles's home for the past two days arrived at the tiny station. As the couple descended there was another of those outbursts of Magyar dynastic emotion which seemed inseparable from all Charles's hours of defeat. The whole company – soldiers, retainers and peasants – broke out in wild cheers of 'Éljen a Király, Éljen a Királyné!' ('Long live the King, Long live the Queen!'). That master of opportunism, General Hegedüs, who had travelled on the train, waved his own cap in the air and shouted with the rest. Indeed as Charles and Zita moved to the waiting coaches, he found the time and the nerve to say to them: 'When Your Majesties come again, please let me know before and then everything will go off all right.' Then when the cavalcade had moved off, Hegedüs promptly telephoned Budapest from the station-master's office, placed himself formally under Horthy's command, and asked for instructions.

The night in Totis was not without incident. A band of six armed men despatched from somewhere with orders to murder the royal couple

---

* At the dying man's insistent pleading, the Emperor's oldest son, Archduke Otto, visited Horthy shortly before his death. The former Admiral and Regent begged for political 'absolution'.

managed to slip through the castle guards in the early hours. Brandishing pistols and hand grenades they got to within a few yards of the King's bedroom when Count Esterhazy, unarmed and in his nightshirt, arrived on the scene, hurled the leading intruder backwards down the spiral staircase and raised the alarm. This ugly episode only underlined what everyone knew. The devotion and hospitality of the Esterhazys was but an interlude. A secure alternative to Tótis had to be found.

From now on, however, the King could no longer go where he chose. Ever since his formal admission of defeat on the railway platform at Torbagy, his personal future was placed in the hands of Horthy – or rather, in those of the *Entente* powers who had been in continuous session through their Ambassadors' Conference at Paris for the past five days. Already on 24 October, after the failure of Charles's initial attack, the French Prime Minister had formally disassociated himself again from his secret protégé. In a telegram sent over his signature to Budapest that day,* Briand, as Chairman of the Conference, had called on the Hungarian Government, 'whatever this may be', to proclaim the deposition of King Charles and to secure his removal from Hungary under conditions to be notified later. Three days later, another message from Briand notified Horthy of the arrangements decided upon. The Hungarian Cabinet was 'invited to hand over the King's person to the British naval Danube flotilla presently in Budapest'. From there, the message concluded, the former King would be conducted to the Black Sea and put on board a British cruiser. The prelude to this decision had been a secret conference held in the House of Commons in London on 26 October, with the Prime Minister, Mr Lloyd George, in the chair. According to the minutes,† Lord Curzon, the Foreign Secretary, reported that 'the ex-Emperor Carl's attempt to regain the throne of Hungary had failed' and stressed that 'it was essential he should be removed elsewhere at once from Hungary, which was a centre of intrigue'. By a coincidence, a British ship would shortly be calling at the Black Sea port of Galatz, so the first step was to take him down the Danube on another Royal Navy vessel to meet it at the coast.

As regards further plans for Charles, the conference discussed Malta as a possible temporary home. But this, it was felt, would be 'peculiarly inconvenient' as the Prince of Wales was about to visit that island. For a permanent home, one of the Balearic or Canary Islands was thought suitable. There was a short discussion as to whether Charles should be interned in a British possession but, as the minutes conclude, 'the majority of those present were opposed to Great Britain being his gaoler'.

* Reproduced in Public Records Office C 21686/180/21.
† Public Records Office CAB 23/27, 26 October 1921.

Nothing could have delighted Horthy more than this decision of the Great Powers. The day before receiving the news, he had moved Charles * from Totis to the famous old abbey of Tihany, which stood isolated and easily guarded on its peninsula above the northern shore of Lake Balaton. The Regent now knew that, without exerting himself further, he would soon be rid a second time of this sovereign who had become his rival. And on this occasion, Horthy guessed, the riddance would be more permanent than a polite train journey back to the Swiss lakes. He was right.

The story of the three-week odyssey that followed can be told entirely in the Empress's own words as she recorded them at the time.

---

* Charles had refused to budge from Totis until his principal political supporters like Rakovsky and Gratz, whom Horthy had arrested, were released from prison and allowed to accompany him. Before arriving at Totis, Charles had ordered Lehar and Ostenburg to go into hiding to escape the Regent's vengeance and had told them to pass the same instructions down to their subordinate officers.

Chapter 17

ROYAL NAVY CAPTIVES

For security reasons, the Empress Zita only rarely kept a diary – and then only in note form – while on the throne and during the first years of exile. From her arrival with Charles at the Abbey of Tihany, as though realizing that security had now become irrelevant, she departed from this practice. The following is her day-to-day account of events.

27 October 1921 (Tihany)

The Emperor learns that three officers of the *Entente* powers are there (a Frenchman, an Englishman, and an Italian). He asks Simenfalvy, the Horthy officer in charge of us, what these three gentlemen are supposed to do. The reply: 'To make sure that the King is kept apart from the others and that no one has contact with him and also to guarantee the personal safety of the King and Queen.'

At this the Emperor retorted: 'You've gone far indeed to lock up your crowned King and then, on top of everything, to call on the *Entente* to guard him in Hungary.'

Around midday the three English, French and Italian officers arrive to present themselves and to take a look at our quarters. I had gone meanwhile into the bedroom but immediately the doors were opened and the three officers came in. They walked through to the King's dressing-room before leaving again. I can't think what they really wanted. They looked at me rather uncertainly and the Frenchman gave a sort of salute. Not one of them spoke a word.

Sunday 30 October

When the Emperor learnt early in the morning that Herr von Boroviczeny had been forbidden to go to Sunday Mass, he asked one of the *Entente* officers to come to him. It was the Frenchman who came. The Emperor protested against the treatment of Boroviczeny and asked for him to be allowed to go at least to the 9 A.M. Mass. The French officer promised to arrange for this immediately and condemned what had happened.

The Emperor asked him to produce the note from the Ambassadors' Conference with the actual signature of the three *Entente* officers at Tihany on it. The Hungarian Government had sent details of it to him yesterday but he was no longer able to believe the word of Budapest. He then added that he was a Hungarian and would only allow himself to be removed from here by force.

31 October (departure from Tihany and arrival at Baja)

On 1 November, arrival by rail in Baja. We stopped at the big bridge over the Danube, from where steps led down to the water. The Emperor and I went down them first, followed by Agnes Boroviczeny and the French officer and then a crowd of unknown officers.

Below, waiting, was the English monitor *Glow-worm*. We crossed over her tiny gangway. The formal 'handover' (into the custody of the *Entente* powers) had taken place before we left the train and that was why the Frenchman was now walking immediately behind us. When we got to the door of the captain's cabin, Simenfalvy stood on one side of us and saluted and the three *Entente* officers did the same on the other side. Then Simenfalvy disappeared and the English officer introduced the acting captain of the *Glow-worm*, as the captain was not at the moment present.

Three-quarters of an hour later, the ship was ready to leave. The Frenchman enquired once more whether there was anything we wanted as he would fulfil every wish that was in his power. The Emperor thanked him and replied his only concern was what he had asked about before – namely the well-being of his loyal followers. Then the ship slowly moved off, the three *Entente* officers saluting from the bank and the Emperor returning their salute.

Before tea a pinnace-boat came upstream, hailed us, and the *Glow-worm*'s captain, who was in it, now came aboard. He had been at Galatz attending a Danube Commission meeting and had been ordered to his ship by telegraph. His name was Captain Snagge.

Soon after coming aboard he spoke with Count Esterhazy and passed on a request that the Emperor should give his word of honour in writing that he would make no attempt to escape as long as he was in the captain's charge. If the Emperor did this, he would be treated as an 'honoured guest'. If he refused, Captain Snagge would have to treat and guard the Emperor 'as a prisoner' which he would greatly dislike doing.

After a lot of reflection and after Count Esterhazy had made sure that Snagge himself would not be coming with us farther than Galatz, the

Emperor gave his word of honour as requested. It thus applied only as far as Galatz and not thereafter.*

This settled, we dined with Captain Snagge and went early to bed.

Wednesday 2 November

A pinnace-boat brought the Abbot of Ujvidek on board. Naturally no question of celebrating Mass. He had welcomed us three years before in Ujvidek.

Lunch at 1 P.M. Captain Snagge reads us extracts out of his war diary. All five of us (the Emperor, myself, Count Esterhazy, Frau von Boroviczeny and Snagge) sit more or less the whole time in this one cabin, because it is warm here.

Five o'clock: tea, and as it gets dark the ship anchors for the night. Dinner 8 P.M.

Thursday 3 November

The ship moves on again at dawn and we pass Belgrade very early in the morning. At about three o'clock in the afternoon we reach Moldava, and wait a little upstream. Impossible to pass through Moldava as the Danube has only about two feet of water in places. Snagge requests a motor boat and telegraphs to all points of the compass for instructions – naturally without result. The Rumanians offer a rail journey instead.

Snagge refuses: he can't stand the Rumanians. Today Snagge told us many long and interesting anecdotes about the work of the English among the Arabs during the war.

4 November 1921

We have stayed here all day (a little upstream from Moldava) and we don't know when and how we can go on. Snagge wants us to go by motor boat to Turnu-Severin and from there with a Rumanian passenger steamer to Sulina, as the British warship cannot get as far as Galatz.

We have explained to Snagge every day that the Emperor's presence will not provoke an outbreak of war because in each of these countries there are too many supporters of the Little *Entente*. He won't believe it.

---

* The text read as follows (I am indebted to Captain Snagge's widow for seeing a copy of the original document):

Je donne ma parole d'honneur au Capitaine Arthur Snagge que, pendant mon voyage, tant que je serais sous sa garde, je m'abstiendrai de toute tentative de regagner ma liberté. En faisant cette promesse au Capitaine Snagge je me considère comme engagé vis-à-vis de lui, personnellement, et pour toute la durée de ce voyage.

Charles
Empéreur d'Autriche
Roi de Hongrie.

Glow-worm
1 November 1921

Today he told me that while the ship was passing Belgrade they had caught a man – a Hungarian – who had set fire to the engine room and fuel stores and caused great damage. The incident was, however, hushed up. Another man tried to do the same in Szabadka, but was arrested beforehand.

I said to him: 'You see, but it would have to be not two men but hundreds and at every frontier. The Little *Entente* could not have declared war because of sabotage acts. That's what we have always told you.'

He replied: 'I think I believe it now myself.'

The Emperor had also repeatedly explained to him that the present policy of the Western Powers meant a victory for Germany. The lands of the Austro-Hungarian Empire would now automatically be forced to group themselves one after the other around Germany because the *Entente* had removed by force their natural head and link. Snagge seems to realize the truth of this more and more.

He also told me now that the British monitor ships had been prevented for two days from carrying out their orders to come to Budapest because they could not provide themselves with Danube pilots. The Serbian pilots had all been taken on board Serbian ships the day before and all the Croats refused to serve as pilots because they had read in their papers that the voyage was to take their Emperor out of the country. This happened in 'liberated' Ujvidek. The authorities bargained with them and offered them enormous sums of money – all in vain. Finally, Snagge said, they had found a Hungarian Serb in Ujvidek who had taken on the job for one thousand crowns a day – not with any enthusiasm, but tempted by the pay.

Today one senior and two junior Rumanian officers came on board to discuss the idea of the special train now waiting at Orsova to take us to Galatz. Snagge told me one of the junior officers had formerly been one of ours. He had exclaimed to Snagge: 'But just imagine, I've often seen the King at the front.' Snagge commented: 'He didn't like the job he had to do now.' A French officer who was detailed for our eventual journey sent me a bouquet of chrysanthemums today. Unfortunately I don't know his name.

The Emperor had a long discussion with Snagge about military affairs. The punishment rate in British naval crews during the war dropped by eighty per cent compared with peacetime – so high were the standards of conduct. There was no mutiny on a single ship. Result of the U-boat war: a blaze-up of English patriotism.

5 November 1921

Awakened at 5 A.M. with the news that we shall have to get to Galatz by car and rail after all. We are supposed to be ready at 7 A.M. for breakfast and disembark in Moldava itself before 8 A.M. Three Rumanian officers were presented to the Emperor.

At the disembarkation there was quite a crowd of harbour officials and workers who greeted us very nicely. A convoy of cars was waiting for us and we immediately got in. The Emperor and myself went in the first car with Captain Snagge and an English nannie next to the chauffeur. There were arguments about which of the Rumanian officers should sit in the second car so that Snagge had to go back and sort things out. The escort consisted – apart from Captain Snagge and his aide – of twenty English Marines under the command of Lieutenant Roberts. A Rumanian officer, a French officer – who controlled this section of the Danube – and an Italian were also there.

While Captain Snagge was dealing with the other car, the window of our own dropped down. One of the workmen leapt forward to shut it and, as he did so, said quickly in Hungarian: 'I kiss your hands. Better times will come.'

Everyone was up and about in Moldava, because that same morning all pro-Hungarian elements had been taken into custody. That had alerted the population to what was happening. All the windows were open and everyone greeted us and waved at us without taking any heed of the police.

The journey to Orsava lasted three hours and everywhere we had the same reception – everyone making a point of waving and saluting – the atmosphere almost festive. Captain Snagge was very impressed by it all. He kept on pointing out the different groups of people to us and expressed pleasure about their loyalty and commented again and again over this obvious devotion to fatherland and dynasty of these areas that had been severed from both. Those peasants and workers who were near to the street even knelt down as we passed, waving with both hands.

In Orsava all the streets were crammed with people wanting to greet us and showing enormous enthusiasm. It was really moving to watch. From all sides came shouts of '*Eljen*' ('Long may he live') and there were cries that the King should come back and free them again. The shop windows had been completely cleared out so that the crowds, who would otherwise have been pushed away from the pavements by the police, could find room to watch us drive past. And Orsava was once such a pro-Rumanian town!

Because of this great demonstration of popular support it was arranged that we would not mount the train at the station of Orsava itself, but at a small station near-by, to prevent further displays. But despite this, quite a lot of people managed to get there in time by running all out, and in order to get our train moving the Rumanian soldiers had to clear the crowds with their rifle-butts and even by threatening to use their bayonets. In this way the train's path was cleared and, around midday, we were ready to leave. This farewell from Old Hungary was really moving. Soon after leaving Orsava we crossed the former frontier (of the Monarchy) and, as the Emperor was now on foreign soil, he took off his uniform and put on civilian clothes instead. . . .

Another moving detail: there was a woman on the train at Orsava who had already loaded on all our baggage. As I was watching her at this heavy work, I noticed that tears kept running down her face. I asked her in German what her work really was. She told me she was a porter and was responsible for all heavy work. When I asked her where she came from she replied that she was born in Bukovina, and was thus an Austrian subject. But now she could get no job in her homeland and had been forcibly moved to Old Rumania, with many others. But the Rumanians didn't trust the people of Bukovina and so she had to take on the heaviest work here to be able to live at all. She was deeply moved by being able to perform some service for us and had done it with all her heart.

The journey by train from Orsava to Galatz lasted twenty hours. We went via Craiowa, Slatina, Ploesti and Braila. We saw lots of Austrian rolling stock *en route*.

At Galatz the local Corps Commander and the Prefect of Police were on the platform. They wanted to be presented to us, but Snagge turned them away. The Rumanian major who had accompanied us by train and the Police President both asked to have our autographs. Captain Snagge kept off the former and our own Count Hunyady the latter.

Sunday/Monday 6-7 November

At about midnight Count Esterhazy came and reported that Count and Countess Hunyady were on their way to Galatz, where they would take over as our suite from himself and Agnes Boroviczeny for the rest of the journey. Captain Snagge had told him, however, that orders had been issued for the Rumanian steamer *Princess Maria* to be boarded at once and that, if the Hunyadys did not therefore arrive on time, they would have to take over in Constantinople. At 9.10 A.M. we arrived in Galatz to find that Count and Countess Hunyady had arrived on time. We had only a few minutes for hasty greetings and farewells.

We'd hardly boarded the ship when it was announced that a Capuchin father was also on board and for a moment we hoped that we would really be able to take Holy Mass on this Sunday morning. These hopes made our surprise all the greater when we were informed that this could not be arranged due to the great hurry that still prevailed. The father came to our cabin and said that unfortunately he had already taken Mass and that in any case he had been told that he could only stay three or four minutes. It was only thanks to an intervention by Captain Snagge that the priest was allowed to come on board to see us at all.

Captain Snagge told the Emperor that while our train had been waiting in one of the suburbs of Bucharest, the [Rumanian] Minister of the Interior had urgently pressed to be allowed to speak with His Majesty. Captain Snagge regarded this as a mockery of his captive and rejected the request. Naturally, the Emperor was terribly sorry to hear about this but it had all happened several hours ago and it was too late now to put things right. He did not of course express his disappointment to Snagge, whose refusal had been made with only the best intentions.

The train that had taken us across Rumania was a former royal train. As long as we were on the train, the English escort was responsible for its protection and jumped off at every stop to surround the coaches we were in. Captain Snagge insisted on us travelling exclusively under English protection and on keeping any Rumanian personnel away from the escort party.

The ship *Princess Maria* was a luxury steamer which the Rumanians had got their hands on somewhere after the war. As we were eating our lunch, it struck us that the dishes had a familiar taste. They might have been prepared any day in our own palace kitchens back in Vienna a few years before. Later we learnt that the cook on this ship was indeed one of our former Viennese Court chefs, and he had tried to convey all his loyalty to us by serving the nearest he could to a proper Court dinner. We were very touched by the good man's gesture; unfortunately we never learned his name. We only knew that as a serving soldier he had once been for a long time cook to Archduke Max, the Emperor's younger brother, in the South Tyrol.

The voyage downstream to Sulina went very quickly – much faster in fact than allowed, as Captain Snagge is a member of the Danube Commission. We arrived at Sulina at 5.30 in the afternoon. This has absolutely nothing to show for itself: one solitary European house belonging to the Commission. Their Excellencies of bygone days used to reside there; now the officers are in it.

We hove to alongside the 5,000-ton [English] cruiser *Cardiff*. Its captain, Maitland-Kirwan, was away shooting snipe in the marshes and most of the crew were ashore. The captain returned about 12.30. He had had no orders indicating we would arrive so soon. Our provisional destination was Constantinople and we were to steam out early the next day. We transferred ship at eight in the evening for supper on the *Cardiff*. I was given the Admiral's cabin, the Emperor that of the Commander.

We took leave of Captain Snagge and were formally taken over by Captain Lionel Maitland-Kirwan. He also asked the Emperor to give his word of honour not to attempt to escape during the voyage. It seems that Captain Snagge in fact asked for it in Maitland-Kirwan's name, in order to avoid any unpleasantness for this very shy and tactful officer in advance. The word of honour was given dated on the *Cardiff* the 7 November 1921.

At 9 A.M. on 7 November the *Cardiff* weighed anchor. We said good-bye to Captain Snagge, who returned upstream to Constanza in the *Princess Maria* and from there back by train to Galatz. We moved out to the open sea with pilots. The water was shallow and we churned up a lot of mud. There was still the danger here and there in the Black Sea of running into loose mines sown in the Turkish–Greek fighting and the *Cardiff* put out mine guards.

A lovely day with blue sky and lots of gulls. We saw Constanza from afar.

8 November 1921

Skies overcast, sea calm. At 8.15 A.M. we enter the Bosphorus and we recall the whole of our [state visit] journey here in May of 1918. It starts to rain quite heavily before Therapia. Still no news of what is to happen to us.

At nine o'clock we steam into Constantinople – past Yildiz, Dolma-Bagche, the Arsenal and the Golden Horn. There were an enormous number of ships there – French, English and Italian men-of-war and merchantmen of every flag on earth.

On our last time here we sailed past Kara-Hissar and the White Palace on the Asian coast, where we took tea. Now, it looked rather dirty and neglected; it was dazzling white then.

This time we sailed past the admiral's ship which played 'God Save the King' as we did so. We stopped right in front of Stamboul. In front of us lies the Hagia Sophia, a little to the right of it the old Seraglio, left the Museum and a large mosque. The sun came out at this moment and there was a wonderful rainbow behind the old Seraglio. A crowd of water-birds flew by continuously – cormorants, sea-gulls, dippers and many others.

The captain went across straight away by motor boat to the admiral, to ask for instructions. Count Hunyady had already warned us that the captain, very worried, had shown him last night a report in *The Times* according to which the Emperor had twice broken his word this year – the first time with Horthy, in that the Emperor had allegedly promised the Regent that he would let him know when he was coming back to Hungary and had in fact arrived at Easter without doing so; and the second time just recently with Switzerland.

The Emperor had managed to get hold of the captain before he left the ship to make it clear to him that both allegations were untrue. He had promised to let Horthy know and he *had* let him know. As for the second case (of not informing the Swiss authorities of his departure in October), the Swiss had only expressed 'a desire' to be told and the Emperor had told them they would be informed forty-eight hours 'before he left for *a new place of asylum*'. This, however, did not describe Hungary. The captain was quite relieved but said even without these assurances he would not have believed the newspaper stories.

After this the captain went over to the admiral's ship and only came back later in the afternoon, though in the meantime he sent word over that the Hunyadys could go ashore at two o'clock and do some shopping.

When the captain returned he told us that there were still absolutely no instructions about us and that Admiral Tyrwight [sic] was distinctly annoyed with the Foreign Office. 'The Commander of the Fleet in Malta sent them a cross telegram, and so did our Admiral.' Perhaps there will be an answer this evening and then we will sail at 8 P.M. or during the night – but where we don't know.

The Hunyadys were back on board for tea and brought a suit of clothes for the Emperor. As it was too tight, the good English steward looking after us altered it that evening into a size larger. They also brought a suit, a blouse and two jumpers for me,* and collars and socks for the Emperor. Also maps, postcards and a pair of shoes for the Emperor – dreadful American ones, but they did fit.

That morning I had written the children quite a short letter in French and handed it, unsealed, to the captain. He had asked the admiral what to do about it and the admiral had asked his diplomatic people. The answer came back: the letter must not be sent. But Admiral Tyrwight sent it none the less on his own responsibility and when the captain asked him how he should handle the question in future, the admiral had told him to do what he thought fit.

At this the captain told us that I could write without hesitation and that he would not read it and that it should be addressed, not in my hand, to someone who would forward it to the children. Joyous news this afternoon: I received a telegram from Colonel Strutt in London that all is well with the children. Our first news of them for eighteen days. [They had remained in Switzerland.]

---

* One of the junior officers aboard the *Cardiff*, Lieutenant (now Commander, retired) Charles Drage, R.N. recalls that an enterprising British sailor on board did a brisk trade by charging 'twopence a peep' to look at 'an Empress's wardrobe'.

9 November 1921

Breakfast with the captain and Count and Countess Hunyady. Weather overcast, sultry and warm. Still no news as to when and where we are going.

Then at ten o'clock a boat comes over from the admiral's ship and soon afterwards we get up steam. The captain appears and tells us he has orders to sail at 12.30: destination Gibraltar. So that means our final destination is probably Madeira.

Of course only fifteen minutes before we are due to go a very dirty Greek ship comes alongside to off-load potatoes – as slowly as it could and with a great deal of noise. They almost fell into the sea delivering the last few sacks as our captain gave orders for us to sail on time and they were left scrambling up and down the side like apes with the last loads.

The journey from Constantinople with the view of Stamboul was as lovely as a fairy-tale. The sun had now come out; only the Museum spoiled the picture. Apart from that one could have imagined oneself back in the time of the Crusaders.

The Turkish coast was soon out of sight. The Sea of Marmora was very calm. A beautiful evening with stars and the moon. Unfortunately we didn't sail into the Dardanelles until about 9.30 and couldn't therefore see anything properly apart from the vague outline of the banks and, to the left, a fairly big building which was on fire.

That evening, I said to the captain that it now looked fairly certain it was going to be Madeira for us as the ship was not putting in at Malta. He replied: 'I hope so for your sakes.' Apparently in the telegram to the admiral there had been some mention of Ascension Island as our destination: a hundred inhabitants, an English officer as Governor, tropical heat and no decent house. Much worse than St Helena! [Napoleon.]

The admiral's reaction was to order the *Cardiff* to steam straight away for Madeira 'before they change their minds!' We are steaming at twelve knots.

10 November

At two o'clock in the morning a frightful storm breaks. The Emperor and I are both dreadfully sea-sick. I go over twice to his cabin to see how he is – and pay dearly for it. The Emperor also comes twice over to me – and removes himself hastily. Our good steward looks after us with touching care. Count Hunyady feels quite well.

At four in the afternoon we hear that the captain wants to heave to as a cable has come from Brindisi saying that a vessel which put out from there had to go back because she couldn't ride the storm heading for Tunis. It's hopeless! We've sailed today past Euboea as far as Belo Boulo (I couldn't read the last name properly) but we cannot get any farther.

11 November

The storm howls and rages on. We are still very poorly . . . the anxious steward brings us toast and champagne. The day lasts for years. We even hope that the ship will put in at Malta after all.

Count Hunyady comes to tell the Emperor that news has been received that the English are simply to hand him over to the Portuguese Governor of Madeira – just like that!

At eight in the morning we round the Cape Matapan, and by evening we are right in the middle of the southern sweep of the Adriatic.

12 November

Thank heavens the storm let up during the night and we feel more or less all right. We go straight away out into the fresh air and take breakfast, though still feeling a little uncertain.

Some time after two o'clock we see Sicily loom up – Cape Passero – and for quite a while we sail alongside the coast. Early this morning we got good news of the children, thank God. Again via the good Colonel Strutt.

13 November

A little stormy during the night but all day today the sea is as calm as a mirror. We sail quite near to the African coast – strange, harsh stone cliffs, mostly bare, though dotted here and there with clumps of shrub and white patches of sand.

At ten o'clock we go into the stateroom, as the crew are holding their service on deck. They have no chaplain so the captain reads the Prayers and then they sing together. We see quite a few ships, which up to now have been quite lacking.

After tea the ship's officers have some clay-pigeon shooting. They invite the Emperor and Hunyady to join them. The latter shoots splendidly. The formerly only moderately – after a pause of nearly $2\frac{1}{2}$ years.

We are making good speed and are catching up for lost time.

14 November

Today we sight the coast of Algeria – the mountains, surprisingly, covered with light snow, like a sprinkling of sugar. It is a calm, grey and rainy day but quite tropically warm. At five we pass Algiers itself in pouring rain. Then we turn away from the African coast towards Spain. The poor captain is still being put through the hoop in history, politics and geography by the Hunyadys.

15 November

At one o'clock the Spanish coast looms up with high jagged mountains. The officers wanted to organize another clay-pigeon shoot but the ship's motion was too great. Big, slow and not unpleasant waves. We are steaming now along the coast: a lot of shipping.

Punctually at 7 A.M. we arrive at Gibraltar and enter the harbour. Thank the Lord we have got this far. We tie up next to a Swedish cadet-training ship. The captain immediately asks the naval authorities – what's next? Gets the reply that they don't know and he should report at 10 A.M. to the admiral: but the admiral tells him that he also has still received no instructions.

The Governor of Gibraltar and his wife wanted to come and pay us their respects, but were forbidden to do so.* Via the admiral in Constantinople came another strict order forbidding the Hunyadys to go ashore to do any shopping. For all these instructions the powers that be have found time, but still not enough time, to tell us, after fifteen days of journey, where we are being taken. We read in one paper that our destination is to be Madeira but that there is no fitting accommodation there, a pretty prospect! The captain cannot even discover what sort of a Government Portugal now has. 'Not that it matters. In a fortnight there will be a different one anyway.'

The Governor sends us a basket with wonderful roses and fruit. The officer who brought it over was only a few weeks ago shooting in Hungary with Count Toni Apponyi. The admiral's adjutant also came to ask on behalf of his chief whether there was anything we wanted, and to present the Admiral's visiting card.

That evening, just as a storm was getting up, the news came: 'To Madeira, and leave immediately!' The captain refused in view of the weather and declared he would leave instead at eight in the morning. Then, if the sea was still too rough, anchor before Tangier. 'It would be unfair on a lady.'

Yesterday the Emperor asked him whether we might celebrate Mass early this morning. He said 'Yes', but naturally the same thing happened as before. The priest, an English naval chaplain, came after eleven o'clock and had already taken Mass. It was arranged that he should come again early tomorrow morning with everything necessary.

* It was Winston Churchill, then Colonial Secretary, who, on 9 November 1921, had passed on to the Foreign Office, with a request for guidance, a telegram from the Governor of Gibraltar asking whether 'he should ignore the former Austrian Emperor and Empress or show them civility'. Lord Curzon, the Foreign Secretary, informed Churchill that 'the visit of an aide-de-camp to the vessel to assist the ex-Emperor in any matter of personal private convenience will be all that is required'. (Public Records Office C 21430/180/21 and C 21575/180/21, telegrams of 9 and 10 November 1921.)

We dined tonight with Commander Thompson, as the captain was invited by the admiral.*

17 November

The English priest arrives at 7 A.M. And so after seventeen days we had our first Holy Mass.

Hunyady tries to give him a money offering after the service but is refused with the words: 'If the Emperor were still where he ought to be, I would accept it gladly; but not here.' At that Count Hunyady said the money was for the poor. The priest replied: 'That I cannot refuse. But I will tell them that it is the Emperor who sends it.'

At 8 A.M. we sail out. The weather looks calm. We see a whole school of dolphins after quite large fish which motor fishing vessels are also trying to catch with their nets. A very pretty view of Gibraltar and Algeciras. The sea gets steadily rougher. Europe disappears. One after the other we all get sea-sick. The captain told me that even he was quite ill early this morning.

18 November

Terribly bad sea. One could hardly sleep for being thrown about so much. The Emperor is dreadfully ill. This *would* have to be the day when the clocks are put back an hour so it all lasts longer.

19 November

The Lord be praised: We have arrived in Funchal. . . .

At nine in the morning Captain Maitland-Kirwan went ashore to complete arrangements for our hand-over on the ship. Whether because he was told to, or because he just made a mistake, he handed us both over to the Portuguese authorities, instead of only the Emperor.

After this the Mayor of Funchal, who is also the Chief of Police, came on board with the British Consul to be presented to us. It was decided, in view of the heavy seas, that we would not be transferred ashore until three in the afternoon. A request by the captain of the *Cardiff* and the British Consul to accompany us was rejected by the Portuguese authorities with the remark that 'this was now no longer a concern of the British'.

Despite the fact that the Portuguese had deliberately announced the wrong time for our landing, quite a large crowd had gathered in the

* Commander Drage's diary (see p. xiii) notes: 'Made Gibraltar at 8 A.M. A Swedish cruiser was in harbour and, while exchanging calls, her Captain pointed out that it was a Maitland who commanded the *Bellerophon* when she took Napoleon to St Helena and now, a century later, another Maitland was taking another Emperor into exile. . . . It is so like the English to need a foreigner to point out such a historical parallel.'

pouring rain to give us a very friendly welcome. We had already that morning taken leave of the ship's officers in the wardroom. They served us champagne and expressed the wish that they might soon be able to come and pick us up again in order to take us back home. They all lined up when we left the ship. The good captain was very moved. Then we were taken ashore.

Journey's end.

Chapter 18

MADEIRA: ENVOI

When Charles stepped ashore from the British pinnace-boat at Funchal he stepped out of history – close on five years to the day in November 1916 that he had entered it with Franz Josef's death. It is perhaps the right moment, before describing his own harrowing end, to write his political obituary first.

The picture usually painted of him is of an exceptionally good, diligent and well-intentioned ruler, but one who was somewhat weak in character, vacillating in his decisions and susceptible to outside influences, above all those of his energetic wife and her energetic Bourbon family. This portrait, while not wholly false, needs drastic re-touching. It also needs hanging in a very different light.

The 'weakness' of Charles was rather a gentleness of personality than a softness of character. For most people who knew the Emperor and Empress well, it was Zita, with her vivacity and her striking looks, who made the greater immediate impact. Even an English outsider like Colonel Strutt, who became equally devoted to them both, had the same reaction on meeting them at Eckartsau for the first time. The Emperor struck him as being good and kind and brave, but without any more remarkable qualities. Of the Empress he wrote: 'As I entered the room I realized that she must always share with the Queens of the Belgians and Rumania the honour of being one of the three great royal women of the war.'*

Yet personality is linked with character only as a flower is to its roots. The two are not identical, and some gentle-looking blossoms can be deceptively well-embedded in their native soil. So it was with Charles. For if by strength of character is meant sticking to the basic aims of one's life through thick and thin; holding on to one's beliefs, however unpopular; and pursuing one's ideals, however elusive, with a dedication that nobody and nothing could ever alter, then this last of the Habsburg

---

* Strutt Diary, *op. cit*. See p. 233.

315

Emperors was no shaky figure but a solid one. His brief reign can serve in this respect as his own apologia.

Charles came to the throne in the middle of a war which he both inherited and loathed. He had inherited with it an Empire as well – the most ancient, most complex and most vulnerable in Europe – which he loved. The problem, that might well have daunted a Napoleon, was how to end the one without winding up the other. Though only twenty-nine when this dual task was placed on his shoulders, Charles had already mapped out his future path both at home and abroad in an attempt to solve it. He had set this course himself while a young Habsburg Archduke and even before his marriage to a Bourbon princess. He never wavered from it when the burden became his to carry as Emperor. The so-called 'vacillations' concerned the methods to be used, of which there were theoretically scores – most of them contradictory and all of them constantly shifting in feasibility with the changing tides of war. But, at high water or low, there was never a shift in his principles.

From his early twenties, for example, he had become a convinced federalist in his approach to the Dual Monarchy's racial enigma. Some of these ideas were unorthodox as well as progressive – like his readiness to see Republics exist side by side with Kingdoms in the new state which he had first explained to his fiancée in the summer of 1911. They were the same ones he finally pushed through, almost unaided, in the autumn of 1918. This consistency was not the stubbornness of a closed mind. Indeed, he was often reproached for listening to too many viewpoints, however little, in the end, they affected his own. It was due rather to his conviction that his federal ideal was both morally just and politically rational to a degree that none of the other would-be 'solutions' could claim to be. All the Habsburg Emperors had talked in turn of treating the many nations under their sceptre as equals, like the children of a family. But all, in fact, treated their first-born – the Austrians and the Hungarians – as privileged, and all had their pampered favourites among the rest. The last Habsburg ruler was the first for whom the equality of his peoples was not a phrase in a manifesto but a passion in his heart.

He could never have said, as Franz Josef was alleged to have said, 'I am a German prince'. He could never have become, as Franz Ferdinand became, a notorious 'champion of the South Slavs'. Nor, on the other side of the coin, could he ever feel that hatred of the Hungarians as such which some of his closest advisers developed. What he fought in Budapest was something quite different: the hypnotic and baleful influence of the Magyar legend on his Empire as a whole. In as much as any man of the Dual Monarchy could think and feel with eleven minds and eleven hearts –

A last gamble that just failed: the 'October Bid'

22 Back on their own forbidden soil again. Charles and Zita (standing centre next to man holding hat) in the midst of an enthusiastic crowd of loyalist Hungarian soldiers and civilians at Sopron (Ödenburg) in Western Hungary on 21 October 1921. The day before they had made a surprise landing by chartered plane on a nearby estate, flying direct from Switzerland. The day after they left with three train-loads of troops for Budapest and the final battle with Horthy.

23 Sopron, 22 October 1921. A guard of honour and dipped standards for Charles and Zita as King and Queen of Hungary on leaving Western Hungary for the capital. The moment of triumph was short-lived. After a brief skirmish outside the capital they were betrayed into surrender. Captivity and final exile followed.

Royal Navy Captives

24 Charles and Zita on the deck of the British cruiser H.M.S. *Cardiff* which took them in November 1921 on the last stage of their journey into exile after the collapse of the second restoration bid in Hungary. Standing are Count and Countess Hunyady, two of the most loyal members of their household, who made the voyage with them. The whole journey is described in the Empress's own diary, made on board, in Chapter 17.

25 Lieutenant-Colonel Edward Lisle Strutt, C.B.E., D.S.O., who in February 1919 was sent by King George V on a special mission to Austria to protect the Emperor Charles and his family from the barbarous fate that had overtaken the Russian royal family the previous year. It was a task which called for the utmost resourcefulness, tact and courage. But Strutt, who became devoted to his ex-enemy royal charges, proved equal to it, as his own account of his adventures in Chapter 15 shows.

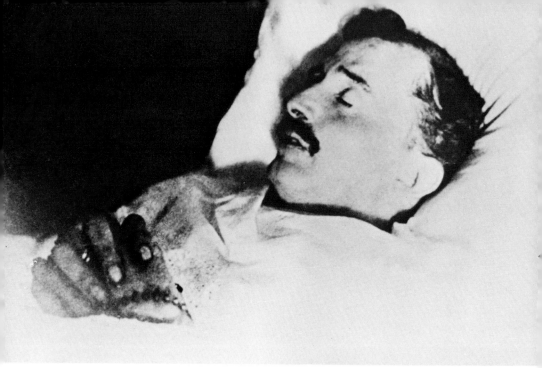

26 Death in exile. Charles on his death-bed in Madeira 1 April 1922, less than five months after landing on the island. Poverty and hardship had soured the last months of his life and had helped to bring about his premature death aged only thirty-five. Though his ancestors lie in Vienna, his own tomb is still on Madeira.

27 Widow and heir: the Empress with her eldest son Otto, a picture taken in San Sebastian, Spain, in May 1923, two years after the Emperor's death. In 1967, nearly fifty years after leaving his father's Empire as a child, Archduke Otto was allowed to return to the Republic of Austria again, though not as a claimant to the throne.

one for each of his peoples – that man was Charles, as Archduke and as Emperor.

It was the same story with his concept of himself as a monarch, which had begun to form in his mind even before the murders at Sarajevo placed him suddenly only one life away from the throne. He had determined while still a youth to rule as a constitutional monarch of the new age, rejecting the 'latent absolutism' of the old Habsburg order, redressing its injustices and reforming its archaic ways. All this too he fulfilled in his bare hundred weeks of power. The temptations of invoking 'Paragraph Fourteen', and of introducing that rule by decree which the existing constitution allowed him were always resisted, despite the constant pressure exerted on him to use this convenient device to 'settle the Hungarian problem' and other Imperial nightmares. The excesses of Franz Josef's military courts he duly tried to amend, and much else besides, with his famous July Amnesty – a radical reform measure about which, incidentally, the Empress herself, as well as his advisers, had misgivings. As for that Court ceremonial which had for centuries lain over Vienna's palaces as thick as the baroque plaster on the ceilings, he did the unthinkable and virtually abolished it. For all this, he became, in less than two years, the 'People's Emperor' to his subjects.

But the greatest consistency, and the greatest call on his own courage and patience, was that which he displayed in his search for peace. Here, in the famous endeavour of the 'Sixtus Affair', he did indeed use his French brother-in-law as chief intermediary to the enemy camp. But, for all that Bourbon Prince's eloquence and cleverness, there was no question of the Frenchman imposing alien views on his imperial relative. On the central problem, which was the need to combat Prussian militarism and to replace, in peace and war, the 'vertical alliance' of Vienna–Berlin with the 'horizontal alliance' of Vienna–Paris–London, both men were separately agreed. Moreover, though they talked about it far into the night often enough in those pre-war family gatherings at Schwarzau, each man had reached his conclusion in his own way. Sixtus came to it as a passionate Frenchman glaring across the Rhine at the victor of Sédan; Charles as the milder Austrian, with the Saxon mother, who hated the Prussian spirit for its intolerance and feared the nationalist credo of the Hohenzollerns for the damage it could do to his own multi-national homeland.

There may have been times in early 1917 when Sixtus urged his brother-in-law to go even faster down the road of concession and compromise than he was travelling already. But he did not set Charles on that road and he could never have drawn him off it. And the one crucial concession made – the Emperor's willingness to support French claims on Alsace-Lorraine at the expense of his German ally – sprang equally from French pressure and Charles's own convictions. He, not Prince Sixtus or the Empress Zita, had been born titular head of the House of Lorraine. It was on a visit with his tutors to those erstwhile Habsburg provinces long before the war that he had convinced himself of their French soul and their French destiny. He knew that their transfer to France, and the sacrifice to Italy of his own beloved Trentino, were the two keys that might open the door to a European settlement; and he went on turning those keys, whatever barricades were erected on the other side of the door.

In the summer of 1917, after the apparent failure of the Sixtus negotiations, the Empress once said to him: 'Well, I suppose this means even you will have to admit defeat and give up your peace moves at least for the time being.' To which Charles replied, with unusual sharpness: 'I shan't even contemplate giving up, not for an instant. You only have to think of the people dying by their thousands every day. I cannot just fold my hands in my lap. We must start up immediately in some other way.' And he did.

Charles was no intellectual in his approach to life. He reached his conclusions by a mixed process of logic, common sense and the dictates of his conscience. This purely moral driving force, always at work inside an intensely religious man who believed with all his being in the triumph of good over evil, cannot be overestimated in explaining and assessing his actions. The two – his Catholic faith and his working life – were fused together by his crown. He saw this and he wore this as a plain man of God as well as a Habsburg ruler. In a way that may seem naïvely old-fashioned to more cynical eyes in a more cynical age, it was the divinity of kingly office which moved him more than its power, and its duties which called louder than its splendour. He was the last of Europe's 'Apostolic Majesties'. But none in the seven-century Habsburg line before him had tried harder to live up to the full meaning and the full challenge of that resplendent title.

Often, this plain uncomplicated moral approach to problems enabled him to see further and clearer than any of the cleverer or more complex people around him. He saw, for example, what all his own generals and admirals did not see about that fateful decision of his German ally to launch an all-out U-boat war: that it would not only fail in itself but, by bringing America in on the *Entente* side, would spell the doom of the Central Powers. This same attitude, that because a thing was evil it was wrong, also explained his refusal to help Lenin back into Russia and his reluctance to mortgage Europe's future by a wartime pact of convenience with Bolshevism. Ludendorff came to admit the truth of this too late in 1920 when he said of the Lenin episode: 'It was a mistake I don't like to remember.'

But a moral approach often brings complications of its own especially when, as in Charles's case, he would never deviate from it one inch. By always seeking for the good and believing in the good, for example, Charles often underestimated the evil, and sometimes failed to see it altogether. In this way, the very virtues of the Christian became the weaknesses of the Emperor who was called on to rule in a desperate and warring world. Being without any trace of ruthlessness or guile himself, he was slow to accept its existence in others. And when, as with General Hegedüs on the outskirts of Budapest in October 1921, he did accept it, he was still reluctant to draw the painful conclusions. When driven to it, Charles could himself master men of iron, as his overthrow of the formidable Count Tisza in Budapest showed. But a little more iron in his own soul, in the shape of politically healthy cynicism, would have helped him as a ruler. His trust in others as a human being was the biggest chink in his armour as a sovereign. He was always being wounded through it. In the end, as with the second restoration bid, the stab was mortal.

He was never inconsistent, at least over essentials. He was condemned by the contrast between his nature and his destiny to be something worse: self-contradictory. Thus he was a pacifist but a proud soldier. He was a Commander-in-Chief but not a war-lord. He was the ally of the Germans, yet their natural rival; the enemy of the Western democracies, yet their natural friend. He was the citizen Emperor who wore the feudal crown. He was born not so much out of his world as between two worlds, the old and the new which he tried to reconcile but which finally crushed him and his Empire to fragments like two counter-revolving mill-stones. Finally, by the greatest irony and tragedy of all, he was born to rule in peace but condemned to rule in war.

These contradictions, which he could neither prevent nor control, meant that he was always suspect as Emperor among extremists of all kinds. To the arch-conservatives, he was too much of a reformer; yet to the socialists, he remained the patriarchal sovereign. For the militarists, he was too much the man of the olive branch; yet, to the outright pacifists, he was still too much the man of the sword. For the chauvinistic Magyars, he held his Budapest Coronation oath too lightly; to the pan-Slavs and many Austro-Germans, he took it far too earnestly. It was to the men of the middle way, the men of tolerance and compromise, that he looked. There were never enough of them even to begin with and they became steadily fewer as his reign moved on, and the spite of war sharpened as every month passed.

Nothing and nobody could have saved the Habsburg Empire he

inherited in its old form and its old scope for very long. But, given settled conditions, Charles might well have proved the one royal reformer who could have led this effulgent ruin forward to make its orderly peace with the twentieth century. It could then have settled into the history of our continent, instead of suddenly dropping out, leaving an uneasy vacuum which is still unfilled today after fifty years have passed. As it was, the philosopher-king had to play the warrior-king instead; the reformer became the liquidator.

The last sad months now began. They were sullied by the addition to all their other troubles of the only affliction the royal exiles had hitherto been spared: poverty. While they were still on the *Cardiff*, their polite jailers, the *Entente* powers, were already tackling the problem of how much money they would decently require to live in Madeira, and where it should come from. The Ambassadors' Conference in Paris decided on 16 November 1921, that an annual sum of 500,000 gold francs, or £20,000, would be appropriate.* Even this point was not settled without considerable argument. One British official consulted, for example, regarded the sum as 'preposterous' and suggested £5,000 a year instead; only to be overruled by his superior at the Foreign Office, Alexander Cadogan, who held that an annual grant of £20,000 was reasonable 'in view of the ex-Emperor's status and the necessity of maintaining a family and some staff, however modest'.

But the difficulties in fixing the sum were nothing compared with those of actually raising it. The Conference eventually decided that neither the victorious *Entente* powers nor the defeated enemy countries (which in this case meant the Republic of Austria and the lapsed Kingdom of Hungary) should contribute to the fund. Instead, it should be fed by equal grants of £5,000 a year each from the four 'succession-states' – Poland, Czechoslovakia, Yugoslavia and Rumania – who would pay the money to Portugal as the administering government.

The idea of making the heirs to the House of Habsburg pay something towards the comfort of the dispossessed owner was a reasonable one, and the sum itself would have spared the exiles any hardship. But it remained an idea. The succession-states simply refused to pay. As the months dragged on, not a farthing was either offered by nor extracted from Warsaw, Prague, Belgrade and Bucharest. The *Entente* powers, who had selected this place of banishment and had themselves agreed on the urgency of making financial provision for Charles and his family there, declined, for their part, to make any temporary advance. In London, the

* Public Records Office C 21853/180/21. Telegram from Paris of 16 November 1921.

Treasury Commissioners flatly declared, on 1 December 1921, that they had no funds available for making such an advance and that they could not undertake to present a vote to Parliament for this purpose'.* The true position was even worse. As the British Consul at Funchal once told the Empress outright, the Great Powers were not only sending no money themselves; they were taking steps to prevent it coming in from any private sources.

Behind this apparently churlish attitude lay the very genuine fear that Charles, like that terrible Corsican a century before him, might somehow find the means to slip away from his island prison and set the whole European mainland in turmoil once more. This concern was expressed at length in a personal telegram which the Foreign Secretary Lord Curzon sent, on 20 December 1921, to Lord Hardinge in Paris for transmission to the Ambassadors' Conference there:

'I am impressed', he wrote, 'with the serious menace to the peace of Central Europe which is perpetuated by uncertainty as to the ex-Emperor's possible movements. For instance, the danger of a monarchical movement in Bavaria, though not immediate, is not unreal. Were it to come to a head, it might well be the signal for an attempt to escape from Madeira of which the consequences would be incalculable.'

Lord Curzon then put two suggestions forward for discussion at the Paris Conference. The first was that an Allied officer should be attached as a watch-dog to Charles's person, 'charged with the duty of reporting any suspicious circumstances'. The second had a strong echo of St Helena about it. The *Entente* powers, Curzon proposed, might adopt a public resolution to the effect that if Charles tried to leave Madeira the attempt would automatically oblige the Allied Governments to transfer him to definite imprisonment in one of their more remote island possessions'. The threat contained in this second proposal was ultimately issued, several weeks later. In the meantime, this fear of another 'Hundred Days' from another and very different Emperor had the effect of depriving Charles of the most modest of suites as well as the most modest of incomes. Loyal followers in the old Empire like Count Revertera and Baron Hye, who applied to go to Madeira and share in his exile, were refused visas for fear that a 'monarchist movement' might be assembled there. Count and Countess Hunyady, who had landed with him, could not remain for long and, for a while after their departure, the 'Court' of the banished Emperor consisted solely of Dom Joao d'Almeida, a Portuguese nobleman who had once served in the Austro-Hungarian Army. Even a small domestic staff –

* Public Records Office C 22679/180/21. Treasury Chambers Memorandum to Foreign Office of 1 December 1921.

a cook, a maid and a married couple – was not allowed to sail for Funchal until Christmas time.

Thus, though he never renounced his claims or titles,* and though he never abandoned hope, Charles was in fact too preoccupied now with the sheer struggle for existence to plan any more political adventures. Early in the new year, when his private purse was nearly empty and there was still no sign of an income from any outside source, he turned in desperation to his last 'nest-egg', the family jewels. Now came the final blow. Even this nest had been raided, by those who should have guarded it.

The bulk of these family jewels – as opposed to all the state gems and regalia, which were left behind in Vienna – had been brought out to safety in Switzerland by Count Berchtold on 1 November 1918, ten days before the final collapse and the flight from Schönbrunn. These heirlooms, the Empress recalls, included the so-called 'Empress's Crown', a family crown of Lothringen jewels; eight Golden Fleeces in different settings; various family diadems, brooches and necklaces and the famous 'Florentine Diamond', said to be the largest pink gem of its type in the world.† Their purely commercial value, which would be astronomic by present-day standards, was vast even in a post-1918 market that was already well supplied with the jewels of the newly dispossessed. A certain Bruno Steiner, an Austrian lawyer who had first entered the Habsburg service in connection with the settlement of the large Este estate of Franz Ferdinand, was the man originally entrusted with the sale of these heirlooms, as and when required. The Emperor had authorized the disposal of some of them to pay, for example, the cost of his Swiss household and to send funds to his retainers and supporters in the former Dual Monarchy. Indeed, the 50,000 Swiss francs deposited for that Junkers monoplane which flew Charles and Zita from Zurich into Hungary in October 1921

---

* His last act on leaving Tihany Abbey for the British monitor had been to proclaim his full rights as the 'Apostolic King of St Stephen's crown' and declare all Horthy's measures illegal. On 6 November 1921, however, the Hungarian National Law Book duly published the 'dethronization' measures which the Great *Entente*, prodded by the Little *Entente*, had demanded of a very willing Horthy. This declared 'the sovereign rights of King Charles IV to be abolished' and declared the Hereditary Succession of the House of Austria in Hungary to have lost its 'legal force'. During the Second World War Horthy tried to establish a 'dynasty' of his own by getting his son elected as his Deputy Regent. The son's death on the Russian front put an end to this plan, just as, two years later, the Red Army itself put an end to Horthy's Hungary.

† This jewel, which weighs 133½ carats, was originally the property of Charles the Bold, Duke of Burgundy, who carried it as a talisman with him into battle. Among its earlier adventures was its loss on the field of Morat on 22 June 1476. Tradition has it that a peasant picked it up and, thinking it was coloured glass, sold it for a florin. It eventually reached the Medici Treasury in Florence; then the House of Lorraine; and so through Maria Theresa's marriage to the head of that House, the Habsburg family.

could have come from the sale of a diamond trinket first given to some Habsburg Archduchess in Prague or Budapest a century before, when imperial aeroplanes were quite unimaginable and imperial exile almost equally so. More than half of these jewels, the Emperor estimated, should still have been intact in their Zurich bank safes at the New Year of 1922. It was to these that his thoughts reluctantly turned after the cheerless and near-penniless Christmas in Funchal.

As the children were still waiting in Switzerland to join their parents, and as one of them, the six-year-old Robert, was due to have an urgent appendicitis operation, a compelling compassionate reason had anyway arisen for the Empress to return to Zurich, where the operation was being carried out. There was a further flurry of anxiety at the Ambassadors' Conference in case Zita might be planning a single-handed descent on Hungary to wrest the crown herself from Horthy's hands (a tribute more to her reputation than to their realism). But permission was eventually given, after she had agreed to travel quite alone, to leave again by 3 January, and to accept strict police surveillance* during the whole of her stay on Swiss soil. So, when the Empress set out for Switzerland in January, Charles told her to bring back not only the rest of the family but also the remaining family jewels.

Prince Xavier, who met his sister in Zurich, sounded the first note of alarm. 'I'll be curious to see,' he commented, 'what actually will be left, as opposed to what should be.' His misgivings were soon borne out. Of Bruno Steiner himself there was in Zurich no sign, nor any information as to where the jewels left in his charge might be. Xavier went after his trail and finally tracked him down one evening living in a Frankfurt hotel under a different name. The lawyer seemed shaken by this unexpected visitation of the exiled Emperor's brother-in-law but assured Xavier that the remaining Habsburg jewels were still quite safe in a Frankfurt bank and that he would fetch them and hand them over at eight o'clock the next morning. Prince Xavier was back at the hotel at 7 A.M., but he was already too late. Bruno Steiner and his family had left during the night, leaving no forwarding address. Though a lawsuit against him was duly lodged, that was the last the royal family saw either of their lawyer or of their gems. Only one important jewel, which had not been left in his keeping, turned out later to have survived: the Florentine Diamond itself, the sole though worthy survivor from one of Europe's great collections.

When, on 2 February 1921, the Empress arrived at Funchal harbour,

* The authorities took this so earnestly, the Empress recalls, that each sister leaving the Zurich nuns' hospital where she stayed had her veil lifted by the police to make sure it was not the royal visitor slipping away in disguise.

bringing with her all the children except the still convalescent Robert, Charles was already waiting like a stranded tourist on the mole to run up the ship's gangway and greet them. Tears of joy shone in the young face that was already old as he welcomed his wife 'home', and carried the two-year-old Rudolf ashore. But the happiness of family reunion was later somewhat dampened by the news that they were now without any resources whatsoever.

On 13 February Charles swallowed his pride and appealed direct to his captors, the *Entente* powers. A letter of that date signed by his one 'equerry' Count d'Almeida and sent to the Emperor's legal representatives reads:

I am commanded to instruct you as follows. Kindly inform the Ambassadors' Conference, as the representative of your client, that he has up till now met the entire costs of his expenses here from his own money which he brought with him. As this money, however, is now exhausted, he is no longer able to continue paying.

The Ambassadors' Conference brought him here against his will and is thus under obligation to meet itself the costs of his stay.

Madeira 13 February 1922.

(signed) Dom Joao d'Almeida.*

This merely set further complicated and fruitless negotiations in motion. The Ambassadors' Conference politely replied, after consulting the four succession-state Governments again, that they 'recognized the necessity of assuring to His Majesty an income which will permit him to meet the expenses incurred by his residence at Madeira, for which purpose his present resources are understood to be insufficient'. Charles was accordingly asked 'to be good enough to indicate the minimum sum necessary for this purpose'. So far so good; yet the sting came in the tail. Before it would be in a position to take a decision, the Ambassadors' Conference concluded, it was 'indispensable' that His Majesty should furnish it directly with 'an exact and detailed statement of his present resources, especially of the real and personal property, wherever situated, of which he disposes'. The estimate was also to include 'all payments which His Majesty considers to be owing to him from whatever source'.

The request was an international lawyer's paradise. It spelled despair to an exiled Emperor who, for the first time in his life, was concerned with how to meet weekly housekeeping bills. In early March, Charles sent written instructions out to his Austrian administrator, Baron Schager, to claim £60,000 a year on his behalf as 'the minimum for the very dear and

* The Habsburg Family Papers.

steadily rising cost of living here'.* (He knew, the Empress says, that this was over-generous, but he also suspected that any figure he submitted would be at least halved.) Schager was also instructed to draw up the necessary catalogue of the Emperor's 'Austrian and Bohemian private, family and Fideikomis estates, with brief and clear notes proving their purely private origin and character'.*

These orders despatched, there was nothing but to sit back in Madeira and wait until such time as all the legal, financial, constitutional and political hurdles which lay between the exiled Emperor and an assured income had been either jumped or knocked down. But he simply could not afford to go on waiting any longer where he was – in a large suite of rooms at Villa Victoria, which was an annexe of Funchal's costly Reid's Palace Hotel. Nor could he afford any of the properties, in Funchal or elsewhere, which were being hopefully offered to him via London by various prospective sellers. The ever-loyal Colonel Strutt, for example, now came again, for the last time, into Charles's life with an offer from a Miss E. Lindon to let her house in Madeira to the Emperor. Hampton's, the London estate agents, enterprisingly approached the Foreign Office with particulars of another British villa on the island. Then there was Mr Alfred Barclay Meidell, a Norwegian subject, who had approached the British Legation in Christiania saying that if ever the Emperor moved to Santa Cruz he had 'a fine palace-like structure' on the hill there whose sanitary arrangements were 'of the very best by London firms' and which 'in outlandishness might suit an ex-Kaiser'. Charles, he told the British Ministers, could have it for £20,000 'including furniture and fittings and stocks of wine'.† Even could he have gone to Santa Cruz, the Emperor by now had not got £200, let alone £20,000, to put on the table.

He therefore accepted with gratitude the offer of a local landowner to put at his disposal without charge a villa, the Quinta do Monte, high above the bay. Before February was out, the royal family and their tiny staff had moved up to the hills. It was this move – and the grinding money shortage behind it – which was to cost the last Habsburg ruler his life. The mountains above Funchal, and the house they now installed themselves in there, were ideally suited for the hot summer months. For the late winter and early spring they could be, and indeed proved, a death-trap.

This, and the royal family's plight in general, are best described in the words of a lady's maid who had come out to Funchal at Christmas to serve in the Empress's household. When the transfer up to Quinta do Monte had been completed, the troubled girl wrote this letter home to Austria:

* Habsburg Family Archives.
† Public Records Office C 20891/180/21.

We have moved from Funchal up here to the mountain. There was hardly any furniture here and we had to borrow almost everything from the hotel 'Victoria'. Our van, with the linen, the kitchen utensils and glass had not yet arrived so we had to borrow all this too from the hotel. Soon, we have to take back to the hotel the greater part of the bedding, wardrobes, all the linen, crockery, glass, pans and kitchen utensils, the household things and the wash-stand and china. That means a lot of work for me.

Down in the town it was very pleasant, but their poor Majesties have no money and were no longer able to pay the expensive hotel and therefore a banker who was a joint-owner of all the hotels on the island of Madeira offered this villa to their Majesties free of charge, and because of their money embarrassment, they accepted this gratefully. Up here on the Monte, the weather is only bearable in May and June. Down below, the sun shines every day and when it rains, it is not for long, but up here we have had only three warm days. The rest has been rain, fog and damp all the time. There is no electric light, water only on the first floor and down in the kitchen. The villa would be quite nice, but there simply is not enough room and this in spite of having only the bare minimum in the way of staff. Our only fuel is green wood which of course smokes all the time. We wash with only cold water and soap. Thank God we brought our washing-machine with us which we set up outside. The people here do their washing with cold water only, the laundry is never boiled as with us at home. The sun is supposed to do that; it is a tropical sun – when it shines. Unfortunately, we have had little sunshine so far; often we look down enviously to Funchal where the sun is always shining. The house is so damp that it all smells of mildew and the mist penetrates everywhere.

The only means of communication are cars and ox carts which we cannot afford, or else a mountain-railway, but that does not run every day. To go to Funchal on foot takes all day there and back. The poor Emperor, who has only three meals, can have no meat in the evening, only vegetables and puddings, which upsets us all very much. We don't mind. I don't miss it, but we really have not enough to eat, we are starving. If we only knew of someone who has some influence with the *Entente*, in order to arrange for their Majesties to rent a proper house. Their Majesties should be given sufficient means, so that they be assured of a decent livelihood. Even the necessities of life are lacking at every turn here. The children's tutor, with a doctor's degree, lives in a tumbledown hut in the garden with only one scrappily repaired room. In another rickety one-room cottage which is divided by a partition, live the servants with their wives. The latter work as housemaids. What seems worst of all to us is the Empress is expecting a baby in May and they cannot afford to have either midwife or a doctor. We have only a children's maid here and she has no experience in that sort of nursing. So there will not be a proper midwife. I am terribly upset about this.

I am writing without their Majesties' knowledge. I just cannot bear that these two innocent people should be left for so long in this completely inadequate house. Someone ought to lodge a protest! Their Majesties won't complain and they wouldn't even murmur if they were locked in a cellar with bread and water. In our chapel, thick fungus is growing on the walls. It is impossible to live in any room without a constant fire. We all do our best to cope with the dreadful situation. Sometimes we do get very low and depressed, but when we see how patiently their Majesties accept all these ills, we carry on again courageously.

On 9 March Charles left the house with Otto and Adelheid for that long walk down to Funchal and back, in order to buy some toys in the town for the little Karl Ludwig, who would be four the next day. Someone ran after him with an overcoat, which he declined. As usual, it was warm and sunny in Funchal. As usual, there was a chill mist gathering over the trees as they climbed back up. Charles caught a cold which he refused at first to treat seriously. Five days later he had to take to his bed, shaking with fever and a severe bronchial cough.

It was another week before they could persuade him to have a doctor called. Every penny, Charles declared, had to be saved, and there was no money to spare for unnecessary expenditure of that sort. When a Portuguese doctor from Funchal was finally fetched on 21 March, he drew a long face and summoned a second colleague for consultation. One of the Emperor's lungs was already affected. They moved him from his cramped bedroom on the first floor of the villa to a large airy room which looked out on the garden downstairs, and which would catch any sun that shone. That short journey on a stretcher was to be the last of his many wanderings.

On 25 March he ran a really high temperature (104°) for the first time and the coughing fits meanwhile became almost incessant. The pneumonia was gaining a hold on his weakened frame and, in 1922, there were no antibiotics to shake it painlessly loose. In the next few days, the two Portuguese doctors tried everything then known to fight the illness. Each treatment was painful. The sum total of them all together was agony. First, turpentine injections were administered in the legs, in order to create local inflammations and draw the infection away from the lungs. Then, when this failed and the disease spread to both lungs, camphor and caffein injections were tried. Next, plasters of linseed with mustard were ordered to be applied to his body every hour. Finally they started to cup his back. By the end of the month his body was a mass of burns, blisters and swellings, but all the pain had brought healing no nearer. He was by now on oxygen to help him breathe – whenever it could be got. The primitive bags had to be fetched up from Funchal, where there were few enough in any case, and each container gave relief for only seven minutes. The patient bore all this without a murmur of complaint; his main concern, indeed, seemed to be the trouble he was causing others. Though Charles had always been as indifferent to pain as he was to luxury (a logical combination) this was not just plain stoicism. He had projected into this last illness that sense of mission, of serving others, which had lit up his whole life. On the very night of his death, during a lull in the delirium, those round the bed heard him say quite calmly: 'I must suffer like this, so that my peoples can come together again.'

Charles was more fortunate than many as he went towards his end. He was, after all, accompanied and consoled by two of the three things which had meant most to him in the life that was now closing: his family and his religion. For almost a fortnight, his wife had sat day and night at his bedside, virtually without sleep, though often pretending to rest to satisfy his own reproaches. It was not as though he was the only patient at the Quinta do Monte. By the end of the month, illness of one sort or another had struck everywhere in the household. Two of the children, Karl Ludwig and Felix, were also stricken with pneumonia; the Archduke Robert was in bed with a gastric infection; and the staff were going down one after the other with influenza. Unbroken and unbent, the royal mistress of the house surmounted it all, and seemed always in her chair at her husband's side when his eyes opened again.

Next to her, the dying man's thoughts were of his eldest son, the ten-year-old Otto. There was no Empire to be handed over to the boy, as his father, and everyone else besides, had so confidently assumed in that far-off November of 1912 at Reichenau when the Crown Prince was born. All that could be transferred now, in this damp villa above Funchal, was the title to a dynasty, and its obligations. Late at night on 27 March, after the Emperor had received the Holy Sacraments, he broke his own rule about never admitting the children to the sick-room for fear of infection, and had Otto fetched.* Between the comings and goings of doctors and priests, the frightened and fearful child had a few minutes together with his father, who was still holding the crucifix. The next day Charles said: 'The poor boy. I would gladly have spared him that yesterday. But I had to call him to show him an example. He has to know how one conducts oneself in such situations – as Catholic and as Emperor.'

As Catholic and as Emperor. It is no reflection on the wife to whom he was so utterly devoted to say that, in these last days, it was his faith which brought Charles an even greater solace than she did. Indeed, neither of them would have questioned that this should be so. For both, their marriage, complete as it was in itself, had been but a part of that faith.

---

* Archduke Otto says this was about the last time he remembers seeing his mother in a coloured dress. From the day of his father's death down to the present, the Empress has worn nothing but black.

All its powers of comfort were mercifully present now. There was a house-priest, Father Zsamboki, living in the villa, and on the Sunday after Charles had been moved downstairs, he was able to listen and watch, through the open door, as Holy Mass was celebrated in the adjoining drawing-room. From then until the end the priest was never far from his side, hearing his confession, giving him Holy Communion, and, when the time came, the last sacraments. And whether the priest was there or not, Charles spent most of his last conscious hours in prayer, often aloud and together with his wife, always with her hand in his. The words occasionally came in Latin: '*Ave Maria, gratia plena . . .*' More often they were in German, the unaffected words of an unaffected man. They helped to carry him in serenity, at times it seemed almost in ecstasy, up to the threshold where emperors and peasants stand in one line.

Yet there was one sorrow that nothing, not even his family and his faith, could completely quell. For the third thing that would have sweetened suffering and death could not be there: his homeland. It was always flitting through his head in different guises. Sometimes, in his full consciousness and clarity of mind, it would appear in all the regalia of the Dual Monarchy which had been his. Thus on the evening of Friday 31 March, when he had been given only a few hours to live, he came out of a feverish ague and said in a calm, emphatic voice: 'I declare yet again that the November Manifesto is null and void since I was forced into it. And no man can take away from me that I am the crowned King of Hungary.' Often, in delirium, he was back in that Empire, fighting its battles again, helping wounded soldiers at the front, healing the strife in Bohemia, finding milk supplies for the children of Vienna. And sometimes he imagined that emissaries from that lost kingdom had come to greet him or to fetch him. On the afternoon of 30 March, for example, he suddenly became convinced that a group of Austrians had arrived at the villa, asking to be received. Humouring his illusion, the Empress said: 'As you are ill, let me go and receive our guests instead.' But Charles insisted: 'No no, they have come such a long way. I cannot refuse to see them. Ask them in. I can at least nod to them.' And before the fantasy passed he had tried to raise himself from his pillow to greet his invisible countrymen.

But usually, when he spoke of Austria, it was not as an Emperor seeing again his vanished Empire, but as an ordinary exile dreaming simply of home – the water meadows of the green Danube where he had been born, the mountain forests of Reichenau where he loved as Archduke and Emperor to walk and hunt, and those savage scented plains of Hungary where, barely five months before, he had gambled everything and lost everything. It was in this vein that, at another moment on that last Friday night, he sighed to the Empress: 'Why, oh why don't they let us go home? I long so much to go home with you.' And then again, early the next morning: 'Let's go home, let's go home together – we are already so near. Why won't they let us go home?'

But right at the end, on this the final day, it was to his present comforters, his wife and his God, that he returned. As the morning drew on, it was clear that death was now standing in the room. His breathing became fainter and more irregular. He had barely the strength left to speak. The heart, that had never been robust, was giving out. To those who stood watching the Empress at his bedside, it seemed as though her own feelings had become too deep for emotion. She attempted no sentimental farewell and spoke no longer of the children or of their life together. Instead, in an attempt to help him slip into his new life, she recited aloud short prayers, one after the other, into his ear. Yet he was not quite oblivious of her. Just before noon, he looked up at his wife and whispered: 'I love you so much.' They were the last words he spoke to her, and the last he addressed to the world around him.

The final half-hour, he seemed already with his God. He pleaded with the priest for Holy Communion again and Father Zsamboki administered it to him as the sacrament of the dying. Charles then tried to lift the crucifix he was holding up to his lips. He no longer had the strength and lowered it with a sigh. In the few seconds that were left, they heard him muttering, as though in a dialogue, the name of Jesus. It was with that word on his lips, spoken the very last time a little louder, that he died. The time was 12.23 P.M. on Saturday, 1 April 1922.

Despite the greying hair and the lined face, he was still only thirty-five. It had been a life short in years yet long in suffering and in frustration. He had inherited the well-nigh insoluble, and attempted the well-nigh impossible with it. Now the young 'Peace-Emperor' had found his own peace at last.

APPENDIX 1

Translation of letter from Charles's father, Archduke Otto (year unknown), to Count George Wallis, about education plans for Charles. It is of interest as revealing a lively behind-the-scenes struggle as to whether these plans should be taken out of the family's hands and controlled instead by 'the state'. (See pages 10–14.)

Dear Count Wallis,

Thank you very much for your letter. I can only reassure you by saying that, in the matter of our enemies, both my wife and myself are quite determined not to give way. I anticipate that, early this winter, there will also be a half-hearted move on the part of the All-Highest, which we are resolved to reject as well!

We are completely satisfied both with you and with your methods of educating Charles and will indeed always be grateful to you. And, so long as we parents are alive, the education of our son will be conducted *only* as *we* think fit!

So please put your mind quite at rest on this point, and when you start up with Charles at the end of October we can discuss everything at leisure and take any necessary steps. . . .

With warmest greetings,

(signed) Archduke Otto

(HABSBURG FAMILY PAPERS)

Translation of letter from Charles's father, Archduke Otto, to Count Wallis, Charles's tutor, on his education programme.

Schonau 22.9.1904

Dear Count Wallis,

As I shall probably be prevented by my illness for some time to come from having a thorough discussion with you about the next stage in the education of my son Charles, I want to tell you in writing of the plans which the Archduchess and I have thought out together.

When Charles is eighteen, he should be posted to a garrison where he can apply himself to a general university education as well as to his military duties. Whoever is appointed to accompany him in these last two years before his majority would be, for all outward purposes, his head of household, but in reality still his mentor who would have to be his guide in everything.

As my wife and I have the completest confidence in you, we would be very pleased if you could continue in this position with our son for these next two years. But – as we asked you once already a year ago – if you accept this plan of ours, you must tell us quite clearly and definitely whether your state of health will really permit you to fulfil these two further years of duty.

There is absolutely no question of appointing a second gentleman for our son. But I must add that it is precisely during this intermediate period between 18 and 20 that our son should enjoy progressively more freedom of movement and should develop greater self-assurance. . . .

As to the choice of garrison town, I shall propose to His Majesty either Prague or Innsbruck, which are the only two suitable garrisons where there is also a university and where, it is to be hoped, this or that reliable professor can be found.

Our son Charles who, with God's help, is destined one day to become Emperor, must firstly be grounded thoroughly in infantry training as our principal military arm: like my brother and me, we all began with the foot-soldiers. The correct relationship with the officers' corps and the discreet isolation from certain less commendable elements in it – this is and remains the task of his tutor, combined with the relevant regimental commander and his staff, and it should be a simple one to fulfil.

I cannot agree with the idea you once put forward, that Charles, after attaining his majority, could still continue to educate himself further in all sorts of ways. That may be so; it may equally not turn out that way. As long as he is under age, I hold it to be our duty to see that he studies all that he needs for his later life – and that is a lot! After he has attained his majority and is serving with his regiment he can study further if he feels so inclined. If not, then at least he will already have absorbed enough to equip him for all his future military situations and positions of State.

For this reason, during the last two years, he must do a thorough course in law, history, and political science alongside his military duties. . . . Prague has the advantage that Charles would cultivate social habits properly there, and get used to giving small dinner parties and so on. Innsbruck on the other hand has more military advantages, in that the Imperial Tyrolean Regiment is such a splendid one and Charles himself is so fond of the Tyrol. And then, there he would have Archduke Eugene as the first of the garrison, which would be quite good for the development of Charles's character! Naturally, this choice of garrison must be very carefully thought out in the ample time we have and at some stage the view of the Emperor himself must be sought. . . .

You are assured always of our complete confidence. The broad outlines of our decision will not be changed. From the coming autumn onwards this is the educational programme that will be carried out.

(signed) Archduke Otto

(HABSBURG FAMILY PAPERS)

APPENDIX 2

The Cabinet discuss the Austrian peace move with the Prime Minister, Mr Lloyd George, pressing for a positive response. He was bound by his promise to Prince Sixtus not to reveal, even to his colleagues, that it was the Emperor Charles who had made his highly secret approach in person. (See pp. 92–4.)

[Secret]

Minutes of War Cabinet meeting 159a held at
10 Downing Street on Friday 8th June 1917 at 12.30.

Present:

The Prime Minister (in the chair).
The Right Hon. Earl Curzon.
The Right Hon. The Viscount Milner.
The Right Hon. G. N. Barnes.
The Right Hon. Lord Robert Cecil.
The Right Hon. The Earl of Derby.
Lt.-General The Right Hon. J. C. Smuts.
General Sir H. W. Wilson.
Major-General Sir G. M. W. Macdonogh.
Lt.-Colonel Sir M. P. A. Hankey.

. . . . The Prime Minister then adverted to the possibility of a separate peace with Austria, which he had no doubt we could secure on terms. The difficulty was that Baron Sonnino had succeeded in manoeuvring the King of Italy out of the proposed Conference between our King, the King of Italy, and the French President. Baron Sonnino had probably suspected that the real object of the Conference was to discuss the possibility of peace with Austria, and had burked it owing to the fact that he himself was for political reasons not in a position to make peace on the Austrian terms. The latter included the cession of the Trentino (but not of Trieste nor Gorizia nor Dalmatia) in return for the cession by Italy of Erythrea, or some colony; and the independence of Serbia was also provided for. Giolitti however was supposed to have received the offer of the Trentino without fighting, hence Baron Sonnino's political difficulties.

The Prime Minister felt that we ought not to allow Baron Sonnino to stand in the way of the possibility of a separate peace with Austria, and we ought to insist on seeing him, even if we could not get the King of Italy to a Conference. At this moment Italy was probably in a chastened mood, as, after taking 25,000 prisoners she had, according to Austrian accounts, lost 27,000. Lord Robert Cecil pointed out that the Italian Cabinet was in all probability likely to break up, owing to the proclamation of a protectorate over Albania. He thought that

333

Baron Sonnino had very likely taken this action, which was a flagrant violation of the Treaty of London, because he saw no reasonable prospect of Italy realizing her desideration in Dalmatia. Unfortunately he had been given an excuse for taking some such action by the extraordinary conduct of General Sarrail in setting up a republic at Koritza under French protection, with two Chambers, an Army and postage stamps of its own. This action had apparently been undertaken by General Sarrail on his own initiative and without the knowledge of the French Government, and the real reason probably was the existence in the neighbourhood of a rich copper mine. Monsieur Cambon and Monsieur de Fleusian knew nothing about it and his own information was derived from Lord Granard, who had just returned from Salonika. Lord Robert Cecil was agreed that no further step could be taken in the Austrian negotiations without discussion with Italy.

It was generally agreed that the Austrian approach ought to be pursued. While not unmindful of the risks that the conclusion of a separate peace with Austria might produce an atmosphere of peace in which the crushing of Germany might become difficult, and while fully conscious of the importance of not being drawn into a trap designed to secure the release of the 2 million Austrian prisoners with a view to a subsequent resumption of hostilities, the War Cabinet were of the opinion that, if properly handled, these negotiations might result in the isolation of Germany and a general peace on the terms sought by the *Entente* Powers, and that, while great caution was necessary, the opportunity ought not to be let slip.

The War Cabinet decided:

(a) That the Acting Secretary of State for Foreign Affairs should send a telegram to Rome asking Baron Sonnino to meet the representatives of the British and French Governments at some French town, or, if preferred, at some English town.

(b) That a Committee on War policy should be set up.

(PUBLIC RECORDS OFFICE, LONDON)

APPENDIX 3

The telegram that launched the Emperor Charles's separate peace bid to President Wilson (see pp. 136–8). Shown is the first page of the secret cypher message to Prince Fürstenberg, Austro-Hungarian Ambassador in Madrid, directing him to approach King Alfonso to act as the Emperor's intermediary in a top-level peace approach to the White House. The bold 'Cz.' on the left is of Count Czernin, the Emperor's controversial Foreign Minister, who soon began to blow cool on the initiative.

(Facsimile of telegram overleaf.)

Telegramm in Ziffern
an Prinz Fürstenberg
in Madrid.

*)
siehe unten

17 Feb. 1918.

< Im Allerhöchsten Auftrage
Seiner k.und k.Apostolischen
Majestät wollen Euer Durchlaucht
Seiner Majestät dem König von
Spanien sofort folgendes mit-
teilen und schriftlich über-
geben:

Die.öffentlichen Reden des
Herrn Wilson einerseits und des
Grafen Czernin andererseits haben
die.europäische Lage wesentlich
geklärt und die wichtigsten strit-
tigen Punkte auf ein gewisses
Minimum reduziert.Es scheint mir
somit der Augenblick gekommen zu
sein,in welchem eine direkte Aus-
sprache zwischen einem meiner
Vertreter und einem Vertreter
Herrn Wilsons die Situation der-
maßen klären könnte,daß dem Zusammen-
tritte eines Weltfriedenskongresses
nichts mehr im Wege stünde.

Deine wiederholt geäußerte
so unendlich großherzige Intention,
in einem solchen.historischen

*)
Wie die in 2 Ausfertigungen
chiffriert sein:

Ausfertig. I sub No 66
fortlaufend als einziges Tlgrm
(vom Anfang bis Schluß)

Ausfert. II
in 3 Teiltelegrammen sein:

Tlgm a) sub No 67 von < bis >
Tlgm b) sub No 68 von < bis >
Tlgm c) sub No 69 von < bis >

Numeriert   Protokoll No
No 66 = 1960
" 67 = 1961
" 68 = 1962
" 69 = 1963

Krieg 25/29

I/964

Pr.No 1960-63/60
Chiff: 17.II 1918.
41

(AUSTRIAN STATE ARCHIVES)

APPENDIX 4

A wartime treaty proposal between the Austrian and German Empires.
The draft of Article II of the fateful Spa Treaty of May 1918 (see pp. 156–60)
which proposed that the new alliance should remain in force 'until
January 1, 1940'. In fact, six months after this draft was drawn up, both
Empires were dissolving for ever.

Artikel II.

Der Bündnis

~~Dieser~~ Vertrag bleibt bis zum 1. Jänner 1940 im Kraft.

Seine Geltungsdauer wird über diesen
Zeitpunkt stillschweigend verlängert, falls
bis zum 1. Jänner 1938 von keinem der hohen
Vertragschließenden eine Kündigung erfolgt.

Vom 1. Jänner 1938 an kann er von jedem der hohen Vertragschließenden mit zweijähriger Kündigungsfrist gekündigt werden.

(AUSTRIAN STATE ARCHIVES)

337

APPENDIX 5

The Emperor William's last message to his Austrian fellow-monarch. A personal telegram sent to Vienna in the last days of the war, on 27 October 1918, containing a desperate appeal to Charles not to sue for a separate peace. The message begins: 'Dear Friend, The announcement of your intention to sue for a separate peace with our enemies has given me the most painful shock. . . .'

It was in fact too late both for separate peace appeals or for protests against them. A fortnight after this telegram was sent, both Emperors had been driven from power. (See pp. 180–90.)

(*Facsimile of telegram on facing page.*)

VOM K. UND K. HOF· TELEGRAPHEN-AMTE.

Ankunfts-
no.. 59

3 Blätter

Telegramm.

№ _____ mit _____ Worten

aufgegeben   SS neues palais 422 27/10 5,-25 n .= Uhr

angekommen in Wien-Schönbrunn   den 27. Okt. 1918 19   um 5⁴⁵ Uhr Am

Dienstliche Angaben

Von _____

An

Seine kaiserliche u. königlich Apostolische Majestät

= teurer freund ! die ankuendigung deiner absicht.,
unseren gegnern einen sonderfrieden anzubieten , hat mich
auf das schmerzlichste ueberrascht . du wuerdest durch
ausfuehrung dieses gedankens dem plan unserer feinde
freie bahn oeffnen , der darauf ausgeht , durch trennung
unserer reiche unsere laender leichter ihrem willen zu
unterwerfen und ihre antimonarchischen ziele zu
verwirklichen .- einen baldigen frieden wuenschen unsere
voelker und regierungen . nach ihm ist mein sinnen ebens
gerichtet wie deins ; ihm zu dienen , habe ich schwere
persoenliche opfer gebracht , denn dem wohl meines volkes

P.A.1866

"Rondo", Wien VI.

118

APPENDIX 6

Two signatures that signed away the Dual Monarchy.

The last page of Charles's 'renouncal of power' as Austrian Emperor, signed at Schönbrunn Palace in Vienna on 11 November 1918. The other signature is that of Professor Lammasch, his last Prime Minister. (See pp. 212–16.)

```
    Nur der innere Friede kann die Wunden dieses
Krieges heilen.


    W i e n , am 11.November 1918.
```

(AUSTRIAN STATE ARCHIVES)

Also: a facsimile of the document in Hungarian, signed at Eckartsau the next day, by which Charles similarly renounced power as King of Hungary. (See pp. 217–19.)

(HUNGARIAN STATE ARCHIVES)

APPENDIX 7

An Emperor thanks his ex-enemy fellow Emperor who had turned into his rescuer.

Charles's personal letter of thanks to King George v for sending a British officer to protect him and his family during the dangerous winter of 1919. (See pp. 224–45.)

Majesté,

Je suis heureux de pouvoir venir remercier Votre Majesté de la si délicate attention de m'avoir envoyé le colonel Summerhayis. Je suis fort touché de cet acte si courtois, et en même temps j'en suis très reconnaissant. Le colonel est un homme charmant qui remplit sa mission avec beaucoup de tact et d'amabilité. La situation dans le monde entier est très difficile; surtout pour nous souverains. Que Dieu ait pitié de l'humanité souffrante et lui rende bientôt le repos dont elle a se besoin!

De Votre Majesté le bon frère et cousin

Charles

Eckartsau, ce 21 février 1919

BIBLIOGRAPHY

Author's Note: It would be easily possible to fill thirty-odd pages with a list of books in various languages which have been read or consulted in connection with *The Last Habsburg,* or which are known to have some relevance from researches on earlier works. I have always somewhat suspected these parades of titles, however, even when appended to the weightiest of volumes; and they are inevitably repetitive.

I have confined myself below therefore to three source categories, in their order of interest to the scholar or the academically inclined general reader.

The first is a list of archives and original sources which had either never been made available in any form before, or else had never been quarried for this specific purpose. The second is a selective list of recent books (i.e. those which have appeared in the last ten years or so) which bear on the subject and of which, in some cases, even the specialized reader may be unaware. I have added brief comments as a guide.

Finally comes a highly selective list of older and mostly familiar works which, despite more recent books, are still 'musts' as regards the Emperor Charles and his times.

A. *Archives and original documents.* (The explanatory references can be found in the Foreword or in footnotes to the text.)

1. *The Habsburg Family Papers*

Invaluable for the youth and education of the Emperor and also for his restoration bids and his time in exile generally. Almost all of his political papers as Emperor were handed over during his reign to the state archives; many have not survived.

2. *The Royal Archives, Windsor Castle*

The papers of King George v include most of the Emperor Charles's personal letters to the British monarch; some other references to the Emperor's secret peace initiative of 1917; and certain documents relating to the Emperor's abortive restoration bids of 1921.

3. *Public Records Office, London*

New material especially on the Austrian peace moves, and British attitudes to Charles and the Habsburg monarchy both during the war and in the immediate post-war years.

4. *State Archives, Vienna*

Valuable for Austro-German relations during the war (including personal relations between the Emperors Charles and William); for the

Emperor's peace bid to Washington in February 1918; for the attempted reorganization and collapse of the Empire in October/November 1918; and for the Emperor's restoration bids of 1921.

5. *Lieutenant-Colonel Strutt, 'Diary of a Special Mission'*
(Full text as deposited by his family at Windsor Castle.) Central eye-witness account of the Emperor's last weeks in Austria, February–March 1919, and his journey to Switzerland.

6. Various private diaries (Commander Drage, R.N. retd; Countess Karolyi; Agnes Boroviczeny, etc.). All of interest for the second restoration bid of October–November 1921.

B. *Some recent works of interest*

Heinrich Benedikt, *Die Friedensaktion der Meinlgruppe*, Graz 1962. (Authoritative account of the activities of one of the principal unofficial peace lobbies in Vienna 1914–1918.)

Heinrich Benedikt, *Die Friedensaktion der Mittelmächte 1917/1918*, Graz 1962. (A good general survey of the Central Powers' wartime diplomacy.)

Gordon A. Craig, *War, Politics and Diplomacy*, New York 1966. (Useful short essays on Austrian military command problems in World War I and on the Austro-German Alliance.)

Edward Crankshaw, *The Fall of the House of Habsburg*, London 1963. (This book is mis-named. It describes the Empire's slow decline. Only the last ten of its 419 pages deal cursorily with its fall in 1917–18. It is a vivid and often perceptive narrative but the final chapters give the impression of having been hurried.)

Vladimir Dedijer, *The Road to Sarajevo*, London 1967. (A modern Communist who became fascinated by a Habsburg Archduke. Some new and valuable material on the pre-1914 Bosnian independence movement and on Franz Ferdinand's reform plans.)

Fritz Fischer, *Germany's Aims in the First World War*, London 1967. (A massive and sober indictment of Germany's dream of hegemony in *Mitteleuropa* and a vindication, fifty years later, of all the Emperor Charles's fears and separate peace endeavours.)

W. W. Gottlieb, *Studies in Secret Diplomacy*, London 1957. (Good chapters on Austro-German tension during World War I and on the secret Treaty of London.)

Nicholas von Horthy, *Memoirs*, London 1956. (Contains one carefully composed chapter on the 1921 restoration bids which is most notable for what it omits.)

Robert A. Kann, *Die Sixtus Affäre*, Vienna 1966. (Brief but highly detailed documentary account with some fascinating new material on Czernin's own 'political testament'.)

Michael Karolyi, *Faith without Illusion*, London 1956. Catherine Karolyi, *A Life Together*, London 1966. (Both of interest for their accounts of life and events in Budapest 1916–19.)

Richard Lorenz, *Kaiser Karl*, Styria 1959. (Balanced and painstaking, but based mainly on secondary sources and therefore repeating many factual errors.)

Arthur J. May, *The Passing of the Habsburg Monarchy*, Philadelphia 1966, 2 volumes. (Strong on American attitudes to and relations with the Dual Monarchy; in general a balanced and lively survey of familiar material.)

F. S. Northedge, *The Troubled Giant*, London 1966. (The first four chapters form a good broad survey of diplomacy in general during World War I.)

Helmut Rumpler, *Das Völkermanifest Kaiser Karls*, 'Österreich Archiv' Series, Vienna 1966. (An excellent and exhaustive research work into the origins and drafting problems of the Manifesto.)

Ladislas Singer, *Ottokar Graf Czernin*, Graz 1965. (A valiant pro-Czernin account which contains little new apart from an interesting exchange of correspondence between Czernin and the Hungarian Prime Minister Count Tisza.)

Wolfgang Steglich, *Die Friedenspolitik der Mittelmächte*, Wiesbaden 1964. (A solid, heavy-going reference work, with 150 pages of source notes for 400 pages of text. All the advantages and disadvantages of writing uncritically from official documents.)

Wmilio Vasari, *Ein Königsdrama im Schatten Hitlers*, Vienna 1968. (The latest work on Horthy, concentrating on the 1921 restoration bids. Basically pro-Charles, but not distorted.)

Ludwig Windischgraetz, *Ein Kaiser kämpft für die Freiheit*, Vienna 1957. (The 'Red Prince's' memoirs, written entirely from memory. Many fascinating details but, on the main issues, highly subjective and far from reliable.)

Z. A. B. Zeman, *The Break-Up of the Habsburg Empire*, London 1961. (An excellent brief survey, which draws heavily on Czech sources, some unfamiliar. The emphasis on the Slav as opposed to the Austro-Hungarian scene sometimes leads to wrong perspectives.)

Hans Karl Zessner-Spitzenberg, *Kaiser Karl*, Salzburg 1953. (Shorter and more uneven than Lorenz's work. Relatively little on politics and diplomacy but a good personal portrait with a detailed and accurate account of the Emperor's last months of exile on Madeira.)

C. *A few older books of particular interest*

Arz, *Zur Geschichte des Grossen Krieges*, Vienna 1924. (Memoirs of Charles's competent but far from brilliant Chief of Staff. Authoritative on military details, e.g. over the Italian campaigns and armistice. Value of book restricted by author's refusal to touch on any political and grand strategy controversies, in which he was in fact very much involved.)

Aladar von Boroviczeny, *Der König und Sein Reichsverweser*, Munich 1924. (Detailed account by one of the Emperor's loyalist followers of both restoration bids. Accurate in most essentials.)

August Cramon, *Erinnerungen*, Berlin 1922. (Memoirs of the German General who was liaison officer at the Austrian Headquarters for most of the war. The difficulties of the alliance, as seen from the Berlin end.)

Ottokar Czernin, *Im Weltkrieg*, Berlin 1919. (An amazingly empty book. The omission of any details on the great 'separate peace' controversy may, however, partly be attributed to the year of publication so soon after the war.)

Edmund von Glaise-Horstenau, *The Collapse of the Austro-Hungarian Empire*, London 1930 (Translation). (It is a mystery why this book ranked for decades with Western historians as the 'classic account'. It is a vivid but hastily written narrative by a man who was never at the real centre of events and whose pronounced and eventually rabid pan-Germanism distorted all his Austrian judgements.)

Aus Kaiser Karls Nachlass, Berlin 1925. (The Emperor's own notes on the first restoration bid, as 'published' by Werkmann after Charles's death.)

David Lloyd George, *War Memoirs*, London 1934. (Volumes IV and V give the fullest survey of Britain's response to the Austrian peace offer of 1917.)

G. de Manteyer, *Austria's Peace Offer*, 1916–17, London 1921 (Translation). (This is as near as anything to Prince Sixtus's own account, and uses many of his notes and diaries. It forms the fullest French version, and is spoiled only by much unnecessary pro-French rhetoric.)

Arno J. Mayer, *Politics and Diplomacy of Peace-making*, London 1968. (Strong on American attitudes to the immediate post-1918 Central European scene and with interesting evidence of some State Department support for the defeated Habsburg cause as an anti-Bolshevik weapon.)

A. Polzer-Hoditz, *The Emperor Charles*, London 1930 (Translation). The memoirs of the Emperor's boyhood mentor who became his influential private secretary. A unique 'inside account', but needs to be read with other versions to get the right balance.)

Herbert Vivian, *Life of the Emperor Charles of Austria*, London 1932. (The only other English biography ever written: a personal and 'non-political' narrative of remarkable accuracy given the sources available at the time.)

Karl Werkmann, *Deutschland als Verbündete*, Berlin 1931. *Der Tote auf Madeira*, Munich 1923. (Memoirs of the Emperor's Press Secretary. Particularly valuable for eye-witness accounts of November 1918; also for the 1921 restoration bids which the author helped to prepare – even if his true role was more modest than he suggests.)

INDEX

INDEX

the House of

FERDINAND I

FRANZ JOSEF I d.1916
Elizabeth of Bavaria

Maximilian d.1867
Emperor of Mexico
Charlotte of Belgium

Marie Valerie d.1924
Archduke Franz Salvator

Gisela d.1932
Prince Leopold
of Bavaria

Rudolph d.1889
Stephanie of
Belgium

Francis Ferdinand d.1914
Sophie, Countess Chotek
Duchess of Hohenberg

Elizabeth d.1963 (Dukes of Hohenberg)
1. Otto, Prince of
Windischgratz
2. Leopold Petznek

Otto
b.1912
Regina of
Saxony-Meiningen
(Heir to present
Habsburg claims)

Adelheid
b.1914

Robert
b.1915
Margaret of
Savoy

Felix
b.1916
Anne, Duchess
of Arenberg